The Heidelberg Catechism

The Mercersburg Theology Study Series
Volume 10

The Mercersburg Theology Study Series presents attractive, readable, scholarly modern editions of the key writings of the nineteenth-century theological movement led by Philip Schaff and John Nevin. It aims to introduce the academic community and the broader public more fully to Mercersburg's unique blend of American and European, and Reformed and Catholic theology.

Founding Editor
W. Bradford Littlejohn

Series Editors
Lee C. Barrett
David W. Layman

Published Volumes

1. *The Mystical Presence and the Doctrine of the Reformed Church on the Lord's Supper*
Edited by Linden J. DeBie

2. *Coena Mystica: Debating Reformed Eucharistic Theology*
Edited by Linden J. DeBie

3. *The Development of the Church*
Edited by David R. Bains and Theodore Louis Trost

4. *The Incarnate Word: Selected Writings on Christology*
Edited by William B. Evans

5. *One, Holy, Catholic, and Apostolic: John Nevin's Writings on Ecclesiology (1844–1849): Tome One*
Edited by Sam Hamstra Jr.

6. *Born of Water and the Spirit: Essays on the Sacraments and Christian Formation*
Edited by David W. Layman

7. *One, Holy, Catholic, and Apostolic: John Nevin's Writings on Ecclesiology (1851–1858): Tome Two*
Edited by Sam Hamstra Jr.

8. *The Early Creeds: The Mercersburg Theologians Appropriate the Creedal Heritage*
Edited by Charles Yrigoyen and Lee C. Barrett

The Heidelberg Catechism

The Mercersburg Understanding of the German Reformed Tradition

By
JOHN WILLIAMSON NEVIN
and JOHN WILLIAMS PROUDFIT

Edited by
Lee C. Barrett

General Editors
Lee C. Barrett
and David W. Layman

Foreword by
Richard Christensen

WIPF & STOCK · Eugene, Oregon

THE HEIDELBERG CATECHISM
The Mercersburg Understanding of the German Reformed Tradition

Mercersburg Theology Study Series 10

Copyright © 2021 Wipf and Stock. All rights reserved. Except for brief quotations in critical publications or reviews, no part of this book may be reproduced in any manner without prior written permission from the publisher. Write: Permissions, Wipf and Stock Publishers, 199 W. 8th Ave., Suite 3, Eugene, OR 97401.

Wipf & Stock
An Imprint of Wipf and Stock Publishers
199 W. 8th Ave., Suite 3
Eugene, OR 97401

www.wipfandstock.com

PAPERBACK ISBN: 978-1-5326-9819-4
HARDCOVER ISBN: 978-1-5326-9820-0
EBOOK ISBN: 978-1-5326-9821-7

12/30/20

Contents

Contributors | vii
Foreword by Richard Christensen | ix
Editorial Approach and Acknowledgments | xi

General Introduction | 1

Document 1: The History and Genius of the Heidelberg Catechism (1847) | 43

    Editor's Introduction | 45
    Preface | 51
    Table of Contents | 55
    I. Introduction | 57
    II. The Palatinate | 64
    III. Occasion of the Catechism | 73
    IV. Formation of the Catechism | 80
    V. War against the Catechism | 87
    VI. The Catechism at Home | 96
    VII. The Catechism Abroad | 106
    VIII. The Catechism in America | 115
    IX. Theology of the Catechism | 129
    X. Church Spirit of the Catechism | 139

Document 2: "Zacharias Ursinus" (1851) | 153

    Editor's Introduction | 155
    "Zacharias Ursinus" | 157

Document 3: "The Heidelberg Catechism and Dr. Nevin" (1852) | 179

    Editor's Introduction | 181
    "The Heidelberg Catechism and Dr. Nevin." | 184

Document 4: "The Heidelberg Catechism" (1852) | 221

    Editor's Introduction | 223
    "The Heidelberg Catechism" | 225

Document 5: "Historical Introduction" to the Heidelberg Catechism in German, Latin, and English: Tercentenary Edition (1863) | 255

    Editor's Introduction | 257
    "Historical Introduction" to The Heidelberg Catechism in German, Latin, and English: Tercentenary Edition | 267

Bibliography | 305
Index | 313

Contributors

Lee C. Barrett earned his PhD degree in Religious Studies from Yale University in 1984. He has taught at Presbyterian theological institutions and at Lancaster Theological Seminary. Much of his research and writing focuses on the thought of Søren Kierkegaard. He is the author of *Foundations of Theology: Kierkegaard*, and *Eros and Self-Giving: Intersections of Augustine and Kierkegaard*. He is the editor of *The T. & T. Clark Reader in Kierkegaard as Theologian*, and *Kierkegaard in Context*.

David. W. Layman earned his PhD degree in Religion from Temple University in 1994. Since then, he has been a lecturer in religious studies and philosophy at schools in south-central Pennsylvania. He is editor of volume 6 of the Mercersburg Theological Study Series, *Born of Water and the Spirit: Essays on the Sacraments and Christian Formation*.

Foreword

Catechisms have a long and varied history in the life of the Church. They have been, at one time or another, the source of fierce debates, the treasured summary of a rich tradition, or neglected documents to which few people paid attention. In the American religious landscape of the nineteenth century, catechisms and historic confessions of faith were frequently downgraded in importance by many American Protestants who favored the individualism of Pietistic revivalism and/or a kind of primitivism (the spurious attempt to bypass most of church history and revive what was purported to be the "original" faith of the early Christians). For many church bodies, conversion of the individual person's heart took precedence over the catholicity and unity of the Church.

In the mid-nineteenth century, at the small seminary of the German Reformed Church in Mercersburg, Pennsylvania, theologian John Williamson Nevin, along with his colleague historian Philip Schaff, championed a more communal and organic view of the Church. The center of his theological system was the incarnation, which he called "the true idea of the gospel." In his 1843 work, *The Anxious Bench*, Nevin argued that revivalist piety—such as the use of the "bench" for sinners to sit on and be exhorted to conversion—was part of an individualistic and unchurchly system that created disorder, reduced faith to feeling, and shifted attention from the mysteries of conversion to the methods of the revivalist. He called for a "system of the catechism" rather than a "system of the bench," lifting up a piety of gradual nurture and instruction under the means of grace of the Church.

Several of Nevin's key essays on the Heidelberg Catechism, here edited, shine light on the centrality of the Incarnation for his theology, on the wholeness and corporate reality of human nature, and on the high significance of the sacraments. Salvation, according to Mercersburg, was not individual, but communal. Resisting the more rigid formulations of the Old School Presbyterianism in which he had been raised, Nevin opposed his teacher, Princeton's Charles Hodge, who had called Christianity a system of truth recorded in scripture "in a definite and complete form for all ages."[1] For Nevin, Christianity was a life in which one participated, not a doctrine

---

1. Charles Hodge, "History of the Apostolic Church," *Biblical Repertory and Princeton Review* 26 (1854): 171.

that a person taught or learned. The church was the bearer of Christ's life throughout history. Salvation was the partaking of this life.

This volume is a publication of the Mercersburg Theology Study Series, an extensive compilation of writings from the Mercersburg heritage. Edited by Lee Barrett, a long-time student of Mercersburg theology, the volume begins with an introductory essay which places Nevin clearly in his historical context, noting his distinctiveness of thought in contrast to the revivalists as well as to the New England and Princeton theologians. Further, Professor Barrett explains both the background of the Heidelberg Catechism of 1563 and how its irenic tone found favor with both Reformed and Lutheran theologians. Four essays of Nevin on the Heidelberg Catechism articulate emphases in his theology which brought a new vigor to theological consideration of the question of the Church and its sacramental character.

As one of the principal Reformed confessions of the sixteenth century, the Heidelberg Catechism has historically been the most widely accepted doctrinal standard among Reformed churches. For years, it served as the standard of instruction in pastors' confirmation classes in the German Reformed Church and several other Reformed bodies. Professor Barrett is the editor and translator for the most recent English translation of the catechism, *The Heidelberg Catechism: A New Translation for the 21st Century* (Cleveland: The Pilgrim Press, 2007).

In the United States today, much is made of the issue of freedom, quite frequently meaning independence from the control of a higher authority. But the Heidelberg Catechism begins its explication of the faith, not with freedom but with belonging: "What is your only comfort in life and in death? That I, body and soul, in life and in death, belong not to myself but to my faithful Savior Jesus Christ . . ." Beginning not with the attributes of God, but with our relationship to the Lord and one another, the catechism places the emphasis on God's gracious action in Christ in the life of the believer. Nevin's insistence on the Incarnation as the center of Christian faith found support in this Reformation document, reinforcing and helping to shape his theological conclusions. The essays herein show forth the evidence of a theology that went against the grain of much of nineteenth century theology and also prefigured the larger ecumenical movement of the twentieth century.

Richard L. Christensen
Associate Professor of Philosophy and Religion (ret.)
Lakeland College, Sheboygan, Wisconsin

Editorial Approach and Acknowledgments

The purpose of this series is to reprint the essential writings of the Mercersburg theologians in a way that is both fully faithful to the original and yet accessible to non-specialist contemporary readers. These twin goals, often in tension, have determined our editorial approach throughout. We have sought to do justice to both by being hesitant to make any alterations to the original texts, while at the same time being very generous with supplemental information in the form of annotations and explanatory footnotes.

We have decided to leave spelling, capitalization, and emphasis mostly as in the original text, except where the antiquated spelling of proper names would make them unrecognizable or flout general contemporary practice. For example, Nevin's occasional and inconsistent use of "Zuingli" has been changed to "Zwingli." Obvious typographical errors have been corrected. We have, however, taken some liberties with altering punctuation, which is sometimes quite awkward and idiosyncratic in the original texts, and which can be confusing to modern readers. In the nineteenth century commas and semicolons were used more extensively and profligately, often in ways that now impede comprehension. In some instances this archaic punctuation has been changed, particularly in regard to the removal of excessive and confusing commas. In several articles the volume editor has added quotation marks to the original author's citations as required by modern conventions. The entirety of the text has been re-typeset and re-formatted to make it as clear and accessible as possible; consequently, the pagination of the original editions has been changed.

The author's original footnotes have been retained, although for ease of typesetting they have been subsumed within the series of numbered footnotes that also include the supplemental informational footnotes added by the editors. Our own supplemental footnotes are wholly enclosed in brackets, while the footnotes of the original author are not. Often material in brackets (such as birth and death dates, biblical citations, or translations of foreign language words) appear within the original author's footnote, because that information has been added by the editors. Sometimes entire sentences in brackets will appear at the end of the original author's footnote; these have been supplied by the editors to provide contextual information.

Source citations in the original text have been retained in their original form, but where necessary we have provided expanded citation information in brackets or numerated footnotes, and have sought to direct the reader to more modern editions of these works, where they exist. Where citations are lacking in the original, or are incomplete, we have tried as much as possible to provide them in our footnotes.

In the annotations that we have added (either in the footnotes or in the form of brackets in the main body of the text) we have attempted to be comprehensive without being overly cumbersome. In addition to offering citations for works referenced in the original text, these additions fall in six major categories:

1. Translation
2. Explanations of unfamiliar terms
3. The identification and brief descriptions of individuals mentioned by the author
4. Additional source material
5. Clarifying commentary
6. Contextual information

We have attempted to be comprehensive in providing translations of any untranslated foreign-language quotations in these texts, and have wherever possible made use of existing translations in standard modern editions. At times the translations have been done expressly for this volume.

Additional annotations serve to elucidate any terms, concepts, or historical figures with which the non-specialist reader may not be familiar. We have also sought to provide references to secondary sources where the reader may find further information. For these additional sources, only abbreviated citations are provided in the footnotes; for the full bibliographical information, see the bibliography.

Throughout the volume we have sought to shed light on the issues being wrestled with by John Nevin and his nemesis, John Williams Proudfit. Much of the commentary and contextual information appears in the General Introduction and in the editor's introductions to each document. Further brief commentary on specific points has been provided in the footnotes in order to facilitate understanding of the significance of the arguments and counter-arguments of the two authors.

Many of the themes articulated in these texts may sound arcane and strange to modern ears. This is to be expected, because the culture of these authors was in many respects markedly different from our own. Nevertheless, the ultimate issues that gripped their hearts and minds are of perennial significance. We hope that our practice throughout will bring these remarkable texts to life for contemporary readers, while also allowing the authors to be heard in their own authentic voices and in the idiom of their era.

Acknowledgments

The libraries that have made the research for this project possible must be recognized. Without the resources of the Library of Lancaster Theological Seminary and the Archives of the Evangelical and Reformed Historical Society this volume could not have been completed. Myka Kennedy Stephens, the Seminary Librarian, has provided invaluable assistance with questions ranging from the most mundane to the most esoteric. Alison Mallin, the Archives Assistant in the ERHS, has helped us locate elusive documentary material in the proverbial cardboard boxes.

The founding editor of the Mercersburg Theology Study Series, Bradford Littlejohn, deserves continuing gratitude for his publishing initiative and his herculean efforts to actualize this project. His enthusiasm for the irenic vision of the Mercersburg theologians is exemplary and contagious.

I am grateful for the labors of my fellow general editor, David W. Layman, whose keen eye for detail removed many infelicities from these pages. His knack for spotting minute formatting irregularities is a sheer wonder to a detail-oblivious personality like myself.

Expansive gratitude must be extended to the members of the Mercersburg Society. Their financial support and their passion for this under-appreciated theological movement have made this series possible. The leadership of Thomas Lush, Carol Lytch, and Deborah Rahn Clemens has been the sustaining pillar of this enterprise. Most of all heartfelt thanks must be extended to Tekoa Robinson, who provided unstinted help with the footnotes and index.

General Introduction

Lee C. Barrett

Nevin Encounters the Heidelberg Catechism

In 1840 John Williamson Nevin left his teaching position at Western Theological Seminary, a financially struggling institution, and accepted a call to the Theological Seminary of the German Reformed Church in the United States, an equally financially beleaguered institution. In many respects this was an odd career decision. The fledgling school in Mercersburg Pennsylvania served a German-descended and often bilingual population, while Nevin was of Scotch-Irish ancestry and had only become proficient at reading German a few years earlier. Mercersburg was affiliated with the German Reformed Church, while Nevin had been raised in the Presbyterian tradition. The school where Nevin had taught for about a decade was theologically very Presbyterian, while his new German constituency had little exposure to Presbyterian doctrine. Nevin had been educated in the Old School Reformed theology and the Common Sense Scottish philosophy of Princeton Theological Seminary, while his new seminary was rooted in the confessional heritage of the Palatinate. Although Nevin was widely read in many strands of Reformed theology and was beginning to become familiar with German philosophy, he was still not entirely conversant with the theological ethos of his adopted denomination.

In spite of these differences, Nevin quickly identified with the spirit of his new religious environment and immersed himself in its history. Retrospectively reflecting on his rapid adaptation, he explained that even before his transition to Mercersburg he had begun to appreciate German culture for being more reflective and poetic than that of the pragmatic Anglo-Saxon world.[1] The perceived mystical bent of the Teutonic mind admirably suited his own spiritual proclivities. Ironically it was a Scots-Irish

---

1. Appel, *The Life and Work of John Williamson Nevin*, 112.

ecclesial *parvenu* who became most forceful in urging the German denomination to be vigilant in preserving its ethnically-linked theological heritage.

With surprising zeal Nevin threw himself into the daunting task of helping his new seminary to flourish. Almost immediately he resolved to help revitalize not only his school, but also the obscure and rather parochial denomination. Even more grandly, he dreamed that its influence upon the religious life of the nation could become significant and salutary. After an initial assessment of the denominational landscape, he concluded that in order to pursue these goals the German Reformed Church first needed to reinvigorate its original and distinctive spirit. Nevin the cultural outsider took on this task himself. He promoted the self-imposed project through a variety of means, including writing articles on the history and uniqueness of the German Reformed tradition for *The Weekly Messenger*, the denomination's periodical. He championed the idea of a centenary celebration of the origin of the German Reformed Church in America.[2] He travelled extensively throughout Pennsylvania and Maryland, preaching, lecturing, and soliciting funds for the seminary, mostly in the English-speaking congregations. He was convinced that a crucial step toward denominational flourishing was to increase the seminary's visibility in the church any way that he could. Without a thriving center of theological education and reflection, he feared that denominational loyalty and identity would not survive in the kaleidoscopic and fluid religious environment of nineteenth-century America.

A major component of Nevin's strategy of religious identity reinforcement was to encourage the denomination's intentional use of its confessional standard and chief pedagogical resource, the Heidelberg Catechism. Nevin's own Presbyterian upbringing had been marked by catechetical instruction, and he continued to cherish that ecclesial nurture. Nevin appreciated catechisms in general. He reminisced fondly about the "regular catechetical training of the young, with reference to their coming to the Lord's Table" that had characterized his childhood.[3] At home he had learned "the Mother's Catechism" and then the Shorter Westminster Catechism, an authoritative confessional document of the Presbyterian tradition. That parental pedagogy was reinforced by the Shorter Catechism's use in the school that he attended, an institution which functioned as an auxiliary to the church. To further strengthen the theological instruction, one year the pastor would catechize each family separately, and the next year would examine neighborhoods in plenary sessions, including both children and adults.[4] This appreciation for his childhood formation by the Presbyterian catechisms remained with Nevin throughout his life, even when he became restive with aspects of the theology contained in them. When he attended Union College, a Presbyterian institution "representing the collective Christianity of the so-called evangelical

---

2. Appel, *The Life and Work of John Williamson Nevin*, 129.
3. Nevin, *My Own Life*, 2.
4. Nevin, *My Own Life*, 4.

denominations," he was disappointed by its doctrinally ill-defined spiritual life.[5] He was not edified by the generic Protestantism of the school's mildly "New Side" Presbyterian administration which, in order to foster cooperation with the Congregationalists, encouraged latitude in subscription to the denomination's doctrinal standards, including the Westminster catechisms.

After moving to Mercersburg Nevin recognized that now his theological ruminations were to be guided by the Heidelberg Catechism, and not by the Westminster Confession and catechisms of his Presbyterian heritage. However, at first he may not have thought that the change in catechisms was all that significant. One of his mentors at Princeton, Archibald Alexander, had advised him that he was merely switching from one expression of the Reformed tradition to another; his new denomination was simply a communion of "German Presbyterians."[6] He initially did not regard the Heidelberg Catechism as being dissimilar to the Westminster Confession, and observed that the Westminster documents were in part based upon it.

However, his appreciation of the uniqueness of the Heidelberg Catechism grew. During a trip to Easton, Pennsylvania in the summer of 1840 Nevin discovered in the library of his host, Rev. Thomas Pomp, a copy of Heinrich Simon Van Alpen's *Geschichte und Literatur des Heidelbergschen Katechismus*, as well as other works about the catechism.[7] Inspired by these volumes, he concluded that the "animus or spirit" of the German Reformed tradition could be most clearly discerned in the venerable catechism.[8] Other events reinforced his engagement with the document. After the death of his senior colleague Frederick Rauch[9] in November of 1840 Nevin had to assume the responsibility of preaching in the college chapel on Sunday mornings.[10] He decided to base the sermons on the catechism's questions and answers. This series enabled him to work through its theology in a systematic fashion and probe more deeply the "inner spirit" of the German Reformed tradition. More ambitiously, he

5. Nevin, *My Own Life*, 8.

6. Dubbs, *History of Franklin and Marshall College*, 192.

7. Heinrich Simon Van Alpen (1761–1830) was a rationalistically inclined historian and pastor who served congregations in the Rhine valley. He was the author of *Geschichte und Literatur des Heidelbergischen Katechismus*. This was later translated by Joseph Berg as *The History and Literature of the Heidelberg Catechism*. Philadelphia: William S. and Alfred Martien, 1863. Alpen's work on the history of the Heidelberg Catechism was regarded as definitive.

8. Appel, *Life and Work*, 132.

9. Frederick Augustus Rauch (1806–41), a German émigré and the first president of Marshall College, was Nevin's colleague at Mercersburg for one year prior to Rauch's early demise. Rauch, who had studied under a variety of German Idealists including Karl Daub, helped introduce the thought of Hegel and Schelling to America. Rauch reinforced Nevin's incipient understanding of the social nature of experience, the shaping power of national and ethnic cultures, and the corporate nature of faith. Nevin edited and wrote the introduction to the second (posthumous) edition of Rauch's *Psychology* and took over the teaching of Rauch's courses, lecturing from Rauch's notes.

10. Marshall College had been founded in 1836 to prepare students for the seminary and for civic careers. It too was originally located in Mercersburg. In the first two decades of their existence the college and the seminary mostly shared the same faculty and administration.

began publishing a series of essays on the history of the Reformed Church and the catechism, twenty-nine in all, in the denomination's *Weekly Messenger*.[11] Although he did not know it at the time, he would continue to write about the catechism for the rest of his life.

The Significance of Catechisms

Nevin commenced this history and exposition of the Heidelberg Catechism because he was convinced that catechetical instruction was absolutely crucial for the well-being of any Christian community. In the history of the church, that opinion was by no means idiosyncratic. For centuries, catechisms, like other confessional documents, had served a variety of vital functions in the lives of churches. They had summarized the essentials of the faith, guided preaching, instructed and oriented new members, and provided a resource for the life of prayer. Some were aimed at children, some were intended for adults, and some were designed to provide a model of instruction for pastors and preachers. During the Reformation era they usually appeared in a Latin version for scholars and the clergy, and in a vernacular version for everyone else. In some contexts they were deemed to be so crucial as to require memorization by all church members. Often the sequence of topics treated in them was employed as a template to structure the doctrinal training of the ecclesial leadership. Catechisms were also used to differentiate sound teaching from dangerous or misleading interpretations of the faith and to polemicize against perceived heretics. The different weights given to these multiple functions shaped the style of the various catechisms, some being pithy and staccato, and others being more prolix and discursive.

In the religious turmoil of the later sixteenth century confessional documents became even more important as markers and shapers of religious identity. In the post-Reformation world catechisms, perhaps even more so than confessions of faith, served as potent catalysts of ideological and social cohesion for both Protestants and Catholics.[12] The vernacular versions were not mere regulatory documents aimed at the religious leadership of the various communions, but were manuals of instruction suited for a much broader audience. Rather than codifying arcane theological points, they were designed to present the essentials of the faith to common people and, in many cases, to children. Through various channels of dissemination, catechisms became not only widely available, but also highly influential. They were used not only for teaching in the home, the school, and the church, but also for the guidance of spiritual formation and preaching. As early as the first generation of Reformers some

11. *The Weekly Messenger*, 1840–42.

12. See Irene Dingel, "The Heidelberg Catechism in Sixteenth-Century Confessional Debates," in Karla Apperloo-Boersma and Herman J. Selderhuis, ed. *Power of Faith: 400 Years of the Heidelberg Catechism*, 41–49.

catechetical preaching had been done in Wittenberg and Geneva.[13] With the Heidelberg Catechism this homiletical function would become increasingly important.

In the late Middle Ages catechetical practice typically employed the Ten Commandments, the Apostles' Creed, and the Lord's Prayer (and sometimes the Ave Maria) as structural elements. In this schema the Law exposed the human predicament, the Creed offered the resolution of the problem, and the Lord's Prayer modeled the appropriate yearning for this remediation. This sequence was thought to correspond to the virtues of love (which is violated by sin), faith (which trusts in the offer of salvation through the ecclesial means of grace), and hope (which longs for sanctification). The Roman Catholic use of the Creed, the Ten Commandments, and the Lord's Prayer in catechisms was continued by many Protestants communities, although the sequence of the component sections was often modified.

The Reformation spawned an intensified concern for theological literacy, and therefore a growing interest in catechetical instruction. Given Protestantism's dual foci on sound doctrine and the priesthood of all believers, it was imperative to ensure that all believers were at least minimally theologically literate. Ordinary Protestant believers should know what differentiated their own communions from Catholics and from sectarian groups. As a consequence, catechisms became an even more crucial and popular confessional genre.

After traveling in German Protestant territories in 1528, Luther was appalled at the lack of the most basic theological knowledge among the general population. He found the ostensibly Protestant peasantry to be riddled with folk superstitions and the remnants of Catholic beliefs and practices. That problem inspired him to compose in 1529 a large catechism for pastors and a smaller one for uneducated adults and children.[14] He retained the medieval structure of most catechisms, but dropped the Ave Maria and added sections on the sacraments and a few other matters. The dissemination of the new catechisms to the laity was facilitated by the prevalence of printing presses in Germany, Switzerland, and the Netherlands. Lay people could purchase inexpensive copies for use at home. Luther's popular *Small Catechism* soon had a plethora of rivals, often inspired by the theological sensibilities of the theological and political elites of a particular political region. As Protestantism fragmented, a frenzy of publication resulted in the proliferation of catechisms, many of which were idiosyncratic and eclectic. The passion for catechesis was transplanted by many Protestant groups to North America and lay behind Nevin's childhood memories of Presbyterian pedagogy.

---

13. See Arie Baars, "'The Simple Heidelberg Catechism . . .': A Brief History of the Catechetical Sermon in the Netherlands," in *The Power of Faith*, 159–67.

14. See Martin Luther, *The Small Catechism*.

GENERAL INTRODUCTION

The Genesis of the Heidelberg Catechism

Given the importance of catechisms to Nevin and their prominence in much of Protestantism, it was natural that he would strive to make the Heidelberg catechism come alive for his new denominational family. That task required illuming its historical context. Nevin knew that the adoption and use of any particular catechism was always entangled with issues of political and cultural power. He was keenly aware that the Heidelberg Catechism was no exception. Whenever he would narrate the history of its genesis, which he did several different times in his authorship, he would always recount the saga of the political machinations that motivated its creation. The Catechism's inception, official adoption, and popularization were intertwined with the history of the Palatinate (the region around Heidelberg) where it was composed and with the history of the vicissitudes of Europe more broadly.[15] In the sixteenth century this enmeshment of politics and religion was inevitable, given the prevalent assumption that political cohesion required religious unity. Consequently, every time that Nevin discussed the catechism he rehearsed in minute detail the political and religious history of the Palatinate and the regions to which the catechism spread.

The ancient city of Heidelberg, the capital of the Palatinate, was situated on the banks of the Neckar River, an important trade route. The Palatinate was a dominant political and economic power in southwestern Germany, being one of the secular principalities that constituted the loose, fractious, and often precarious political amalgam known as "The Holy Roman Empire," which stretched from Austria to the Baltic Sea. The Palatinate's influence was even greater than its size would suggest, for its ruler, known as the "Elector," was one of the four (later five) secular magnates who, along with three ecclesiastical rulers, chose the Holy Roman Emperor.

In the mid-sixteenth century the religious situation in the Palatinate was confusing and troubling. While the state still recognized the authority of the pope during the first decades of the Reformation, Lutheran influences from Saxony had been felt ever since the 1520s and had become stronger during from the 1540s. Segments of the population had been influenced by humanism, and anticlericalism was popular and widespread. In many places Lutheran forms of worship were practiced, but only clandestinely, for the influence of the Holy Roman Emperor, who was staunchly Catholic, was considerable in the region. No matter what they might privately believe, the successive Electors needed Emperor Charles V's support in their struggles against rival

---

15. The Palatinate, "*Pfalz*" in German, included two regions of Germany, one that bordered on Bohemia and Bavaria (the "Upper Palatinate"), and one that was situated on the Rhine between Alsace, Baden, and Württemberg (the "Lower Palatinate"). The premier city of the region near the Rhine was Heidelberg, renowned in the sixteenth century for its university and impressive library.

German princes.[16] During the 1540s and 50s the Electors Ludwig V[17] and Frederick II[18] tried to accommodate the opposed Protestant and Catholic factions, allowing some Protestant-like reforms, including communion in both kinds and sometimes even clerical marriage, without overtly breaking with the Roman Catholic Church. Frederick quietly staffed his administration with Protestants who were willing to be relatively nonpolemical. The ascension of Elector Otto Henry[19] in 1556 triggered more profound religious changes. The new elector, who looked to Philip Melanchthon for theological guidance, declared the Palatinate to be Lutheran. He proclaimed that the Lutheran Augsburg Confession was its new doctrinal norm and authorized the use of a Lutheran catechism by Johannes Brenz.[20]

In theory the embrace of Lutheranism was a legitimate move on Otto Henry's part. A brutal series of wars between the Catholics and Protestants in Germany had been ended in 1555 by the Peace of Augsburg, which recognized both the Catholic and Lutheran faiths as permissible religions for the empire's principalities. This did not mean that both Lutheranism and Roman Catholicism were tolerated side-by-side throughout the German territories, for only one of those communions could be established in a given principality, depending on the religious proclivities of its

---

16. Charles V (1500–58) was Holy Roman Emperor and Archduke of Austria from 1519. He had already become Lord of the Netherlands in 1506, and King of Spain in 1516. The boundaries of his domain extended from Germany to northern Italy. He is remembered for his efforts to revitalize the medieval concept of a universal Christian imperium and was committed to safeguarding the integrity of the Holy Roman Empire from the Protestant Reformation. However, he eventually agreed to the Peace of Augsburg and relinquished his efforts to entirely eliminate the Protestant threat to unity. In his last years as Emperor his policy toward German Protestants drifted toward containment.

17. Elector Ludwig V (1478–1544) was not adverse to Protestantism, even though four of his brothers were Roman Catholic bishops. He often tried to mediate in religious controversies.

18. Elector Frederick II (1482–1556) was Elector of the Palatinate from 1544 to 1556. He actually embraced the Lutheran faith in 1546 but did not actively support the Schmalkaldic League of rebellious Lutheran princes. He was outlawed by Emperor Charles V, which motivated him to return to the Catholic fold.

19. Otto Henry (or Otho-Henry), the Magnanimous (1502–59) was Elector of the Palatinate from 1556 to 1559. He is remembered for his generous support of the arts and sciences and for the establishment of the Bibliotheca Palatina in the 1550s. He converted to Lutheranism in 1541 and overtly supported the Lutheran Schmalkaldic League.

20. The Augsburg Confession of 1531 was largely composed by Philip Melanchthon (1497–1560), a Wittenberg theologian who worked closely with Martin Luther. It was presented at the Diet of Augsburg to explain the new faith to Emperor Charles V. It became such an influential confessional document in Lutheranism that it was often used to define genuine Lutheran doctrine. Johannes Brenz (1499–1570), a theologian active in neighboring Württemberg, had composed the *Landescatechismus*. He had become an avid supporter of Luther's views after meeting him at the disputation at Heidelberg in 1518. He is remembered for his *Syngramma Suevicum* (1525), in which he attacked Œcolampadius and presented his theory concerning the way in which the body and blood of Christ are actually present in the Sacrament. He participated in many of the important theological conferences that shaped Lutheranism, including the Colloquy of Marburg and the Diet of Augsburg. See Gunnoe, "The Reformation of the Palatinate and the Origins of the Heidelberg Catechism," in Bierma, ed., *An Introduction to the Heidelberg Catechism*, 15–47.

ruler.[21] Given that arrangement, it was entirely permissible that Lutheranism could be recognized as the religion of the Palatinate, if its ruler so decided. In the eyes of the Emperor, the main criterion for counting a form of Christianity as Lutheran was adherence to the Augsburg Confession. Besides Catholicism and Lutheranism, no other form of Christianity was to be tolerated as an established religion in any of the Empire's principalities.

The legalization of Lutheranism as the only permissible Protestant option for a territory generated problems for the Elector. Although Otto Henry had opted for Lutheranism, the religious situation in the Palatinate was too complex for Lutheranism to triumph easily. Adherents of Catholicism remained in the territory and some residual monastic establishments continued. Anabaptist and spiritualist teachings were gaining an audience. Moreover, Reformed influences had been introduced, emanating from neighboring Switzerland and Strasbourg. Reformed-style iconoclasm, including purging sanctuaries of devotional objects and simplifying clerical vestments, was tacitly sanctioned by the state. Otto Henry himself was partly responsible for this theological pluralism, for he had invited not only Lutherans but also followers of Ulrich Zwingli, the influential reformer of Zurich, to teach in the university.[22] These realities sowed the seeds for bitter religious controversy and social factionalism.

When Otto Henry died in 1559 his heir, Frederick III (known as "the Pious")[23] began to show favor toward Reformed theology, or at least toward the Reformed-leaning

---

21. The policy was a decision of the imperial Diet meeting in Augsburg that ended the recurrent hostilities between the Catholic territories of the Empire and the various Lutheran military alliances. The right of each prince to determine the nature of religious practice in his own territory became popularly known as *"cuius regio, cuius religio"* ("whose religion, his religion").

22. Ulrich (Huldrych) Zwingli (1481–1531) was the leading Reformer of Zurich in Switzerland. He had been deeply influenced by the humanist writings of Erasmus. He was more extreme than Luther in his condemnation of many Roman Catholic liturgical practices, often denouncing them as idolatrous. As the pastor of the Grossmünster in Zürich he introduced a controversial new communion liturgy to replace the Mass. His new liturgy denied that an actual sacrifice occurred during the ritual as the Roman Catholic wording suggested. According to Zwingli, Christ had already made the sacrifice for sin once and for all in eternity. In his view the Eucharist was "a memorial of the sacrifice" and not a repetition of the sacrifice. In 1529 at the Marburg Colloquy he failed to reach an agreement with Luther on the presence of Christ in the Lord's Supper and thereby made it obvious that his reform movement was different from Luther's. Nevin would often be critical of the influence that Zwingli had on the development of the Reformed tradition.

23. Elector Frederick III, the Pious (1515–76), was attracted to the Protestant faith long before he became Elector Palatine of the Rhine in 1559. When he did become the Elector he sought to get a clearer understanding of the controversy raging between the strict Lutherans, the followers of Melanchthon, and the different strands of the Reformed tradition. As Frederick immersed himself in theological studies he gravitated to the Reformed faith. A disputation held in 1560 between Lutheran and Reformed theologians solidified Frederick's antipathy to Lutheran hyper-orthodoxy, particularly in regard to the Lord's Supper. After the Naumburg Convention in 1561 Frederick fully endorsed Reformed doctrine, and made the Reformed faith the official religion of his domain by supervising the composition and promotion of the Heidelberg Catechism. His backing gave the German Reformed movement a secure position from which to spread within the Holy Roman Empire.

theology of the followers of the moderate Lutheran, Philip Melanchthon.[24] The drift toward the Reformed pole of the theological spectrum, including the encouragement of the Reformed practice of "breaking the bread" in the Lord's Supper, alarmed the highly orthodox Lutheran Duke Christopher of neighboring Württemberg, who protested that the Reformed faith violated the tenets of the Augsburg Confession, and therefore was not a licit religious option according to the Peace of Augsburg. Duke Christopher argued that Reformed teachings could not be tolerated as the religion of any German principality because they did not accord with the Augsburg Confession. If this accusation stuck, the Palatinate would be vulnerable to reprisals from the Empire.

In order to avoid a confrontation, it was incumbent upon Elector Frederick to convince the Holy Roman Emperor Maximilian II, a Catholic, that the faith that he sought to foster was congruent with the Augsburg Confession.[25] Ironically, a Catholic ruler would have to judge whether Frederick was sufficiently Lutheran or not. There was some reason to be optimistic about this prospect, for Maximilian was a moderate Catholic who hoped to avoid another round of lethal religious civil war. Moreover, most of the Lutheran rulers of German principalities did not relish the prospect of a costly conflict with the Palatinate, or of a dangerous fracture in the German Protestant united front. It was politically advantageous for Frederick to portray his theological leanings as at least being compatible with Lutheranism. Consequently, Frederick needed a confessional document that appeared to be, if not exactly Lutheran, at least Lutherish. The Heidelberg Catechism which he had recently commissioned was his primary evidence of his theological credentials. Happily, in 1566 Maximilian at a meeting of the Imperial Diet at Augsburg did indeed judge the Heidelberg Catechism to be within the bounds of the Augsburg Confession and confirmed Frederick as a prince of the Holy Roman Empire.

The Palatinate's religious problems were not merely a function of its external relations to other German states or to the Empire. Domestic religious feuds and rivalries also disrupted the tranquility of the region. Under the succession of electors, divergent religious orientations had emerged in the region, with ministers who held different doctrinal positions condemning one another in sermons and in print. With

---

24. Philip Melanchthon (1497–1560) was a Wittenberg theologian who worked closely with Martin Luther. He was the principal author of the Augsburg Confession and wrote *Loci Communes,* the first sketch of a Protestant systematic theology. His views on Christ's presence in the Eucharist, the relation of grace and freedom, and the nature of divine election earned him the reputation of being a Lutheran moderate. The "Philippist" faction in Lutheranism soon raised the suspicions of the strict Lutherans, the Gnesio-Lutherans, who insisted upon an unequivocal identification of the body and blood of Christ with the physical bread and wine.

25. Maximilian II (1527–76) was Holy Roman Emperor from 1564 until his death. His reign was vexed by the Protestant and Catholic trends toward stricter confessional identity that followed the Peace of Augsburg (1555). Although he remained Catholic, he had been educated by non-doctrinaire humanist scholars and maintained cordial relations with many prominent Lutherans. He refused to allow the publication of the decrees of the Council of Trent in Austria, and worked for religious reconciliation.

few trained Protestant ministers, eclectic, home-grown doctrinal opinions proliferated. As Nevin always noted, by the 1560's several different catechisms, some Lutheran and some Zwinglian, were in circulation in the Palatinate region of Germany. The tension between the Lutheran and Reformed factions grew, exacerbated by the tension within Lutheranism between the more irenic party of Melanchthon, and a more doctrinally precise group. Melanchthon and his supporters, known as "Phillipists," proposed that some Catholic ceremonies could be retained by Protestants because they were "adiaphora," matters that did not jeopardize salvation. This alarmed the "Gnesio-Lutherans," including the very pugnacious Flacius Illyricus,[26] who fought to preserve Luther's original teachings in their alleged purity. The factions clashed over the differences between the 1530 version of the Augsburg Confession, known as the *Invariata*, and Melanchthon's somewhat more open-ended revision of 1540, known as the *Variata*. The Gnesio-Lutherans insisted upon acknowledging the *Invariata* as the only doctrinal standard, while the Philippists accepted the authority of the *Variata*. Both types of Lutherans were present in the Palatinate.

Much of this tension in the Protestant world was ultimately rooted in the divergence of Luther and Zwingli on the significance and understanding of Eucharist. The followers of Zwingli were accused of mere memorialism by the strict Lutherans, while the strict Lutherans were denounced by many of the Reformed party as crypto-Catholics who believed that Christ was physically present in the elements of the bread and wine. The situation was complicated by the fact that within the Lutheran fold the Gnesio-Lutherans followed the *Invariata* which described the body and blood of Christ as being "under" the form of bread and wine, while the Philippists adhered to the *Variata* which stated that the body and blood "are truly exhibited" with the bread and wine. Many Reformed clergy and theologians balked at the focus on the physical elements of the *Invariata*, but found Melanchthon's revised formulation to be acceptable.

Elector Frederick was disturbed by the cacophony of theological voices in his principality. He, and other German princes, were motivated not only by a desire for ideological solidarity, but also by a concern to protect what they took to be the central tenets of Christian faith and practice from the corrosive effects of theological chaos. (Nevin, of course, was not blind to the parallel with his own day.) The unity of the faith and its transmission to the next generation could be jeopardized by the general confusion. Frederick desperately needed something to unify his domain and safeguard his vision of orthodox faith. He also needed something that would satisfy the moderate

---

26. Matthias Flacius Illyricus (1520–75), born in Croatia, was a theologian, church historian, philosopher, and Lutheran zealot. He opposed Melanchthon's efforts in the 1550s to find a way of coexisting with the Catholics who had just emerged victorious from the Schmalkaldic war. Illyricus rejected the notion that many Lutheran practices were not necessary for salvation, supported the doctrine of total depravity, claimed that the image of God in humanity had been completely destroyed, and insisted upon the physical presence of Christ in the Eucharistic elements. His often extreme views were the cause of much opposition from many of his fellow Lutherans.

Lutherans without alienating the Reformed party. In the eyes of Frederick, the Palatinate needed a confessional document that could achieve several different goals: foster a common faith, promote social cohesion, and nurture new generations of believers. It had to have enough latitude to be acceptable to a range of divergent theological factions, but also have enough specificity to promote identity-definition. An authoritative catechism could serve these purposes by displacing the myriad Lutheran and Reformed catechisms then in circulation.

Accordingly, Frederick enlisted the services of Zacharius Ursinus, a twenty-eight year old theologian who had recently been called to the University of Heidelberg, to participate on a team charged with composing a new catechism for the Palatinate.[27] Ursinus had been a student of Philip Melanchthon, the irenic Lutheran leader who had been advising Frederick on theological matters. Ursinus had fallen afoul of the rigid Lutheran party, and had already been exposed to Reformed thought, to which he was sympathetic. This made him ideally suited to perform a mediatorial role between the moderate Lutherans and most of the Reformed groups. Ursinus was assisted to some extent by Caspar Olevianus,[28] a talented young preacher who had studied under John Calvin in Geneva and was on good terms with Theodore Beza,[29] Calvin's successor. Following the recommendation of Melanchthon, who died shortly thereafter, the two theologians sought to strive for biblical simplicity and to avoid the potentially divisive speculative claims of the emerging Protestant scholasticisms. Although Ursinus was the principal author, other university professors and leading ministers served on the authorial team. Church superintendents and lay leaders, including Frederick himself, worked prominently as consultants and editors toward the end of the process of composition.

The final product approximated Frederick's goal, for it focused attention on themes that united the Lutheran and Reformed communions, and avoided most of the issues that divided them. The text synthesized elements of the moderate Lutheranism of Melanchthon with the irenic Reformed thought of Martin Bucer[30] and Peter

---

27 Zacharias Ursinus (1534–83) was a sixteenth-century German Reformed theologian and Protestant reformer who became the leading theologian of the Reformed Protestant movement in the Palatinate. He is best known as the primary author of the Heidelberg Catechism.

28 Frederick Caspar Olevianus (1536–87) was a Reformed theologian who was called to teach at the University of Heidelberg in 1560. Olevianus was one of the pioneers of Reformed "covenant theology" that revolved around the distinction of the "covenant of works" and the "covenant of grace." He was regarded as being more eloquent and rhetorically adept than Ursinus, with whom he worked on the composition of the Heidelberg Catechism.

29. Theodore Beza (1519–1605), a French Protestant scholar and reformer, assumed John Calvin's mantle of Geneva's spiritual leader. He polemicized against the Gnesio-Lutherans on the doctrine of the Eucharist and developed a thoroughly supralapsarian understanding of God's sovereign will. He is known for his treatise *Summa totius Christianismi*, which exhibits the centrality of the extreme predestinarian perspective in his theological system.

30. Martin Bucer (1491–1551) was the leading Reformer of Strasbourg. Although he became known as one of the progenitors of the Reformed tradition, he sought to mediate between the positions of Luther and Zwingli. He worked with Melanchthon on the Wittenberg Concord, a statement

Martyr.[31] The implicit emphasis of common ground was attractive to all Protestant parties except the hard-liners on both sides. Its acceptability to Melanchthonians, Calvinists, and mild Zwinglians appealed to Nevin's desire to find common ground among "churchly" Protestants. Frederick, Ursinus, and Melanchthon would emerge as the irenic heroes of Nevin's frequent narrations of the Catechism's genesis.

Frederick's campaign to promote the Catechism began immediately. A German version of the text was prepared for use in the churches, and a Latin text was composed for scholars, since Latin was the *lingua franca* of the European academic world. In January 1563 the Catechism was officially approved by a Heidelberg synod. With the backing of Frederick, its wide dissemination in the churches of the Palatinate commenced.

Nevin applauded the Heidelberg Catechism's success (in most instances) in finding common ground between the moderate streams of the Lutheran and Reformed traditions. A Lutherish flavor can be detected in some features of the Catechism. Like many of the Lutheran confessional documents it makes Christ's gracious redemptive activity the linchpin of everything else. Like the Augsburg Confession it concentrates on the individual's alienation from God and need for reconciliation. Unlike some other Reformed catechisms and confessions of faith from this era, it does not begin with an abstract definition of God's nature and attributes. Nor does it deal extensively with the sequence of God's eternal decrees, or speculate about the hidden purposes of God. For example, in the Catechism God's sovereignty is not treated as a speculative problem involving the relation of God's agency to creaturely actions and events, but rather as a pastoral matter concerning the reassurance of troubled and frightened human beings. As Nevin repeatedly pointed out, the logic of a metaphysical system, with axioms and corollaries, and premises and implications, does not determine the flow of topics in the document. Practical pastoral concerns, and not the architectonics of a systematic theology, dictate the Catechism's structure. It follows the sequence of questions and concerns that would naturally arise in any effort to embrace and enact the Christian life.

Nevin appreciated the Catechism's existential and self-reflexive mood, and hailed that as a characteristic of all genuine theology. He lauded it for avoiding the pitfalls of "metaphysical Calvinism," by which he meant the tradition stretching from the Synod

---

of common articles of belief. He was lauded by Nevin for his ecumenical efforts toward bringing doctrinal unity to the various Protestant traditions of his time.

31. Peter Martyr Vermigli (1499–1562) was an Italian-born Reformed theologian who taught in Strasbourg, Oxford, and Zürich. He vehemently denied that Christ was locally present in the eucharistic elements and defended with equal vigor a consistent doctrine of double predestination. He influenced the Edwardian Reformation through the eucharistic liturgy of the 1552 *Book of Common Prayer*. His *Loci Communes* (1576) became a standard Reformed theological textbook.

of Dort,[32] through seventeenth century Reformed dogmaticians like Turretini,[33] to the systematic theologians of Princeton Seminary like Charles Hodge.[34] That theological trajectory was obsessed with speculations about God's primordial plan for the universe, including God's decisions to save certain individuals, damn others, create humanity, permit or ordain the fall into sin, and become incarnate. The relation of God's will to human actions figured prominently in those doctrinal systems, many of which suggested divine predeterminism. Nevin critiqued this orientation for at least three reasons. First, the relation of infinite agency to finite agency could not be conceptualized. Nevin exhibited a Kantian humility concerning the powers of pure reason, and was conscious of reason's limitations. Secondly, attempts to authoritatively stipulate answers to such elusive questions needlessly divided Christian communions. Thirdly, metaphysical probings of the divine mysteries distracted Christians from the important task of living out the Christian life. The mysteries of God could not be conceptually grasped, but the contours of the Christian life could be known, and were manifested in the worship and nurture of the church.

Appropriate to this personal, existential orientation is the Catechism's celebrated opening question, "What is your only comfort in life and in death?" The metaphysical perfections of God are not its starting point. Following the lead of this first question, the mood of reassurance, hope, and confidence pervades the text. According to the Catechism, Christians do not need to secure their own earthly or eternal well-being, for God, through Christ, has claimed them as God's beloved children. The Catechism follows the flow of Christian experience, moving from the exposé of sin and misery to the celebration of God's remedial grace, and finally on to the response of gratitude for that grace. This basic three-fold structure has been famously summarized as "guilt, grace, and gratitude." That structure was thought to be discernible in the Epistle to the

---

32. The Synod of Dort (1618–19) was an international synod called by the Dutch Reformed Church to settle objections to the Belgic Confession that had been raised by the "Remonstrants," the followers of the theologian Jacob Arminius (1560–1609). Arminius had voiced concerns that the Calvinists were interpreting God's sovereignty in regard to salvation in ways that suggested absolute divine determinism. The synod decided against most of the Remonstrant positions, and affirmed the doctrines of total depravity, unconditional grace, limited atonement, irresistible grace, and the perseverance of the saints.

33. François Turrettini (Francis Turretine, 1623–87) was a Genevan-Italian Reformed theologian who defended the decisions of the Synod of Dort and articulated the theory of the plenary verbal inspiration of the Bible. His three-part *Institutio Theologiae Elencticae* (1679–85) was widely used as a textbook of conservative scholastic Reformed theology, and shaped many early-nineteenth century Reformed theologians in America.

34. Charles Hodge (1797–1879) was a celebrated Presbyterian theologian at Princeton Theological Seminary, who in the 1820's had taught Nevin and had allowed him to be his replacement while he engaged in an academic tour of Europe. Hodge developed a scholastically orthodox version of Calvinism known for its logical rigor and its effort to deduce doctrines from biblical "facts" in the way that physical scientists derive conclusions from the data of the natural world.

Romans, an authoritative precedent. It had also been anticipated by many Lutheran and Reformed doctrinal texts which were well-known to Ursinus.[35]

A more distinctive Reformed orientation can be perceived at other points, although it is often muted. For example, the Catechism frequently stresses the fact that God is sufficiently powerful to ensure that all will be well with us, thereby sounding the characteristic Reformed note of divine sovereignty. However, it refuses to speculate about the mechanisms of God's providential activity and avoids a detailed discussion of predestination, as do many other Reformed confessional and catechetical documents. Also in a Reformed manner it asserts that although Christ is in solidarity with humanity (a Lutheran emphasis), Christ is also reigning in heaven with sovereign power over the universe. Again following a Reformed trajectory, in its third section the Catechism presents obedience as an integral part of our grateful response to God's grace, and in this context explicates the Ten Commandments.[36] The Law is not just a threat that terrifies the conscience and awakens the longing for forgiveness, nor is it only a deterrent that restrains sin through the threat of punishment. Luther had emphasized these "two uses of the Law," and subsequent Lutherans continued to stress them. But in the structure of the Heidelberg Catechism the Law has a crucial "third use," for it is also a welcomed guide to direct the lives of the saints. (Although this "third use of the Law" became a hallmark of Reformed theology, Melanchthon and even Luther himself had espoused it, with careful qualifications, and it is affirmed in the Lutheran Formula of Concord.) With confidence in God's grace and a delight in doing God's will, the Christian life of obedience unfolds as an act of gratitude. Nevin was keenly aware of the significance of the Heidelberg Catechism's positioning of the questions concerning the Ten Commandments. He appreciated the fact that this structure implied that joyful obedience to God followed from union with Christ through faith.

More controversially, on the issue of the Eucharist the Heidelberg Catechism has been regarded as much more Reformed than Lutheran. In 1529 at the Marburg Colloquy Luther and Ulrich Zwingli, the reformer of Zurich, had attempted to reach a consensus on all theological points, but had discovered that they could not agree on the understanding of the Lord's Supper. Luther insisted upon a real physical presence of Jesus Christ in some way associated with the physical elements of bread and wine, while Zwingli maintained that the ritual makes vividly available to faith the remembrance of the life, death, and resurrection of Jesus of Nazareth. John Calvin of Geneva later taught that through the sacred meal believers' hearts are spiritually "lifted up" to be united to Christ in heaven in order to feed on his glorified life. Further complicating matters, the view of Melanchthon the Lutheran was perceived by many to have affinities with Calvin's "real spiritual presence." In this controversy the Heidelberg

---

35. Bierma, "The Sources and Theological Orientation of the Heidelberg Catechism," in Bierma, ed., *An Introduction to the Heidelberg Catechism*, 81–86.

36. Bierma, "Sources and Theological Orientation," 89–91.

Catechism seems to lean toward the Melanchthon/Calvin end of the spectrum. The Catholic view is forcefully rejected and the staunch Lutheran position seems to be ruled out, while the Zwinglian interpretation is not clearly excluded. In Question 75 the Catechism speaks of being nourished and refreshed by Christ's body and blood just as surely as tasting the bread and the wine, but it hesitates to assert that the bread and the wine are instruments of that spiritual feeding.[37]

Nevin's own Eucharistic theology clearly approximated that of the Calvin/Melanchthon camp. He disparaged the physicalism of the Lutheran position as well as the "subjectivism" and "rationalism" of the Zwinglian view. Consequently, he found the teaching of the Heidelberg Catechism, suggesting some sort of real spiritual presence of Christ, to be quite congenial. In fact, the Catechism may have helped him clarify and consolidate his own thinking about the Lord's Supper.

On most issues the authors of the Catechism succeeded in identifying doctrinal themes upon which moderate Lutherans, Calvinists, and even some Zwinglians could agree. But in spite of its irenic nature, by no means was the Catechism greeted with universal acclaim. Almost immediately in 1563 and 1564 it became the subject of polemical attacks by the conservative Lutheran theologians Heshusius[38] and Flacius Illyricus. They protested that any attempt to replace Luther's *Small Catechism* was nothing less than diabolical. The Lutheran critics objected to the new catechism's teachings about the Eucharist which did not adequately link the presence of Christ to the physical elements. For them, the mode of Christ's presence was not an *adiaphora* (a matter of indifference in regard to the issue of salvation) about which a variety of opinions could be tolerated. Rather, the precise formulation of the doctrine of the Eucharist was essential to the well-being of the church. On this topic the Heidelberg Catechism failed their test. These "Gnesio-Lutherans" also denounced the fact that the Catechism was imposed on the Palatinate church by the elector, who was thereby assuming undue authority in ecclesial doctrinal affairs.

Catholics, of course, were even more hostile and alarmed. In neighboring Alsace it was feared that an accessible, well-written Protestant catechism would lure lay people away from the Catholic Church. Seeking an antidote to the popular Palatinate catechism, they responded in 1564 by publishing a new edition the catechism of Canisius,[39] whose Catholic orthodoxy was beyond reproach. A small summary was even appended to reach a broader and less sophisticated audience. Nevin admitted that the ecumenical appeal of the Catechism was limited to Protestants, but he did

---

37. Bierma, "Sources and Theological Orientation," 100.

38. Tilemann Heshusius (1527–88) was a vehement Lutheran controversialist. In 1559 while he served as superintendent of the churches in the Palatinate he quarreled publicly with his Reformed-leaning deacon, Wilhelm Klebitz, so viciously that they both were dismissed from office. In Bremen and other cities Heshusius became the implacable foe of any Lutherans whom he suspected of being Crypto-Calvinists.

39. Peter Canisius (1521–97) was a Dutch Jesuit who did much to oppose the spread of Protestantism in the Netherlands and the German-speaking lands.

marvel that, given the religious animosity of the era, the document was so restrained in its critique of Catholicism.

Part of Nevin's strategy in promoting the Heidelberg Catechism was to make the case that it was the premier Reformed confessional document, treasured by all Reformed churches around the world. He wanted to make it clear that for Reformed theology it was even more foundational than the Genevan Catechism, the Belgic Confession, the Second Helvetic Confession, the Canons of the Synod of Dort, or the Westminster Confession and its corresponding catechisms. Here he could appeal to ample historical evidence to support his contention.

Becoming immediately popular, the German text of the Heidelberg Catechism went through four different editions in 1563 alone. In that same year it was placed in the newly created Church Order of the Palatinate, in between the order for baptism and the order for the Lord's Supper. That position in the church's worship book is significant, for it displayed the link between baptism and the Eucharist. It stipulated that baptized children seeking to be admitted to the Lord's Table should be required to profess their faith in the presence of the church. That profession should be guided by their internalization of the teachings of the Catechism. In effect, the first question of the Catechism functioned as an affirmation and appropriation of the individual's baptismal covenant. In the Palatinate the Catechism was introduced to the church as vital instruction concerning how believers should live as baptized children of the covenant. That role guaranteed its importance. Nevin's defense of the Catechism would capitalize on its role as part of the on-going nurture of the church, closely tied to the church's sacramental life.

One of the distinctive characteristics of the Reformed churches in the Palatinate was the attention given to catechetical preaching. As early as 1563 the *Kirchenordnung* of the Palatinate stipulated that a portion of the Catechism should be read aloud at every Sunday service, and that the entire Catechism should be covered in nine Sundays.[40] Even more daringly, sermons to expound the Catechism's questions and answers were mandated for every Sunday afternoon service. In spite of disruptions caused by invasions, warfare, and eventual Catholic political hegemony, the practice of catechetical preaching continued in many Reformed congregations in the Palatinate through the eighteenth century. Although this type of preaching had become rare in Pennsylvania, the historical model of regular catechetical preaching would inspire Nevin to advocate its use in local churches.

To demonstrate the unique status of the Heidelberg Catechism Nevin devoted almost as much attention to its reception in the Netherlands as he did to its popularity in the Palatinate. Much of the population of the Protestant portions of the

---

40. See Carl Ullmann, "Sketches from the History of the Heidelberg Catechism in the Land of Its Birth," in Henry Harbaugh, ed., *Tercentenary Monument in Commemoration of the Three Hundredth Anniversary of the Heidelberg Catechism*, 125. Ullmann (1796–1865) was a German Calvinist theologian and professor of church history, dogmatics, and symbolics who is noted for the nuanced distinction of faith and dogmatics elaborated in his most famous work, *Das Wesen des Christenthums* (1845).

Netherlands, struggling against the attempt by their Hapsburg overlords to forcibly preserve Catholicism, quickly became ardent devotees of the Heidelberg Catechism. The Protestant-leaning city of Emden, a center of the printing industry, had strong commercial ties with the Palatinate. Religious influences followed the trade routes. A Dutch translation of the Catechism complete with a Psalter appeared as early as 1566. At the Synod of Emden in 1571 the Catechism was adopted by the nascent Dutch Reformed church as an instructional tract. Along with the *Confessio Belgica* by Guido de Bres it was accepted as an authoritative confessional standard.[41] The Catechism was mandated for use in the church, the school, and the family. As the role of the Catechism in civil society as a marker of cultural identity became more prominent, catechetical classes were held in churches during weekdays with special instructors. To enhance its effectiveness, a shorter version of the Catechism for children, the *Kort Begrip* by Herman Faukelius, was published in 1608. By 1618 the Synod of Dort had stipulated that two days of catechetical teaching should occur in the schools each week.

Like the Palatinate, the Reformed churches in the Netherlands encouraged catechetical preaching, and achieved lasting success in implementing it.[42] The Synod of the Hague in 1586 authorized preaching on the Heidelberg Catechism during a Sunday afternoon service. This injunction was reiterated by Synod of Dort (1618–19), which added that such sermons should be simple and easily understandable. The requirement of such preaching was incorporated into the Church Order of Dort. The practice of catechetical preaching continued through the eighteenth century and was transplanted to the Dutch settlements in the American colonies. Nevin could assume that the Dutch Reformed Church in America, with its theological center in neighboring New Brunswick, would have a deep attachment to the Catechism and would preserve its own traditions of interpreting it. The enduring power of that virulently anti-Catholic Dutch tradition would one day cause Nevin some vexation.

However, the Dutch attachment to the Heidelberg Catechism was never uniform. The reasons for disenchantment with it were multiple. In the more rural areas of the Netherlands, the practice of catechetical preaching was not widespread, for gathering on Sunday afternoon was not practical. On the theological front, the Arminian Remonstrants protested that the church had elevated the Catechism above Scripture itself. They eventually produced their own instructional document, the Goudse Catechism of 1607, as an alternative. In the later seventeenth century a Pietist movement, the *Nadere Reformatie*, sometimes emphasized catechetical instruction, but sometimes downplayed it. To further complicate the situation, a scholastic hyper-Reformed party, virulently opposed to the Remonstrants, expressed disappointment that the

---

41. Guido de Bres (1522–67) was a Flemish theologian who was eventually executed by the Inquisition during the early days of the Dutch revolt against the Catholic Hapsburgs. He had studied under Calvin and Beza, and their influence was evident in the confession of faith that he authored.

42. See Arie Baars, "'The Simple Heidelberg Catechism . . .': A Brief History of the Catechetical Sermon in the Netherlands," in *Power of Faith*, 159–67.

catechism had not adopted the doctrine of double predestination as an organizing principle. Meanwhile, by the early eighteenth century the Enlightenment, particularly influential in cosmopolitan Amsterdam, eroded attachment to any doctrinal system.

For all these reasons attendance at catechetical instruction and catechetical preaching in the Netherlands declined in the late eighteenth century. That decline was accelerated by the impact of the French Revolution which led to the constitutional separation of church and state in 1795. After the Napoleonic wars the New Church Order of 1816 still upheld the Catechism as a confessional norm, but mandated that agreement with the doctrinal standards was only necessary in so far as they agreed with Scripture. Institutional support for the Heidelberg Catechism was declining in the Netherlands. In 1863 local pastors were permitted to decide for themselves whether they would preach from the Heidelberg Catechism or not. In spite of this diminishment of official ecclesial authority, spiritual autobiographies from the nineteenth century testified to the Catechism's enduring power. Nevin was aware of the Catechism's continuing (although somewhat reduced) significance in the Netherlands, and used its lingering popularity as an argument for its preeminent status in the Reformed world.

It was also important for Nevin's context that a hyper-orthodox Dutch Reformed group adhered doggedly to the church order of Dort. This faction, disgruntled by the relaxation of confessional authority, seceded from the main ecclesial body in 1834, forming an independent synod. These Netherlandish Christians did continue the practice of regular catechetical preaching. Many of these more traditionalist Dutch Reformed people immigrated to the United States and joined the Reformed Church of America. They would infuse into that body an intensified commitment to the use of the Catechism. They would also promote a tendency to interpret the Catechism in the light of the Canons of the Synod of Dort. Nevin would welcome their enthusiasm for the Catechism, but not the hermeneutic lens through which they interpreted it.

Nevin noted that the Heidelberg Catechism also had an impact on the English-speaking world. In this he was not mistaken, although he did exaggerate the extent and depth of its influence. The Catechism was translated into English in 1572 and immediately began to inform English Puritanism and Scottish Presbyterianism. Thomas Goodwin, who became a participant in the Westminster Assembly, remarked that it was required reading for the Puritans at Oxford. During the early seventeenth century it was also much in use in the Puritan colleges of Cambridge, particularly Emmanuel College.[43] In Scotland the Heidelberg Catechism had been published in 1591, 1615, and 1621, and was well-known in Presbyterian theological circles. The Scottish

---

43. Fesko, *The Theology of the Westminster Standards*, 60–61. Thomas Goodwin (1600–80) was a celebrated English Puritan pastor who served as Oliver Cromwell's chaplain. A champion of congregational polity, he helped amend the Westminster Confession to make it more acceptable to the non-Presbyterian Independents in a document known as the Savoy Declaration.

theologian Robert Rollock was known for using it extensively in his pedagogy.[44] In the early seventeenth century the Scottish Church officially approved its use, along with several indigenous catechisms and the Geneva Catechism. However, by the late seventeenth century most of these catechisms, including the Heidelberg document, were largely supplanted by the Westminster Longer and Shorter Catechisms. It was the Westminster texts, and not the Heidelberg Catechism, that would shape the faith of generations of Presbyterians, including those, like Nevin's family, who were transplanted to North America.

Nevin knew that the Heidelberg Catechism was not unknown in Congregational circles, although it was not widely influential. The Puritan-descended Congregational churches of New England employed a plethora of catechisms. Because each congregation could decide for itself which, if any, to use, many of these catechisms were either local, home-grown texts, or were the products of their English origins. The most popular of these was William Perkins' "Six Principles of the Christian Religion," which dated from the late sixteenth century. This was eventually supplanted by the *New England Primer*, based on the English *Protestant Tutor*. Many of the editions of the primer also contained the Westminster Shorter Catechism, or John Cotton's Shorter Catechism, or both.[45] Given this pluralism of confessional documents, it was mainly just the clergy who were familiar with the Heidelberg Catechism as a theological resource. In his narration of the Catechism's influence, Nevin, of course, did not emphasize its relative neglect by Congregationalists, although he did acknowledge their eventual lack of interest.[46] This neglect, he would argue, was one of the problems with "Puritanism."

Declining Interest in Catechetical Instruction in Nineteenth Century America

However, in spite of the high esteem in which the Heidelberg Catechism was held by the various Reformed traditions, during the eighteenth and early nineteenth centuries enthusiasm for any sort of catechism had waned in many North American Protestant circles. Several cultural developments, some rooted in Europe and some unique to the New World, conspired to motivate this decline of enthusiasm for catechisms in general and the Heidelberg Catechism in particular. Nevin's effort to rehabilitate the Heidelberg Catechism placed him with a small but vocal collection of American confessional theologians who, often for very different reasons, were swimming against the

---

44. Robert Rollock (1555–99) was an influential professor of theology at Edinburgh who trained a generation of pastors.

45. John Cotton (1585–1652) was the premier theologian of Massachusetts Bay Colony during its formative period. A strict Puritan, in England he had denounced the use of "Romish" vestments and ceremonies. Cotton helped conceptualize and defend New England's congregational polity.

46. See Wilberforce Eames, *Early New England Catechisms*.

prevailing cultural currents. Nevin's writings show that he was keenly aware of many, if not all, of these potent cultural trends.

Some of the cultural and theological shifts that predisposed many Americans to dispense with catechisms in general and the Heidelberg Catechism in particular (or at least to minimize its significance) had remote roots in tensions in European ecclesial politics, even though the United States did not have a European-style state church. This was particularly true of the ethnic populations from Continental Europe that had migrated across the Atlantic most recently.[47] Many of these transplanted tensions had been generated by the complicated and troubled relations of the church and the state in the various German principalities. In Germany three different attitudes toward the Heidelberg Catechism emerged that would have an impact upon the American religious landscape.

In the wake of the Napoleonic wars powerful and increasingly centralized states like Prussia aspired to forge a comprehensive national church untroubled by confessional differences.[48] It was widely believed by certain German political elites that only a unifying national theology could serve as a counterweight to the aggressively secular ideology spawned by the French Revolution.[49] For example, in 1817 King Frederick Wilhelm III of Prussia issued a series of decrees that created the United Church of Prussia, the state-sponsored union of Reformed and Lutheran traditions. The implementation of this governmentally mandated union required a reformulation of the respective churches' liturgical, political, and doctrinal foundations. Many of the civil and ecclesial leaders sought to emphasize the commonalities of the Reformed and Lutheran traditions, as well as their shared divergence from Catholicism. Consequently, many members of this faction looked with favor upon the Heidelberg Catechism because it had been intended to be an irenic document. While showing traces of its mild Reformed genesis, it could be acceptable to moderate Lutherans. However, others wanted a clean sweep of all the older confessional documents, for all of them, including the Heidelberg document, were associated with particular historic traditions. In their eyes, the problem was that the Heidelberg Catechism was not part of the folk memory of German Lutherans. This party called for the creation of new pan-Protestant confessions and catechisms that would supplant those of the Reformation era. The older more irenic catechisms could continue to be honored, but the prospect of a new confession and a new catechism that could unify the Prussian state (and the other German principalities that had formed union churches) generated the most excitement and controversy.

---

47. Annette Aubert has drawn attention to the importance of the German philosophical, theological, and literary heritage for the development of the Mercersberg Theology. See Aubert, *The German Roots of Nineteenth Century American Theology*.

48. See Conser, *Church and Confession*, 13–96.

49. See Purvis, *Theology and the University in Nineteenth-Century Germany*.

When some of these German Lutherans and Reformed people migrated to the United States, they brought with them a yearning for a trans-denominational evangelical alliance. Although most of these Reformed immigrants settled in Missouri and other parts of the Midwest and eventually formed the Evangelical Church Synod of the West in 1840, some remained in Pennsylvania and Maryland. They often sought to downplay confessional differences, including those associated with the historic confessions of faith from the post-Reformation era. They preferred the latitude of Luther's Catechism and the Heidelberg Catechism, and encouraged even greater latitude in interpreting them. By 1847 those in the Mid-West had produced their own very latitudinarian North American catechism.

However, the desire for national theological unity could point in a very different direction if its vision of a comprehensive state church was even more expansive than an integration of the Lutheran and Reformed traditions. The party of Ernst Ludwig von Gerlach,[50] who enjoyed the support of the very conservative Prussian king, hoped to include Roman Catholics in its more ecumenical vision of the established church. Consequently, this faction championed the concept of *"evangelische Katholizität"* (evangelical catholicism),[51] and advocated for a return to the early creeds, particularly those jointly recognized by magisterial Protestantism, Roman Catholicism, and Eastern Orthodoxy. It was hoped that such a recovery of the alleged unity of the patristic church would help unite the conservative monarchies of Europe, including Prussia, Austria, and Russia, against the corrosive forces of liberalism and revolution. Therefore Gerlach's faction sought to restrict ecclesial authority to the pre-Reformation ecumenical creeds. Ideally the Reformation era catechisms that had sowed so much Protestant/Catholic discord could be quietly forgotten.

Both of these ecumenizing movements, of course, triggered a reaction from the stalwart Lutheran parties in the various German states. Lutheran traditionalists insisted upon preserving their own unique doctrinal heritage and theological ethos, and therefore looked to the confessional documents of Lutheranism, particularly the Augsburg Confession, Luther's Catechism, and the Formula of Concord, to ground their specific identity. They echoed the earlier suspicions of the Heidelberg Catechism that their Gnesio-Lutheran ancestors had voiced in the sixteenth century, objecting that the Catechism was much too Reformed, particularly on the mode of Christ's presence in the Eucharist.

Many of these disgruntled confessional Lutherans would eventually immigrate to North America, injecting their catechetical sensibilities into the general religious flux of the United States. To complicate matters, large groups of Prussian and Saxon Lutherans who opposed the Union Church arrived in the United States in 1839. Many of

---

50. Ernst Ludwig von Gerlach (1795–1877) was an extremely conservative jurist, monarchist, and Prussian nationalist. He had been on friendly terms with Philip Schaff while Schaff had been living in Berlin.

51. Nichols, *Romanticism in American Religion*, 72–74.

these would found the Missouri Synod, known for its fierce attachment to the doctrinally strict Formula of Concord, and not just to the Augsburg Confession or Luther's Catechism. Even within the older Lutheran bodies in the United States a party arose, eventually theologically led by Charles Krauth, calling for a heightened allegiance to all the Lutheran confessional documents, including the catechisms.[52] Nevin later admitted that in his younger, more evangelical days he had harbored some contempt for these "Old Lutherans" and found their attachment to their confessional documents to be atavistic.[53] While some of these orthodox Lutherans could sympathetically appreciate Nevin's valorization of the Heidelberg Catechism as a parallel confessional movement in the Reformed tradition, they certainly could not countenance the Catechism's use in Lutheran congregations.

Besides these opposing drives for an expansive evangelical ecumenism on the one hand and a stricter confessional identity on the other, other dynamics began to militate against the use of the Heidelberg Catechism in the lives of many American congregations. The most potent of these dynamics were generated by evolving cultural movements that were more characteristic of the United States than of most European countries. In the absence of an established church the Protestant imperative that all Christians should read Scripture for themselves, in conjunction with an augmented trust in the perspicuity of Scripture, rendered creeds and catechisms unnecessary in the minds of many Americans. In the early nineteenth century a plethora of restorationist movements, simply calling themselves "Christians" or "Disciples," were the most vociferous and visible exponents of this tendency. Proclaiming such slogans as "No creed but Christ" and "Where the Holy Scriptures are silent, we are silent," they rejected the catechetical traditions of the church as superfluous and deleterious human innovations. The Campbellites,[54] who helped form the Disciples of Christ, and the followers of John Winebrenner,[55] who founded the Church of God, epitomized

---

52. Charles Porterfield Krauth (1823-83) was a Lutheran pastor and editor who championed the movement to rehabilitate Lutheran confessionalism. He was somewhat influenced by Nevin and Schaff, and shared their conviction that the Reformation had organically grown out of the church of the Middle Ages and the Patristic period.

53. Nevin, *My Own Life*, 148.

54. Thomas Campbell (1763-1854) was a former Presbyterian minister who was influenced by both John Locke and the Second Great Awakening. After having had his ministerial credentials revoked by the Presbyterians, he eventually formed an independent congregation that helped inspire the "restorationist" movement. This movement hoped to reduce the tenets of Christianity to the essentials upon which reasonable, descent individuals could agree and which could be clearly demonstrated to be based on Scripture. Campbell sought to return Christianity to what he imagined was the theological simplicity of the apostolic church and therefore rejected the contentious creeds that had allegedly disrupted the unity of the primitive Christian community.

55. John Winebrenner (1797-1860) was a German Reformed pastor who was disaffiliated from that tradition because of his enthusiasm for the "new measures" of radical revivalism and for his insistence upon a personal conversion experience as a hallmark of genuine Christian faith. His commitment to the doctrine of the clarity of Scripture eventually led him to reject the use of all creeds and catechisms. His views were adopted by the Church of God, General Conference, which he helped

this deep-rooted suspicion of the corrupting and divisive impact of humanly authored creeds and catechisms. The pristine and unified church of the apostolic era had required no such hermeneutic inventions. The Bible needed to be liberated from its theological bondage to the tradition-minded ministerial elites and restored to the common people, just as it had been in apostolic times.

According to these groups, the Bible was a transparent text, requiring no authoritative ecclesial interpretation, summary, or supplement. Surely, it was argued, a benevolent deity would necessarily have provided humanity with a clear, unambiguous revelation, for God cannot hold people responsible and culpable for failing to do something that they are actually incapable of doing. Therefore, if God morally evaluates people according to whether they respond to God's revelation in Scripture or not, people, including the unlearned, must be capable of understanding that revelation without the aid of human catechisms and confessions. If divine revelation involves the communication of saving information, then that information cannot be so cryptic as to baffle an ordinary individual's interpretive capacities. It was argued that the need for a catechism as a supplemental interpretive key is incompatible with belief in divine revelatory benevolence. This belief in the perspicuity of Scripture provided fertile soil for the flourishing of private interpretations of the Bible untethered from any creedal or catechetical tradition. In 1849 Nevin, who had long been critical of this radicalized view of "Scripture alone," polemicized against it most stridently in his critical review of a book by John Winebrenner, a former German Reformed pastor who had founded the Church of God.[56] "An open Bible and private judgment," Nevin warned, leads only to "excess, extravagance and superstition, in the name of religion."[57]

This intensified sense of the clarity and sufficiency of Scripture was fueled by a deep cultural trend in the United States. The birth of the new American Republic was seen as the triumph of simple, ordinary citizens over the hierarchies and elites of Europe. In the Jacksonian era confidence in the abilities of ordinary people to think for themselves and to make their own decisions came to full blossom. The right of private judgment in religious matters seemed to be the self-evident analogue of the right of private judgment in political matters. It was natural that the lionization of the cognitive and volitional capacities of ordinary, unlearned people in the political sphere would be extended to the religious sphere. According to the popular sentiment, it was obvious that laypeople can and should discern the meaning of Scripture for themselves. Nathan Hatch has persuasively argued that the early nineteenth century witnessed an upsurge in egalitarianism, epitomized by the Jacksonian idealization of the "common man."[58] Alleged religious elites whose authority was based on their mastery of bibli-

---

found with five other pastors in 1830.

56. See Nevin, "The Sect System," *Mercersburg Review* 1 (1849): 487. See Nevin, *One, Holy, Catholic, and Apostolic: Tome One*, ed. by Sam Hamstra Jr., The Mercersburg Study Series, vol. 5, 235–71.

57. Nevin, "The Sect System," *One, Holy, Catholic, and Apostolic: Tome One*, 247.

58. Hatch, *The Democratization of American Christianity*.

cal, doctrinal, and historical lore were not to be revered or automatically obeyed. In the new nation, the older European habit of deference to authoritative institutions waned as individual initiative and self-reliance were celebrated. Catechisms could be relegated to the category of traditional impediments to the unhindered operation of the common sense of the average person.

The belief in the exclusive authority of the Bible coupled with confidence in the capacity of all believers to grasp its clear message not only inspired the proliferation new religious groups, but also impacted the more established Protestant traditions. Even the theologically orthodox factions among the Congregationalists denounced the confessional heritage as an idol venerated by Papists and the other enemies of the Puritan spirit.[59] This downplaying of historic catechisms did have some roots in the Puritan heritage, for New England congregations had sometimes used their own individual covenants for catechetical instruction (some of which were based on the Westminster documents of the seventeenth century). By the early nineteenth century, even some Lutheran and a few Dutch Reformed ministers had joined in the minimization of the normativity of historic catechisms. (However, they usually grudgingly conceded that the documents did have limited pedagogical utility.)

The separation of church and state at the federal level and the gradual spread of this disjunction to all the states also contributed to the erosion of loyalty to historical traditions.[60] The magisterial Protestant traditions were forced to adapt to a situation in which they no longer enjoyed the protection and support of the civil government. The disestablishment of religion inadvertently favored informal religious groups and movements and disadvantaged those that had previously relied upon traditional confessional allegiance. In the new voluntaristic environment, ministerial authority was often based on personal charisma, and not on institutional endorsement. The religious leader was not primarily valued as the representative of an historic tradition, but rather as an inspirational speaker, emotional catalyst, and event mobilizer. In such a context, familiarity with the theology informing a catechism was not regarded as a particularly desirable requisite for pastoral leadership. In the new world of the revivals religious affiliation was a function of persuasion rather than loyalty, and catechisms were not perceived to be very persuasive evangelistic tools. Because lay people were not subject to legal sanctions for failing to be a member of a particular church or to subscribe to a particular statement of faith, their power to choose a religion was implicitly augmented. As a consequence fewer people regarded the church with its unique clergy, creeds, and catechisms as an essential channel of grace. Rather, affiliation with a church was increasingly seen to be a matter of the individual's preference.

---

59 Cited in Nevin, "Puritanism and the Creed," in *The Early Creeds*, ed. by Charles Yrigoyen and Lee C. Barrett, The Mercersburg Study Series, vol. 8, 105. See also Nichols, *Romanticism*, 175.

60. Congregationalism was not fully disestablished in Massachusetts, the last state with an established religion, until 1833.

In more extreme populist circles, the view arose that immersion in the life of any church might not be a necessary part of the God-ordained means of salvation.

The expansion of the range of available religious options eroded unquestioned allegiance to any single one of them. Given the kaleidoscope of conflicting denominational doctrines, the plausibility of each one of them was diminished. Even in small villages in Pennsylvania, a German Reformed farmer knew that his neighbors might be Moravian, Lutheran, Mennonite, Methodist, or Presbyterian. It was obvious that not all Christians shared an attachment to the Heidelberg Catechism. Many of these neighbors may have seemed to be morally upright and spiritually healthy people. Inevitably the suspicion arose that perhaps a particular catechism was not necessary for the living of a sound Christian life. The conjunction of religious voluntarism with America's ever-expanding religious pluralism undermined any automatic ascription of authority to the normative teachings any particular historic religious institution. In the welter of options, many Americans felt that if they did place themselves under the authority of a particular ecclesial body, that subscription could only be their own deliberate and reversible choice.

The ascription of authority to catechisms and other confessional documents was also impeded by the enthusiasm for dramatic personal conversion experiences that was the legacy of the American religious awakenings. The surge of episodes of intense religious emotion at mass gatherings probably had complex roots in the "holy fairs" of Scotland, the enthusiastic "New Light" preaching in some Dutch Reformed circles, the pan-congregational meetings of the Pietists, and the Puritan focus on conversion narratives. These influences sparked the First Great Awakening of the early eighteenth century, epitomized in the preaching of the Congregationalist Jonathan Edwards,[61] the Presbyterian Samuel Davies,[62] the Anglican George Whitefield,[63] and the Dutch Reformed Theodor Ferlinghuysen.[64] At the very end of the eighteenth century and gaining intensity during the early nineteenth, the Second Great Awakening rekindled the fires of corporate religious fervor in prayer groups in such disparate contexts as

---

61. Jonathan Edwards (1703–58) was a celebrated colonial American minister, theologian, and philosopher. The diverse components of his complex thought ranged from Lockean epistemology, to Platonic metaphysics, and to orthodox Calvinism. He was a proponent of the Great Awakening in its less frenzied forms, a critical analyst of religious experience, a Reformed ethicist, and an evangelical preacher.

62. Samuel Davies (1723–61) was an oratorically powerful evangelist active in Virginia. He was an early advocate for the separation of church and state.

63. George Whitefield (1714–70) was an Anglican minister and evangelist who itinerated throughout England, Wales, and the American colonies, preaching to huge and very responsive crowds. Even worldly and skeptical Benjamin Franklin was moved by his rhetorical abilities, and the two became unlikely friends. He is best remembered for his emotionally evocative revival preaching that played a significant role in the "First Great Awakening" and the beginnings of the evangelical tradition in North America.

64. Theodor Frelinghuysen (1691–1747) was a Dutch Reformed "Awakener" of the Raritan Valley in New Jersey. A passionate evangelistic preacher, he was also fiercely devoted to the Heidelberg Catechism.

Bible studies in New England colleges and camp meetings in the Kentucky frontier. As the movement gained momentum, many Second Great Awakening revivalists employed high pressure and even confrontational techniques to trigger conversions. Among these was the notorious "anxious bench" popularized by the maverick Presbyterian Charles Finney, who become celebrated for the size and fervor of his huge revivals, many of which were urban.[65] These waves of revivalism shifted the center of gravity of the Christian life away from the church's gradual nurture to the sudden transformation of the individual's heart. Cathartic episodes of being moved by grace to make a personal decision to embrace Christ began to displace the identity-shaping power of historic communal traditions. The church became less a channel of grace through its worship, liturgies, catechisms, and confessions, and more the site where individuals gathered to be spiritually energized. The trans-denominational experience of Christ's saving grace diminished the importance of potentially divisive catechetical instruction and fostered a generically Protestant ecumenism.

No denomination was left unaffected by the revivals. Often they divided into rival factions, formed new congregations, and sometimes experienced painful schisms. In Congregationalism some of the spiritual descendants of Jonathan Edwards and other defenders of the First Great Awakening developed the "New England Theology" which provided an apologia for a mild form of revivalism. Samuel Hopkins advanced the controversial claim that unconverted individuals actually grew worse by partaking of the means of grace offered by the church, including prayer and catechesis.[66] Against this the Old Calvinists, many of whom were "Old Light" opponents of revivalism, protested that the visible church should include the unsaved, for even they could benefit from its nurture. They argued that the life of the church is transformative for both children and unregenerate adults, and that the testimony of a conversion experience is unnecessary.[67] In their view, the illumination of the mind through catechesis can prepare the souls even of the unregenerate, for the growth of faith is a gradual process. Nevin had much sympathy for the Old Calvinist position, for it resembled his own upbringing.

The Presbyterian Church (of which Nevin was a member until his call to Mercersburg) was by no means immune to the allure of revivalism and the danger of schism. In 1834 in Pittsburg, a city thick with confessionally inclined Scots-Irish Presbyterians, Nevin was exposed to the revivalist James Gallaher, known as "the Kentucky operator," who employed Charles Finney's controversial "new measures" in an emotionally charged evangelistic campaign that lasted for six weeks. Three years

---

65. Charles Finney (1792–1875) was a persuasive preacher and ardent revivalist who became a professor and president of Oberlin College. The most famous evangelist of his era, he vociferously advocated Christian perfectionism, social reform, and abolition, and developed a confrontational "decisionist" style of mass evangelism.

66. Samuel Hopkins (1721–1803) was a student of Jonathan Edwards who served pastorates in Connecticut and Newport, Rhode Island. He emphasized the need for a total renovation of the soul by God's grace so that God could be loved with no spiritual self-interest.

67. See Holifield, *Theology in America*, 149–56.

later, in 1837 while Nevin was still teaching at the Presbyterian Western Seminary, the denomination formally split along Old School (insisting upon doctrinal orthodoxy) and New School (tolerant of more doctrinal latitude and sympathetic to experiential forms of piety, including revivalistic ones) lines. The more revival-friendly party (who usually only favored the older and more restrained evangelical style of the disciples of Jonathan Edwards) was expelled from the denomination by those who advocated full subscription to the denomination's doctrinal standards. In effect, the denomination's General Assembly, dominated by those who wanted stricter adherence to confessional standards, were so alarmed by the rise of revivalism that they disenfranchised the New School congregations. The Old School proponents saw a return to their historic confessions and catechisms as an antidote to the perceived subjectivism and individualism of the revivals. Nevin lived through this painful schism; his heart was with the Old Schoolers even though he deplored their uncharitable, divisive, and possibly unconstitutional actions.

Even the Lutherans, with their own history of fierce attachment to the Augsburg Confession and Luther's catechisms, felt the influence of revivalism. Samuel Schmucker, who was steeped in Lutheran Pietism and had himself had a conversion experience at a revival, advocated for the relaxation of the demand for strict adherence to Lutheran confessional documents. His willingness to diverge from the tradition was evident in his denial of such essential doctrines as the corporeal presence of Christ in the bread and wine.[68] His publications concerning what he called the "American Lutheran Church" articulated the sensibilities of the more revival-friendly Lutherans.[69] In reaction to this, the tradition-oriented Lutherans in Pennsylvania, many of whom were recent immigrants fleeing from the Prussian unionist church, rallied under the theological leadership of Charles Porterfield Krauth and Julius Mann.[70] Mann had been a friend of Philip Schaff in Germany and at one point in his career had hoped to teach with him at Mercersburg. In spite of doctrinal differences that surfaced as Mann became more strictly Lutheran, both Schaff and Nevin spoke favorably of his attachment to catechetical instruction. Predictably, the two Lutheran parties, one wedded

---

68. Samuel Schmucker (1799–1873) was a low-church Lutheran pastor who was instrumental in the founding of both Gettysburg Seminary and Gettysburg College and helped organize the General Synod of the Lutheran Church in America. While he taught theology at Gettysburg Schmucker became notorious for downplaying the distinctive doctrines of Lutheran confessionalism, particularly in regard to the sacraments as instruments of grace. He even toyed with the idea of replacing the Augsburg Confession with a declaration of faith that would be more acceptable to Reformed denominations. Rather than being pleased by this ostensible ecumenism, Nevin and Schaff dismissed him as a doctrinally anemic combination of revivalism and rationalism.

69. See Samuel Schmucker, *The American Lutheran Church*.

70. Julius Mann (1819–92) was a German emigré Lutheran pastor and theologian who had studied at Tübingen before settling in Pennsylvania. Much of his career was spent teaching at Lutheran Theological Seminary in Philadelphia where he defended Lutheran confessionalism and combatted the doctrinally lax views of the Schmucker camp.

to catechetical pedagogy and the other less enthusiastic about it, became increasingly antagonistic and generated on-going tension within the Lutheran Church.

The German Reformed Church in Pennsylvania was certainly not impervious to the various Awakenings' surges of evangelical piety. Nevin's enthusiasm for the Catechism was partly inspired by his aversion to the revivalism that was gaining ground in his newly adopted denomination. The origins of the German Reformed heritage in Pennsylvania must be considered in order to appreciate the unique challenges that Nevin faced in his efforts to revitalize catechetical instruction. Those origins gave the catechetical/revivalistic struggles and tensions in the denomination a particular flavor.

The roots of this heritage were in the migration of Reformed people from the Palatinate, Alsace, and German-speaking Switzerland. Fleeing from the devastation caused by the wars of Louis IV and the consequent ascendance of Catholicism in these regions, the refugees often settled in small villages and farms in south-central Pennsylvania. Few of them migrated as cohesive religious communities. The development of a robust religious life among the struggling Reformed population was hampered by a chronic shortage of clergy. Their dispersal in rural areas, their difficulty in adjusting to the absence of an established church, and the rigors of primitive conditions inhibited their ability to organize a vital ecclesial life. Some gathered in religious meetings led by lay "readers," but even that leadership could only imperfectly recall the teachings of their Reformed heritage.[71] The Heidelberg Catechism was often used, but its doctrines were not always well-understood.

The Heidelberg Catechism figured prominently in the birth of the denomination as an organized body. In 1729 a German-born lay schoolteacher who had immigrated to Pennsylvania, John Philip Boehm, was ordained by the classis of Amsterdam to serve three small German congregations in eastern Pennsylvania.[72] By ordaining him, the synods of North and South Holland assumed responsibility for the German Reformed population. Boehm's ordination pledge included acceptance of the Heidelberg Catechism, which he did gladly. In 1731 his instructions to all German congregations recognizing the authority of the classis of Amsterdam stipulated that their ministers must expound the Heidelberg Catechism regularly.[73] In 1747 twelve congregations formed the first German Reformed coetus, adopting the Heidelberg Catechism and the canons of Dort as their confessional documents. Until 1791 they remained organized as a mission of the Dutch Reformed Church, which was strongly represented in the Raritan Valley of neighboring New Jersey. That arrangement made a certain amount of sense, because both groups recognized the Heidelberg Catechism as a

---

71. Richards, *History of the Theological Seminary of the Evangelical and Reformed Church*, 25–28.

72. Although he was neither theologically trained nor ordained, after he arrived in Pennsylvania John Philip Boehm (1683–1749) was called by the three German Reformed congregations to preach and administer the sacraments. Because the celebration of the Lord's Supper by a layperson caused considerable consternation, Boehm sought ecclesial authorization from the Dutch Reformed Church.

73. See Richards, *History*, 32–33.

confessional standard, although the Dutch often interpreted it through the lens of the Synod of Dort. Even after they organized as a self-sufficient synod in 1793 with 178 congregations, the German Reformed Church still had no journal, no mission board, few ministers, and no seminary until 1825. The organs that foster a sense of denominational identity were either weak or missing entirely.

Such an amorphous situation made the original German Reformed congregations and later the fledgling denomination ripe for the allurements of the Awakenings. Settlers of German Reformed ancestry often defected to sectarian groups, including the apocalyptic and monastic Ephrata community. The experiential and irenic piety of the Moravians promoted by Count Zinzendorf syphoned off other members.[74] The awakening among the "New Side" Presbyterians (those who favored the revivals) in Pennsylvania also encouraged a more cavalier attitude toward church doctrine and fostered a disenchantment with traditional catechesis. Over the subsequent decades sympathy for revivalistic ardor motivated two major denominational secessions. The first was led by the Pietist Philip William Otterbein,[75] an émigré German Reformed pastor who became much enamored of the Wesleyan movement, and who helped found the United Brethren in Christ. Later in 1823 the extreme revivalist and opponent of infant baptism John Winebrenner led another schismatic group out of the denomination and founded the Church of God.[76]

In less disruptive ways revivalism even affected the churches that remained in the German Reformed Church. In 1827 Finney-style revivals under James Reiley in York Pennsylvania enthralled much of the local German Reformed population. From 1828 to 1844 enthusiasm for more demonstratively experiential religion increased and attachment to more formal religiosity decreased. Many local pastors began to adopt for use in their own congregations the highly emotive strategies employed in

74. Count Nikolaus Zinzendorf (1700–60) was a Pietist German aristocrat who enabled the Moravian Brethren to organize the colony of Herrnhut on his estate. He became a zealous propagator of Moravianism, and spent considerable time in Pennsylvania organizing Moravian communities. His trans-denominational vision (of a Pietist sort) put him at odds with confessional Lutherans and much of the nascent Reformed leadership in Pennsylvania.

75. William Otterbein (1726–1813) was a university-trained German immigrant and a pastor in the German Reformed tradition. Although he never formally left that denomination, along with the Mennonite Martin Boehm he organized and inspired the more revivalistic and more Wesleyan religious communities that evolved into the United Brethren. John Wesley (1703–1791) was an English cleric, theologian, and evangelist who founded the Methodist movement within the Church of England. He emphasized such Arminian theological doctrines as the human ability to resist grace, the impartation of righteousness, and entire sanctification as a culminating work of grace. He focused on the development of intensive personal accountability, discipleship and religious instruction through the formation of small prayer groups.

76. John Winebrenner (1797–1860) was a German Reformed pastor who was disaffiliated from that tradition because of his enthusiasm for the "new measures" of radical revivalism and for his insistence upon a personal conversion experience as a hallmark of genuine Christian faith. His commitment to the doctrine of the clarity of Scripture eventually led him to reject the use of all creeds and catechisms. His views were adopted by the Church of God, General Conference, which he helped found with five other pastors in 1830.

the camp meetings.[77] The revivalistic fervor was widespread enough to alarm some of the denominational leadership. As late as 1843 the annual Report of the Synod warned against "mere excitement, produced by the agency of men," and "the ecstasies of fanatical feelings," and recommended as an antidote "the study and teaching of the Heidelberg Catechism."[78] It urged ministers and all the people to "increased attention to and study of this beautiful yet simple compend of divine truth as the rallying point of our Reformed Zion."[79]

Nevin was aware that his critique of ahistorical and a-confessional revivalism was contrary to powerful currents in American culture. Although he had no quarrel with the experiential piety of someone like Jonathan Edwards, throughout his mature career he excoriated the subjectivism and individualism of the "baptistic" sensibility. In 1863 he wrote, "For what have been supposed to be the objective factors of the new creation in Christ Jesus, they throw themselves upon the purely subjective side of the process; making the work of Christianity to be an inward transaction wholly between each individual singly considered and his Maker, on the outside of the Church altogether . . ."[80] Nevin began to expose the dangers of Finney-style revivalism almost as soon as he began to teach at Mercersburg. In 1842 he was much disturbed by the homiletical strategies of William Ramsay, a Presbyterian minister who was a candidate for the pastorate of the German Reformed congregation in Mercersburg. Much to Nevin's chagrin, Ramsey even used the "anxious bench" and did persuade several people to respond to the altar call. (Ramsey was offered the position by the congregation, but Nevin wrote him a stern admonishing letter, and Ramsey declined to accept the call.) Feeling obliged to explain his antipathy to "the system of the bench," Nevin penned *The Anxious Bench* in 1843.[81] In that pamphlet, particularly in its second edition, Nevin contrasted the use of high-pressure revivalistic techniques with the steady inculcation of faith through the "system of the catechism." Among the many faults of the system of the bench, Nevin noted its tendency to manipulate transient emotions, isolate individuals from the life-giving presence of Christ in the ecclesial community, promote sectarianism and the valorization of private judgment, and cater to the prejudices of the popular opinion. In many ways, these criticisms could be expanded into a condemnation of the populist mood of the Jacksonian era.

In a very different way the rationalism of the Enlightenment had also undermined confidence in the authority of catechisms. The *philosophes* in France, the Deists in England, and the "neologians" in Germany all encouraged skepticism about religious traditions and cautioned rational individuals to be wary of the superstitions

---

77. See Good, *History of the Reformed Church in the Nineteenth Century*, 130–34.
78. See Richards, *History*, 218–19.
79. Richards, *History*, 219.
80. Nevin, in this volume, [placeholder: ##].
81. Nevin, *The Anxious Bench*, in Hamstra, ed., *One, Holy, Catholic, and Apostolic: Tome One*, The Mercersburg Study Series, vol. 5, 27–103.

perpetuated by creeds, confessions, and catechisms.[82] The more ardent proponents of the Enlightenment often voiced the theme that truth must be discovered by the autonomous rational individual and cannot be legitimately acquired by trusting the testimony of third-parties, particularly not the allegedly authoritative teachings of the church officials. Moreover, the proliferation of rival catechisms, all of whose claims to truth were dubious, only served to provoke needless dissensions within the body politic. Domestic tranquility and international peace would be well served if Christians would embrace a tolerant skepticism toward most doctrines and restrict their convictions to a minimalistic "reasonable" core.

The general spirit of Enlightenment skepticism did not exempt the Heidelberg Catechism from suspicion and critique. In a document addressed to the classis of Amsterdam in 1728 the precarious German Reformed communities in Pennsylvania complained that their members were being influenced by the "errors of those among whom they dwelt," most notably "the most dreaded of heretics, the Socinians."[83] Upon taking up his teaching position at the nascent German Reformed seminary in 1832, Rauch was sufficiently alarmed by the inroads that Enlightenment-style rationalism had made among Pennsylvania Germans that he penned a detailed critique of it in the denominational newspaper, *The Messenger*.[84]

Nevin frequently mentioned rationalism as a perennial temptation lurking in the background of Protestant culture. He described the "modern rationalism of Germany" as "the liberty of the Reformation run mad."[85] In Nevin's eyes rationalism was to the mind what sectarianism was to the will.[86] Both elevated the powers of the autonomous individual to the position of ultimate arbiter of truth. Rationalism was simply the epistemic manifestation of sectarianism. Nevin objected that this severed the ties between the individual and the spirit of a community and its historical traditions. In 1863 Nevin linked rationalism with the decline of catechetical instruction, writing "With the triumph of Rationalism in later times, it [catechetical instruction]

---

82 "Neology" was a term originating in Europe in the eighteenth century to denote any form of theology that stressed the compatibility of the basic contents of reason and revelation, the rational justifiability of central Christian beliefs, and the need to employ reason to critique traditional doctrinal formulations and to reconstruct biblical history. Unlike more skeptical rationalists, most of the thinkers labelled as neologians saw revelation as playing an essential role in reinforcing truths discoverable by reason.

83. Richards, *History*, 213. Socinianism was a cluster of nontrinitarian movements that arose in the sixteen and seventeenth centuries, often associated with the work of Faustus Socinus (1539–1604). Strong in Poland and Transylvania, Socinians were identified with the denial of the pre-existence of Christ, original sin, and Christ's substitutionary atonement. As a term of abuse, eventually "Socinian" was used almost interchangeably with "Unitarian."

84. Rauch, *Messenger of the German Reformed Church*, Sept. 1, 1834, pp. 83–84.

85. Nevin, "Catholic Unity," in Hamstra, ed., *One, Holy, Catholic, and Apostolic: Tome One*, The Mercersburg Study Series, vol. 5, 130.

86. Nevin, "Antichrist," in Hamstra, ed., *One, Holy, Catholic, and Apostolic: Tome One*, The Mercersburg Study Series, vol. 5, 198.

became more and more an empty name, till we find it sunk at last into almost universal neglect. Indifference to all positive religion, and contempt for the Catechism, went hand in hand together."[87]

Nevin was less worried about the overt and extreme rationalists, like the Unitarians, than he was about the "rationalistic supernaturalism" that he feared had infected many forms of Christian theology. Although Nevin sometimes singled out the neologians of Germany as the culprits, in Reformed circles in the United States this theological orientation was more characteristically indebted to Scottish Common Sense philosophy and British empiricism more broadly. This rationalistic supernaturalism, a hybrid offspring of the Enlightenment, sought to justify Christian beliefs by appealing to "evidences," such as the testimony of biblical miracles and the fulfillment of prophecy, or to the agreement of revelation with the dictates of an allegedly universal moral sense. By such arguments the supernaturally revealed data of Christianity could be validated by human reason. Nevin was particularly critical of this strategy as practiced in *Biblical Theology* by Storr and Flatt, an influential work that had been published in an English translation in 1826.[88]

This rationalistic supernaturalism that Nevin critiqued also sought to arrange and interpret biblical material according to the logic of a metaphysical system. Certain theological propositions would serve as axioms and others as derivative corollaries. The theological style of argumentation and organization usually mimicked the inductive method of the natural sciences, with biblical passages serving as the raw data that supported the axioms. Often the contents of the resultant theological systems were quite orthodox according to the standards of their respective denominations. Even so, the assumption was that faith was the product of the interaction of the individual's free cognitive processes and the revealed biblical data. Throughout his mature career Nevin vigorously critiqued this percolation of rationalism into the Reformed tradition in his exchanges with Charles Hodge of Princeton concerning the hermeneutic importance of the creedal traditions of the church. [89] As we shall see, Nevin also clashed with this sensibility in the Dutch Reformed Church in regard to the interpretation of the Heidelberg Catechism.

In spite of all these countervailing cultural trends, Nevin resolved to champion the intensified use of the Heidelberg Catechism. His task was a bit peculiar. He found himself in the midst of a denomination that theoretically accepted the authority of

---

87. Nevin, in this volume, 303.

88. Nevin, *My Own Life*, 106. Gottlob Christian Storr (1746–1805) was a German theologian who defended the Bible as a supernatural revelation, but used reason to demonstrate its truth. Johann Friedrich Flatt (1759–1805) was his student and collaborator.

89. Charles Hodge (1797–1879) was a celebrated Presbyterian theologian at Princeton Theological Seminary, who in the 1820s had taught Nevin and allowed him to be his replacement while he engaged in an academic tour of Europe. Hodge developed a scholastically orthodox version of Calvinism known for its logical rigor and its effort to deduce doctrines from biblical "facts" in the way that physical scientists derive conclusions from the data of the natural world.

the Catechism, but in practice (at least in many congregations) tended to downplay it. His new denomination typically espoused the value of clergy who embodied its doctrinal and liturgical heritage, but actually lacked enough trained clergy for their ministries be effective. Nevin discovered that many congregants seemed to be concerned for doctrinal integrity, but nevertheless were vulnerable to the blandishments of the revivalists. His new religious family cherished their German ethos, but were swiftly accommodating themselves to American-style populism. The situation that Nevin faced was more complex than the one-dimensional hostility to catechesis that had animated the restorationists and many Finneyites. His task was to rekindle a passion for something that his constituency still claimed to cherish but whose value it did not fully comprehend.

As we have seen, the Mercersburg Theology, as the movement that Nevin helped initiate came to be known, had a natural affinity for the practice of catechetical instruction in general. However, Nevin's enthusiasm for the Heidelberg Catechism was not simply motivated by his conviction that ecclesial traditions were essential for the cultivation of faith. For Nevin, the Catechism was more than an antidote to untrammeled religious individualism and emotional self-indulgence. More importantly, it was fueled by his belief that the essential features of the theology that he was formulating were in accord with the contents of the Catechism. Nevin harbored a special fondness for this catechism in particular. In fact, to some extent the Heidelberg Catechism influenced the genesis of Nevin's theological vision. To appreciate Nevin's apologia for the Catechism, the contours of that theological vision must be sketched.

The Distinctiveness of the Mercersburg Theology and Its Catechetical Emphasis

In the 1840's an obscure village in Pennsylvania witnessed the blossoming of a remarkable theological phenomenon. During that decade John Nevin and his theological compatriots were busy articulating an understanding of Christianity that diverged significantly from the spiritual world of most of their North American Reformed cousins. Even as the Mercersburg Theology was just beginning to congeal it triggered a vehemently hostile reaction. Nevin and his colleague Philip Schaff were caught somewhat off guard by the virulence of the critiques. While at the time Nevin probably thought that he was only reminding the church of the power of its sacraments, liturgy, creeds, and catechisms as channels of soul-shaping grace, he had inadvertently initiated what could have been a Copernican revolution in North American Reformed theology (although its immediate impact was limited). He implicitly shifted the center of gravity of the Christian faith away from the atonement and toward the incarnation. This move had far-reaching consequences for every theological topic.

The incarnation, the keystone of Nevin's theology, was construed as the perfecting of human nature through its union with the Second Person of the Trinity. According to Nevin the joyful spiritual union of the faithful with Christ's glorified life would animate growth in godlikeness for individuals, the church, and the human race. The eschaton would complete a process of development that had begun with the creation itself. Nevin reconceived the church as the Body of Christ that enables participation in the life of the Second Adam; he regarded the universal ecclesial community as being much more than a local voluntary association of the faithful. The sacraments were treasured as the primary vehicles for the communication of Christ's transformed and transforming life. Nevin gave the worship of the church new prominence as an essential channel of grace that regenerated and sanctified believers. Along with his colleague Schaff, he celebrated the organic and progressive development of the church through the centuries toward its eschatological consummation.[90]

Several aspects of this vision offended the prevailing sensibilities of American evangelical Protestantism. Perhaps most obviously, its embrace of the organic development of the church implied a positive evaluation of the church's patristic and medieval heritage. This, of course, meant that the historic Roman Catholic tradition could not be dismissed as being entirely the work of Antichrist. Nevin and Schaff's view contradicted the popular theory that the only bearers of genuine Christianity, the faithful remnant, had been the dissident medieval groups like the Waldensians.[91] This positive reappraisal of much of medieval Catholicism did not sit well with a Protestant population that was frightened and angered by the influx of Irish and German Catholic immigrants into the cities of the eastern seaboard, including neighboring Philadelphia and Baltimore.[92]

Further upsetting their American Reformed brothers and sisters, the Mercersburg theologians rooted the conviction of the truth of Christianity in the immediate experience of Christ's self-communication in the life of the church. Nevin rejected the notion that Christian faith was based on a logically prior belief in the Bible's inspiration and veracity.[93] In his nineteenth century context, Nevin's assertion that the authority of the Bible was derivative from the authority of Christ was shocking. While his scholastic Reformed contemporaries were insisting that authority should be ascribed to the Bible because its reliability can be demonstrated by the fulfillment of prophecy and the public nature of the miracles, Nevin grounded the Bible's authority in its ability to make Christ's presence experientially available to the church.

Even more momentously, the Mercersburg movement implicitly reconceived the basic plot line of the Christian narrative as the drama of the perfecting of creation

---

90. See Nevin, in this volume, 129-151.

91. The Waldensians were a Christian movement that arose in France in the twelfth century. Because they embraced apostolic poverty they were declared to be heretical. Surviving in the Alpine valleys of France and Italy, most of the Waldensians were absorbed by various Reformed churches during the Reformation era.

92. See Feldberg, *The Philadelphia Riots of 1844: A Study of Ethnic Conflict*.

93. See Nevin, "Puritanism and the Creed," in *The Early Creeds*, 103–121.

rather than as the story of redemption from sin. The more wide-spread Reformed view was ably articulated by Charles Hodge of Princeton Theological Seminary, Nevin's erstwhile theological mentor. In Hodge's theological paradigm, the essential leitmotif of the biblical narrative is the movement from paradisiacal innocence, through the fall into sin and guilt, and on to forgiveness and sanctification.[94] In the words of the Westminster Catechism the "chief end" of human life was perfect obedience to the will of the righteous God, an obedience which was identified with the "enjoyment" of God. According to this scenario, such enjoyment included the adoration of God's glorious ordering power and delight in submitting to it. In this prevalent version of the Reformed faith, prelapsarian Adam and Eve had been created with the capacities to understand God's will and to obey God in perfect righteousness. However, humanity's primal ancestors had lost those abilities through their catastrophic fall into sin and had bequeathed their debility and corruption to all their descendants. To make matters worse, by violating God's law humanity has rendered itself culpable and deserving of condemnation and punishment. The good news of Christianity is most basically that through the sacrifice of Christ the punishment for sin has been lifted, a right forensic relation with God has been restored, and the power to obey God has been recovered.

Reformed theologians in America could quarrel among themselves about the details of the story. They could disagree about the transmission of original sin, about the basis for the imputation of Adam's guilt to the rest of humanity, and about the severity of the primal corruption. They could disagree about the relation of the power of God's redemptive grace to human responsibility and freedom. They could disagree about the role of the fall into sin and redemption in Christ in God's providential design, and about the relation of sin, damnation, and salvation to the eternal decrees of God. They could disagree about the logistics of the atonement. But for almost all of them Christianity was fundamentally a tale of restoration, or at least of the rectification of an opportunity that Adam and Eve had squandered. It is the story of paradise lost and paradise regained, even when that loss was construed as part of God's mysterious plan.

Nevin, while by no means rejecting the paradise lost/paradise regained pattern, recounted the more basic outlines of the Christian story in a very different way. Influenced by patristic sources, devotional literature, and German Idealism and Romanticism, Nevin narrated the essential plot of the Christian saga as the movement from creation to glorification. The pivot of the drama was Christ's incarnation and ascension. Nevin wrote, "The world, from its extreme circumference, looks inward to this fact [the Incarnation] as its true and proper center, and presses towards it continually, from every side, as the end of its entire constitution."[95] In Christ supernatural life has entered the natural realm and transformed it. The infinite has embraced the finite and initiated a process that would culminate in incorruptibility and the consummation

---

94. See A. A. Hodge, *Life*, 181.
95. Nevin, *The Mystical Presence*, ed. by Linden J. DeBie, The Mercersburg Study Series, vol. 1, 176.

of all things. Time was being transmuted into eternity and the earth was being transformed into heaven. For Nevin and his theological allies, humanity's fall into sin, reprieve, and the recovery of righteousness were no longer the absolute centerpieces of the Christian story; rather, they were complications of the more basic narrative of the old creation's sublation into the new creation. The motive force driving the whole cosmic drama was not sin (although sin was a major derailment) but the more basic ontological incompleteness of Adam and Eve's original human nature. Finite creatures, attaining self-consciousness in humanity, long for union with the infinite God. Only that consummation will ultimately satisfy their restless hearts. Nevin remarked in *The Mystical Presence* that people are brought to God "only by being made to participate in the divine nature itself."[96] In lectures delivered some time before 1850, Nevin declared, "The whole world, in the deepest sense, is longing and striving after union with God. Nothing less than a union with its divine creator can satisfy the soul."[97]

It must not be thought that Nevin minimized the problem of sin and redemption. He was aware that the Heidelberg Catechism's basic structure of guilt, grace, and gratitude for redemption seemed to mirror the plot of the paradise lost/paradise regained narrative, and he frequently professed appreciation for that pattern. Like any Reformed theologian, he wrote passionately about the horrifying nature and frightful extent of human depravity. With equal ardor he rhapsodized about the inestimable value of God's gratuitous gift of the justification of the sinner. Moreover, he was quite comfortable with the fact that the Catechism's discussion of Christ's redemptive work described it as the bearing of the burden of God's eternal wrath against sin.

However, Nevin did not remain exclusively fixated on sin, atonement, and redemption, as much of American Protestantism tended to be. Unusually for his American context, Nevin was even more interested in Christ's ascension than he was in his crucifixion. He wrote, "The glorification of Christ then, was the full advancement of our human nature itself to the power of the divine life . . ."[98] He noted with approval the prominence of the theme of Christ's ascension in the Heidelberg Catechism. For example, he praised the Catechism for stressing the believer's participation in the resurrected Christ's new life (Question 45).[99] Similarly, he lauded its proclamation that in Christ our human flesh has ascended into heaven (Question 49),[100] and that our human bodies will be made conformable to the glorious body of Christ (Question 57).[101]

The shift in Christological focus was evident to many of Nevin's readers. With much consternation, the leadership of the German Reformed classis of North Carolina perceived that Nevin's writings refocused the faith on the incarnation and the

---

96. Nevin, *The Mystical Presence*, 188.
97. See Erb, *Nevin's Theology, Based on Manuscript Class-Room Lectures*, 131.
98. Nevin, *The Mystical Presence*, 197.
99. Nevin, in this volume, 271.
100. Nevin, in this volume, 271.
101. Nevin, in this volume, 273.

ascension. They cited the Mercersburg theologians' downplaying of the atonement as one of the reasons for their withdrawal from the denomination in 1852.[102] They valued the Heidelberg Catechism just as much as Nevin did, but they saw the drama of sin, atonement, and redemption as the Catechism's leitmotif. Nevin was surprised by the commotion that he and Schaff had unwittingly triggered. He himself was probably unaware of the way in which his shift in theological emphasis was an implicit modification of the basic structure of Reformed theology as it had developed in America.

This reconceptualization of the basic Christian narrative required a revision of most of the central topics in Christian theology. Without much fanfare, the language about God was subtly transformed by Nevin. The more traditional Reformed theologians like Archibald Alexander and Charles Hodge of Princeton as well as the southern Old School Presbyterians like James Thornwell had preferred to describe God using the vocabulary of sovereign power, royal majesty, and ordering will.[103] Thornwell was famous for insisting that the goal of the pious life was not happiness, but was the glorification of the awesome God.[104] Much enamored of the Calvinist scholasticism of the seventeenth century, they foregrounded God's metaphysical perfections, including immutability, omniscience, and omnipotence, and proclaimed God's absolute transcendence of all finite limitations. They stalwartly upheld the traditional Reformed dictum that the finite cannot contain the infinite and attacked any theological discourse that even remotely smacked of pantheism.[105] Along with this concentration on God's transcendent power, Reformed theologians in America characteristically articulated the relationship of God and humanity by employing judicial language, favoring concepts like law, disobedience, guilt, punishment, and reprieve. The New England theology associated with the second generation of followers of Jonathan Edwards shifted the discourse slightly toward a more constitutional vocabulary, describing humanity's relationship with God in "federal" categories. But even here the emphasis fell on God's ordering power over the cosmos.

While by no means rejecting any of these concepts, Nevin more typically spoke of God in terms of love, relationality, and the power of unity-in-difference. The language of reconciliation and the union of the infinite and the finite pervaded his writings.[106] He spoke of the need for a "bridge [Christ] over the awful chasm which before separated earth from heaven."[107] Consequently, Nevin valued the Heidelberg Catechism's opening question and answer that introduced the concept of God in terms

---

102. "North Carolina Classis, Minutes," in Charles Hambrick-Stowe, ed., *Living Theological Heritage*, vol. 3.

103. James Thornwell (1812–62) was an "Old School" Presbyterian theologian who taught at Columbia Theological Seminary. A strict adherent to the Westminster documents, he is most remembered for his defense of slavery as a biblically mandated institution.

104. See Thornwell, "Lectures on Theology," 462.

105. See Hodge, *Systematic Theology*, I, 366–441.

106. See Nevin, "Christianity and Humanity," and Schaff, *Christ and Christianity*.

107. Appel, *Life and Work*, 622.

of parental care. Although the Mercersburg theologians did not abandon the forensic conceptuality of their Reformed cousins, they employed more frequently an interpersonal vocabulary of alienation, reconciliation, and union.[108] God, while still being the judge, became more prominently the lover. This refocusing led Nevin to qualify the sharp metaphysical dualisms that had pervaded the theological systems of theologians like Charles Hodge.[109] The natural and the supernatural, time and eternity, flesh and spirit, and earth and heaven did remain ontologically different for Nevin, but they were not irreconcilable.

These theological shifts became most evident in Nevin's treatment of Christology and soteriology. The Princeton theologians, following the lead of seventeenth century Reformed scholasticism, explained God's atoning act in Christ as a legal transaction between the first and second persons of the Trinity. Christ's suffered the penalty of sin that humanity had incurred and enacted the perfect righteousness that humanity owed God. Both of these things were accomplished *extra nos*, outside us sinful human beings. According to the covenant between God the Father and God the Son, the benefits of Christ's work are imputed to the elect, who are also given the faith to trust in the reality of those benefits.

Nevin, on the other hand, proclaimed that the entirety of Christ's life, death, resurrection, and ascension was the glorification of human nature. Christ's atonement for sin is ascribed to believers because they participate in every aspect of Christ's life, including his death on the cross.[110] The atoning work of Christ is efficacious for Christians because it lives in them through their mystical union with Christ. Nevin certainly did affirm that Jesus had satisfied God's justice, but he more characteristically spoke of Jesus's earthly career as the infusion of his theanthropic life into humanity. That new life brought with it not only redemption from guilt and spiritual debility, but also victory over corruption, death, and all the ills that afflict finite humanity. For Nevin the incarnation of God in Christ's human nature was not just a necessary precondition for the accomplishment of Christ's atonement for sin, as it seemed to be for many American Reformed theologians. Rather, for Nevin the essence and root of salvation was located in the very constitution of Christ's divine/human personhood. It was Christ's very being that possessed saving power, for in Christ's person the universal form of human nature was glorified and suffused with divine life. In a sermon delivered in 1863 at the tercentenary celebration of the Heidelberg Catechism, Nevin proclaimed, "His [Christ's] Incarnation—the act of His coming in the flesh—was itself redemptive, and may be said to have included in itself, from the beginning, all that was needed for the full salvation of the world."[111] From the perspective of Mercersburg, Christ is the Second Adam in whom the divinely intended actualization of human nature, a

---

108. See Erb, *Nevin's Theology*, 125–32.
109. See De Bie, *Speculative Theology and Common Sense Religion*, 93–99.
110. See Evans, *Imputation and Impartation*.
111. Appel, *Life and Work*, 622.

process derailed by Adam and Eve, has been finally achieved. Nevin explained, "He [Jesus] was man more perfectly than this could be said of Adam himself, even before he fell; humanity stood revealed in his person under its most perfect form."[112]

Nevin's new emphasis of the soteriological efficacy of Christ's personhood transformed the way that Christ's atonement for sin was understood. The righteousness of Christ is imputed to believers because that righteousness has been imparted to them through their living union with Christ.[113] According to Nevin the only basis for the imputation of Christ's righteousness and his satisfaction of divine justice to sinners is the believer's participation in Christ's life.[114] God pronounces Christians to be righteous and justified because the life of Christ the righteous one has entered them. Because of that union, Christ's possessions have become theirs. For Nevin, this mutual indwelling of Christ in the believer and the believer in Christ is the basis of actual sanctification as well as forensic justification. The Christian's life-long growth in sanctity is the organic unfolding and blossoming of the new life of Christ that has been implanted in her, like the maturation of a tree from a seed. Christ lives in the faithful person's heart, gradually permeating and transforming her spiritual core. The believer introjects Christ's affections, motivations, and dispositions, slowly being recreated in the image of Christ. For Nevin, the union with Christ is a "new life" that "is deeper than all thought, feeling, or exercise of will."[115] Faith's identification with Christ initiates a slow process of "putting on the mind of Christ." Although Nevin knew that the Heidelberg Catechism described Christ's atoning work in terms of a "satisfaction" that is imputed to us (Question 60), he also discerned in it the centrality of the language of participating in the life of Christ and all his benefits (Question 53), of being "grafted into Christ" (Question 64), and of sharing in "his anointing" (Question 32).

Nevin's focus on union with Christ had profound ecclesiological consequences. The believers' participation in the life of Christ was effected through the ongoing agency of Christ's life in the church. Nevin articulated a concept of the church, uncharacteristic of most of American Reformed theology, as the continuation of the vital energy of the incarnation. For Nevin, the glorified Christ had not abandoned the finite realm. Rather, the ascended Lord continues to be active in it through the medium of his body, the ecclesial community. This was a sharp departure from the ecclesiology of his revivalistic brothers and sisters, and even from the Reformed scholasticism of Princeton. According to most of his Reformed contemporaries, the church was either an aggregate of converted individuals or an association of individuals manifesting righteous behavior and espousing orthodox belief. Nevin's alternative vision was that the Holy Spirit, working through the church, brings about the union of believers with the ascended Christ, enabling Christ's theanthropic personhood to become

---

112. Nevin, *The Mystical Presence*, 149.
113. Again, see Evans, *Imputation and Impartation*.
114. See Erb, *Nevin's Theology*, 226, 296.
115. Nevin, *The Mystical Presence*, 151.

soteriologically effective. He explained, "Forth from the person of Christ, thus 'quickened in the Spirit,' the flood of life pours itself onward continually in the Church . . ."[116] Nevin reconceived the church as the Body of Christ rather than as a voluntary society or as a congeries of elect individuals. In this regard the Heidelberg Catechism supplied him with support. Although it did not define the church as a continuation of Christ's presence, the Catechism did describe it as a community chosen for eternal life of which the individual is a living member (Question 54), and as members of Christ who share in one fellowship with Christ (Question 55).

The sacramental life of the church was an essential and foundational way through which Christ's vitality was communicated, and Nevin accordingly wrote frequently and passionately about the power of the sacraments. This became one of the more obvious and controversial differentia of the Mercersburg Theology. Nevin was predictably thrilled with the Catechism's teachings about baptism and the Lord's Supper, which he saw as a synopsis of the positions of Calvin and Melanchthon. For Nevin, the Catechism provided a corrective to the "rationalism" of Zwingli and the crude physicalism of the Gnesio-Lutherans.

But in addition to that sacramental emphasis, Nevin insisted that Christ was also communicated through the church's communal nurture in general, including its historic liturgies, creeds, confessions, and catechisms.[117] At the conclusion of second edition of *The Anxious Bench*, Nevin contrasted "the system of the catechism" with "the system of the [anxious] bench," much to the detriment of the bench. By "catechism" in this treatise he sometimes meant catechisms in general, but often he was intending the Heidelberg Catechism in particular. For Nevin the system of the catechism fostered dependable, steady, long-term growth while the system of the bench merely catalyzed ephemeral and unreliable emotional episodes. The system of the catechism was intrinsically communal, for it was embedded in familial and ecclesial nurture, while the system of the bench was private and narcissistic. This valorization of the transformative power of the communal, historical traditions of the church would have implications for almost every ecclesial practice, and would make glaringly obvious the divergence of the Mercersburg movement from the sensibilities of the majority of Reformed Protestants in the United States.

All of these themes converge in Nevin's articles on the Heidelberg Catechism which follow. In these disparate writings that span almost two decades he pursues several different purposes. Most importantly, he uses his exposition of the Catechism as an occasion to develop the theological themes that were characteristic of the Mercersburg Theology. In doing so he also voices his discontent with those churches that did not recognize the critical importance of the Heidelberg Catechism, did not understand its content, and failed to employ it for instruction purposes. To counter

---

116. Nevin, *The Mystical Presence*, 156.

117. See Barrett, "The Distinctive World of Mercersburg Theology: Yearning for God or Relief from Sin?" See also Evans, *A Companion to the Mercersburg Theology*.

their failures, he makes a case for the crucial need for catechetical instruction in the church as an alternative to the spiritually superficial revivalism of zealots like Finney. To strengthen his argument he contends that the Heidelberg Catechism is the most representative and the most profound of all Reformed confessional documents. And, most importantly, he tries to show the reader that the Catechism's theological contents proclaim the central Christian affirmation that in Christ human nature has been united to the very life of God.

Document 1

The History and Genius of the Heidelberg Catechism (1847)

(by John Williamson Nevin, D. D.)

Editor's Introduction

When John Nevin began teaching at Mercersburg in 1840 he discovered that the German Reformed churches in Pennsylvania and Maryland were not uniformly committed to the catechetical traditions of their own heritage. Almost immediately he noted that revivalism's cavalier attitude toward confessional traditions had infected many congregations, with the result that many of them only owed a "modicum of allegiance to the Heidelberg Catechism."[1] Much to his consternation, in many places the practice of confirmation and even the celebration of the Lord's Supper had become infrequent.[2]

Nevin became increasingly aware of this situation after the end of the summer term of 1840 as he travelled from Mercersburg to Harrisburg and then to Easton in order to become familiar with the more rural German Reformed churches of eastern Pennsylvania. He was pleased with their Germanic traditionalism, but alarmed by the paucity of clergy and the weakness of pastoral oversight. He discovered that although many congregants were familiar with the Heidelberg Catechism, they did not necessarily comprehend it well. He observed that in many places confirmation had become a mere formality, with little examination of candidates before their admission to the church.[3] More shockingly, other catechisms were being used in German Reformed communities, and in some of them none were being used at all.[4] Nevin feared that his new denomination was in danger of losing its German Reformed confessional identity. He became even more convinced that the church needed to adhere to its own historic standards, particularly the Heidelberg Catechism, if it wanted to preserve its precious distinctive character.[5] Nevin's awareness of the continuing attractions of John Winebrenner's revivalism, and his polemical exchange with Winebrenner in

---

1. See Hart, *John Williamson Nevin: High Church Calvinist*, 63.
2. See Hart, *John Williamson Nevin*, 69.
3. Appel, *Life and Work*, 112.
4. Appel, *Life and Work*, 149.
5. Appel, *Life and Work*, 112.

Document 1: The History and Genius of the Heidelberg Catechism

1842–43, reinforced his antipathy to Finney-style proselytizing and his commitment to the "system of the catechism."[6]

In some sectors of the denomination the mood was ripe for a catechetical revival. In 1840 the German Reformed Church, having adopted a proposal by the Maryland classis that Nevin himself may have inspired, began planning a centennial celebration of its founding (the coetus had been formally organized in 1747). At least some church leaders shared a conviction that the denomination needed to rediscover its historic roots in order to safeguard its imperiled identity. Nevin capitalized on this sentiment, insisting that that those roots extended further back than the last hundred years in America. The sources of the distinctiveness of the German Reformed heritage stretched back at least to the Reformation in Europe (and for Nevin even to the medieval and early church). In addition to recovering a consciousness of its own uniqueness, Nevin was convinced that his new denomination needed to learn to see itself as a branch of the broader body of Christ. Consequently, Nevin published a series of articles about the German Reformed Church and the Heidelberg Catechism in *The Weekly Messenger*.[7] It was a massive undertaking, totaling twenty-nine numbers and taking almost two years. Together the essays constituted a brief history of the Reformation in general and the German Reformed Church in particular. Many of the articles focused on the dominating figures of the Reformation, like Luther, Zwingli, and Calvin. Only in the last few installments did Nevin deal in depth with the Heidelberg Catechism.

The series of articles did spark a revival of interest in the Heidelberg Catechism, at least in some quarters. In many congregations the use of other catechisms was discontinued. In light of that ostensible success, Nevin's friends urged him to make his reflections on the Catechism more widely available. Responding to their request, in 1847 he used some of the material from his essays as the basis of a short book, *The History and Genius of the Heidelberg Catechism*.[8] He omitted much of his treatment of the earlier reformers and added more information about the Catechism's composition.

In these articles Nevin argued for the general theological importance of the Reformation era and the confessional documents that it produced, particularly the Heidelberg Catechism. Nevin's exposition of the Reformation and its significance was often dialectical. On the one hand, he described it as seismic shift in the collective consciousness of Western Christianity.[9] He dismissed the "great man" theory of the Reformation's origins, for that would trivialize the phenomenon. The Reformation had not been the brain-child of any single religious hero, not even Luther himself. Rather, it was the efflorescence of the corporate spirit of the church at that point in history. Leaders like Luther and Zwingli merely epitomized that general consciousness and gave eloquent voice to it. On the other hand, no matter how revolutionary

---

6. Winebrenner, "Letter 4," *Gospel Publisher* (Nov. 1, 1843).
7. *The Weekly Messenger*, December, 1840–August, 1842.
8. Nevin, *The History and Genius of the Heidelberg Catechism*, this volume.
9. Nevin, *The History and Genius of the Heidelberg Catechism*, this volume, 57.

the Reformation might seem, it was rooted in the soil of the patristic and medieval church, and was the organic development of dynamics present within Roman Catholicism. It was not a complete rejection of the medieval past, nor was it a return to the pristine church of the era of the Apostles. The Reformation was both something novel and something rooted in the past.

In a similar dialectical manner Nevin discussed the relation of the various strands of Protestantism to the characteristics of the territorial cultures in which they arose. On the one hand he insisted that the shift in Christian sensibilities was not just the fruit of German or Swiss national movements.[10] Luther was not merely addressing spiritual problems or cultural conditions that were unique to Saxony, nor was Calvin dealing with issues that were restricted to Geneva. The spirit of Protestantism could not be limited by ethnicity or geography; rather, it was of universal significance. Similarly, the Heidelberg Catechism should not be of interest only to western German and Dutch Christians. All Protestants, including those in America, could benefit from its profundity. On the other hand, Nevin was emphatic that the national characteristics of the Saxons, the Palatines, the French, and the Swiss were not irrelevant to the religious traditions that arose in their territories. Ethnic cultures did leave their stamps upon the various forms of Protestantism. Therefore the German Reformed folk of North America should treasure the Heidelberg Catechism as a bearer of their distinctive spiritual identity. The Heidelberg Catechism was both universal and particular.

Nevin also wrote dialectically about the relation of Lutheranism and the Reformed tradition. On the one hand he insisted that the Reformed heritage was different from Lutheranism, the other great branch of the Protestant family.[11] He emphasized the fact that the Reformation in Switzerland arose independently from that in Saxony; Zwingli's battle to cleanse the church of the corruption of the papacy had not been influenced by Luther initially. Moreover, Luther and Zwingli had very different personalities and even different shortcomings, for Zwingli was too rationalistic and Luther was too polemical. Having differentiated the Saxon and the Swiss Protestants, Nevin then proceeded to treat French Protestant religious culture (including Calvin's Geneva) as a significantly different variation on the Reformed theme. On the other hand, Nevin argued that the differences between the Lutheran and Reformed traditions should not be exaggerated to the point of irreconcilability, as Luther had tragically done at the Colloquy of Marburg in 1529. Nevin lauded the aspirations of Philip of Hesse, who had called for the conference, for he had been wise to seek a rapprochement between the two divergent Protestant families.[12] The villains in Nevin's

---

10. Nevin, *The History and Genius of the Heidelberg Catechism*, this volume, 57-63.

11. Nevin, *The History and Genius of the Heidelberg Catechism*, this volume, 58.

12. Philip I, Landgrave of Hesse (1504–67) was one of the premier political leaders of the Protestant cause in Germany. He converted to Protestantism in 1524 and spent much of his reign attempting to unite Lutheran and Reformed Christians in a common front against the Catholic Hapsburgs. While claiming to be a Lutheran, he showed much sympathy toward the Swiss Zwinglians. He was the guiding spirit of the Protestant Schmalkaldic League, a military alliance that was defeated by the Catholics

Document 1: The History and Genius of the Heidelberg Catechism

subsequent historical narrative were the Gnesio-Lutherans[13] who anathematized everyone except themselves in order to safeguard their favorite doctrinal fine points, and the hyper-Calvinists who also condemned everyone whose metaphysical speculations about God's decrees differed from their own. In Nevin's pages Melanchthon and Calvin emerged as the champions of wisdom and mediatorial virtue. According to Nevin, the Lutheran Melanchthon and the Reformed Calvin were not that different from one another on the doctrine of the Lord's Supper. Nevin concluded that non-doctrinaire Lutherans and Calvinists who did not fixate upon unknowable and unedifying metaphysical issues should be able to find common ground.

Nevin's genealogy of the Lutheran and the Reformed traditions served as an apologia for the Heidelberg Catechism. According to Nevin the Catechism should be situated in the irenic strand of Protestantism associated with Melanchthon and Calvin. He reiterated that the Catechism's authors, although sympathetic to the Swiss reformers, intended no break with the Augsburg Confession. Nevin concluded that the Catechism should function in two very different ways. It should be the glue that holds the unique German Reformed tradition together, and it should be a crucial basis for pan-Protestant unity.

---

in 1547. After that debacle, Philip spent his remaining years trying to clear a path to the coexistence of Protestants and Catholics. Nevin admired his efforts to promote the unification of Christianity, even though they largely failed.

13. "Gnesio-Lutherans" fought to preserve Luther's original teachings in their alleged purity. Alarmed by the differences between the 1530 version of the Augsburg Confession, known as the *Invariata*, and Melanchthon's revision of 1540, known as the *Variata*, they insisted upon acknowledging the *Invariata* as the only doctrinal standard for the Lutheran church.

HISTORY AND GENIUS

OF THE

HEIDELBERG CATECHISM.

By J. W. NEVIN, D. D.

Prof. of Theol. in the Seminary of the Ger. Ref. Church,

Mercersburg, Pennsylvania.

CHAMBERSBURG:
PUBLICATION OFFICE OF THE GERMAN REFORMED CHURCH.
1847.

Preface

The small work here offered to the public owes its origin, in some measure, to the latter portion of a series of Essays, which appeared during the years 1841 and 1842, in the WEEKLY MESSENGER, under the general caption of the *Heidelberg Catechism*.[1] The publication was called forth by the occasion of the late Centenary of the German Reformed Church in this country; and was designed to serve the object of that celebration, in the way of bringing home to the consciousness of the Church, in popular form, an imperfect sketch at least of her own history and constitution, as unfolded in Europe first and afterwards on this side of the Atlantic. There was an earnest call at the time for the whole, in the form of a separate volume. It has been judged best not to comply with this request; but it seemed important, at the same time, to throw into a more permanent form so much at least of the articles in question as had respect to the direct history of the Catechism itself. This is now done in the present publication; which however is not a reprint simply, to any extent, of what was previously published, but in all respects another work, in which the old material is taken up, with the addition of a good deal that is new, into a much more thorough and complete form.

The series of Essays in the Messenger was prefaced, Dec. 9, 1840, with a short introduction, in which occurs the following passage, worthy for various reasons to be repeated in this place.

> The whole is intended to be a contribution to the celebration of our *Centenary Year*. One great object of this observance, it seems to me, should be to make the Church properly acquainted with herself, by connecting in her consciousness as far as possible the present with the past. We need, not only to look back on our history, as it belongs during the last hundred years to this western continent, but to follow it still farther back, to its commencement in the old world. We need to feel that we *have* a history, as old and as honorable to say the least as that of any other Protestant denomination; embodying a vital spirit of its own; enshrining principles and ideas, which are worthy of being cherished by us, as a precious legacy, through all coming time. The more we can be brought to commune familiarly and freely with the spirit of the Reformation,

---

1. [*The Weekly Messenger*, December, 1840–August, 1842.]

as it wrought mightily in the deeds, and uttered itself powerfully in the words, of our ecclesiastical ancestry, the better is it likely to be with us in all respects at the present time. In every community, whether it be religious or civil, it is of immense account to keep a firm hold in this way on the original life of the organization, by which it exists; so far as this deserves to be looked upon as wholesome and sound.[2] Reverence for the past, a history worthy of being cherished and honored, and a disposition to do filial homage to its authority, may be regarded as an indispensable condition of all spiritual greatness. In the affairs of religion, this inward sentiment of sympathy and union with the life of other ages is specially important; and all that tends to make it active, should be carefully and religiously encouraged, in opposition to every form of opinion or practice, which by a vain affectation of improvement, would impair the force of so sacred an association. Let us have progress, by all means; but let it be progress *upwards,* within the sphere of the original life of the Church itself, as a tree unfolds itself in growth and is the same tree still; not progress *outwards,* by which the life of the past, together with its form, is renounced, and "another gospel" is introduced in the room of the old.

It has not been considered necessary to accompany the text of the work, from page to page, with particular references to the authorities, which have been made use of in its compilation. I may state here, in a general way, that I stand indebted for facts mainly to H. S. van Alpen's *Geschichte und Literatur des Heidelbergischen Katechismus,*[3] the 2nd volume of Planck's *Geschichte der protestantischen Theologie,*[4] and several articles in the large *Encyclopædie der Wissenschaften und Kuenste* now in course of publication by ERSCH and GRUBER.[5] Other less considerable helps it is not necessary to mention. ALTING's *Historia Ecclesiæ Palatinæ,*[6] LENFANT's

---

2. [The notion that every culture has a unique spirit, present at its point of origin as a seed which then grows and unfolds, was common to most forms of Romanticism and to Hegelianism. Nevin was probably influenced here by Frederick Augustus Rauch (1806–41), his German émigré colleague at Mercersburg for one year who had been immersed in Hegelian thought. In his *Psychology* (the second edition of which Nevin edited and for which he wrote the introduction) Rauch stressed the power of different ethnic and national cultures to shape the experience of individuals in distinctive ways (*Psychology*, 66–80). Rauch also used organic, collective language to describe the maturation of the potentialities latent within a culture.]

3 [Heinrich Simon van Alpen, *Geschichte und Literatur des Heidelbergischen Katechismus* (Frankfurt am Main: Hermannischen Buchhandlung, 1800).]

4. [G. J. Plank, *Geschichte der protestantischen Theologie*. 2 vols. (Göttingen: unknown publisher, 1831). Planck (1751–1833) was a German Protestant theologian and historian as well as the great-grandfather of physicist Max Planck. He is remembered for his volumes, *Geschichte des protestantischen Lehrbegriffs* (*History of the Protestant Teaching Concept*) and *Geschichte der christlich-kirchlichen Gesellschaftsverfassung* (*History of the Christian Church's Social Constitution*).]

5. [Johann Samuel Ersch and Johann Gottfried Gruber, *Encyclopädie der Wissenschaften und Künste* (Leipzig, 1818–42).]

6. [Heinrich Alting, *Historia Ecclesiæ Palatinæ*. Groningen, 1728 (originally published 1644). Alting (1583–1644) was a German Reformed theologian who taught at Heidelberg until he had to flee from the sack of the city by the Imperialists. In the Netherlands he served as a tutor to the son of the

PREFACE

L'innocence du Catechisme de Heidelberg,[7] J. C. KŒCHER's *Katechetishe Geschichte der Reformirten Kirche*,[8] and other works in relation to the general subject which it would have been desirable to consult, have unfortunately not been within my reach.

Such as it is, the work is now committed to the Church, with the prayer that it may serve, under God's blessing, the interest of a sound church feeling, within its communion.

J. W. N. Mercersburg, February 1847.

---

disposed Elector Palatine and resumed his teaching of theology. While not endorsing the Arminian party, he expressed reservations about some of the extreme doctrines of the hyper-Calvinists.]

7. [Jacques Lenfant, *L'innocence du Catechisme de Heidelberg*. Amsterdam: Pierre Humbert, 1723 (originally published 1688). Lenfant (1661–1728) was a French Reformed theologian who fled from France after the revocation of the Edict of Nantes and eventually settled in Berlin. Throughout his career he polemicized against the Jesuits and defended the Heidelberg Catechism against their complaints that it departed from the teachings of the early church.]

8. [Johann Christoph Kœcher, *Katechetishe Geschichte der Reformirten Kirche* (Jena: Cröker, 1756). Kœcher (1699–1772) was a Dutch-German Reformed theologian who wrote a comprehensive history of German, Dutch, Swiss, and French catechisms, including the Latin versions.]

Table of Contents

I. Introduction

The Reformation. Luther. The two Confessions. Reformed Church. Symbolical books. Heidelberg Catechism.

II. The Palatinate

The Province. Heidelberg and its University. Luther at Heidelberg. Frederick the "Wise." Otho-Henry. Frederick the Pious. Confessional agitations. State of the German Church in general. Bremen.

III. Occasion of the Catechism

Hesshuss and Klebitz. Response of Melanchthon. The Palatinate becomes Reformed. General emotion in Germany. John Brentz in Wirtemberg. Stuttgard Synod and Confession. Violent controversy. Lutheran principle fully developed.

IV. Formation of the Catechism

The Elector Frederick. Caspar Olevianus. Zacharias Ursinus. Provincial Synod. First editions. Established use.

V. War against the Catechism

The pacific spirit. Angry reception by Romanists and Lutherans. Theological assaults. Remonstrance of princes. Diet of Augsburg. Noble stand taken by Frederick. Triumph. His piety and happy death.

Document 1: The History and Genius of the Heidelberg Catechism

VI. The Catechism at Home

Relapse of the Palatinate to Lutheranism. Restoration under prince Casimir. Death of Olevianus and Ursinus. David Pareus. Thirty Years' War. Philip William. Decline of the Reformed Church in the Palatinate. 80th Question.

VII. The Catechism Abroad

General reception in the Reformed Church, Switzerland. France. England. Hungary. Poland. Germany. Holland. Arminian opposition. Synod of Dort. Commentaries. America. Reformed Dutch & German Reformed Churches.

VIII. The Catechism in America

Reformed Dutch Church. Historical sketch. Present state. German Reformed Church. General view of its history in America. Relations of the two Churches at this time.

IX. Theology of the Catechism

Seal of general approbation. Ecumenical character. Objectiveness. Earnest practical spirit. Doctrinal reserve. Opposed to all Pelagianism. Theory of sin and redemption. Relations to high Calvinism on the subject of the decrees. Theory of the sacraments, and of good works.

X. Church Spirit of the Catechism

German origin. Relations to Lutheranism and the Augsburg Confession. Prussian Church, positive and catholic. Historical basis in the Apostles' Creed. Sacramental feeling. Churchly associations. Old Palatinate Liturgy. Baptismal educational religion. Confirmation. Conclusion.

I. Introduction

The Reformation. Luther. The two Confessions. Reformed Church. Symbolical Books. Heidelberg Catechism.

The Reformation may be regarded, in one view, as an entirely new life in the history of Christianity. More deeply considered, however, it will be found to stand in the closest living connection with this same history, as it had been regularly developed in the bosom of the Catholic Church for centuries before. It formed no absolute rupture with the old life of the body bearing this title; on the contrary, it was only its true and legitimate continuation, through the vast convulsive crisis which threatened at the time its total dissolution. In no other light can it be vindicated as the work of God.[1]

Thus viewed, its origin cannot be referred to any particular man or men. Not to LUTHER or ZWINGLI, nor with the great age itself even to which they belonged, can it be said, strictly speaking, to have taken its start.[2] The Middle Ages formed its womb. Through long centuries, the life of the Church had struggled previously toward this grand magnificent issue. The sixteenth century was but "the fullness of time," for the *revelation* of a process, which was before hidden indeed from the world, but had long wrought mightily nevertheless as a mystery of God, in the direction of the very result which was now reached. It was the life of the Church then as a whole, which, by the help of God's Spirit, gave birth to the Reformation, as a new form of existence with which it had been pregnant for ages before. LUTHER and the other Reformers, with all their activity in furthering the work, were themselves in one sense the product of its

---

1. [Nevin's claim that the Reformation grew out of the Catholic Church contradicted the widespread Protestant view that the Reformers were the heirs of anti-papal sectarian groups like the Waldensians, who had survived as a faithful remnant of the true church during the Middle Ages.]

2. [Nevin was arguing against theories such as that held by the British essayist and historian Thomas Carlyle (1795–1881) who argued that "great men" are the decisive factors in historical developments. Nevin's colleague Philip Schaff mentions Carlyle's interpretation of Luther in *The Principle of Protestantism*, which Nevin translated from German to English in 1845. See *The Development of the Church*, ed. David Bains and Theodore Trost, The Mercersburg Theology Study Series, vol. 3 (Eugene, Or: Wipf & Stock, 2017), 117.]

power; being comprehended in fact in the general movement over which they seemed to preside, as a restless world force, which they were insufficient either to fathom or control.[3] They did not make the Reformation. The Reformation made *them*.

We find accordingly a sort of simultaneous outburst of the same great work in different lands, that makes it difficult to say precisely where it took its rise. The movement in Switzerland stood in no connection externally, at first, with the movement in Germany; and in some sense its presence in both these countries might seem to have been anticipated by the open action of the same general power in France. The proper cradle of the Reformation indeed was Germany; and its central personality, beyond all doubt, is presented to our view in the colossal figure of MARTIN LUTHER. But the work was not bound to him, in any way, as a whole. In France and Switzerland in particular, its course was altogether separate and free.[4]

The movement from the beginning, was in a general view one and the same. It included in itself however two different ground tendencies, which, starting asunder at the very outset, came finally to full opposition, and so resolved themselves into two distinct communions or confessions. Hence, to characterize these divergent interests, the great denominational titles LUTHERAN and REFORMED.

This division sprang immediately from the sacramental question; especially as concerned with the point of Christ's presence in the holy eucharist. But the difference which here came to view may be said to have affected the theory of Christian doctrine throughout. It shows a most poor and superficial way of thinking, to look upon the sacramentarian controversy of the sixteenth century as something only externally or accidentally related to the proper life of Protestantism—an arbitrary, isolated difficulty, created by the caprice of superstition simply, or merely blind self-will.[5] To the religious consciousness of the time, the question stood intertwined with the entire scheme of the gospel, and was felt to reach out, in its bearings and consequences, to the farthest limits of theology. However then we may deplore the unhappy strife, we have no right to denounce it as unreasonable and wrong. It was unavoidably necessary, in the circumstances of the age. The question was in no sense factitious or supererogatory. It lay actually and broadly present in the religious movement of the period itself, whether men might choose to regard it or not. To have smothered it, or thrust it aside, as an interest of small account, would have been to betray the cause of truth, and wrong the whole work of the Reformation. There might have been controversy indeed, without a formal rupture of the Church. But this was hardly to be expected in

---

3. [The theme of a "restless world force" operating through individuals was indebted to the reflections of G. W. F. Hegel (1770–831) on history, which were partly mediated to Nevin by his colleague Frederick Rauch.]

4. [Nevin was arguing against the view of many conservative Lutherans that only Luther should be credited with the origin of the Reformation.]

5. [The minimization of doctrinal differences on the Eucharist between the Lutherans and the Reformed had been a strategy of those who were enthusiastic about the Prussian Union church. It was also typical of Pietists and many American "awakeners."]

I. INTRODUCTION

the case of an agitation so earnest and deep. Where two sides of a vital, fundamental truth thus fall asunder for the understanding, it seems to be in general necessary, that the difference should be pushed out to the point of a full formal contradiction, before the way can be opened for a final reconciliation, in which proper justice may be secured to the rights of both.[6]

The origin of the *Reformed Church*, as distinguished from the *Lutheran*, is sometimes traced to the person of ULRICH ZWINGLI, the illustrious Reformer of *Zurich*, who led the way in the spiritual emancipation of Switzerland. This view however is in no proper sense correct. His relation to the Reformed Church historically, is not at all parallel with that of LUTHER to the body distinguished by his name. He occupies indeed a very prominent position in its history, as the father we may say of the Helvetic Reformation, and the leading organ at the start of the anti-Lutheran tendency with regard to the Lord's Supper. In this last view, however, he was only the center or nucleus, around which externally the opposition to Luther's doctrine on this subject was first brought to take shape and form; while at the same time, the Reformation had already begun, as we know, to reveal itself in France, under the same general character, without any dependence on him whatsoever.[7] The Protestant movement, as such, included in its very nature, the Reformed tendency as well as the Lutheran; and it prevailed accordingly, under this complexion, in certain sections of the Church, from the beginning, irrespective of all direct hostile reference to the opposite system. In this way, the Reformed Church appeared in different parts of the Christian world at the same time, simultaneously with the rise of the Lutheran Church. It owes its origin to France full as much, to say the least, as it does to Switzerland. It was simply one great leading form of the Reformation itself, which in the nature of the case could not fail to display its presence, in different directions, in full parallel with the other great form of it, in every part of its progress. The man, who beyond all others unquestionably, in the sixteenth century, contributed to give solid form and character to the Church, under this aspect, was JOHN CALVIN, the founder of the Reformed faith in *Geneva*. Still CALVIN is not to be considered the father properly of the Reformed Church. It existed as a different interest before he appeared on the stage of the Reformation: and with all his vast influence, his theological system never became universally prominent in its communion.

The *Reformed* Church acquired its distinctive title first in France; not with any reference of course to the Lutheran Protestantism of Germany, which was regarded

---

6. [Here the influence of Hegel's dialectical view of historical development is evident. Seemingly opposed positions, each containing some truth, must develop to their respective logical conclusions, and then strive to be resolved in a higher synthesis that preserves the partial truths of both of them.]

7. [It was important for Nevin to differentiate the impact of Zwingli in much of Switzerland from the rise of a different kind of Reformed tradition in France and the French-speaking cantons. According to Nevin, the French variety was less rationalistic and subjective. He also appreciated the fact that the French movement continued for years to see itself as a reform of the Catholic Church, a view that held attractions for Nevin.]

Document 1: The History and Genius of the Heidelberg Catechism

as in all material respects one and the same interest; but in opposition wholly to the Church of Rome, against whose exclusive pretentions it claimed to be the true Church of Jesus Christ, now purged from the errors and abuses under which the truth had been previously so long oppressed. It was simply the *Catholic* Church Reformed. Afterwards however the title as transferred to the Church in Switzerland, and then to other countries, came to be distinctive particularly of that part of the Protestant world which refused to be called *Lutheran*. By assuming this last name, the body thus denominated, divided itself openly from the other Confession; which was thus left in exclusive possession of the original general appellation, the *Reformed Church*; and this became accordingly thence-forward a technical title, carrying in it a reference to Lutheranism on the one hand, as well as to Romanism on the other.

Under this general title was comprehended, in the sixteenth century, the national Protestantism, not only of *Switzerland* and *France*, but of the *Netherlands* also and *Scotland* and *England*. The same faith substantially became triumphantly established after a short time, in the German *Palatinate*; and in the end it prevailed extensively in other parts of Protestant Germany also, in competition with the other Confession [Lutheranism].

ZWINGLI commenced his ministry in Zurich, in the year 1519. The work of reformation went forward afterwards rapidly, under his influence. As early as 1525, all was thoroughly Protestant. Bern, Basel, Schafhausen and St. Gall, soon followed in the same course; and before the death of ZWINGLI, who was slain in battle, A. D. 1531, more than half the Helvetic confederacy had become Reformed. Geneva threw off the authority of Rome in 1535. Here CALVIN, who had been forced to retire from his native France by persecution, found himself constrained to settle the following year; and through the vast force of his character, Geneva soon became the acknowledged center of the entire Reformed Church. The first national Synod of the French Protestant Church was held at Paris, in the year 1559. About the same time, the Reformation became fully established in England, by the accession of Queen Elizabeth to the throne. Scotland soon after threw off the yoke of Rome under the guidance of JOHN KNOX.[8] Through long years of civil war, the Church of Holland accomplished finally the same freedom. The Palatinate, previously Lutheran, passed over to the Reformed faith, A. D. 1560.

These different sections of the Reformed Church were regarded, in the beginning, as one and the same Confession. They were not however, like the Lutheran Church, bound together by subscription to a common creed. With an independent organization, each national branch of the general body had its own ecclesiastical standards. Hence [there arose] a variety of Confessions and Catechisms; which serve

---

8. [John Knox (1513–72) was the leader of the Scottish Reformation and the author of many of its confessional documents. During a period of exile he had studied with many of the Swiss Reformers. He is remembered for his role in the composition of The Scots Confession.]

strikingly, however, by their general agreement, to attest the substantial unity of the faith to which they owe their existence.

The *First Confession of Basel*, supposed to be the production originally of ŒCOLAMPADIUS, was published, A. D. 1534.[9] The Second Confession of Basel, known commonly as the *First Helvetic Confession*, made its appearance in 1536, under the sanction of a general ecclesiastical convention representing all Protestant Switzerland. The *Gallic Confession* was formed by an assembly of delegates from the Reformed churches of France, held in Paris, in the year 1559. With the religious revolution of 1560, was introduced in Scotland the *Old Scotic Confession*. The *Belgic Confession* became public in the Netherlands in 1562. In this same year, the *Thirty Nine Articles* of the Church of England (a modification of the system previously projected in the reign of Edward VI by CRANMER[10] and RIDLEY,[11]) were clothed with formal symbolical authority. The *Second Helvetic Confession*, drawn up by HENRY BULLINGER in the year 1562,[12] became of established general force for Switzerland A. D. 1566. The *Westminster Confession* belongs to the middle of the following century.

Along with these Confessions, various *Catechisms*, larger and smaller, appeared on all sides, as rules and helps for religious instruction. These it is not necessary to note in detail. Among others, an excellent Catechism was composed for the use of the Church in Geneva by CALVIN. It appeared in the French language A. D. 1541, and four years later in a Latin translation by the author. It surpassed decidedly all previous catechisms in the Reformed Church, and soon acquired a widely extended credit. BEZA styles it an admirable work;[13] and tells us, that it was so highly approved even in foreign lands, as to be not only translated into the principal living tongues, such as German, English, Scotch, Belgic, Spanish, and honored besides with versions into

---

9. [Johannes Œcolampadius (1482–1531), a humanist scholar, was the Protestant reformer of Basel. He engaged in theological disputes with Eramus, Zwingli, Luther, and Martin Bucer. He was closely aligned with Zwingli's theology of the Eucharist.]

10. [Thomas Cranmer (1489–1556) was an English reformer who served as Archbishop of Canterbury during the later reign of Henry VIII and the reign of Edward VI. Somewhat influenced by Swiss and French reformers, he was the primary architect of the liturgical and doctrinal reforms in Britain. He supported the principle of royal supremacy, which entitled the king to sovereign rule over the Church within his realm. Most importantly, he authored the first two editions of the *Book of Common Prayer*. He was martyred during the Catholic resurgence under Mary I. Nevin frequently argued that the origins of the Church of England were to be found in the Reformed tradition.]

11. [Nicholas Ridley (1500–55) became the Protestant Bishop of London, working closely with Cranmer. He too was martyred during the Marian persecutions. Nevin typically valorized Reformed martyrs.]

12. [Heinrich Bullinger (1504–75) was a Swiss Reformer who succeeded Zwingli as the ecclesiastic leader of Zürich. His somewhat more moderate theology was widely influential. He is best remembered for drawing up the *Second Helvetic Confession* in 1561, which was translated into German and published in 1566.]

13. [Theodore Beza (1519–1605), a French Protestant scholar and reformer, was Calvin's theological successor in Geneva. He polemicized against the Gnesio-Lutherans on the doctrine of the Eucharist and developed a thoroughly supralapsarian understanding of God's sovereign will. He is known for his treatise *Summa totius Christianismi*.]

Document 1: The History and Genius of the Heidelberg Catechism

Greek and Hebrew; the first by the celebrated printer *Robert Stephens*, and the last by *Immanuel Tremellius*.[14]

Still more important however than this formulary, for the Reformed Church as a whole, was the memorable CATECHISM OF THE PALATINATE, or the HEIDELBERG CATECHISM; which appeared in the year 1563, and soon won for itself a sort of universal authority in the Church, that no similar system has since been able to supplant. Its relation to the Reformed Church was soon allowed to be parallel, in this respect, with that of the venerable *Catechism of Luther* to the Lutheran Church; a distinction not admitted before, in favor even of the Catechism of Geneva. Hence it is denominated at times the *Reformed Catechism*, as representing by general acknowledgement, the faith of the entire communion, distinguished by the same title in the sixteenth century. It is much more indeed than a Catechism, in the ordinary sense; being so constructed as to serve, at the same time, the purpose of a full church confession. It stands forth accordingly with special prominence, not only among the Catechisms, but among the regular Confessions also, of the period to which it belongs. In this view, it holds, we may say, the very highest distinction. If the question be asked, which among all the symbolical books that have appeared in the Reformed Church, has the best claim to be regarded in the light of an œcumenical or general symbol; the answer must be given undoubtedly, that it is the Heidelberg Catechism.

Such as we find to be, in fact, the clear judgment of history itself. Though formed originally for the use of a particular territory only, the Catechism proved to be a true and happy expansion of the faith of the Reformed Church in general; and in a short time accordingly, it came to be recognized and honored as such all over Europe. Where it was not exalted formally to the rank of a symbolical book, it was at least invested with the highest credit, as a word embodying in the most approved form, the doctrines of the Church at large. The authority of the prince under whose direction it was prepared was sufficient indeed to bring it to general use in the Church of the Palatinate; but this authority could have no force beyond these limits. Its favorable reception in other lands could be owing only to its own intrinsic worth, and the ready concurrence in its doctrine and spirit, which it met with from the Reformed Church in every direction. It was received indeed with a sort of universal homage, as an ornament to the creed which it was felt so well to represent. Switzerland, France, Scotland and England, joined in testifying toward it their admiration and respect. It was translated for the use of schools and churches of Hungary. It became the basis of religious instruction for the Reformed Church generally in Germany. In the Netherlands it was clothed in the highest authority in being made to constitute, along with the Belgic Confession, the national rule of faith. Finally by the Synod of Dort, the general council of the entire Reformed Church in the beginning of the seventeenth century, it was formally acknowledged and sanctioned, as a fair and proper representation of the

---

14. [Immanuel Tremellius (1510–89) was an Italian Jewish convert to Christianity who became a leading translator of the Old Testament.]

I. INTRODUCTION

Reformed faith in all lands. It became thus in form, to a certain extent, the accredited standard of the Church as a whole.

In all this we see the true importance of the Heidelberg Catechism. The relation which it now bears to the whole Reformed Church of the sixteenth century is full of interest, and such as may well make it an object of special regard in all ages. No other Catechism or Confession comes down to us, under the same broad catholic character, or with equal claims, in the view just mentioned, to historical attention and respect.

The history of the Catechism requires, in the first place, a brief review of the religious history of the Palatinate itself, in the age of the Reformation.

II. The Palatinate

The Province. Heidelberg and its University. Luther at Heidelberg. Frederick the Wise. Otho-Henry. Frederick he Pious. Confessional agitations. State of the German Church in general. Bremen.

The title PALATINATE (in German *Pfalz*,) belonged formerly to two adjoining provinces of Germany, which were distinguished as *Upper* and *Lower*. The first (*Oberpfalz*), bordered on Bohemia and Bavaria; the other (*Unterpfalz*) was situated on both sides of the Rhine, touching on different sides Mayence, Wirtemberg [Württemberg], Baden, Alsace and Lorraine. It is frequently styled the *Palatinate of the Rhine*; and in spite of the horrible devastations to which it has been subjected in different ages, from the ruthless hand of war, is known as one of the most fertile and productive sections of Germany. Down to the year 1620, the two provinces belonged together; but when the Elector, Frederic V [1596–1632] was put under the ban of the empire, after the battle of Prague, the Upper Palatinate was made over to Bavaria. In consequence of the great changes that took place in Europe after the French Revolution, the country which formerly constituted the Palatinate on the Rhine is now possessed by Prussia, Bavaria, Baden, Hesse-Darmstadt, &c. It is not easy of course to identify it on a modern map.

Heidelberg, the ancient capital of the Palatinate,[1] early became conspicuous in learning, by its celebrated university, established about the middle of the fourteenth century.[2] The founder of this noble institution, to whose influence Germany is indebted for so much of her cultivation, was the elector *Rupert* [1309–90], surnamed from the color of his beard the *Red*. At least forty years were needed, to bring the princely enterprise to its completion; and then large sums were sent to Rome, to

---

1. Since 1802, a city of the grand-duchy of Baden; distinguished for its charming situation, at the foot of the beautiful Kœnigstuhl, and on the left bank of the lovely Neckar, over which is a bridge 700 feet long, and from which a most superb view extends, between high mountains, over the valley of the Rhine, to the Vosges.

2. [Much of this information was gleaned from Heinrich Simon van Alpen, *Geschichte und Literatur des Heidelbergischen Katechismus*. This was later translated by Joseph Berg as *The History and Literature of the Heidelberg Catechism*. See pages 11–19.]

procure the sanction of the Church in its favor. This was granted by a bull of Pope Urban VI, A. D. 1385, in which Heidelberg is declared especially worthy, by the salubrity of its air and the fruitfulness of the surrounding country, to become such a general fountain of science.[3] The new university was required to conform to the model of the institution at Paris, and was endowed also with the same rights and privileges. The fostering care of his successors continued subsequently, to sustain and enlarge the work thus happily commenced by Rupert. Throughout the following century, we find, in connection with this university, a wholesome influence at work in the Palatinate, in favor of letters and religion; which, in the midst of all adverse agencies, contributed largely, beyond all doubt, to the general movement which ushered in subsequently the glorious age of the Reformation.

The electors, Frederick I [1425–76], and Philip the Upright [1448–1508], spared no pains to advance the credit of the university. Under the generous patronage of the latter, toward the close of the fifteenth century, we find in Heidelberg such men as *John Wessel, Rudolph Agricola,* the two *Reuchlins, Jacob Wimpheling,* &c., all warmly devoted to the cause of learning, and powerfully efficient in its advancement.[4]

Philip died in the year 1508, and was succeeded in the government by Louis, the Pacific [1478–1544].

During this reign, in the year 1518, a general convention of the Augustinian monks was held at Heidelberg. Among others, MARTIN LUTHER, the monk of Wittenberg, as one of the most distinguished men of his order, was summoned to attend. He had shortly before, in the case of Tetzel,[5] taken the first step in the great work of the Reformation, and was now fast becoming an object of earnest attention for all Europe. His friends used their influence to prevent him from undertaking the journey; for it was felt generally to involve no inconsiderable risk of his personal safety. He considered it his duty however to go; and under the protection of a warm letter of recommendation addressed by the elector of Saxony to the elector of the Palatinate, he made his appearance at the appointed time in Heidelberg, having performed a good part of his journey on foot. Through the influence of Œcolampadius, who was at this time connected with the electoral court, as instructor to the young prince, a favorable impression had already been created towards the extraordinary stranger. He found himself accordingly well received. On the suggestion of some of the brethren of his order, he offered himself to hold a public disputation on the merit of good works and the value of the Aristotelian philosophy. The discussion attracted great attention; and the spirit and force with which Luther maintained his views failed not to produce a deep impression

---

3. Prince Rupert's zeal for the university amounted to the character of a passion. He was accustomed to speak of it as his "beloved daughter" and watched over it with a father's care to the end of his life.

4. [All of these scholars were celebrated humanists; their presence in Heidelberg made the university an intellectual center for northern Europe.]

5. [Johannes Tetzel (1464–1519) was a Dominican preacher who famously promoted the sale of indulgences. This infuriated Luther, who denounced the practice in his Ninety-Five Theses.]

Document 1: The History and Genius of the Heidelberg Catechism

on the minds of many who were present. Among his hearers were found, *John Œcolampadius, Martin Bucer, Ehrhard Schnepf, John Brentz* and *Theobald Billican*; men, whose names appear conspicuous in the subsequent history of the Reformation.

Luther returned to Wittenberg. But the seed which he had been permitted to sow in the Palatinate remained behind, and soon began to reveal its power in the way of growth. From this time onward, such men as those whose names have been mentioned, exerted themselves in the work of disseminating evangelical principles; and the cause thus favorably introduced continued steadily to gain ground, till it was felt finally that the old system of religion was in danger of being entirely subverted. This led to persecution. Complaints were urged so successfully that the public lectures of Luther's friends were at length altogether prohibited, and two of them, Brentz and Billican, were required to appear, and answer for their alleged errors, before the academical senate and the electoral chancellor; which resulted however in nothing worse than the suspension of their lectures. Louis the *Pacific*, as he was called, devoted mainly it would seem to hunting and building, did not allow himself to be much disturbed with the religious questions of the time; while his constitutional goodness of heart rendered him averse to all rigorous measures in the way of persecution. He discovered no particular zeal against the new doctrines, and the Reformation continued to diffuse itself accordingly like leaven, from Heidelberg as a center throughout the Palatinate and into the adjoining territories.

Louis was succeeded in 1544 by his brother, Frederick II, the Wise.[6] This prince showed himself to be decidedly favorable to the Reformation; and under his auspices, the work immediately began to go forward with full power, in a more open way. In Heidelberg indeed, the people did not wait for the regular action of the government. As the mass was being celebrated in the church of the Holy Ghost, early in the year 1546, the whole congregation suddenly struck up the hymn in German "Es ist das Heil uns kommen her." The elector now ordered, that the mass should be in the future held in the vernacular language, that the Lord's Supper should be distributed in both kinds, and that priests should be allowed to marry. The unfortunate issue of the war of Schmalkald put a full stop indeed, the very next year, to the movement thus auspiciously commenced. The so called *Interim* of the emperor, Charles V, was forced upon the Palatinate, and along with it came back once more, in full authority, the errors and superstitions of Rome. But God did not suffer the enemies of his cause to triumph long. Maurice, of Saxony,[7] became unexpectedly the avenger of his country's wrongs,

---

6. [Elector Frederick II (1482–1556) was Elector of the Palatinate from 1544 to 1556. He actually embraced the Lutheran faith in 1546 but did not actively support the Schmalkaldic League of rebellious Lutheran princes. He was outlawed by Emperor Charles V, which motivated him to return to the Catholic fold.]

7. [Maurice (1521–1553) was Duke and later Elector of Saxony. Although he was a Protestant, he fought against the Lutheran Schmalkaldic League because he needed the political support of Charles V. However, he came to distrust the Hapsburgs, championed the Protestant cause, and forced Charles V to allow Lutheranism in the territories ruled by Lutheran princes.]

II. THE PALATINATE

and in 1552 the emperor found himself constrained, in the famous Pacification of Passau, to consent to the religious freedom of the German states.

The next elector, Otho-Henry, the Magnanimous,[8] 1556, showed a still more active zeal in favor of the Reformation. Under his administration, the Augsburg Confession was fully established in the Palatinate. Old superstitions were abolished. A new system of church government was introduced. The city of Heidelberg became, in a short time, almost entirely Protestant. Warmly devoted besides to the cause of science and art, Otho-Henry distinguished his reign also by his generous endeavors to improve the university and city. "He was resolved," he said, "to place the university and city on right footing, if it should cost him his last cent."[9] Heidelberg was adorned with new magnificence, in the way of architecture and sculpture, under his princely hand.

Unfortunately however, the triumph of the Reformation brought along with it the seeds of a new division. Protestantism was itself distracted, by conflicting views, and the idea of religious toleration was foreign from the genius of the age. The Palatinate included already three different parties, ranged under the names of Luther, Zwingli, and Calvin, or Melanchthon—for these last two were held to be substantially the same, on the main question at issue.[10] This of course was in relation to the Lord's Supper, the great central question of the age for the whole Protestant world. The division of sentiment was not allowed indeed, during this period, to come to an open rupture. But it was the source of much unquiet feeling, in a comparatively quiet way; and the elector was subjected to no small embarrassment at times from the sense of its refractory presence.

Otho-Henry died, A. D. 1559. Few princes have been more deserving of respect. Without children himself, he transmitted his electoral dignity to his cousin FREDERICK THE THIRD, whose honorable distinction it is to be known in history under the surname of the *Pious*.[11]

---

8. [Otto Henry (or Otho-Henry) the Magnanimous (1502–59) was Elector of the Palatinate from 1556 to 1559. He is remembered for his generous support of the arts and sciences and for the establishment of the Bibliotheca Palatina in the 1550s. He converted to Lutheranism in 1541 and overtly supported the Lutheran Schmalkaldic League.]

9. While yet a young man, he purchased, in his visit to Palestine, a large number of Greek and Oriental manuscripts for the library. The first copy that had been brought to Europe of Abulfeda's work on geography, he procured at the price of 1000 dollars. Afterwards, under his administration, great additions were made to it from various quarters: so that it became, as the *Bibliotheca Palatina*, famous through all Europe.

10. [The similarity of Calvin and Melanchthon was a theme that Nevin stressed throughout his career. It was part of his strategy to find common ground between moderate Lutherans and moderate (non-Zwinglian) Reformed factions.]

11. [Elector Frederick III, the Pious (1515–76), was attracted to the Protestant faith long before he became Elector Palatine of the Rhine in 1559. When he did become the Elector he sought to get a clearer understanding of the controversy raging between the strict Lutherans, the followers of Melanchthon, and the different strands of the Reformed tradition. As Frederick immersed himself in theological studies he gravitated to the Reformed faith. A disputation held in 1560 between Lutheran

Document 1: The History and Genius of the Heidelberg Catechism

Under the administration of this prince, the Palatinate, previously Lutheran, passed over formally to the *Reformed* Confession. To understand fully the nature of this important change, to which immediately the Heidelberg Catechism owes its formation, it is necessary to glance at the religious posture of Protestant Germany in general at the time it took place.

The great sacramental controversy of the sixteenth century includes in its history two entirely distinct periods. As carried on in the first place between Luther and the Swiss divines, with Zwingli so long as he lived at their head, it was brought ostensibly to a close by the memorable Wittenberg Concord, in 1536.[12] This was not considered satisfactory indeed, on either side. But men's minds had become weary with contention; and it was held desirable at all events to make the most of the present truce, where it seemed so difficult to come to a true and lasting peace. The result of all [this] had been undoubtedly moreover a partial moderation of extreme views on both sides. It was felt, more widely of course than it was expressed, that Luther on the one hand, as well as Zwingli on the other, had gone too far; and that the truth was to be sought in a middle position, rather than with either of the champions separately considered. Luther probably saw himself that the truce involved some feeling of this sort; and this may have had its influence in the effort by which he sought toward the close of his life to have the controversy renewed. The effort however produced no effect. Ten years after the date of the Concord, A. D. 1546, he was taken to his rest. The truce still continued. Many flattered themselves that it had become in fact, the grave of all former theological hostilities. But this expectation was vain. The general difference of the two Confessions had not yet been brought to a true inward reconciliation; and the question was too important to be permanently sacrificed to the interests of a mere prudential compromise. It might slumber for twenty years; but it could not always sleep. In due time accordingly, the truce as a matter of course came to an end. We may find much to quarrel with, in the spirit of those who led the way in the new rupture that followed. The rupture itself however was necessary.[13] It lay in the religious position of the age. It belonged of right to the history of the Reformation.

---

and Reformed theologians solidified Frederick's antipathy to Lutheran hyper-orthodoxy, particularly in regard to the Lord's Supper. After the Naumburg Convention in 1561 Frederick fully endorsed Reformed doctrine, and made the Reformed faith the official religion of his domain by supervising the composition and promotion of the Heidelberg Catechism. His backing gave the German Reformed movement a secure position from which to spread within the Holy Roman Empire.]

12. [The Wittenberg Concord was intended to forge a consensus among Lutheran and Reformed theologians concerning Christ's presence in the Eucharist. To please the Reformed party the document denied that Christ was "enclosed" by the physical elements, but to satisfy the Lutherans it did affirm that a sacramental union of Christ and the elements took place during the performance of the ritual. Although the Reformed theologian Martin Bucer signed it, most Reformed pastors later rejected it.]

13. [It was a commonplace of Hegelian philosophy that dialectical tensions must develop to their logical conclusions before a higher synthesis can be achieved.]

II. THE PALATINATE

This second period of the controversy, was ushered in by a sort of trumpet blast on the part of the memorable Lutheran polemic[ist], JOACHIM WESTPHAL,[14] preacher in Hamburg; who felt himself called, in the year 1552, to sound an alarm throughout Germany against the errors of the Swiss churches, in a special tract devoted wholly to the subject. The immediate occasion of this assault, seems to have been the way in which some distinguished theologians, whose standing might be counted intermediate or neutral with regard to the old controversy, had been led to declare their mind on the general subject. Specifically prominent among these were *Peter Martyr*[15] and *John Calvin*. In openly expressing their views, they had no thought of course of provoking controversy. It was not felt probably that there was any danger of giving material offense in any direction, with the moderate tone of thinking which seemed to have become so generally prevalent at the time, in the Lutheran Church itself. Calvin had good reason to believe that not only Melanchthon, but very many others also who belonged to the same communion, held in truth the same view substantially with regard to the Lord's Supper that he held himself; and at all events, his own view was not something which he had now brought forward for the first time. He had held it all along in an open and public way; and had no reason to anticipate, that it would prove particularly offensive at this time. The truth was however, [that] the cause of Westphal's displeasure, as well as of the general war that followed, lay much deeper than any such outward and accidental occasion. There had been, since 1536, in the Lutheran Church itself, a broad though quiet, and to a great extent unconscious, falling away from the extreme view of the great Reformer. The tenth article of the Augsburg Confession had come to be held very extensively in a simply Calvinistic sense. At the same time, the spirit of the old orthodoxy was not yet by any means extinct. It existed still, under a latent character, and as the event proved, in great strength. The progress of more liberal views, naturally served to rouse it finally, first to jealousy, and then to open resistance. In these circumstances, it needed no great provocation to bring on a war. Westphal was but the organ of the interest he represented, in its first show of violent reaction against a tendency which was now felt to threaten its own life. It was some consciousness of this, no doubt, that served to inspire him with confidence and courage, in the daring responsibility he ventured to assume in this case before the Christian world.

14. [Joachim Westphal (1511–74) became the leader of the Gnesio-Lutheran party of Hamburg. He is best known for his participation in several theological controversies, including those concerning Christ's descent into hell and, most importantly, the nature of the Lord's Supper. He published *Farrago confusanearum et inter se dissidentium opinionum de coena Domini, ex Sacramentariorum libris congesta* (1552), as a warning against those who denied the presence of Christ in the Lord's Supper. He argued against the notion of adiaphora and resisted anything that he feared would compromise belief in the corporeal presence of Christ in the Eucharist. He figures in Nevin's narratives as one of the chief exemplars of narrow dogmatism.]

15. [Peter Martyr Vermigli (1499–1562) was a Reformed theologian who taught in Strasbourg, Oxford, and Zürich. He vehemently denied that Christ was locally present in the Eucharistic elements and developed a doctrine of double predestination.]

The *Farrago*, as his tract was styled, passed at first notice without reply.[16] Men seemed to pause, in anxious suspense, as with the secret feeling that they had come to stand on the eve of a great conflict, whose consequences no one could calculate or foresee. Westphal renewed his attack, the following year, in a second publication; and the year after again, in a third. Calvin found himself now compelled to take up the pen in self-defense. Gradually the controversy began to assume a more general character. Other champions appear in the field. The true state of the Lutheran Church, as a house inwardly divided against itself, comes more and more into view. It is no longer Germany at war with Switzerland; but Germany convulsed with the elements of discord and division in her own bosom. The whole land is agitated, in every direction, with the presence of a second sacramental war, more terrible than the first, carried on by rigid Lutherans and Crypto-Calvinists beneath the banner of the Augsburg Confession. By such vast critical process, reaching through many long years of strife, were the two great Protestant Confessions conducted finally to the full sense of their original difference and distinction. Lutheranism became complete in the Form [Formula] of Concord; and the faith of the Reformed Church, as exhibited in the several Calvinistic Confessions which appeared in the midst of this controversy, and particularly we may say as embodied comprehensively in the Heidelberg Catechism, was openly acknowledged in large sections of Germany, where the Reformed Church as such had been previously unknown.

A full account of these agitations and conflicts would carry us far beyond the limits that belong properly to our present design. They form altogether one of the most strange and interesting chapters in the church history of the sixteenth century.

The great point at issue in the controversy, as it now stood, was the *mode* simply of Christ's mystical presence in the holy eucharist. The fact of a real communication with his true mediatorial life, the substance of his body and blood, was acknowledged in general on both sides. The rigid Lutheran party however were not satisfied with this. They insisted on a nearer definition of the manner, in which the mystery must be allowed to hold; and contended for the formula, "*In, with, and under*," as indispensable to a complete expression of Christ's sacramental presence. He must be so comprehended in the elements, as to be received along with them by the *mouth*, on the part of *all* communicants, whether believers or unbelievers.[17] It was for refusing to admit these extreme requisitions only, that the other party was branded with the title *Sacramentarian*, and held up to malediction in every direction as the pest of society.

16. [Joachim Westphal, *Farrago et Confusanaerum et inter se Dissentium Opinionum de Coena Domini* (Hamburg, 1552).]

17. [The doctrinally conservative Lutheran party insisted that the objective presence of Christ in, with, and under the elements of bread and wine is in no way contingent upon the faith of the communicant; even the unfaithful receive the body and blood of Christ (although it is not efficacious for them). This became known as the doctrine of the "*manducatio impiorum*." Calvinists generally rejected that belief, asserting instead that during the Lord's Supper Christ is only spiritually present for faith.]

II. THE PALATINATE

The heresy of which it was judged to be guilty stood simply in this, that the presence of Christ was held to be, after the theory of Calvin, not "in, with, and under" the bread, but only *with* it; not for the mouth, but only for *faith*; not in the flesh, but only in the *Spirit*; not for unbelievers therefore, but only for *believers*. This was the nature of the question that now filled Germany with conflagration. It respected wholly the mode of Christ's substantial presence in the Lord's Supper, not the fact of the mystery itself.

The intestine war broke forth first in the city of Bremen; where it soon became very violent, and gradually involved the whole country in commotion. The immediate occasion of it was furnished by the distinguished preacher, *Albert Hardenberg*,[18] a man, who stood in the highest credit for learning and piety, and was considered in some respects the main ornament of the place to which he belonged; but who, unfortunately for himself, was suspected of being more Reformed than Lutheran in his view of the Lord's Supper. It was not the least consideration in his prejudice that he was known to be in regular correspondence with Melanchthon, as one of his most intimate and confidential friends. The movement against him was commenced in 1555, by *John Timann*,[19] one of his colleagues in the ministry of Bremen, who now came forward with great zeal to the assistance of Westphal, in his crusade against heresy. The other preachers were after some time fully engaged also in the process of persecution. Every effort was made to bring the man into discredit with the magistracy and the people, as an enemy of the orthodox Lutheran faith. The pulpits, in the end, were made to ring with long loud reproaches, hurled upon his head. For years, conspiracy and intrigue knew no rest. Timann himself died in the midst of the controversy; but his mantel fell upon others, who showed themselves well able to supply his place. Other cities and states, Hamburg, Lubeck [Lübeck], Lunenberg, Saxony, Mecklenburg, Wirtemberg [Württemberg], Denmark, were secretly engaged to interpose their mediation in the case, as though the whole Lutheran world were brought into reproach and peril by the spiritual pestilence so long harbored in the bosom of Bremen. In the end Hardenberg saw himself compelled to retire. The controversy however was still continued, and came to a more favorable result ultimately than might have been expected. It lasted altogether thirteen years, holding the city of Bremen in violent disturbance the whole time.

In close connection with the religious struggle of Bremen, so far as its interior history was concerned, stands the religious revolution of the Palatinate, which fell like a thunderbolt on the ears of Lutheran Germany, while that struggle was still in progress. We have seen already that the elements of distraction were at work here also during the reign of Otho-Henry; and we may now understand more fully the true ground

18. [Albert Hardenberg (1510–574) was a Reformed theologian and the main Protestant reformer of Bremen, Cologne, and Emden.]

19. [John Timann (1500–75) was a leading Lutheran theologian in northwestern Germany who insisted that the ministers of Bremen sign a document upholding a conservative interpretation of Luther's eucharistic teachings. He accused his colleague Albert Hardenberg of heresy concerning the latter's views on the Lord's Supper.]

of this difficulty, as well as its proper constitution and character. It was no isolated or accidental commotion that had thus begun to agitate the life of the Palatinate. It was the result simply of that more general agitation, with which all Germany at this time was coming to be convulsed spiritually to its very center. The same forces which were at violent issue in Bremen, and throughout the empire, were now revealing themselves in the same form in the Palatinate also, to resolve that appointed problem. With the accession of Frederick the Pious, this problem came to a decision, whose glorious monument is still with us in the Heidelberg Catechism. To the history of its origin and formation, we are now prepared to direct our attention.

III. Occasion of the Catechism

Hesshuss and Klebiz. Response of Melanchthon.
The Palatinate becomes Reformed. General emotion in Germany.
John Brentz in Wittenberg. Stuttgard Synod and Confession.
Violent controversy. Lutheran principle fully developed.

One of the most violent, unsettled spirits of this turbulent time was *Tilemann Hesshuss*;[1] rendered memorable, if by nothing else, at least by the merciless castigation inflicted upon him by Calvin, in his last tract on the Lord's Supper. He was a man of inordinate ambition, fond of money, constitutionally intolerant and overbearing; and withal, whether by conviction or accident, a perfect zealot in the cause of Lutheran orthodoxy. In the year 1558, he was appointed by Otho-Henry first professor of theology in the university of Heidelberg, and general superintendent of all the churches in the Palatinate. Six months however had not elapsed, before he had made himself here, as in all places where he had lived before, an object of very general dislike. In particular, he was drawn into strong collision with one *William Klebiz*,[2] who occupied the situation of a deacon at the time in Heidelberg; a man also, it would seem, of most unclerical temper, and but little inclined to maintain friendly relations with the new superintendent. It soon came between them to an open, most violent rupture; in which the sacramental question was made the prominent subject of quarrel. Hesshuss charged Klebiz with heresy, as openly favoring the Calvinistic view of Christ's presence

---

1. [Tilemann Hesshuss (or Heshusius, 1527–88) was a Gnesio-Lutheran theologian and Protestant reformer who insisted upon strict Lutheran orthodoxy and helped instigate several theological controversies throughout his lifetime. One of his most notorious conflicts was his controversy with Wilhelm Klebitz in Heidelberg over the Lord's Supper that resulted in both ministers being expelled from their ecclesial positions. Because of his doctrinaire stance, he is cast by Nevin as one of the chief villains of the saga.]

2 [William Klebiz (or Klebitz, 1533–68) was a Lutheran reformer who served as a deacon at the Church of the Holy Spirit in Heidelberg while Hesshuss was the chief minister and superintendent. His Reformed understanding of the nature of Christ's presence in the Lord's Supper catalyzed an ongoing controversy with Hesshuss. The dispute was only terminated when both antagonists were removed from their offices.]

Document 1: The History and Genius of the Heidelberg Catechism

in the Lord's Supper, rather than the strict Lutheran. The point of his apostasy was found mainly in this, that he affirmed the participation of Christ's body in the Supper to be by faith only, and not by the mouth. Hesshuss grew savage in his denunciations; the more so probably as he could not fail to see that the reigning influence around him was on the side of his adversary, and not with himself. In stormful style, Sabbath after Sabbath, he poured forth his indignation from the pulpit, upon the new Arius, as he styled him (or "Zwinglian devil,") who had made his appearance in the Heidelberg church, not sparing, at the same time, the university and the authorities of the city for their supine indifference to the portentous evil that was threatening in their very midst the whole Palatinate with ruin. Klebiz returned violence for violence. The whole city was thrown into commotion.

It was in the midst of this tempestuous outbreak that Frederick III succeeded to the electorate. The moderate measures he employed, in the first place, to allay the strife, proved unavailing. Hesshuss set his authority at defiance; played the pope, in truly frantic style; and proceeded in the end to thunder from the pulpit a sentence, first of suspension, and then of excommunication, against the deacon Klebiz; solemnly laying it on the conscience of the civil government to expel him from the city and state, under pain of the most heavy divine judgments upon the whole land. The elector interposed again, enjoining on both parties mutual forbearance and silence, till such time as a proper Synod might be convened to examine the whole question. The very next time that Hesshuss appeared in his pulpit, he began to rave again in his old style. The elector himself came in for a share of the abuse, as an apostate from the true faith of the Augsburg Confession. Klebiz felt himself absolved from the duty of silence also, by this example of his adversary; and in this way, things were at once as bad as before.

In these circumstances, the elector found it necessary to resort to more vigorous measures. Without farther process, Hesshuss and Klebiz were both dismissed from office, on one day; and by this means, the public quiet was once more restored.

Frederick was now made to feel the importance of having the subject of this controversy brought to some such settlement, in his domains, as might preserve the peace of the country in time to come. He conceived the design accordingly of establishing a rule of faith for the Palatinate, that would reduce its conflicting views to some common measure, to which all might be required subsequently to conform. The Augsburg Confession, it was plain, could not supply the wants of the case. He had subscribed [to] it himself indeed in good faith; and it was the established Confession of the land. But it was not so, in the sense which was put upon it by the rigid party, now making so much noise in the Lutheran Church. If this was to be taken as its true construction, the elector felt that he belonged inwardly himself to a different creed, and that the same thing was true of the Palatinate generally. It was not difficult for him then of course, to make up his mind in general, with regard to the ecclesiastic position which it would be proper to assume, in the new formulary of faith.

III. OCCASION OF THE CATECHISM

To sustain himself however in the movement which he had in view, he deemed it proper to write to Melanchthon in the first place, for his judgment in relation to the difficulty with which he was called to deal; knowing well enough beforehand the state of mind in which he stood at this time to the theological agitations generally with which he was surrounded. This drew forth the celebrated *response* of Melanchthon; which became public soon after, when he had himself descended to the grave, and served to involve his memory in no small reproach, with the stiff party to whose views it was found to be opposed. It approved the elector's course, in silencing the sacramental controversy, and also his purpose of excluding strife by establishing some common formula in the case, to which all should be required to submit; while at the same time it very decidedly condemned the use of any such terms for this purpose, as were pressed upon the Church by Hesshuss and men of the same stamp. Such a judgment coming from such a quarter was of great account for Frederick and his divines, in the posture in which they now stood. Melanchthon did not design of course to recommend a formal transition to the Reformed Church; and had he anticipated any such movement on the part of the Palatinate, we may well suppose that his response would have been expressed in more guarded terms. As it was however, it virtually justified this step. For it involved a full sanction of the proper Reformed or Calvinistic doctrine, and condemned the Lutheranism of such men as Westphal and Hesshuss as extravagant and extreme; while at the same time, this very form of Lutheranism was successfully asserting in fact its title to be considered the true and legitimate orthodoxy of the Church. In declining its authority then, it was altogether reasonable that the Church of the Palatinate should at once pass over to the other confession. To this issue accordingly it now came.

The event could not fail, of course, to create the most earnest attention. Among others, the son-in-law of the elector, Duke John Frederick of Saxony, was much disturbed and troubled at the tidings.[3] He immediately took a journey to Heidelberg, carrying along with him, in his orthodox zeal, two of his most expert theologians, *Morlin*[4] and *Stossel*,[5] to rescue his relative, if possible, from the dangerous snare of Calvinism, into which he had so unhappily fallen. For this purpose a public disputation was proposed, in the spirit of the age, to be held between the two theologians just mentioned, and any the elector might see fit to nominate for the defense of his own cause. The proposal was readily accepted; and a disputation followed accordingly, which was continued for five full days in the presence of the two princes. It was held in the month of June, 1560. The Calvinistic cause was maintained by *Peter Bocquin*, one of the most distinguished theologians connected at the time with the

---

3. [John Frederick II, Duke of Saxony (1529–95) was a staunch Lutheran who later defied the Emperor and, from 1566 on, spent his life in captivity.]

4. [Maximilian Mörlin (1516–84), the Lutheran superintendent of Coburg, had studied with Melanchthon but later became one of his most vehement critics.]

5. [John Stössel (1524–78) was the Gnesio-Lutheran superintendent of Heldburg.]

Heidelberg university.[6] The whole debate seems to have been occupied exclusively with the *mode* of the Eucharistic presence; the divines of John Fredrick contending for the high Lutheran doctrine, while *Bocquin* asserted the Calvinistic theory, "that the true substance of the true body" of Christ is received indeed in the sacrament, but only by believers through faith, by the power of the Holy Ghost, and not in a corporeal way through the mouth.

The result of the whole disputation was that the elector found himself only more confirmed than before, in his resolution to establish the Reformed doctrine in the Palatinate.

Two other princes, John Frederick of Gotha[7] and Duke Christopher of Wirtemberg [Württemberg],[8] the first another son by marriage and the last his own god-father, addressed him also on the subject, with letters of earnest remonstrance. But all had no effect, in the way of unsettling his purpose. His replies, full of attractive simplicity, still remain as noble monuments of the pious spirit that governed him in this whole transaction. He acted throughout, not from passion or self-will, but in obedience to what he himself at least believed to be the truth.

There was no violent revolution, in the change which took place in the Palatinate. The case did not require this; for the reigning spirit of the university, as well as of the Church in general, was already more Reformed than Lutheran. Here and there indeed a minister might be found, who was disposed to act the zealot on the Lutheran side. Such naturally were obliged in the end to relinquish their places; not directly for their faith itself, but because they were not willing to submit silently to the order of things with which they were surrounded. Some changes too were introduced into the public worship; such as the removal of altars and organs at least from a part of the churches, the substitution of the breaking of bread for the wafer, &c.; the object of which was undoubtedly to transfer the religious associations of the people from the one communion to the other, that they might be led thus to a more full correspondence with the Reformed Church in doctrine also as well as rites. A still more efficient and direct policy toward this end was exhibited in the introduction of decidedly Calvinistic teachers into the university. All new appointments were of this kind. Among them

---

6. [Peter Bocquin (d. 1582) had been influenced by Calvin, and was regarded as the premier Reformed theologian of Heidelberg before the advent of Ursinus.]

7. [Johann Frederick III of Saxe-Gotha (1538–1565), a devout Lutheran, was genuinely passionate about theology, having studied it at Jena.]

8. [Christoph, Duke of Württemberg (1515–1568), was sympathetic to the Gnesio-Lutherans. His territory bordered the Palatinate, and therefore the two regions were often suspicious of one another, although they had previously cooperated on matters of religion and imperial politics.]

III. OCCASION OF THE CATECHISM

we find the names of *Caspar Olevianus*[9] and *Zacharias Ursinus*,[10] whose agency soon after became so prominent in the formation of the Catechism; the great work, in which finally this whole revolution may be said to have become complete.

Meanwhile all Germany was like a forest on fire. It is impossible to describe the sensation that was produced throughout the whole Lutheran world by the now manifest defection of the Palatinate. To the view of thousands it seemed a case of the most horrible apostasy, like the fall of Lucifer from heaven. Hesshuss on his flight from Heidelberg, having found a more congenial element in which to breathe in Bremen, had immediately raised the most doleful cry of the elector's treason to the Augsburg Confession; which was loudly re-echoed from all sides by the Westphals, Wigands and Morlins of Lower Saxony, before it was dreamed that matters might become still so much worse. When now at last the full truth came, the effect was absolutely overwhelming. At first, for a short time, men seemed to pause, as though they had been fairly stunned into silence. But it was only that the strife which was already at work might collect itself into a more intense force, to roll forward afterwards upon its stormful career more stormfully than before.

Parallel with the movement in the Palatinate from the start, and in the way of reaction to it no doubt in some measure, another most important movement had taken place in the neighboring province of Wirtemberg [Württemberg]; which it is necessary to notice here, as entering largely into the tumultuating drama. The man who led the way in it was JOHN BRENTZ,[11] the principle theologian of Wirtemberg [Württemberg], and one of the few survivors of the original band of reformers. His whole character gave him immense weight, with the new generation that had come forward upon the stage; and on the sacramental question particularly, he was allowed to be entitled to preeminent respect, as one who had stood nobly by the side of Luther himself, through the whole course of the first war with the Helvetic divines. During twenty years he had kept silence, faithful to the truce of Wittenberg, and piously intent upon the peace of the Church. He had not changed his former views; he was Lutheran still to the very core; but he had learned to exercise more moderation toward those who were not able to go as far in this direction as himself. Now however his moderation was found once more to give way. When Hesshuss first raised the war whoop,

---

9. [Frederick Caspar Olevianus (1536–87) was a Reformed theologian who was called to teach at the University of Heidelberg in 1560. Olevianus was one of the early pioneers of Reformed "covenant theology" that was based on the distinction of the "covenant of works" and the "covenant of grace" as an organizing principle. He was regarded as being more eloquent and rhetorically adept than Ursinus, with whom he worked on the composition of the Heidelberg Catechism.]

10. [Zacharias Ursinus (1534–83) was a sixteenth-century German Reformed theologian and Protestant reformer who became the leading theologian of the Reformed Protestant movement in the Palatinate. He is best known as the primary author of the Heidelberg Catechism.]

11. [Johannes Brentz (1499–1570) was early converted to Protestantism through his interactions with Luther at the Heidelberg Disputation in 1518. Although he had initially been sympathetic to Melanchthon's irenicism, he became more inflexible as he concluded that the original vision of Luther was being compromised by a variety of revisionist movements.]

Document 1: The History and Genius of the Heidelberg Catechism

Brentz had probably as little inclination as his friend, the mild and gentle Melanchthon, to take part in the renewal of hostilities; although he shared no doubt in the offense, that had been taken by many with the open alliance particularly into which Calvin had shortly before entered with the Swiss divines in the famous *Consensus* of Zurich. As the controversy proceeded, new occasions of provocation of course came in his way, to which he could not be insensible. But it was the course of things in the Palatinate, which at length fairly roused his zeal into full action. He might endure Calvinism on its own field; but it was too much, that it should pretend to supplant the holy faith of Luther, in the German Church itself. The Palatinate too was close at hand; and he had himself been widely honored among its churches; his own catechism being in fact in use with them extensively as a text book of religious instruction. We need not wonder then, that he beheld with strong emotion the change which was taking place, and felt himself called upon to oppose it with a strenuous counter movement in his own quarter. If Calvinism prevailed in the Palatinate, Wirtemberg [Württemberg] must carry out Lutheranism in return to its full consequence and force. Only in this form, might justice be done to it now in the eyes of the world. There must be an ecclesiastical synod convened, and a new formula of faith established, that should run the limits of the system so clearly, as to leave no room for equivocation or mistake. In the middle of September, 1559, Hesshuss was driven from Heidelberg. In December following, the superintendents and theologians of the province of Wirtemberg [Württemberg] were called to meet in solemn synod at Stuttgard; for the purpose of framing, or adopting rather from the hand of Brentz, the new symbol that should assert and guard thenceforward the orthodoxy of the land. It was one of the most startling and pregnant events of the time.

By this Stuttgard confession, the peculiar distinctions of high Lutheranism, as distinguished not simply from the Zwinglian, but also from the Calvinistic, theory of the sacraments, were formally proclaimed as the true faith of the Church. In particular, the full consequence of the system, the *ubiquity* of Christ's body, as a result of the so called "*communicatio idiomatum*," was now for the first time unshrinkingly exhibited as a necessary part of the Lutheran creed.[12] It was in fact the first step taken toward the celebrated "Form [Formula] of Concord," in which fifteen years later, through storm-rocked seas, the development of Lutheranism became complete for the empire at large.

12. [The doctrine of the ubiquity of Christ's body was intended to explain how Christ could be present in, with, and under the physical elements in many different locations at the same time, whenever the Lord's Supper was celebrated. The theory proposed that the divine quality of omnipresence was communicated to Christ's human nature, so that even his corporality could share in the divine ubiquity. This belief would become a litmus test of orthodoxy for doctrinally conservative Lutherans. Most Reformed theologians would counter this with the claim that the body of Christ is not omnipresent on earth, but is seated at the right hand of the Father in heaven. In general, the Lutherans tended to gravitate toward a more Alexandrian Christology that emphasized the unity of Christ's person, while the Reformed were attracted to a more Antiochene Christology that stressed the distinction of the two natures.]

III. OCCASION OF THE CATECHISM

As a matter of course the bold demonstration, was followed with immense excitement. It constituted an epoch in the sacramental war. The whole controversy acquired a new importance, from the imposing character of the actors here brought into view, with such a man as Brentz at their head, as well as from the desperate, uncompromising spirit of the action itself. It was a broad affront offered to the whole Reformed Church. It struck directly at the position of a large and respectable party in the Lutheran Church itself, who either held the Calvinistic theory themselves, or at least considered it perfectly compatible with good Lutheranism; and who deprecated of course all action that should tend to bring in a more narrow rule of orthodoxy. Chief among these stood the venerable author of the Augsburg Confession himself, still living at Wittenberg. The Stuttgard confession cut off all room for neutrality, and emboldened the rigid party in the Church to lay out all their strength, from this time onward, for the erection of the same severe test in all parts of the land.

Polemical tracts, in the rough style of the age, full of theological acrimony and gall, flew fast and thick on all sides. Melanchthon slept in Jesus, just soon enough to be spared the necessity of taking part in the strife. His colleagues in Wittenberg were in due time fairly overwhelmed by its surging billows. Geneva and Zurich both came actively forward in their own defense. Calvin's last tract was against Hesshuss. In the close of it, he curiously transfers the management of the "incorrigible bull" to his friend and colleague Beza. Hesshuss was honored accordingly with two tracts from this last; one entitled "*Cyclops or Creophagia*"[13] and the other "*Sophistica or The Syllogizing Ass*." Bullinger was at the same time prominent upon the field. Also Bocquin and Ursinus of Heidelberg. On the other hand, Hesshuss of course was not idle; nor were active and able pens wanting in support of the same cause. Among them all however there was none more active, than that wielded by Brentz himself. The aged reformer seemed to renew his youth, in the zeal with which he contended for the "*ubiquity*," against all opposers far and near. He was the center of the spiritual storm.

It was in the midst of this commotion, while the two confessional tendencies, which had previously been joined together in the Lutheran Church, were coming to their necessary rupture, by the evolution of the true Lutheran principle out of its last consequence, that the Heidelberg Catechism came to its birth. It forms, in this view, the proper historical counterpart of the Stuttgard Confession. This last, the *Form of Concord* in embryo, sundered the proper Lutheran consciousness from all foreign mixture, while the Calvinistic tendency was conducted also to its corresponding public expression, *beyond* the pale of the Lutheran Church entirely, in the Heidelberg Catechism.

---

13. [Theodor Beza, *Kreophagia sive Cyclops* (Conradus Badius, 1561).]

IV. Formation of the Catechism

The Elector Frederick. Caspar Olevianus. Zacharias Ursinus. Provincial Synod. First editions. Established use.

The Catechism of the Palatinate is to be ascribed, in the first place, to the pious zeal of the elector Frederick.[1] The reasons by which he was moved to provide such a formulary for the use of the Church in his domains are given by himself in a general way, in a preface which accompanied the original publication. It is the duty of princes, he says, not only to consult for the quiet and prosperity of their people, by the wise regulations in regard to their common social and political relations, but especially to take measures for imbuing them with a proper knowledge of Almighty God, and a wholesome respect for his word, which is the only ground of all virtue in a community; thus having an eye to the eternal, no less than to the temporal welfare, of all who may be under his care. His predecessors of happy memory had endeavored by various Christian ordinances and institutions to secure this end; but as yet no sufficient result had been reached, in the way of meeting the wants of the land as a whole. Hence he felt himself called upon, not simply to renew former measures, but to go beyond all that had been previously done for the promotion of religious knowledge. The youth of his land, he goes on to say, might be said especially to suffer, as it regarded their religious training, both in the schools and in the parish churches; being in some cases altogether neglected, and in other cases taught so irregularly from various catechisms according to the free fancy of their teachers, and with no established method; the result of which was much confusion and deficiency of sound views.[2] On this account, he had considered it one of the first duties he owed to the Church and State, as ruler of his people, to correct the evil of such wrong and insufficient teaching by providing,

---

1. [Frederick, along with Ursinus, is a chief protagonist of Nevin's drama.]

2. [Nevin was obviously discerning a parallel between Elector Frederick's situation in sixteenth century Germany and his own in nineteenth century Pennsylvania. For both sets of problems part of the remediation was the Heidelberg Catechism. Nevin's historical narrative is saturated with an overtly contemporary ecclesial purpose.]

with the assistance of the whole theological faculty, and other distinguished divines, a suitable summary of the Christian doctrines; which was now published, both in the German and Latin tongues, not only for the use of the young in schools and churches, but as a directory also for all concerned in the business of religious instruction.

Such a formulary was in fact indispensable, to complete and establish under a properly solid form, the religious revolution of the Palatinate. The circumstances of the country moreover required that the work should spring from its own bosom, and not be derived from abroad. The case called for a peculiar composition. In becoming Reformed, the Church of the Palatinate was still German. There was a large amount of Lutheran feeling, along with the properly Calvinistic, in her communion; with some mixture too of Zwinglianism, it would seem, as an interest distinct from both. The new Catechism must go so far as possible, in mediating between these different systems. It must be irenical, conciliatory, catholic.

Having resolved on the introduction of such a new symbolical book, Frederick's next care was to select suitable persons, for the deeply responsible task of its composition. His choice however was soon made, and if we may judge from the result, with great wisdom. It fell on CASPAR OLEVIANUS and ZACHARIAS URSINUS. They were both comparatively young, the first but twenty-six, the other only twenty-eight years of age; which might seem to indicate a want of ripeness for such service as this. But the period was one that gave birth to strong minds, and brought them early to maturity. Melanchthon published his Greek Grammar when he was but sixteen years old; and in his seventeenth year, read lectures on the classics and the philosophy of Aristotle. From the age of twenty-one, as professor at Wittemburg, he stood conspicuous to the eyes of all Europe, as one of the most accomplished scholars of the time, with hundreds of admiring pupils, gathered from every civilized land, sitting at his feet and hanging upon his lips. In his thirty-third year, he was held by all to be the fittest man living to prepare a statement of evangelical faith for the memorable diet of Augsburg; by which means he became the father of the Augsburg Confession. But it was nearly ten years before this that he gave to Europe the first edition of his *Loci Communes*, the primary text-book in divinity for the whole Lutheran Church. Calvin too was only twenty-six years of age, when he surprised the world with his *Institutes*, before whose towering greatness the entire Reformed church has since continued to bow with the deepest respect. Ursinus and Olevianus are less conspicuous names, it is true; but they were worthy notwithstanding of the age to which Melanchthon and Calvin belonged. At the time now under contemplation, they stood in the first rank of Protestant theologians, and were counted an ornament of the University of Heidelberg, into whose service they had been not long before called.

Olevianus was the son of a respectable banker at Treves, the city of the "Holy Coat."[3] In his fourteenth year he was sent to Paris, to complete his education. Here

---

3. ["The Holy Coat of Treves" was a much venerated relic said to be the seamless robe that Jesus wore before his crucifixion. It was a pilgrimage attraction for Treves, a city located along the

Document 1: The History and Genius of the Heidelberg Catechism

he studied law. But God intended him for the Church, and by a solemn dispensation of his providence accordingly constrained him to change the whole plan of his life. He had gone to Bourges; and while there was returning one day from a walk, in company with two friends, one of them a son of the palatine, Frederick III. About to cross the Loire, some drunken students forced themselves into the same boat with them for passage. By their wild folly, the boat was upset. The young prince, with others, found a watery grave. Olevianus, while endeavoring to save his friends, was brought into imminent peril of losing his own life. Out of these depths, his serious spirit inwardly cried unto God; and by a solemn vow, he engaged, if spared, to renounce the law, and devote himself to the work of preaching the gospel in his native city. The Lord heard, and delivered him out of his distress. He was already joined in spirit with the persecuted Huguenots; and now he addressed himself actively to the study in particular of the theological writings of Calvin. His admiration of this great theologian, led him afterwards to Geneva, to enjoy his oral instruction. Here he formed an intimate friendship with *Theodore Beza*,[4] which continued unbroken to the end of his life. While in Switzerland, he made the acquaintance also of that indefatigable enemy of the priests, *William Farel*;[5] who, very characteristically, made him give his hand in the way of pledge, that he would not fail soon to go back and preach Christ in the city of his birth. True to this promise and his former vow, he commenced his ministry in Treves early in the year 1559. The gospel, here as elsewhere, soon began to display its power. Treves seemed almost ready to throw itself into the arms of the Reformation. This led to interference on the part of the reigning authority, and finally to no small popular commotion. Olevianus, with others, was cast into prison; from which, at the end of ten weeks, he was set free, under the condition of a heavy fine and immediate banishment from the city. Thus ended the work of the Reformation at Treves. Olevianus was now welcomed to a new sphere of labor in Heidelberg. In the year 1561, he received an appointment as professor of theology in the Heidelberg university, and not long after as court preacher also in one of the principal churches of the city.

Ursinus[6] was a native of Bresslau, in Silesia.[7] At the age of sixteen he had been sent to Wittenberg; where he spent seven years in the character of a student, helping

---

Moselle River.]

4 [Theodore Beza (1519–1605), a French Protestant scholar and reformer, was Calvin's theological successor in Geneva. He polemicized against the Gnesio-Lutherans on the doctrine of the Eucharist and developed a thoroughly supralapsarian understanding of God's sovereign will. He is known for his treatise *Summa totius Christianismi.*]

5 [Guillaume Farel (1489–1565) was one of the major reformers of the Republic of Geneva. Twice he persuaded a reluctant John Calvin to work with him in Geneva. The two colleagues turned Geneva into the center of the French-speaking Reformed world and an important missionary training ground for the Protestant cause in Europe.]

6. His proper family name was *Beer* (Bear), which according to the fashion of the learned world in that period was exchanged for the more sonorous corresponding Latin title Ursinus. So the name Olevianus also is a similar substitution for the proper corresponding German name of this divine.

7 [Nevin gleaned much of this information from Heinrich Alting, *Historia Ecclesiæ Palatinæ.*

himself during a part of the time by private teaching; for his means were slender. During this period, he made great acquirements in classical literature, philosophy and theology. He was considered besides quite a master of poetry; and composed himself various productions in Latin and Greek verse, which were much admired. Melanchthon, the ornament of the university, conceived a very high regard for his abilities and attainments, and continued on terms of intimate personal friendship with him to the end of his life. This itself forms as high a recommendation of the character of Ursinus, as we could well have in the circumstances. In the year 1557, he accompanied Melanchthon to the conference at Worms; after which he visited Geneva and Paris. On his return to Wittenberg, he received a call from the magistracy of his native city to the rectorship of the principal school, the Elizabethan gymnasium. Here his services gave great satisfaction. But the clergy of the place soon raised an alarm with regard to his orthodoxy. As in the case of Hardenberg in Bremen, so here, one great ground of suspicion was Melanchthon's friendship and favor. It seemed to be taken for granted by the zealots for high Lutheranism, that no one could be in close intimacy with Melanchthon who was not at bottom a Crypto-Calvinist. Ursinus published a small tract, in his own justification; but it did not allay the spirit of persecution. He was still held up to reproach, as a *Sacramentarian*.[8] Finally he resolved to withdraw. The magistracy would gladly have retained him, in spite of all the clamor of his enemies. But he had an aversion to all strife and commotion; and with an honorable dismission, he retired accordingly, a voluntary martyr to the holy cause of peace, to seek a more quiet sphere of action in some different quarter. As Melanchthon was now dead, he betook himself to Zurich. Here soon after he was honored with a call from Heidelberg; where he became settled in consequence, A. D. 1561, as theological professor in the university, and principal in particular of the divinity school belonging to it, under the title "Collegium Sapientiae." He is represented as a man of much modesty; quiet, though ardent at the same time, and even passionate, in his natural spirit; uncommonly assiduous and laborious in the prosecution of his proper work. He had no talent for preaching; but as an academic lecturer, he was exceedingly popular; being distinguished for his vivacity, fullness of learning, and happy power of communication.[9]

Because that volume was very old and rare, he probably found the entire text contained in the anthology *Monumenta Pietatis & Literaria*, ed. Ludwig Christian Mieg (Franfurt am Main: Johann Maximilian, 1701), 129–250. Alting stressed the dual authorship of the Catechism by Ursinus and Olevianus, which probably was an exaggeration of Olevianus' role. Nevin partly followed Alting on this point, but added that the unified style suggested that Ursinus was the main author and ultimate redactor. Some of the material was also sourced from Heinrich Simon Van Alpen's *Geschichte und Literatur des Heidelbergschen Katechismus*.]

8. ["Sacramentarian" was a Lutheran term of abuse directed against Reformed people in general, and Zwinglians in particular.]

9. With all his learning, he made it a point to be very cautious in his judgments; and was not ashamed to adopt the rule that questions put to him in the lecture room should not be answered ordinarily till the following day. Over the door of his study, he is said to have had in full view the inscription: "Amice, quisquis huc venis, aut agito paucis, aut abi, aut me laborantem adjuva." That is:

Document 1: The History and Genius of the Heidelberg Catechism

These were the men on whom Frederick devolved the trust of preparing his new formulary of religious instruction. Their commission was to form a catechism that should suit the wants of the Palatinate. It must represent the Reformed faith, and yet be true at the same time to the general spirit of the Augsburg Confession. The elector had signed this Confession only the year before; and it was not in his heart now to erect within his domains a standard that might be considered hostile to its true substance. The catechism must be such a system, as Melanchthon if living might join with Calvin to subscribe; in testimony of their common faith.[10]

The work is to be considered strictly the joint production of the two men, with whose names it is associated. The conception or plan of it is to be referred mainly, it would seem, to Olevianus; though no doubt, the judgment of his colleague was duly consulted also in the case; while both took part together in settling the material that should enter its composition. The task of reducing the whole to actual form was made to fall exclusively on Ursinus. This was wise. Two different pens could not have been employed upon the work with advantage. A catechism, creed, or liturgy, to be of true force, must spring indeed from the religious life of many. As an isolated birth of the closet, it can have no power. But it is just as true, on the other hand, that as the product of a general life, no such work can ever spring properly, in the last instance, from more than a single author. Only where the general life is carried to some good extent in the consciousness of some one man, who is thus capable of acting as its organ, can the requisitions of the case be fully met. The creed, like a poem, should be all spiritually cast from the living mold of the same mind. Only so can it exhibit, with proper unity and universality combined, the character of a full, symmetrical, organic whole.[11]

The elector is said to have taken an active interest personally in the whole progress of the work, even assisting occasionally in the way of suggestion or advice; so near did it lie to his heart. The circumstance deserves notice, not of course as being of any account to the work itself, but as it serves to illustrate the religious character of the prince.[12]

In the course of the same year, the Catechism was completed and placed in the elector's hands. The next step was to clothe it with suitable ecclesiastical authority and force. For this purpose, he immediately convoked at Heidelberg a synod of superintendents and principal pastors of the entire Palatinate. This was in the year 1563. Along with the German original, appeared at the same time a Latin translation, made also by authority, as a text-book of divinity for the higher institutions. As before intimated,

---

"Friend, entering here, be short, or go away, or else assist me in my work."

10. [By emphasizing this point Nevin was trying to set the stage for closer relations between the German Reformed Church and moderate Lutherans in America.]

11. [The theme that a beautiful literary work should be an organic, unified harmony of diverse parts was a commonplace of Romantic and Idealist aesthetic theory, which Nevin sometimes taught to students at Franklin and Marshall College.]

12. [See Heinrich Simon Van Alpen's *Geschichte und Literatur des Heidelbergschen Katechismus*, trans. Joseph Berg as *The History and Literature of the Heidelberg Catechism*, 23–26.]

IV. FORMATION OF THE CATECHISM

the work was introduced, in the way of a preface, by a sort of special proclamation under the hand of the elector himself.[13] As many as four editions of it seem to have been published, from the same press, in the course of one year; so wide and rapid was the circulation to which it came at once in the bounds of the Palatinate.

One remarkable distinction characterized the first edition, as compared with all which have been published since. The 80th Question, in which the Roman mass is denounced as an "accused idolatry," was not suffered to make its appearance. In the second edition, it is found in its place, only the *accursed idolatry* is still suppressed. Finally however, as in the same year the decrees of the Council of Trent came out anathematizing all who would not own the mass to be divine, the elector took pains to have the Question restored in full to the form in which it was originally composed; while the previous text was allowed to go out of use as defective and incorrect. This gave rise subsequently to no small controversy and reproach.

In these first editions, the questions and answers follow each other in unbroken succession, without division or number. The biblical proof passages are indicated in the margin, by a reference simply to the *chapters* in which they occur, as though the verse were of no account. It was not till ten years later that this inconvenience was removed by the introduction of proper distinctions, and more full references. These appear in the edition of 1573, which contains also the Liturgy of the Church, or its formulary of public services and prayers. In this edition also, the questions are found distributed into fifty two sections, or *Sundays*, according to the order which has since prevailed, for the use of the pulpit; for it was required that every minister should go over the whole Catechism every year, by preaching once upon it on each Lord's Day. A similar arrangement is presented to us in the case also of Calvin's Catechism. Catechetical instruction was a business with which the Church in these days went earnestly to work. The family, the common school, the weekly pulpit, the gymnasium, and the university, were all expected and required, in the Palatinate, to co-operate continually, in carrying out with efficiency the great design of the Heidelberg Catechism.

To assist in the accomplishment of the general object, a *Shorter Catechism* was subsequently prepared and published, for the use of plain people and children, for whom the larger work was too full and not sufficiently easy of comprehension. This was not a new formulary, properly speaking, and was not intended of course to supplant in any measure the authority of the other. On the contrary, it was nothing more than a compend of the larger catechism itself, exhibiting always the same doctrines, and to a great extent also in the same words.

The Catechism was thus fully enthroned in the Palatinate of the Rhine, as the rule and measure of the public faith. It was made the basis of theological instruction in the university. A regular system of catechization was established in all the churches. The afternoon of every Lord's day was devoted to this service, which was made to include

---

13. [Ursinus, *Catechismus oder christlicher Underricht* (Heidelberg: Johann Mayer, 1563).]

grown persons as well as children. Fifty years after this, we find from the report made at the Synod of Dort, that it comprehended in fact three distinct courses of instruction; the first for children, the second for youth, and the third for adults of every age.[14]

---

14. [The Synod of Dort (1618–19) was an international Reformed synod called by the Dutch Reformed Church to settle objections to the Belgic Confession that had been raised by the "Remonstrants" and to regularize church order.]

V. War against the Catechism

Its pacific spirit. Angry reception by Romanists and Lutherans. Theological assaults. Remonstrance of Princes. Diet of Augsburg. Noble stand taken by Frederick. Triumph. His piety and happy death.

The Heidelberg Catechism was designed, as we have already seen, to serve the cause of union and peace. Towards Rome of course it could not turn a friendly aspect; although if we leave out of view the 80th Question, and one or two others polemically pointed in the same direction, it must be allowed to breathe a tone of great moderation even on this side. But with the Lutheran Church, it seemed to avoid all direct controversy. Its reigning character here was apologetic and conciliatory. It sought, in the first place, by a fair and true representation of its own system, to vindicate the Church in whose name it appeared from the aspersions that were plentifully cast upon it from abroad. It aimed, in the second place, to do this in such a way that as little offense as possible should be given to the friends of the Augsburg Confession. As a clear statement of the Reformed faith, it could not fail of course to come into occasional collision with the faith of Luther, at least in a silent and negative way. But it could not be charged with a polemical intention, in any such case. When we examine the Catechism, we find it to be wonderfully free from the spirit of controversy, as well as from its form. From beginning to end, it is occupied with what is positive in truth; rather than with its negative aspects and relations. Nothing can well be more beautiful and dignified indeed, than the straight-forward simplicity and earnestness, with which truth after truth is presented, as it were for its own sake simply, without any sinister, unnecessary reference to the opinion of others. This is truly remarkable, when we consider the particular period in which it appeared, and the tone that had come to characterize too generally at the time the thinking and speaking of the different parties in the Protestant world.[1] No parade whatever is made of the points of difference between

---

1. [The parallel to the theological polemics of Nevin's own era is obvious.]

the Reformed and German [Lutheran] Churches; no polemic thrusts at the weak or exposed parts of the sister communion come into view.

Clearly it was not the object of the Catechism at all to set forth the Reformed or Calvinistic system as such, in broad opposition to the Lutheran system as such; but simply to digest and embody in a popular symbolical form what were considered to be the great leading principles of the evangelical faith for the use of the churches in the Palatinate. That the work itself came in the end to a much wider use was owing simply to its extraordinary merits. As there was still a considerable party in the Palatinate which favored the views of Luther, a disposition had been felt to make the new platform as broad and catholic in this direction, as might at all comport with its own distinctive scheme of doctrine. Among all symbolical books of the Reformed Church accordingly, the Heidelberg Catechism is the one which has ever found the most favor with the friends and adherents of the Augsburg Confession. Candid and liberal Lutherans at least, have not refused it their praise. "I must confess," says one of the older writers of this denomination,

> that leaving out of it the peculiar doctrines of Calvin contained in it, the Reformed are not without reason in their boast, that as Ursinus in his other writings excels almost all the rest of their theologians, so he has in the composition of this Catechism gone also beyond himself. The method, as it regards the three parts, is suited to the subject; the questions are well framed, and lucidly answered; the proof-texts subjoined are happily selected, and the whole arrangement such as to promote edification.[2]

A like favorable view of the work has been taken by many others in the same communion.[3]

But notwithstanding all that has now been said, the Catechism was received far and wide, at the time of its appearance, as a loud declaration of war; and became at once the signal for an angry, violent onset, in the way of opposition and reproach, from all parts of the Lutheran Church. The high toned party which was now filling the whole empire with its alarm of heresy could not have expected of course to tolerate

---

2. [This remark was written by Heinrich Ludolph Benthem. Nevin found the statement quoted in van Alpen, *Geschichte und Literatur des Heidelbergischen Katechismus*. See the English translation *History and Literature of the Heidelberg Catechism*, 84–85. Benthem (1661–1723) was a Lutheran theologian and consistorial counselor from Hanover. He is most remembered for his descriptions of the Reformed and Mennonite faiths in the Netherlands and northern Germany.]

3. So Guerike, the zealous advocate of old Lutheranism in our own day: "Die durch viele Lehrweisheit, Wærme und Geschicklichkeit ausgezeichnete symbolische Schrift der deutschen Reformirten Kirche." *Kirchengesch.* II. p. 1125.

[Trans: "the wisdom, warmth, and aptness of the outstanding symbolical book of the German Reformed Church." The text to which Nevin refers is Heinrich Ernst Ferdinand Guerike, *Handbuch der Allgemeinen Kirchengeschichte*, 4th ed. (Halle, 1840). Guerike (1803–78) was a Lutheran theologian and leader of the "Old Lutheran" party that in Prussia refused to join the Church of the Prussian Union and in the non-unionist German principalities resisted even the partial amalgamation of Lutheran and Reformed theology.]

V. WAR AGAINST THE CATECHISM

patiently any religious formulary that might fall short of its own rigorous measure of orthodoxy. From this quarter accordingly the Catechism was assaulted, more fiercely than even from the Church of Rome itself. Its very moderation seemed to magnify the front of its offense. Had there been more of the lion or tiger in its mien, and less of the lamb, its presence might have proved possibly less irritating to the polemical humor of the times. As it was, there was felt to be provocation in its very meekness. Its outward carriage was held to be deceitful and treacherous; and its heresy was counted all the worse, for being hard to find, and shy of coming to the light. The winds of strife were let loose upon it accordingly, from all points of the compass.

Not only the unity and quiet of the German Church, but the peace also of the German empire, seemed in the eyes of the high Lutheran party to be brought into jeopardy by the new confession. It was not only heresy in religion, bur treason also in politics. Both the elector and his theologians found their faith severely tried by the general outcry which was raised at their expense. But they were men of faith, and they stood the trial nobly and well.

In a very short time, the Catechism was attacked, in the way of formal review and censure, by different pens. Among others, as was naturally to be expected, Tilemann Hesshuss assailed it with open mouth, in his "*True Warning*;" which was allowed to pass however without the honor of an answer.[4] A much more respectable adversary appeared, in the person of the celebrated *Matthias Flacius Illyricus*;[5] a man of great learning, who seems however to have had his very being in the element of religious controversy. His self-styled "*Refutation of the Calvinistic Catechism of Olevianus*" was published in the year 1563.

Meanwhile the elector was taken solemnly to account, in a more private way, by several of his brother princes, who seemed to think [that] the whole empire [was] scandalized by his unorthodox conduct. Prince *Wolfgang* of Neuburg[6] and margrave *Charles* of Baden,[7] both felt themselves constrained to address him on the subject. A still more active concern was taken in the case by *Christopher*, duke of Wirtemberg,[8] between whom and Frederick there had subsisted heretofore a more than common intimacy, based upon a general similarity of character and disposition. It was urged that a special conference or debate should be held publicly, between the leading theologians of Wirtemberg [Württemberg] and the Palatinate, for the purpose of bringing this whole difficulty, if possible, to a proper resolution and settlement. The Heidelberg divines were not in favor of the measure. They apprehended more evil from it than

---

4. [See Tilemannus Hesshusius, *Trewe Warnung* (Eisleben, 1564).]

5. [Matthias Flacius Illyricus (1520–75), born in Croatia, was a theologian, church historian, philosopher, and Gnesio-Lutheran zealot.]

6 [Wolfgang of Zweibrücken (1526–69) was an important German Protestant ruler who died in battle while fighting for the French Huguenots.]

7 [Charles II, Margrave of Baden-Durlach (1529–77) established Lutheranism in his territory in 1556, and supported adherence to the unaltered Augsburg Confession.]

8. [Christoph, Duke of Württemberg (1515–1568), was sympathetic to the Gnesio-Lutherans.]

Document 1: The History and Genius of the Heidelberg Catechism

good. The elector however gave way to the pressure of the princes; and the conference was held accordingly, April 1564, in the convent at Maulbron.

Among the disputants from Heidelberg were the professors Bocquin, Olevianus, and Ursinus. On the other side, appeared Brentz, two of the Tübingen professors, and other distinguished divines. The burden of the debate however was thrown mainly upon Ursinus in the one case, and wholly upon James Andreæ, the great and good chancellor of the University of Tübingen, in the other.[9] Two questions, it was agreed in the beginning, should be thoroughly discussed; first: Is the body of Christ in all places? And secondly: Must the declaration, *This is my body*, be understood literally as the words sound? Five days long the patient princes, Christopher and Frederick, listened to a discussion of the *first* topic, which seemed at last as little at an end as when it started. On the sixth day however, it was deemed proper to press forward to the second point. But unfortunately, the parties soon found themselves back again to the old question! The elector, in dismay, proposed now that the conference should break up in the middle, as never likely to come of itself to a natural conclusion. As usual, in cases of this sort, the whole occasion served only to add new fuel to the flame of controversy as it raged before. Both parties of course claimed the victory. On both sides were published "true and full reports" of the debate; in the case of which, each side charged the other with grievous misrepresentations. The colloquy itself became a subject of war.

As the Heidelberg Catechism was beyond all doubt the occasion, so to many it appeared now to be the culpable cause of all this commotion. The neighboring princes already mentioned came forward against it in form, with a joint epistle it would seem to the elector, pointing out its supposed errors, and severely reprehending its publication. This was forwarded by Frederick to Bullinger of Zurich, who wrote a defense of the Catechism against the princely attack.

In the year 1565, came out the great "Declaration and Confession of the Theologians of Tübingen on the Majesty of the Man Christ."[10] Then a "Solid Refutation of the Sophisms and Cavils of the Wirtemberg Divines," on the part of the Palatinate.[11] Then Replies and Rejoinders, all round, as fast as one could well make room for another. It was hard, of course, in such circumstances, to exercise toleration on either side. The authority of the Catechism was rigorously enforced in the Palatinate. In Wirtemberg [Württemberg], an order was published forbidding all persons to read a Calvinistic book!

---

9. [James Andreæ (1529–90) was an allegedly moderate Lutheran theologian who sought to reconcile the Gnesio-Lutherans and the Philippists. However, he sided with Westphal in the controversy with Calvin over the Lord's Supper, thereby showing that he leaned toward the conservative position. He was the principal German editor of the *Formula of Concord* (1580).]

10. [See also a similar work: *Confessio et Sententiae Ministorum Verbi in Comitatu Mansfeldensi* (Gaubisius, 1565).]

11. [*Verantwortung Wider die ungegründten auflagen und verkerungen* (Heidelberg: Maier, 1564).]

V. WAR AGAINST THE CATECHISM

Ursinus drew up in popular form an *Apology* for the Catechism, against the objections particularly of Matthias Flacius [Illyricus]. He wrote also a tract in its defence, in reply to a *Censure* upon eighteen questions contained in it by Brentz and Andreæ. Both these apologies appear joined with the Catechism itself in the Neustadt edition of 1595, which has always been highly prized on this account.[12]

It began to be a question now, whether the Palatinate could remain politically included in terms of the *Religious Peace*, by which, in the year 1555, the free exercise of their religion was secured to the Protestants of Germany, against the authority previously claimed over them by the Church of Rome.[13] The protection of the empire had been pledged in this case, only to those who followed the Confession of Augsburg. Must not the elector Frederick then be held to have forfeited, by is present position, all right and title to be reckoned in this connection? Could he be allowed to claim in future the privileges which it secured? Much talk was raised on this subject, in view especially of the imperial diet, which was expected to meet at Augsburg in the year 1566. Counsel was taken against the elector in secret; and it was hoped by many, that some decisive political blow would be made to fall at this time upon his head. Representations were made against him to the emperor; whose displeasure, once fairly roused, might cost him not only his kingdom but his life. Rumors of impending mischief surrounded him on all sides, which became the source of no small uneasiness to his friends, as well as of solemn reflection to himself. He endeavored, however, like David, to strengthen himself in the Lord his God.

So serious did the danger appear that his brother, prince Richard of Simmeren, thought it necessary to dissuade him most earnestly from attending the diet at all.[14] But he would not yield to this advice. His magnanimous soul is touchingly displayed, in the two letters, still extant, which he wrote to his brother on this occasion.[15] He admitted that there might be cause for anxiety; but his trust was that his heavenly Father would make him an instrument of his own glorious power, if need be, for the confession of his name in these last days, not only in word, but in deed also, before the whole Roman empire of the German nation. He would not presume indeed to compare himself with his honored relative, Duke John Frederick, Elector of Saxony,[16]

---

12. [*Catechismus, oder kurtzer underricht christlicher lehre* (Neustadt: Herborn, 1595).]

13. [The policy was a decision of the imperial Diet meeting in Augsburg in 1555 that ended the recurrent hostilities between the Catholic territories of the Empire and the various Lutheran leagues. The right of each prince to determine the nature of religious practice in his own territory became popularly known as "*cuius regio, cuius religio*" ("whose religion, his religion").]

14. [Richard of Simmeren (1521–1598) was the Count Palatine of Simmern-Sponheim from 1569–98 and brother of Frederick III, the Pious.]

15. [This was reported in G. J. Planck, *Geschichte der protestantischen Theologie von Luthers Tode bis zu der Einführung der Konkordienformel* (Leipzing: Siegfried Crussius, 1799), vol. 2, part 2, 490.]

16. Defeated and taken prisoner by the emperor Charles V in the memorable battle of Muehlberg, April 14, 1547. He was condemned to death, and afterwards pardoned again; but robbed of his electoral dignity, he remained for five years a captive in the emperor's camp. [Elector John Frederick of Saxony (1503–1554) had been a friend of Martin Luther, and had helped consolidate the Lutheran

now deceased; but the same God from whom this noble witness derived his strength still lived, and could easily uphold him also, insignificant as he was, even if it should come so far as to the shedding of blood: "an honor," he added, "for which, if my God and Father should so please to use me, I could never be sufficiently thankful in this world or in the next."[17]

In this spirit he went to the diet.[18] It was soon manifest, that an active interest was at work in the body to his prejudice. Complaints were preferred against him by the ecclesiastics present, with whom too many of the Protestant princes seemed disposed to make common cause, in their zeal for the extirpation of the Calvinistic doctrine. Finally it came to a formal declaration against him in open council, with the requisition that he should change and set aside again, in virtue of the *Religious Peace*, all that he had admitted into his churches and schools under the seducing form of Calvinism, and in particular do away with his Catechism and other books containing Calvinistic error; otherwise his imperial Majesty must feel himself bound to take the case into serious account. On this, the elector withdrew to one side, as it were to collect his soul for the occasion; but soon returned again to his place, where one of his sons, the prince John Casimir was directed to bring him a bible. Thus prepared, he entered upon his defense.

Modestly but firmly, he replied to each complaint that had been urged against him in the diet. When he came to the main point, his alleged defection from the Augsburg Confession, he did not hesitate to remind the emperor that in matters of faith and conscience he could acknowledge but one Master, the Lord of lords and King of kings. Where the salvation of the soul was concerned, it was God only who could properly command or be obeyed. Still he was ready to give answer to his imperial majesty, as the case required. Calvin's books he had never read, and could not pretend of course to know precisely what Calvinism was. On the other hand, he had signed the Augsburg Confession at Naumburg, in common with a number of princes who were now present, and could easily testify to the fact; and he continued in the same faith still, as believing it to be grounded in the holy scriptures; nor did he believe that any one could convict him of having swerved from this profession in anything that he had done. As for his Catechism, it was all taken from the bible, and so well-fortified with marginal proof-texts that it had not yet been overthrown, and he had good hope never would be, in all time to come. If anyone could show it wrong from the holy bible, which he now held in his hands, he was ready to hear him, great or small, friend or foe. Till this were done, he trusted in his majesty's gracious forbearance. Should this expectation be disappointed however, he said, in conclusion, he would still comfort himself in the sure promise of his Lord and Savior Jesus Christ made to him as well as

---

Church in Saxony.]

17. [See Planck, *Geschichte der protestantischen Theologie von Luthers Tode*, 2, 490.]

18. [Much of this information was taken from Heinrich Alting, *Historia Ecclesiæ Palatinæ*.]

to all saints, that what he might lose for his name in this life should be restored to him a hundred fold in the next.

This bold and manly address made a deep impression upon the assembly. All were silent; only one of the popish bishops murmured something about the 80th Question and the mass. But this received now no attention. Even Augustus of Saxony, who especially piqued himself on his Lutheran orthodoxy, was so moved by the elector's speech that he came up to him, striking him on the shoulder: "Fritz, you are more pious than the whole of us!" A similar remark was made afterwards by the Margave of Baden, to some of the princes: "Why trouble the elector? He has more piety than all of us together."

It was in fact a complete victory, over all the plans and expectations of his enemies. When the question was submitted in the end by the emperor, whether the elector of the Palatinate was to be regard as an ally of the Augsburg Confession, the members of the diet, through the influence especially of the elector of Saxony, decreed an affirmative answer. He was held to be of sound faith, according to the main substance of this standard; and especially on the great cardinal article of justification. On the article of the Lord's Supper, he appeared to show indeed some variation from the Confession. But this was not of such a character, by any means, that it ought to work his exclusion from the terms of the "Religious Peace." The whole decision was highly honorable to the diet, though it gave much umbrage of course to the hot headed theologians, who hoped to see German Calvinism completely crushed in the person of the heroic Frederick.

The elector returned to Heidelberg, amidst the general joy of his people, safe and sound, on the Friday before Whitsuntide. On the evening before the sacred festival, being present at the preparation for communion in the church of the Holy Ghost, he grasped Olevianus by the hand in the presence of the whole congregation, and exhorted him to continue steadfast in the faith. It was an affecting and impressive spectacle. The next day, he partook of the sacrament, in company with his son Casimir and the whole court.

The emperor Maximilian seems to have been favorably affected towards him by the honest plainness of his behavior at the diet. We find them subsequently on the best terms with one another. In the year 1570, Frederick had the honor of entertaining his majesty as a guest in Heidelberg, on his way to Spire; at which time much weighty business was discussed between them that served to give the emperor a high opinion of the elector's uprightness and ability. As he was about to leave, his princely host presented him with a copy of the bible in the Spanish language, as that which the emperor liked best, begging him to accept it in token of his regard. It is the treasury of all wisdom, he said, by whose guidance only, emperors, kings, and princes, can learn to govern well. Maximilian not only received the book kindly, but promised to read it diligently.

The Reformed Church of the Palatinate had internal difficulties to encounter, as well as opposition from without. Much commotion and distraction arose from the introduction of the Calvinistic system of order and discipline, as established at Geneva. Still worse was the disturbance created by the appearance of the anti-trinitarian heresy, within the bounds of the Church. The poison of Arianism,[19] proceeding originally from Italy, had already diffused itself extensively, in different directions, throughout Europe, in connection with the moral ferment of the Reformation. Finally it insinuated itself in the Palatinate. On the 15th of July, 1570, three ministers were cast into prison as patrons of the heresy. *Adam Neuser*, pastor of St. Peter's church in Heidelberg, saved himself from a similar fate, only by flight. In the end, the most conspicuous offended, *John Sylvan*,[20] superintendent of Ladenberg, after a long confinement, was publicly beheaded in the market place. Thus was the tragedy of Geneva re-enacted, in the streets of Heidelberg.[21] It was the spirit of the age, in each case, that demanded the sacrifice.

The last four years of the elector's life, were characterized by comparative peace. To the end, he continued to show a noble zeal for the interests of the Church. His death, which took place on the 26th of October, 1576, in the sixty-first year of his age, was marked by the same piety that distinguished his life. As he felt his end approaching, he said to those who stood around his bed: "I have lived here long enough for you and the Church; I am now called to a better life. I have done for the Church what I could; but my power has been small. He who possesses all power, and who has cared for his Church before I was born, still lives and reigns in heaven; and he will not forsake us. Neither will he allow the prayers and tears, which I have so often poured forth to God upon my knees in this chamber, for my successors and the Church, to prove without fruit." Shortly before his dissolution, he had the 31st psalm and the 17th chapter of John's gospel, read to him by Tossanus, with prayer. He then sank gently into the arms of death.

---

19. [Arianism was an interpretation of the person of Christ associated with the teachings Arius (256–336), a priest of Alexandria, who proclaimed that the Son was subordinate to the Father. Arians typically believed that the Son was neither coeternal nor coequal with the Father, but had been created at some point in time. This doctrine was rejected by the First Council of Nicea in 325 which declared that the Son and the Father are one in essence ("consubstantial"). A cluster of Arians, some of them Anabaptists, arose in northern Italy during the early decades of the Reformation.]

20. [John Sylvan (died 1572) was a Reformed pastor, theologian, and a superintendent of the church of Heidelberg who clashed with Olevianus on the issue of church discipline, which Sylvan did not want to be enforced by the civic magistrates. Sylvan became convinced that the doctrine of the Trinity was not implied by the Bible. Convicted of the heresy of Arianism, he was executed in 1572. The Elector probably felt that given the fact that the orthodoxy of the Palatinate was already under suspicion because of its eucharistic teachings, his territory could not tolerate beliefs that were even more unsettling. Nevin got this account from Heinrich Alting, *Historia Ecclesiæ Palatinæ*, in Ludwig Christian Mieg, ed., *Monumenta Pietatis & Literaria* (Franfurt am Main: Johann Maximilian, 1701), 208–9.]

21. [Nevin was referring to the execution of the non-trinitarian Michael Servetus for heresy in Geneva in 1553.]

He left a will; in which was found, written with his own hand, his dying confession of faith. A document of so solemn a character, that it was afterwards printed both in Latin and German, and appended to the general Confession of the Church.[22]

Altogether, the elector, Frederick the Third, was a great good man, and an extraordinary prince. Emphatically might he be styled a "nursing father" to the Reformed Church.

---

22. [See "The Confession of Frederick III (1577)," in James T. Dennison, ed. *Reformed Confessions of the 16th and 17th Centuries*, vol. 3 (Grand Rapids: Reformation Heritage Books, 2012), 439–57.]

VI. The Catechism at Home

Relapse of the Palatinate to Lutheranism. Restoration under prince Casimir. Death of Olevianus and Ursinus. David Pareus. Thirty Years' War. Philip William. Decline of the Reformed Church in the Palatinate. 80th Question.

With the death of the elector Frederick, the whole religious state of the Palatinate fell once again into disorder. He was succeeded in the electorate by his eldest son, *Louis*;[1] whose previous relations in the Upper Palatinate had inspired him with a strong zeal for Lutheranism, in opposition to the whole religious course of his father. Before his death, the old prince had sought an interview with his son; wishing to bring him under an engagement, if possible, to respect his views in regard to the Church as expressed in his last will and testament. Louis thought [it] proper to decline the interview, and showed no regard subsequently to his father's directions. On the contrary, he made it his business from the start to turn all things into an entirely different train. The clergy together with the mayor and citizens of Heidelberg addressed a petition to him, praying for liberty of conscience, and offering one of the churches for the particular use of those who belonged to his confession. His brother, duke Casimir, lent his intercession also to sustain the request.[2] But it answered no purpose; Louis declared that *his* conscience would not suffer him to receive the petition. The following year he came with his court to Heidelberg, dissolved the ecclesiastical council, dismissed the preachers, filled all places with Lutheran incumbents, caused a new church service to be introduced, and in one word changed the public religion into a wholly different aspect from all that it was before. The Heidelberg Catechism of course was set aside.

1. [Elector Louis (or Ludwig) VI (1539–83) was a devout Lutheran who supported the unaltered Augsburg Confession. Raised by his Lutheran mother, he had long disapproved of his father's Reformed proclivities.]

2 [Duke John Casimir (1543–92), the younger son of Frederick III, remained staunchly Reformed after his father's death, unlike his Lutheran older brother. He led troops from the Palatinate in the Dutch revolt against the Catholic Hapsburgs and kept the German Reformed academic tradition alive in his small territory after Louis had purged the University of Heidelberg of Calvinists.]

VI. THE CATECHISM AT HOME

The booksellers were forbidden indeed to sell any book whatever, in favor of the Reformed faith.

The more prominent theologians were soon compelled to leave their places; among whom were the authors of the Catechism, Olevianus and Ursinus.

The first, who had made himself particularly obnoxious to the new elector by his somewhat intemperate pulpit zeal, received a call not long afterwards to Berleberg. Here he continued in the service of the gospel, the remainder of his days. His death took place, March 15, 1587, in the full triumph of Christian salvation.[3]

Ursinus found an honorable refuge with the prince Casimir, second son of the late elector, who exercised a small sovereignty of his own at Neustadt, and made it his business to succor and encourage there, as much as he could, the cause now persecuted by his Lutheran brother. The distinguished divine was constituted professor of theology in the Neustadt gymnasium; which the prince now proposed to raise to the character of something like a substitute for what the Heidelberg University had been previously for the Reformed Church.

He was soon furnished with the opportunity of making his institution still more important, as an asylum for letters and religion. In the year 1580 Louis signed the Form [Formula] of Concord, and proceeded immediately to enforce its authority in his dominions. With the exception of a single man, all the professors in the University of Heidelberg refused to accept the new symbol, and so of course lost their places. Nearly all the students withdrew at the same time. The university was in fact dissolved;

---

3. "Here have I first learned aright," he said on his deathbed, "what sin is, and how great is the majesty of God!" On one occasion, he fell into a sort of trance or rapture of four hours; which he described afterwards as a state in which the dew of heaven was made to descend upon him, not in drops, but in full overflowing showers, refreshing soul and body with inexpressible joy. As the comforting promises of God were read to him, he would say often: "Would that my home-return to the Lord might soon come; I long to depart and be with Christ." Toward the end, one said to him: "You are doubtless, my brother, well assured of your salvation in Christ." He replied: "Perfectly sure!" laid his head upon his breast, and quietly expired.

Various works from his pen were published after his death, consisting mainly of sermons and commentaries on the Bible. His friend, Theodore Beza, honored his memory with a Latin poem, in his usual elegant style, which begins:

"Eheu, quibus suspriis,
Eheu, quibus te lacrymis,
OLEVIANE, plaxero?
Nam dotibus pares tuis

Doloribus pares meis,
Questus modosque flebiles
Non pectus hoc suggesserit,
Non istud os effuderit." &c.

[Trans: Ah, with those who sigh, / Ah, with those who cry / will I have mourned you, Olevian, / for your talents are equal to my sorrow . . ." See R. Scott Clark, *Caspar Olevianus and the Substance of the Covenant.*]

Document 1: The History and Genius of the Heidelberg Catechism

though it was soon resuscitated again with Lutheran faculties. Prince Casimir received into his college such of the dismissed professors as were not provided for elsewhere. With such names as *Ursinus, Jerome Zanchius,*[4] *Francis Junius,*[5] *Daniel Tossanus,*[6] *John Piscator,*[7] in its theological faculty, and others of the like order in the other departments, the *Cassimirianum*, as the school was now styled, acquired at once a very respectable standing. Here Ursinus continued to labor, true to the faith of his own dishonored Catechism, till the day of his death.

The triumph of Lutheranism in the Palatinate proved in the end to be short. Before the plan could be fully executed, by which it was proposed to extend the revolution of the capital throughout the province, prince Louis died in the midst of his days; and at once the whole face of things was brought again to assume a new aspect. His son, the proper heir to his power, was still a minor, and it devolved accordingly on his uncle, the duke John Casimir, to act as his guardian, and administer the government in his name. He entered upon his office with as little respect for the views and wishes of his deceased brother, as he himself had shown eight years before for the views and wishes of their common father. The Reformed faith was once more restored to honor. Casimir made some effort indeed at first to harmonize and unite the two conflicting confessions; but not being able to succeed in this, he took measures gradually to remove from all places of trust the incumbents appointed by his brother, and to fill them again with appointments from the Reformed Church. As far as possible, the old professors were once more restored to the university. The Casimirianum saw itself shorn by degrees of its transient glory. The Form [Formula] of Concord sunk into disgrace; while its rival standard, the Heidelberg Catechism, rose gloriously into view again as the ecclesiastical banner of the Palatinate.[8] In a short time, the whole order of the church was restored, as it had stood at the death of Frederick the Pious.

But there was one among the banished theologians of Neustadt, who did *not* return at this time with his colleagues, to the scene of his former labors. The author of

---

4. [Jerome Zanchius (1516–1590) was an Italian-born Protestant Reformation theologian, minister, and educator who influenced the development of Reformed theology during the decades following the death of John Calvin. He employed a scholastic method reminiscent of Aquinas to organize and elaborate Reformed doctrine. Although Nevin appreciated Zanchius' intellectual stature, he was not sympathetic to his theological method.]

5. [Francis Junius (1545–1602), who had studied under Calvin and Beza, also helped pioneer Reformed scholasticism. He taught for a time at Prince Casimir's Neustadt gymnasium when the University of Heidelberg replaced its Reformed faculty with Lutheran faculty in 1580.]

6. [Daniel Tossanus (1541–1602) was a French Reformed theologian who fled from the St. Bartholomew's Day massacre of Protestants in Paris and Orleans. He pastored French refugees in Basel, and later moved to Heidelberg, where he eventually taught theology.]

7. [John Piscator (1546–1625) was a prolific and somewhat mercurial German Reformed theologian, active in Heidelberg and Herborn, who transitioned from being a double predestinarian to being an Arminian. He is most remembered for his philosophical and theological textbooks.]

8. [It is characteristic of Nevin to juxtapose the Heidelberg Catechism and the Formula of Concord to the detriment of the later.]

the Catechism itself, the learned and pious Ursinus, was not permitted to behold the triumph to which it was now advanced. He died, on the 6th of March 1583, the very year in which prince Casimir came into power. The event took place in the 59th year of his age.

He had written a number of theological treatises suited to the wants of the time; among the rest a special dissertation entitled the "True Doctrine of the *Holy Supper* of our Lord Jesus Christ, faithfully expounded from the principles and sense of the divine Scriptures, the ancient and orthodox Church, and also of the Augsburg confession."[9] This was published originally, in the name of the whole theological faculty of Heidelberg. His works were issued collectively, some time after his death, in three folio volumes, by his friend and disciple *David Pareus*.[10]

We are indebted to the same faithful and competent hand for another important service, in this case. As long as Ursinus continued at Heidelberg, he had been in the habit of reading regularly lectures on the Catechism, going over the whole of it in this way during the course of each year. Notes of these lectures were taken down by students, which were allowed afterwards in several cases to appear in print. As much injustice was done to him by the defective character of these publications, David Pareus was called upon to revise the whole, and put the work into a form that would be more faithful to the name and spirit of his illustrious preceptor. This he undertook accordingly, and accomplished with great success.[11] The work appeared first in the year 1591, at Heidelberg, in four parts, each furnished with a separate preface by Pareus; since which time it has gone through numerous editions, in different countries. The Heidelberg Catechism has been honored with an almost countless number of commentaries of later date; but this first one, derived from Ursinus through David Pareus, has been generally allowed to be the best that has been written. As he was himself the author of the Catechism, his commentary must be considered at all events the most authoritative exposition of its true meaning.

Prince Casimir's administration was characterized throughout by an enlightened and liberal zeal in favor of both letters and religion. Pains were taken at the same time to educate his nephew, the heir to the throne, in the same principles and spirit; so that when he came to power, under the name *Frederick the Fourth*[12] no change of policy

---

9. [See *Gründlicher bericht Vom Heiligen Abendmal unsers Herren Jesu Christ* (Heidelberg, Meyer, 1564).]

10. [David Pareus (1548–1622) was a student of Ursinus who became a major Reformed theologian in his own right. He served as a faculty member of Old and New Testament at Prince Casimir's Collegium Sapientiae (1598–1602) and is known for publishing the collected works of his former mentor, Ursinus, in three volumes following the latter's death. Like Ursinus, he sought to find common ground between the Lutherans and the Reformed. His irenic overtures to the Lutherans did not bear lasting fruit. See *Corpus doctrinae Orthodoxae Sive Catecheticarum Explicationum D. Zachariae Ursini Opus absolutum*, ed. David Pareus (Rhodin, 1612).]

11. [See *Explicationum catecheticarum D. Zachariae Ursini Silesii* (Heidelberg: Harnish, 1591). See also *Explicationum catecheticarum D. Zachariae Ursini Silesii* (Neustadt, 1593).]

12. [Frederick IV (1574–1610) had been raised by John Casimir to be fervently Reformed.

took place in any respect. He was heartily devoted to the interests of the Reformed Church; and under him particularly, the university seems to have attained its greatest splendor. The principal ornament of the theological faculty at this time was David Pareus, of whom we have just spoken as the most distinguished disciple of Ursinus, and the editor of his works.

The fortunes of the Catechism after this in the Palatinate, were very variable; being always more or less controlled by the eventful political history of the country.

Frederick IV was succeeded by his son, *Frederick the Fifth*.[13] In an evil hour, against the advice of his best friends, this prince consented to accept the crown of Bohemia; which had been offered to him on the part of that country when it had resolved, after the death of Matthias, to refuse submission to the Austrian yoke. His coronation took place at Prague, with great pomp, on the 25th of October, 1619. In the course of the following year he was terribly defeated by the imperial army before the same city, and deprived not only of his new crown, but also of his hereditary dominions. It was the first act in the bloody drama of the *Thirty Years' War*, for which the elements of discord had been mustering their strength for years before, and which now made room for a long series of horrors, which the pen of the historian finds it difficult to describe.

The Palatinate soon lay completely humbled, beneath the strong hand of imperial power. This was of course the full triumph of Romanism, at the same time, over the Protestant institutions of the land. In the year 1622, the Bavarian general Tilly laid waste the beautiful environs of Heidelberg,[14] and finally after a severe siege forced his way into the city by storm. A terrible scene followed of burning, pillage and slaughter. Melancholy to relate, the treasures of the university were not permitted to escape the fury of this Vandal assault. For four days, the noble library, which so many princes had made it their ambition to enrich, and from whose stores so many learned men had drawn nourishment for their intellectual life, stood openly exposed to the ravages of the common soldiery;[15] and it was only the rush for booty of another kind that saved it from entire destruction. As it was, the whole of it became lost from this time forward to Heidelberg. It was devoted as a trophy of war to the pope; and not

---

Although afflicted with alcoholism, he continued his uncle's religious policies and became the leader of a Protestant military league.]

13. [Frederick V (1596–1632), known as the "Winter King," continued his father's support for the Reformed faith in the Palatinate. He unwisely accepted the crown of Bohemia (which was undergoing a Reformed revolution) and was promptly defeated by the Catholic Hapsburg forces at the battle of White Mountain. Forced to flee from the Palatinate, he spent the rest of life in exile in the Reformed regions of the Netherlands.]

14. [Tilly (Johann Tserclaes, 1559–1632) was a military commander who led the Catholic League's forces in the middle stages of the Thirty Years' War. He led the bloody eleven-week siege that captured the Protestant city of Heidelberg on September 19, 1622. That victory left the Electorate of the Palatinate under Imperial control temporarily.]

15. A portion of the manuscripts are said to have been used by stupid dragoons as straw for their horses.

VI. THE CATECHISM AT HOME

long after, borne on a long train of mules, it was seen making its way over the mountains, to rest finally in the chambers of the Vatican.[16] The whole religious aspect of the Palatinate was now changed. Crowds of foreign monks came in, laying claim to the property that had belonged formerly to the monasteries. The Reformed ministers were expelled. The Catechism fell. All assumed once more the Roman aspect. Sad to relate, large numbers of the people consented to change their faith in order to save themselves from expatriation and worldly loss. The university was transformed into a Jesuit college.

By the heroic courage of *Gustavus Adolphus*,[17] king of Sweden, the afflicted province was restored again in great part to its Protestant state; but only for a short season. After the defeat of the Swedish army in 1634 all the fair prospects of the country were a second time completely and cruelly blasted. Famine and pestilence were now added to the scourge of war. Rapine and violence filled the land; and for twelve long years the Palatinate groaned beneath a constantly accumulating weight of sorrows, which it is impossible fully to describe.

By the *Peace of Westphalia*, A. D. 1648, these calamities were at length brought to an end. The Bavarian supremacy now ceased, and the government of the land fell once more into the hands of its true and proper sovereign. The Reformed Church was seen rising again, as it were from the ashes of her former glory, a spectacle of mournful interest to churches of the same faith in other lands. Of three hundred and forty seven preachers who had been settled in the Palatinate of the Rhine at the beginning of the war, only forty-two were found remaining in it when the war closed, in a few towns and villages occupied by the Swedes; and only fifty-four returned from the general

16. The ruin of the "Bibliotheca Palatina" formed one of the most sad disasters of the Thirty Years' War; and was deplored as a public loss by learned men throughout all Germany. "The mother of all libraries," says one, "not only for Germany but for many other lands also, is gone! A treasure not to be told in price, such as the Roman Empire will no longer be able to create! The manuscripts alone were valued at 80,000 crowns. Well did it deserve, in one word, the title: Optimus Germaniae literatae thesaurus!" Efforts were made, after the war, to recover the library from the court of Rome; but without success. It is interesting to know however, that an effort of the same sort made in our own century, has had a somewhat more favorable result. At the close of the war of 1815–1816, the University of Heidelberg again put in its old claim for the restitution of the captive library. With some trouble, nearly a thousand manuscripts were recovered. [This information is found in *Rhenus Fluminum Princeps,* by Johann Jakob Senfftel (Augsburg, 1689), 20. The original estimate of the value of manuscripts was proposed by Joseph Scaliger (1540—1609). Scaliger was a French religious leader and scholar whose *De emendatione temporum* (1583) broadened the perception of classical history to include Persian, Babylonian, Jewish and ancient Egyptian history in addition to annals of the Greeks and Romans. Much of this was reported in *The Classical Scholar* (author unknown), (London: A. J. Valpy, 1816), vol. 13, 212.]

17. [Gustavus Adolphus (1594–1632) was the Lutheran King of Sweden from 1611 to1632 who championed the Protestant cause during the middle period of the Thirty Year's War that had been triggered by Frederick V's rash decision to accept the crown of Bohemia. He is known for his role in leading Sweden to a position of military primacy during his reign, thereby redistributing political and religious power in Europe. After a string of stunning victories over the imperial forces, Gustavus was killed at the battle of Lützen. During the period of Swedish ascendency much of the German territory occupied by the Catholic forces was reclaimed for Protestantism, at least temporarily.]

Document 1: The History and Genius of the Heidelberg Catechism

banishment to resume the work of ministry in their native land. Gradually however the state of the Church improved, along with the return of prosperity to the province in general. This restoration of the Reformed faith included of course the erection of the Catechism to its former authority as the religious ensign of the nation. But greater toleration than before was now exercised toward other confessions. Some attempt was made even, on the part of the government, to unite the two Protestant confessions in a common form of worship, though without success.

This interval of rest and peace endure, however, only about forty years. By the death of prince *Charles* in 1685, the direct line of succession failed, and the electorate passed over to a different branch of the same house, in the person of *Philip William, Duke of Neuburg*.[18] He belonged unfortunately to the Roman Church; and although he stood pledged to respect the religious constitution of the land, the administration necessarily operated in various ways to make Romanism respectable, and to extend its influence. His connection with the house of Orleans moreover served as a pretext for France to lay claim to the whole of the Palatinate;[19] and the consequence was a new war from this quarter, which for a time revived the fully horror of the "Thirty Years." In the year 1688, Heidelberg was taken by the French and handled with the most savage barbarity. Not only was the surrounding country laid waste, and the city abandoned to general plunder; but a spirit of the most wanton destruction was let loose at the same time upon the whole strength and beauty of the place. Walls, towers and palaces, were blown up, and whole streets consumed by fire. Immense cruelties were inflicted besides on the inhabitants. At the end of eighteen months the army was forced to retire; but a new invasion followed three years later. In May, 1693, Heidelberg again fell into the hands of the French; the old cruelties were renewed; and to crown all, the whole city was involved finally in flames, and became thus a heap of blackened ruins. Even the sepulchers of the dead found no respect; the bones of honored princes and heroes, long departed, were barbarously dragged from their resting place, and scattered in the streets.

The whole war was made to bear the character of a religious persecution. It affected something of the merit of a crusade, in the service of the Roman Catholic Church, against Protestantism. The Protestants were compelled in many cases to fly the country. Colonies of the Reformed Church of the Palatinate were now formed, in this way, in different parts particularly of Prussia. Roman Catholics, on the other hand, crowded in to fill up the room which was thus made vacant.

Peace was again restored in 1697, and the city which had suffered so many wrongs began to rise once more, with vast activity, from its own ashes. But the Protestant cause was not able to recover its lost advantages and rights. Romanism was

---

18. [Philip William (1615–90) was related to the Catholic rulers of Bavaria, the most powerful Catholic German state.]

19. [The Duchess of Orleans, the sister-in-law of Louis IV, also had a plausible claim to be the rightful ruler of the Palatinate.]

now become a strong interest in the land, and had usurped in many cases the power and wealth which had once belonged to the Reformed Church. It began accordingly to assume a hostile bearing toward this last, which showed itself particularly in a sort of angry quarrel with the Heidelberg Catechism. The 80th Question, which had long been a cause of offense, was held up now to special odium, as not merely calumnious to the Church of Rome, but insulting to the government of the country.[20] It was in reply to such assaults on the part of the Jesuits that the celebrated *Lenfant* wrote his work entitled, *The Innocence of the Heidelberg Catechism*.[21] This had not served however to silence the complaint. The controversy grew more and more serious. In the year 1707, counsellor *Rittmeyer*, Protestant originally, who had sense become a zealous convert to the Church of Rome, assailed the Catechism with great severity.[22] Not only the 80th Question, but the 94th, and the 97th and the 98th also, fell under censure, as false and disrespectful to the religion of the prince; and the Reformed were taken to task sharply for not at once so altering their formulary as to expunge from it all offense of this kind. Rittmeyer was answered by two of the Heidelberg theologians. Replies and rejoinders followed as usual; and the whole land was filled with excitement. On the side of the Reformed Church, it was maintained that the catechism had existed in its present form long before the Palatinate had come into the circumstances in which it now stood; and its age, no less than its origin, as a symbolical book, entitled it to be held inviolate; that other church symbols, and especially the Articles of the Council of Trent, employed language full as severe toward dissenting systems of faith; and finally, that the hard expressions which were complained of in this case, must be referred at all events to doctrines only, and not to the persons by whom they might happen to be held. On these grounds, it was said, the Church could not consent at this time to introduce into the Catechism any such alteration, as was required from the other side.

Thus things proceeded until the year 1719, when all at once an electoral decree appeared prohibiting the use of the Heidelberg Catechism in the Palatinate altogether. Some Roman Catholic bookseller, who was authorized to print Protestant books, had issued an edition of the Catechism, to which was inconsiderately prefixed the elector's coat of arms, with the words underneath: *By the order of his electoral Serene Highness*.[23] The appearance of this publication proved extremely offensive, and the occasion was improved by the active friends of Romanism, to secure the decree now mentioned, in which the Catechism was condemned in form, as injurious to the electoral dignity, as

20. [This was the question that described the Roman Mass as idolatry.]

21 [Jacques Lenfant (1661–1728), *L'innocence du Catechisme de Heidelberg* (Amsterdam: Pierre Humbert, 1723; originally published 1688).]

22. [Christian Rittmeyer, *Catholische Anmerkungen uber den Heydelbergischen Catechismus* (Heidelberg: J. Mayer, 1707). Nevin discovered this account in Heinrich Van Alpen's *Geschichte und Literatur des Heidelbergischen Katechismus*, which was later translated by Joseph Berg as *The History and Literature of the Heidelberg Catechism*.]

23. [This imprimatur, the Catholics feared, made it seem that the Elector had approved of the theological contents of the Catechism.]

Document 1: The History and Genius of the Heidelberg Catechism

well as to the laws of the empire and the authority of the emperor, and therefore necessary to be suppressed. Remonstrance was made against the order, in vain. No regard was shown to the most reasonable considerations. The decree was declared to be final; and it was made known at the same time that any attempt which might be made to vindicate the Catechism, or to sustain its authority in any way, would be visited with special punishment.

This tyrannical measure drew upon the Palatinate the attention of the Protestant courts of Europe generally. By letters and embassies from all sides, the elector was called upon to restore to his Reformed subjects the public and free use of their symbolical book. In the end the pressure became too heavy to withstand; and with a bad grace the entire point was yielded. By direction of the emperor, who had sense enough to see that the elector was on ground that could not be maintained, a new inquiry was instituted on the whole case. Two distinguished theologians of the Reformed Church were called in, to assist in the conference. It was proposed, in the first place, that they should modify the 80th Question, so as to make it more smooth and conciliatory. This however they refused to do, as not being authorized to make the slightest alteration in the case. But they protested that the Catechism had regard here to doctrines only, and carried in it no disrespect to persons; on which count, it was hoped that the elector would be pleased to withdraw the order, which he had issued against its use. To this accordingly, with due show of formality, the negotiation finally came. It was agreed to look upon the whole difficulty, as one that had grown out of misunderstanding and mistake. The Reformed Church was authorized to use her Catechism again, with the same liberty as before; only it must not carry the elector's coat of arms any more in front; and pains must be taken besides to let the people understand, in the schools and churches, that the 80th Question had respect to the doctrine of the Mass merely, and not at all to the persons holding it, who were not to be stigmatized as *idolators*, though the mass itself be there pronounced "*an accursed idolatry.*"

This distinction between doctrine and person, it may be added, was held by many to be disingenuous on the part of the Palatine divines, and a curious controversy sprang out of it concerning *idolatry in the abstract and idolatry in the concrete*; of which however it is not necessary here to take any further notice.[24]

Had the Catechism stood for the Palatinate only, it must have risen and fallen wholly with the fortunes of the Reformed Church in that interesting land. In this case, its historical importance would be circumscribed by comparatively narrow bounds. The Church of the Palatinate had its glory, for the most part, in the beginning. It never recovered itself in full from the shock of the Thirty Years' War; and from the year 1685, when a Roman Catholic prince was raised to the electorate, it declined still more and more; till finally, instead of being as it was at first the head of all Reformed Churches in Germany, it became the least considerable of the whole, and sunk indeed almost entirely out of sight.

24. [See Van Alpen, *Geschichte und Literatur des Heidelbergischen Katechismus.*]

VI. THE CATECHISM AT HOME

But the Catechism had a wider history than that of the particular Church to which it owes its birth. It very soon passed over the limits of the Palatinate, and became the property of the Church also in other lands.

VII. The Catechism Abroad

General reception in the Reformed Church. Switzerland. France. England. Hungary. Poland. Germany. Holland. Arminian opposition. Synod of Dort. Commentaries. America. Reformed Dutch and German Reformed Churches.

The Heidelberg Catechism, as soon as it became known, commanded not only the respect, but the admiration of the entire Reformed Church. On all sides, it was welcomed as the best popular summary of religious doctrine that had yet appeared, on the side of this confession. Distinguished divines in other lands united in bearing testimony to its merits. It was considered the glory of the Palatinate, to have presented it to the world. The great Bullinger of Switzerland[1] wrote a friend: "I have read the Catechism of the elector palatine, Frederick, with the greatest interest, and have blessed God, while doing so, who thus perfects his own work. The arrangement of the book is clear; the matter is true, and beautiful and good; all is full of light, fruitful and pious; with the greatest brevity its contents are manifold and large. In my judgment, no better catechism has heretofore been published."[2]—This is only a specimen of the way, in which the work was received generally throughout the Reformed Church. It rose rapidly into the character of a general symbol, answerable in this view to the popular standard possessed by the other confession in the Catechism of Luther. Far and wide it became the basis on which systems of religious instruction were formed by the most excellent and learned divines. In the course of time, commentaries, paraphrases, and courses of sermons were written upon it without number. Few works have gone through so many versions. It was translated into Hebrew, Ancient Greek

---

1. [Heinrich Bullinger (1504–77) succeeded Zwingli as the ecclesiastic leader of Zürich. His somewhat more moderate theology was widely influential.]

2. [This quotation comes from Van Alpen, *Geschichte und Literatur des Heidelbergschen Katechismus*, English trans. Berg, 84.]

and Modern Greek,[3] Latin, Low Dutch, Spanish, French, English, Italian, Bohemian, Polish, Hungarian, Arabic, and Malay.

SWITZERLAND, from the first, held the Heidelberg Catechism in the highest esteem. Various catechisms had been in use here, before its appearance; one by Leo Juda,[4] another by Œcolampadius, the Catechism of Zurich by Bullinger, the Catechism of St. Gall, and particularly Calvin's Catechism, of which some notice has been taken before. In the midst of these established formularies however, the new text book of the Reformed faith was soon invested with a sort of universal authority, as a bond of religious profession for the land in general. In St. Gall it was introduced into the schools and churches. The Catechism of Zurich was so revised, in the beginning of the following century, as to be brought more near to it than before. In most of the other cantons, it was admitted, sooner or later, to at least a partial public use. The high credit in which it stood appears also from the numerous editions of it published in that country, and from the many commentaries and expositions with which it has been honored by eminent Swiss divines.

In FRANCE, the Reformed Church, as already mentioned, made use of the Catechism of Calvin; which was often simply called the *French Catechism*. The Heidelberg Catechism of course was not introduced into the homes and schools. Still various translations were made of it into the French language, and it was always held in very high respect. Great attention was given by this Church to catechetical instruction. For a whole century, we find in the acts of almost every Synod, some reference to the subject.

In ENGLAND also and SCOTLAND the Catechism of the Palatinate was held in the same high regard. Immediately after its formation, it was translated into the language of these countries, and became thus extensively read and admired in both of them. A variety of catechisms appeared in England, at an early period; till at length one was prepared, a. 1572, under special appointment, by Alexander Nowel, which took the place of all others, and continued in permanent force afterwards as the standard catechism of the established Church.[5] The Puritans, as they were called, by means of the famous Westminster Assembly, produced about the middle of the next century the *Larger* and *Smaller* Catechisms, which have since held so high a place in the Presbyterian Church, both in Great Britain and in this country. Special respect was shown by this venerable body, in the execution of their task, to the Heidelberg Catechism.[6]

---

3. Both into ancient and modern Greek. Into the first by *Frederick Sylburg*, Heidelberg, 1597. This translation was sent to the Greek patriarch at Constantinople. The version into modern Greek took place in Leyden, 1648, under the direction of the States General of Holland.

4 [Leo Jud (1482–1542) was a Swiss Reformer who worked closely with Zwingli in Zurich.]

5. [Alexander Nowell (1507–1602) was an Anglican priest and dean of St. Paul's, London. During the persecutions of Queen Mary he fled to Strasbourg and Switzerland where he encountered Calvin and the Scottish Reformer John Knox. Under Queen Elizabeth, who disliked his admonition that she should get married, he remained oriented toward a moderate form of the Reformed tradition. He is also alleged to have invented bottled beer. See *A Catechisme* (London: John Daye, 1573).]

6. [The Heidelberg Catechism was consulted by the divines of the Westminster Assembly, but

Document 1: The History and Genius of the Heidelberg Catechism

In HUNGARY, the same formulary soon supplanted, with the Reformed Church, all other catechisms, and was introduced into general use as a symbolical book. Teachers as well as ministers were required to take an oath that they cordially embraced the system of truth contained in it, and that they would follow it truly in all their religious instructions.

A like favorable reception was given to the Catechism in POLAND. It was translated into the Polish language by *Andrew Prasmovius*; and soon came into general use, as an authoritative exposition of the faith of the Reformed Church.

In GERMANY, the Reformed confession gained ground gradually far beyond the bounds of the Palatinate. This was owing partly to the influence exercised by neighboring countries, particularly Switzerland and Holland; but still more no doubt to the process by which Lutheranism itself became complete, in being carried forward to the last consequence, the *Form [Formula] of Concord*. A large amount of Calvinistic feeling, which had prevailed in the Church as moderate Lutheranism, was forced by this onward movement to seek a different position. In all directions accordingly, we discover with the advance of time the presence of Reformed views and principles, in conflict with the rigid orthodoxy of the other confession, and a more or less full and open profession of the Reformed faith.—In *East Friesland*, the struggle between the two confessions commenced, with the entrance of the Reformation itself into the country.—Some account has already been given of the religious commotion in *Bremen*.—All along the Rhine, in different cities and provences, *Juliers, Cleves, Berg*, &c., the principles of the Reformed Church unfolded themselves more or less successfully, in conflict with the high toned Lutheranism of the day. The Form [Formula] of Concord, a. 1576 as just intimated, served greatly to strengthen the tendency in this direction. Thus in the close of the century, the Churches of *Nassau, Hanau, Isenburg*, and others of smaller note, seceded formally from the Lutheran ranks, and became Calvinistic. *Anhalt*, in the year 1597, made a similar transition. Still more important was the change which took place in the beginning of the next century, when Maurice, Landgrave of *Hesse*,[7] and John Sigismund, Elector of *Brandenburg*,[8] embraced the Reformed communion. In this last case indeed the revolution was not at once so entire as in the other; since the prince was disposed to allow the free profession of Lutheranism as before, in his dominions, The bigotry of the party however soon made it necessary for him to suppress the Form [Formula] of Concord, by public authority. In

---

not to any particularly great extent. Nevin was exaggerating its impact.]

7. [Maurice, Landgrave of Hesse (1572–1632) attempted to change the established religion of his two different territories from Lutheranism to the Reformed faith in 1605. By doing so he incurred the enmity of the Emperor.]

8. [John Sigismund, Elector of Brandenburg and eventually Duke of Prussia (1572–1619), converted from Lutheranism to the Reformed faith. He considered making the Reformed church the established religion of his territory, but encountered considerable opposition from the Lutheran population (including his wife). Consequently, his domain became officially bi-confessional; individuals could choose to be either Lutheran or Reformed.]

VII. THE CATECHISM ABROAD

other respects, the liberal and tolerant policy of Sigismund continued the permanent order of the state.[9]

In the Reformed Church, as thus prevailing in different principalities throughout Germany, various catechisms appeared, and secured to themselves a more or less extensive use. In the end however all of these were either cast aside, or sunk into a secondary rank; while the Catechism of the Palatinate attained to a sort of universal authority, as the leading symbol of the Church. In Juliers, Cleves and Berg, it was early introduced into the churches and schools; and in 1580 we find it made of full force by law, as an ecclesiastical standard. So afterwards in Hesse-Cassel, Anhalt, and the several free cities which had embraced the Reformed faith. It became the acknowledged confessional standard of the *German Reformed Church* at large, as distinguished from the other great Protestant confession. Hence we find even in Prussia, at the beginning of the last century, a royal order, requiring all ministers of Reformed churches to lecture every sabbath afternoon on the Heidelberg Catechism, according to the practice observed in Holland.

Germany of course has not failed to do her full share towards the literature of the Catechism. It has passed through an almost incredible number of editions in her hands. Commentaries of all sorts, in long succession, have appeared in its service. Among all these however no one seems to have proved so popular as the "*Golden Treasure*" of John D'outrein,[10] translated into German from the Dutch, and furnished with annotations and additions by Frederick Adolphus Lampe.[11] This large work has been honored with edition after edition, and may be said indeed to have carried with it, for a time, a sort of symbolical authority for ministers and teachers, both in Germany and Holland. Widder's work on the Catechism has also been held in high repute.[12] Others too deserve special praise; but it is unnecessary, in the present place, to be more particular.

In the midst of its honors, the Catechism still encountered in Germany at large no less than in the Palatinate, no small amount of angry opposition. Romanists and high Lutherans joined, in crying out against it as heterodox and pernicious. The notable 80th Question proved a constant stench, in many nostrils. In some cases, when it was known that the minister was to preach upon this question, troublesome persons

---

9. [Nevin believed that if the narrow-mindedness implicit in the stance of the doctrinaire Lutherans was allowed to develop according to its inner logic, then most Protestants would gravitate to the more latitudinarian expression of the Reformed tradition.]

10. [Johannes D'Outrein (1662–1722) was a Dutch theologian and devotional writer. See *Het Gouden Kleinroot* (Amsterdam: J. Boom, 1719).]

11. [Frederick Adolphus Lampe (1683–1729) was a Reformed pastor, theologian, and professor of domatics who was influenced by D'Outrein and by Cocceius's "covenant theology." He wrote extensively about the "inner life" and helped introduce Pietism, which had been a largely Lutheran phenomenon at first, into Reformed circles. He recommended that the Heidelberg Catechism be used for personal devotional purposes.]

12. [See J. Widder, *Erbauliche Betrachtungen uber die in dem Heidelbergischen Catechismo* (Frankfurt, 1753).]

Document 1: The History and Genius of the Heidelberg Catechism

would slip into the church, for the purpose of creating interruption and disorder. Not unfrequently, at the public fairs fanatical well-fed monks might be heard, from some elevated place, haranguing the populace in the lowest billingsgate style; at which times the Heidelberg Catechism, and the 80th Question in particular, were very apt to come in for a special share of abuse. In the year 1621, a certain Jesuit of Cologne, by the name of Coppenstein, attracted some attention, by publishing the "*Calvinistic Heidelberg Catechism Discalvinised;*" in which the questions were all furnished with Roman Catholic answers, with the true text thrust by way of contrast into the margin.[13] Another writer put forth, "*Four Dialogues on the Catechism, between two Reformed citizens, Samson and Job.*" In this production, every question is taken up and embarrassed with subtle, far-fetched difficulties; till in the end the honest worthies find themselves involved in impenetrable smoke, and are glad to take refuge in the Church of Rome. In other cases, where there was not perhaps the same ability to wield the polemic pen, the Catechism was subjected to violence of a different kind; cast into the fire; solemnly flogged with rods in the pulpit; or maltreated in some similar dramatic way; to show how heartily it was hated, and how richly it deserved to be extirpated from the world as a work of the devil.

In no country, however was the Heidelberg Catechism more generally received, or more highly honored, than it was in the NETHERLANDS.[14]

The Reformation was matured in this land, amid the storms of political revolution. The same convulsions which set the Church free, gave birth also to a new, and powerful Republic. From the beginning various influences conspired to incline the country towards the Calvinistic rather than the Lutheran creed. In the end, this tendency completely prevailed. The celebrated *Belgic Confession,* prepared mainly at first by Adrian Saravia,[15] in the spirit and very much in the form also of the Confession used by the Reformed Church in France, was publicly adopted in Flanders in the year 1562; after which, it came into authority by degrees throughout the Church. Especially did the Reformed faith predominate in the seven northern provinces, which in the year 1579 constituted themselves into an independent state.

In the Walloon churches of the Netherlands, using the French language, the Catechism of Calvin was in common use. The Dutch congregations used at first the

---

13. [See the German edition, Johann Andreas Coppenstein, *Uncalvinisch Heydelbergische Catechismus, Veruncalvinisiert* (Heidelberg: Leonhart Neander, 1624).]

14. [Nevin stressed the Netherlands not only because its use of the Heidelberg Catechism was historically important, but also because he hoped to forge stronger ties with the denomination if its leadership could be weaned away from the more rigid forms of the "metaphysical Calvinism" of the Synod of Dort.]

15. [Adrian Saravia (1532–1612) was a Reformed pastor and theologian who worked both in Holland and England. He was latitudinarian on matters of polity (a characteristic that pleased Nevin) and wrote a treatise defending episcopacy. He translated some of the Old Testament books for the King James Bible.]

VII. THE CATECHISM ABROAD

Catechism of Emden, drawn up originally by Lasco,[16] and translated into the Dutch language by John Utenhoven. As soon however as the Catechism of the Palatinate came to be known, it took precedence of both, and continued to grow in credit, till it became in a short time of acknowledged symbolical authority throughout the Church. As early as the year 1566, Peter Gabriel made use of it for public religious instruction, at Amsterdam.[17] In the year 1568, a general synod held at Wesel recommended that in the French churches of the Netherlands the Catechism of Geneva (Calvin's) should continue to be employed, and that where the Dutch tongue prevailed, use should be made of the Heidelberg Catechism; though it was still left free to the particular congregations to follow their own judgment in the case. The same recommendation was renewed in somewhat stronger terms, A. D. 1571. Finally by the national synod of 1574, held at Dort, the advice became a formal decree, and the Catechism was clothed with absolute ecclesiastical authority for the whole Church. After this we find the regulation established that the ministers should everywhere preach upon it on Sunday afternoons, so as to go over the whole of it once a year. The city of Gouda in South Holland undertook, some time afterwards, to introduce a new compend of religious instruction into its schools. But the ministers of the place were called to account, and publicly censured for the attempt. Various other catechisms appeared in the country during the seventeenth century; but they had no weight whatever against the general use and authority of the Heidelberg formulary. This continued in force as the standard text book of the Church, and became at last so identified with its life as to pass often under the title simply of the *Belgic Catechism.*

Here again however, as in other lands, the Catechism drew upon itself the active opposition of many enemies. The Romanists burned it, or whipped it with rods. One Martin Duncan wrote a sort of opposition catechism, on the Roman side. Argument and wit were both employed to bring it into discredit. Among others, some unknown person put forth the "*Thumbscrew;*" in which two weavers are introduced, discoursing of their business at a tavern, when upon a boast made by one of his skill in sorting tangled thread, the other to test his powers brings forward the Heidelberg Catechism, and engages him, in the presence of the landlord and wife, to unravel and adjust certain parts of it according to the rule of faith given in the Bible. The task of course proves desperate; and so all runs out at last into a flood of reproach upon the Catechism, as a most perverse and unsound production. There was opposition to it besides however, from a different quarter. The case of the city of Gouda has just been mentioned. Certain ministers at Utrecht also refused to give it their subscription. In the year 1583, *Dirck Volkartz Coornhart* openly attacked it, in a publication which

---

16. [John à Lasco (1499–1560) was a Polish-born Reformed theologian who was active in the Netherlands, England, and Poland.]

17. [Peter Gabriel (d. 1573) was a Dutch Reformed field preacher who began delivering Sunday afternoon services based on a Dutch translation of the third edition of the German version of the Heidelberg Catechism.]

he dedicated to the States General.[18] He objected particularly to the 5th and 114th Questions, in which so strong a statement is given of the inability of men to fulfil the demands of God's law. A leaven of Pelagianism was secretly active, at different points, in the bosom of the Reformed Church itself; which seems to have been the source of all this unfriendly feeling, towards the Catechism as a rule of faith. The opposition came to its full force finally in the rise of Arminianism, and its revolutionary attempt to overthrow entirely the established faith of the Church.

ARMINIUS, as professor of divinity at Leyden, seemed to be fully satisfied at first with the doctrines of the Heidelberg Catechism.[19] Soon however he began to have scruples with regard to several points; and expressed his wish that there might be a revision of it, for the purpose of removing its objectionable features. Then towards the last again, he insisted that the doctrine of predestination, as commonly held in the Reformed Church, was not to be found in the Catechism, and that his own views here were in full harmony with its teaching. After his death, his friends, the *Remonstrants*, as they were called, discovered the same instability with regard to this point. At times they contended that their own system, and not that of their opponents, was the one contained in the Catechism. But soon again, they would be found taking all sorts of exception to its contents, and objecting to its use in the churches. They urged that it was defective, and needed at least a thorough revision; the more especially as it had been introduced into the Netherlands at the first without any formal, public trial of its merits, such as the importance of the case required.

It was concluded finally on the part of the government to call a general Synod of the Reformed Church, for the purpose of taking this whole difficulty into consideration. In the year 1618, accordingly, was convened the memorable *Synod of Dort*; which resulted in the condemnation of the views held by the Arminian party, and their exclusion from the bosom of the Reformed Church. At this Synod, delegates were present not only from the United Provinces, but also from England, Switzerland, the Palatinate, Hessia, Nassau, East Friesland, and Bremen. The Church in France would have been represented too, had not the French monarch interposed his authority, requiring her delegates to stay at home. The Synod continued its sessions for six months.

Among other matters acted upon, the Heidelberg Catechism was brought under the special review of this venerable body; as the question was now formally submitted, on the part of the Dutch Church, whether it called for any correction or emendation

18. [Dirck Coornhert (1522–1590) was a Dutch humanist scholar, artist, and essayist. He criticized the dogmatism of both Protestants and Catholics, and argued for religious toleration. The state's sponsorship of the Heidelberg Catechism aroused his ire, as did its apparent denial that humans could perform good works apart from grace. His resistance to the Catechism was typical of a liberal movement in the church led by Herman Herbertsz (1540–1607). See Dirck Coornhert, *Proeve van de Heydelbergische Catechismus* (Gouda: Jasper Tourny, 1583).]

19. [Jacob Arminius (1560–1609) voiced concerns that Calvinists were interpreting God's sovereignty in regard to salvation in ways that suggested absolute divine determinism. Against this view, Arminius argued that God's grace can be resisted. He was regarded as the chief theological inspiration of the "Remonstrant" party.]

to make it a fair exhibition of the Reformed faith. The whole being first read over, each delegate was called upon to declare his judgment honestly with regard to this point. The result was a full and unanimous approval of the work; and a formal declaration was filed accordingly, in the name of all present,

> that the doctrine contained in the Catechism of the Palatinate was found to be conformable at all points to the word of God; that there was nothing in it that needed in this view to be changed or corrected; and that altogether it formed a most accurate compend of the Christian faith, being with singular skill not only adjusted to the apprehension of tender youth, but so framed also as to serve the purpose of instruction at the same time in the case of older persons.

When we reflect upon the constitution of the Synod, and consider the circumstances under which this testimony and ratification were given, they must be felt to be honorable to the Catechism in the highest degree, and to invest it with an authority which may well challenge the respect and veneration of the whole Reformed Church.

The greatest attention was paid to catechetical instruction in the Netherlands.[20] The duty was pressed upon heads of families. Schools were required to cooperate with the churches in carrying the system into full effect. The pastors must preach on the Catechism every sabbath afternoon; besides visiting the schools frequently, and holding catechetical exercises, if possible once a week, in private houses. All pains were required to be taken to secure in this way to old and young the benefit of religious knowledge.

It is not strange that such a country should abound in commentaries on the Catechism. Holland seems to have surpassed even Germany itself in this kind of literature. Among all these expositions, none has been more extensively used than that of *Festus Hommius*; which however is more a compilation from various other works, than an original treatise by Hommius himself.[21] The principal contributor to it may be said indeed to have been Ursinus himself, whose expositions, published by Pareus after his death, were to a great extent translated and incorporated into this work. The celebrated English divine *William Ames*, who after leaving his own country for the sake of truth came to stand so high in Holland, published among his other numerous works a *Skiography* also, as he called it, of the Heidelberg Catechism.[22] Of other

---

20 [Much of this material on the use of the Catechism in the Netherlands is based on Van Alpen's *Geschichte und Literatur des Heidelbergischen Katechismus*.]

21 [Festus Hommius (1576–1642) was a Dutch Reformed theologian who opposed the Arminian Remonstrants. See Hommius, *Schat-boeck der verclaringhen over de Catechismus der christelicke religie* (Leiden: Andries Clouck, 1617).]

22. [William Ames (1576–1633) was a Reformed theologian, philosopher, and controversialist who wrote and taught first in England, and then in the Netherlands. His Puritan leanings and consequent clashes with the Anglican Church led him to give up a promising scholarly career in his home country. In the Netherlands he participated in the disputes between the Calvinists and the Arminians, and became a vehement critic of the Arminian faction. The New England Puritans were deeply indebted to his work. See Ames, *Christianae catecheseos sciagraphia* (Franekeræ: Berentsma, 1635).]

Document 1: The History and Genius of the Heidelberg Catechism

names, honorably associated with the work in the same way *Theelinck, Diest, Poudrayen, Heussen, Beltsnyder, Van Leren, De Witte, De Bouma, Bekker, Cocceius, Marets, Vorster, Hakvoord, Van Huttem, Vander Hoocht, Breuklanı, Van Hæke, Venhuysen, Van der Kemp, Van der Steeg*, and a whole legion besides, it cannot be pretended of course to speak here in detail.

It remains to notice briefly the authority of the Catechism in AMERICA.

VIII. The Catechism in America

Reformed Dutch Church. Historical sketch. Present state.
German Reformed Church. General view of its history in America.
Relations of the two Churches at this time.

At a very early period, the Catechism of the Palatinate made its way to the wilds of America. It is now more than two centuries, since it was erected as a standard of evangelical orthodoxy on the island of Manhattan, where the city of New York has since acquired such great importance. Around it rallied the faith and worship of thousands, transplanted through successive years from the old world to the shores of the new. In the midst of ecclesiastical convulsions and political storms, the *Reformed Dutch Church* of America, clinging fast to her hereditary creed, has since struck her roots deep into the soil, and spread forth her boughs luxuriantly to the face of heaven, till she has become known and honored throughout the whole Christian world.[1] A century later in its origin, the American *German Reformed* Church, sprung indeed, in a certain sense, from the same womb, or at least nursed in the beginning by the same maternal arms, comes forward also to claim our attention. She too has had her deep waters to pass through, whose billows had well-nigh swallowed her up. But the favor of "Him who dwelt in the bush,"[2] has accompanied her notwithstanding, in the midst of her most gloomy seasons of trial. Though sorely tossed, during a long night of desolation, on raging chaotic seas, with little notice and less sympathy, she has not abandoned still the martyr faith of her fathers. No force has yet proved sufficient to wrench from her grasp the precious legacy bequeathed to her in the Heidelberg Catechism. At this hour, she cleaves to it with an attachment that promises to grow stronger only as it becomes more intelligent; rejoicing and glorying in it, as at once the true key to the spirit of her organization, and the bond also by which alone she may

---

1. [Nevin used the example of the Dutch in America as evidence of the flourishing that could occur if the Heidelberg Catechism became a significant component of religious identity.]

2. [See Deut 33:16.]

Document 1: The History and Genius of the Heidelberg Catechism

expect to gain new strength and become fully compacted together, in time to come, as a holy temple unto the Lord.

As early as the year 1609, the Dutch found their way into what now forms the harbor of New York, and up the great river which has since borne the name of *Hudson*, the famous sea captain who conducted the expedition. The communication thus opened at this point with the new world, was kept up from year to year, for the purposes of trade; till at length, in 1614, a fort and trading house were erected near the spot on which Albany now stands; about which time also a similar settlement was permanently established on the south-west point of Manhattan island.

The first emigrants were drawn across the Atlantic, of course, by the hope of acquiring wealth. With all their zeal for making money however, they brought with them also their attachment for the principles and order of the Reformed Church, in whose bosom they had been educated; and measures were soon taken to secure religious privileges under the same form in the land of their pilgrimage. There is reason to believe that a church was organized at Fort Amsterdam *(New York)* as early as the year 1619; although no authentic records of its history are to be found, reaching farther back than 1639. The first minister of this church was the Rev. Everardus Bogardus.[3]

The church at *Albany* may claim perhaps as high an antiquity, as that of New York. In the course of years, with the growth of the colony, churches were established also at other points.

The ministers of these churches were ordained by the Classis of Amsterdam, and continued under its ecclesiastical supervision with the approbation of the Synod of North Holland, to which that Classis belonged. In this way the American Church felt almost entirely under the control of this body; and remained thus, through filial respect, in a relation of spiritual wardship to the Classis of Amsterdam, long after their interests required them to form a Classis of their own, and transact their ecclesiastical affairs for themselves. This servile dependence lasted indeed for more than a century. In the end it was an opinion with many that no ministerial authority could be legitimate that did not come from beyond the seas; that no ordination was valid, unless it had impressed upon it the broad seal of the Classis of Amsterdam.

In the year 1664, the colony passed into the hands of the English, and came under the government of the Duke of York. This served in the end to advance the Church of England, at the cost of the Dutch Church. Many families passed over from the last communion to the first. Still the Dutch interest continued to prosper, in close connection with the mother Church in Holland, on to the middle of the following century.

Now however the whole body was convulsed, and threatened with destruction, by the proposal to establish an independent American Classis. Two nearly equal parties, for and against the new movement, were immediately developed in broad battle array; and for fifteen years, the Church became a scene of such ecclesiastical conflict

---

3. [Everardus Bogardus (1607–47) was one of the earliest, if not, the first minister of the Dutch Reformed Church in the Dutch colony in New York.]

and confusion as it is still humiliating and painful to report. In many cases, the general quarrel was carried among the people to actual tumult and deeds of disgraceful violence. On all sides, bitterness and wrath prevailed. The Church rocked, like a crazed vessel in the storm, ready to fall asunder.

To make things worse, the question of *language* now came forward also for practical decision. Must the Dutch Church continue here in America to worship God in Dutch forever; or might it be proper, now that a large part of the people, the young people in particular, were coming to use English only in every other case, to admit this tongue also with proper restrictions into the pulpit? That was the question. Sufficiently easy of answer, one would think, even for a child, in the abstract; but tremendously difficult, as we all know, in actual practice. Strange to tell, the American Dutch Church had contrived to hold it at bay, down till the middle of the last century, sacrificing hundreds of her children, but faithfully upholding the mother tongue in all her places of worship. It was in the year 1764 that English preaching was heard for the first time in the collegiate church of New York. But now the crisis had come. The question, "Shall we allow English preaching in Dutch Churches?" must be met and settled. It must be settled in the affirmative too, if the Church itself were to be saved. But the settlement was not effected without loud, wild uproar. To many, the introduction of English seemed a grand heresy or treason. Did it not strike at the *root* of the Dutch Church? For how could the Church be Dutch, and yet speak English?

In the end however, the controversy *was* settled, on the side of reason and common sense. It was found that the attempt to stem the influx of the English language was about as wise as to think of turning the Hudson up stream. The Church has long since acquiesced in the necessity of sacrificing her old language in order to preserve her old faith; and at this time accordingly, there are but few among all her children to whom a Dutch sermon would be more intelligible than one in Hebrew or Chinese.

The other question came also at length to a happy adjustment; through the agency mainly, we are told, of the late very venerable JOHN H. LIVINGSTON, whose name became so conspicuous subsequently in the history of the Church.[4] An amicable settlement of difficulties, with which both parties now wearied with their own long contention professed to be fully satisfied, was regularly consummated in the year 1772, under the auspices and favor of the Classis of Amsterdam itself. A certain subordination to her authority of the mother Church in Holland was admitted, on the one hand; while on the other, regular judicatories were established for the transaction of all ecclesiastical business in this country. Soon after this, the Revolutionary War took place; which of course suspended, for the time, all communication between the two Churches. Some disposition was shown afterwards by the Church in Holland to

---

4. [John Henry Livingston (1746–1825) was an American Dutch Reformed theologian who had studied in the Netherlands. He was appointed president of Queen's College (now Rutgers) and also taught in the seminary in New Brunswick, New Jersey. He was the most influential American Dutch Reformed church leader of the early nineteenth century.]

exercise still a sort of ecclesiastical supremacy over her American daughter. But this last had now attained to such maturity and self-reliance, as no longer to be satisfied with any such foreign supervision. She proceeded accordingly to take the management of her affairs entirely into her own hands. This was done conclusively, in the end, by the adoption of an independent church constitution, A. D. 1792, suitable to the circumstances and wants of the Church in this country. The Church consisted at this time of about one hundred and twenty congregations, under the care of five Classes.

Previously to this, it had been determined to establish a professorship of theology, with the view of training up a properly learned ministry at home now that all foreign supply was in the nature of the case coming to an end; and on the recommendation of the Classis of Amsterdam, which had been governed in the case by the advice of the theological faculty of Utrecht, the Rev. Dr. Livingston was appointed to take charge of this responsible trust.[5] The Reformed Dutch Church was the first thus to form the scheme of a theological seminary among all the religious bodies of this country. It was long however before the scheme was crowned with any tolerable success. A college had been established at New Brunswick before the Revolution, with which it was intended to connect the professorship of divinity. But the college itself through want of funds soon sank into insignificance; and the professorship, more nominal than real, kept up for a number of years by the gratuitous services of Dr. Livingston in New York, was suffered also to fail at length altogether. An effort was again made in 1807 to resuscitate both interests; but it was not before the year 1825, and after the college had failed in fact a second time, that the whole enterprise was placed finally on a sure and solid foundation. That same year, the patriarch Livingston died.

Since this time, the College and Theological Seminary have both continued to prosper; and with the prosperity of her institutions, the life of the Church has steadily advanced also in other respects. Her organization includes now a General Synod, two Particular Synods, upwards of twenty Classes, and about two hundred and forty congregations, with a membership which is put down in round numbers at twenty-five thousand. As a body, the Church is possessed of great wealth, not being surpassed in this view, according to its size, by any other in the country. It includes also a large amount of intelligence and respectability. No denomination in the country is so fully supplied with ministerial service; nor can any boast of a ministry which as a whole perhaps may be said to be better educated. The Church is accustomed to glory also in its orthodoxy; which is of the high Calvinistic order, according to the measure of the Belgic Confession and the Articles of the Synod of Dort. She places a high value of course on catechetical instruction, and cherishes a special veneration for the Heidelberg Catechism.[6] It may be added that her Liturgy

---

5. [The parallel between Livingston's situation and Nevin's is obvious, including the feature of leading a college linked with a seminary. The relatively happy continuation of the Dutch Reformed seminary's history functioned to give his German Reformed constituency hope for its own future.]

6. It is expressly required by the Constitution of the Church, that everyone who takes a pastoral

VIII. THE CATECHISM IN AMERICA

is based to a great extent, as far as it goes, with some significant modifications, on the old German Liturgy of the Palatinate.

The history of the GERMAN REFORMED Church in America commences a full hundred years later than that of the Reformed Dutch. The oldest congregation is supposed to be the one at *Goshenhoppen*, in Montgomery County, Pennsylvania; whose existence dates as for back at least as 1717. Its first pastor, it would seem, was the Rev. Henry Gœtschy; whose labors however included, in the end, a very wide field besides.[7] He preached statedly to congregations at *Skippack, Falconer Swamp, Saucon, Egypt, Maccungie, Moselem, Oley, Bern,* and *Tulpenhocken*; his circuit comprising a district, which is now covered by four counties, Montgomery, Chester, Berks and Lebanon. *Bæhm's* church, so called after its first pastor, is of like early date. The Rev. Mr. *Weis* began to labor in Philadelphia about the year 1721; though the congregation there did not succeed in completing their first house for public worship before the year 1739. The emigration out of which these churches were formed, seems to have been mainly from the Palatinate.[8]

The Rev. Mr. Weis,[9] in the year 1730, visited Holland, and other parts of Europe, in company with an elder of the name of *Reif,* to make collections in aid of the feeble churches in Pennsylvania. Great interest was taken in their mission; particularly

---

charge shall explain a portion of the Heidelberg Catechism on every Lord's Day, so as to go over the whole if possible every year.

7. [Nevin was wrong about this. Most of the congregations that he mentioned were started by John Philp Boehm (1683–1749). John Henry Goetschy (1718–74) was a German Reformed pastor of the next generation. See Richards, *History of the Theological Seminary*, 25–36. Throughout this section Nevin seems to rely on verbal accounts.]

8. "There is besides in this Province a vast number of Palatines, and they come in still every year. Those that have come of late years, are mostly Presbyterian, or as they call themselves, Reformed; the Palatinate being about three-fifths of that sort of people. They did use to come to me for baptism for their children, and many have joined with us in the other sacrament. They never had a minister till about nine years ago, who is a bright young man, and a fine scholar. He is at present absent, being gone to Holland, to get money to build a church in this city; but they are scattered all over the country . . . They are diligent, sober, frugal, and rarely charged with any misdemeanor . . . There is lately come over a Palatine candidate of the ministry, who having applied to us at the Synod for ordination, 'tis left to three ministers to do it. He is an extraordinary person for sense and learning. We gave him a question to discuss about Justification, and he answered it, in a whole sheet of paper in a very notable manner. His name is John Peter Miller, and speaks Latin as readily as we do our vernacular tongue; and so does the other, Mr. Weis."—[*Extract from a letter of the Rev. Jedidiah Andrews to the Rev. Tho. Prince of Boston, dated "Philadelphia, 8th (October,) 14th 1730."—Hazard's Register, Vol. XV. p. 200 et seq.*]

This extract I owe to Mr. Rupp of Lancaster. The John Peter Miller, it may be added, of whom such favorable mention is here made, united a few years after with the *Sieben-Tæger* or *Dunkers* at Ephrata. [John Peter Miller (1709–1796) was a minister in the German Reformed Church in Ephrata, Pennsylvania who had immigrated to America from the Palatinate in 1730. He is remembered for his excellent translation skills, defection from the Reformed Church, and subsequent participation in the Seven Day Baptist Cloister in Ephrata.]

9. George Michael Weiss (1700–61) came from Heidelberg to Pennsylvania in 1727 and immediately objected to the fact that John Philip Boehm was pastoring congregations without having been ordained. As a result Boehm sought and received ordination by the Dutch Reformed in New York in 1729.]

Document 1: The History and Genius of the Heidelberg Catechism

on the part of the Church in Holland; which was led now in fact to assume a sort of missionary maternal care over this German plantation in America, as earnest at least as any she had ever shown towards her own children in the American Dutch Church. "How many tokens of voluntary beneficence were bestowed upon them," say the Classis of Amsterdam in the year 1751, "both by church judicatories and by private members of our churches, is yet fresh in the recollection of many among us. The impulse of zeal and love in our Christian synods and lower judicatories, and among private members also, seemed to be wrought up even to emulation, in the good work of relieving these necessities."[10] There was still however no regular communication with the infant colony; and for a number of years it appears to have passed again very much out of sight.

In the year 1746 however, the Lord stirred up the heart of one of his faithful servants in Switzerland, the *Rev. Michael Schlatter* of St. Gall,[11] to an extraordinary interest in its behalf. What he learned in various ways of the spiritual destitution of the German churches in America, so affected him with sympathy and sorrow that he found himself, like Nehemiah in the palace at Shushan, no longer able to enjoy any of the comforts that surrounded him at home. He felt himself bound to visit in person, as a missionary, his brethren in the new world; resigned his charge accordingly in Switzerland; travelled to Amsterdam; and received, first from the Amsterdam Classis, and afterwards from the Synods of South and North Holland conjointly, a general commission to visit the American churches, report upon their state, and take such action generally as the case might allow for advancing their spiritual welfare. Particularly he was to ascertain what could be done by different congregations, for the support of the gospel among themselves, in case additional ministers should be sent over from Europe to occupy the ground. Mr. Schlatter arrived in Philadelphia the same fall; became settled at once as pastor of the churches in Philadelphia and Germantown; and from this point, made broad excursions from time to time, as a sort of general superintendent, among the congregations in the country, endeavoring to carry out the general object of his mission. He kept a regular journal of his proceedings, which was submitted to the Dutch Synods, on his return to Holland in the year 1751, and became public afterwards both in the Dutch and German languages. It forms in this way the

---

10. Introduction to Schlatter's Journal. [Schlatter, *The Case for the German Protestant Churches Settled in the Province of Pennsylvania in North America* (London, 1753). This was reprinted in Henry Harbaugh, *The Life of Rev. Michael Schlatter* (Philadelphia: Lindsay and Blakiston, 1857), 118–226.]

11. [Michael Schlatter (1716–1790) was a Reformed minister who had studied in the Netherlands and in Germany. He answered a request from the Dutch Reformed Church for ministers to serve the Reformed congregations in Pennsylvania and the surrounding areas of Maryland, Virginia, New Jersey, and New York. He is most remembered for raising funds in England and Holland for the support of ministers through the circulation of the German and English translations of his journal in 1751, which detailed the dire state in which he found the Reformed congregations in America. Besides organizing the German Reformed churches more effectively and attempting to improve their finances, he initiated educational programs, many of which proved to be unpopular.]

only record we have on the general state of the American German Reformed Church in the middle of the last century.

By means of its light, we perceive the destitutions of the Church to have been deplorably great. There were but four ministers besides Mr. Schlatter himself on the field; all laboring in Pennsylvania; a most insufficient supply, even for the congregations already organized; while the call was heard in every direction, for the formation of new churches. Besides the destitution in Pennsylvania moreover, there was a cry now for help also from New Jersey on the one side, and from Maryland and Virginia on the other; where large German settlements had come to exist, without any pastoral care whatever. It is interesting to find however, in the midst of all this destitution, a general disposition to place a high value on the blessings of the gospel.

The ministers showed much missionary zeal in their work. On the 12th of October, 1746, they held a convention in Philadelphia, the first time they had thus met; and here constituted themselves, by certain articles of agreement, not without many tears, into a formal church association; which grew the following year, September 9, 1747, into what has been since styled the first regularly organized Synod of the German Reformed Church in this country. All hung still however in direct ecclesiastical dependence upon the Church of Holland; and the organization was distinguished afterwards simply as the *Pennsylvania Cœtus.*

Answerable to the zeal of the ministers, seems to have been the readiness of the people also in general to welcome all efforts made for their spiritual benefit. Mr. Schlatter was received everywhere with the most lively demonstrations of interest and regard. The people were melted to tears of thankfulness and joy to find that the Church in Holland was so actively concerned, away beyond the ocean, in their behalf; and the prospect of being able to secure a proper supply for their religious wants, stimulated them to new and extraordinary exertions to accomplish this great object.[12] Mr. Schlatter testifies that he met with a strong desire for evangelical ministrations in every direction; and Christian parents especially were affectingly urgent, in many cases, in their solicitations for help.

> They entreated and implored, with floods of tears, by all that was holy, that I would through the help of God assist them, as far as possible, and provide consolation for forsaken souls. I have observed everywhere the highest regard for the impressive and consoling instructions, given me by the Synod of Holland. Scarcely have I read them in any church, without seeing tears of joy on a

---

12. *Schlatter's Journal.* At Tulpenhocken, he preached to a congregation of more than 600 persons, in a wooden building; the Rev. Mr. Weis and the Rev. Mr. Bœhm both present at the same time; in the midst of much devout attention; the desire and hope of the congregation to secure at last a stated minister plainly legible on their countenances. "They could not conceal the exceeding joy and surprise they felt, in seeing three preachers together, a sight never witnessed there before. The old and the young shed tears of joy. I can truly say that this was to me, and to my brethren, a day of much refreshment. I thought of the blessed Netherlands, where the company of those that preach the gospel is so great; while this extensive country is perishing for lack of teachers."

number of cheeks; while God was praised, for having put it into the hearts of Christians in the Netherlands to care thus for their orphan state.

Before the end of two years, as many as a dozen new charges were organized in Pennsylvania, which declared themselves willing to support pastors as soon as they could be furnished. Deputations came from a distance, in some cases two or three hundred miles, in the middle of winter, to negotiate for spiritual help.

Mr. Schlatter, in the exercise of his missionary trust, visited also the congregations which had begun to be formed in New Jersey, Maryland, and Virginia; all of which appear to have exhibited the same lively interest in the general object of his mission. At Frederick especially, there was much melting of heart, on the occasion of his presence.[13]

Unfortunately however the supply of new ministers from Europe kept no pace with this call for service in America. Of sixteen pastoral charges comprising 48 congregations in 1751, only five were provided with regular preaching. Mr. Schlatter returned to Holland to enlist if possible additional help. His agency was followed with good results. Ministers and schoolmasters were sent over from time to time; as also German Bibles and other religious books. Still the supply was far from being sufficient; for with the rise of new settlements, the emigration still going forward from the Palatinate and Switzerland, the field to be occupied became continually more wide; so that the increase of ministers fell greatly short always of the actual wants of the Church.

With the close of Schlatter's Report, we lose sight of the German churches in America almost entirely again, for the rest of the century. The Pennsylvania Cœtus continued to hold its meetings; and from year to year a regular report of its *"acta"* were forwarded to the Classis of Amsterdam; which had a standing committee *ad res Pennsylvanienses*, whose business it was particularly to look after the interests of this remote spiritual dependency. New ministers came over occasionally. Remittances of money were not infrequent. Altogether [it was] a missionary relation between the two Churches; while at the same time, a very considerable independence was allowed to the American Cœtus; which passed to the exercise of all ecclesiastical powers, ordaining men of its own to the ministry and acting as a synod in other respects, as far as circumstances were felt to make it desirable; all as a matter of course, and without any of that difficulty which had attended the same transition in the case of the American Dutch Church.

This connection with the Church of Holland continued till about the year 1792, when it was interrupted by the wars growing out of the French Revolution.

---

13. "As I was collecting my mind for the introductory prayer, and saw the tears flowing over the cheeks of the people, hungering for the bread of life, my heart was singularly taken and inflamed with love; so that I fell on my knees (as did also the whole congregation), and was enabled with much power and love, and earnest supplication, to commit to the great God the house and worshippers, and to implore upon them his blessing," [*Schlatter's Report.*]

VIII. THE CATECHISM IN AMERICA

The German Reformed Church in America was now thrown entirely upon her own resources, to govern herself and take care of her own affairs as she best could.

The condition of the Church at this time was by no means cheering. Most inadequately supplied with the means of grace, the people had come extensively to undervalue what they did not possess. The forms of religion supplied the place too generally of its life and power. All religious interests moreover had been made to suffer greatly, in the nature of the case, by the agitations connected with the revolutionary war. Left in these circumstances to provide for itself, the German population was but poorly prepared to keep pace spiritually with the progress of the English community around it. Things grew worse indeed, instead of better. The Church lay exposed for years, like an ecclesiastical waste, to the irruption of all kinds of evil; so that many were brought to despair of its ever being recovered again to fruitfulness and life. For a full quarter of a century, and more, the tendencies of the people with regard to religion, seemed to be prevailingly downward rather than upward. On all sides [there was] great spiritual destitution; but no proper feeling now of the fact; a disposition rather to acquiesce in it as proper and right. Increasing wealth; large thriving farms, big barns, abundance of cattle; but along with all, an increase also of covetousness and worldliness, leading men to grudge every dollar given to the gospel as so much money thrown away.[14] The old Catechism and Liturgy [were] held in unrighteousness; associated with the notion of mere outward rites and forms; in broad opposition to personal heart religion, as something fanatical, methodistical, and mean. Well may we say that the German Reformed Church had fallen into a state of great spiritual declension, approximating even to death itself. To the view of many indeed, she appeared to be dead altogether.[15]

After all, however, the desolation was general only; not universal and complete. There was still a living spirit at work in the Church, at least at certain points; and with some persons, we may trust, at all points; which in due time began to make itself felt as a regenerating power in the ecclesiastical life of the body. In this character it became necessarily an effort in favor of spiritual religion, in opposition to a religion of mere dead forms. Naturally too it stood more or less closely connected with the religious life of the surrounding English denominations, and seemed to accompany in this way the introduction of the English spirit into the Church. It was hardly to be expected, in these circumstances, that due account would be made always of what was good in the original constitution of the German Church itself; the temptation was strong rather to identify this with the abuses into which it had been found to run, and to seek help from a different quarter. This however could not fail of course to call forth a violent reaction again on the opposite side; an anti-English, anti-Puritan, anti-Methodistical movement; not without *some* feeling of right; but blindly hostile at bottom to all serious godliness, at least for the most part. Such we find to have been the course of things

---

14. [Nevin encountered this phenomenon in his own fund-raising efforts for the seminary.]

15. [It is significant that here Nevin identified the main problem with the denomination as being dead formalism rather than the excesses of revivalism.]

Document 1: The History and Genius of the Heidelberg Catechism

in fact; and in this form the Church was brought gradually to assume, after some time, a more encouraging aspect; the new spirit, as it might now be called, proving too strong, linked as it was with the inward life of religion, to be controlled and repressed by the old spirit and its dead forms.

In the year 1817, the minutes of the Synod were printed for the first time. Two years later, the body was divided into subordinate judicatories, under the appellation of *Classes*. The first *Delegate Synod* was held in 1820. The Church consisted now of about fifty ministers, and six times as many congregations.

The year following, 1821, a small party in East Pennsylvania seceded from the general body of the Church, and assumed a separate organization; not satisfied with the English tendencies that were coming to prevail; jealous for old usages and forms; deprecating in particular the project of a theological school; afraid of synodical consolidation, tyranny and oppression. Much of the same feeling prevailed, for a number of years subsequently, in a large part of the Church; closely connected with a similar spirit of jealousy, awakened by similar causes in the Lutheran communion. The agitation indeed became at last exceedingly great; revealing itself in public popular meetings, speeches and resolutions; full of indignation and violence towards the church movements of the time; as though they belonged to a general conspiracy against liberty itself.[16]

It deserves to be noticed as a remarkable fact in the history of the Church, that the secession now mentioned, which was known henceforward as the *Free Synod*, after a separation of sixteen years, applied as a body to be restored again to its old connection, and was received accordingly. This event took place in the year 1836, at the meeting of the Synod in Baltimore.

The measure of establishing a Theological Seminary, long talked of, went into effect finally in the year 1825; the Rev. Dr. LEWIS MAYER acting as professor;[17] first in Carlisle; soon afterwards in York. [This was] a most important interest; involving in fact the existence of the Church itself in the end; which was left however for years to hang in painful jeopardy, through the want of proper support; and which cannot be said, even to this hour, to have become fixed on any sure and solid foundation. It has grown notwithstanding into considerable importance. Out of the High School to which it gave rise at York, sprang finally *Marshall College*, in whose connection it now stands at Mercersburg. Both institutions were permanently located here, in the year 1836.

Along with this movement, other evangelical interests came in now also for their share of attention. Something was done towards the cultivation of a missionary spirit.

---

16. [This schism may have been due to a desire to preserve local identity and autonomy on the part of some congregations, which generated a fear of centralized control, including centralized control of the training of ministers. See Steven Nolt, "Liberty, Tyranny, and Ethnicity: The German Reformed 'Free Synod' Schism," 35–60.]

17. [Louis Mayer (1783–1849) was the first professor of the German Reformed seminary. Favoring an amalgam of Reformed theology and mild Enlightenment rationalism, he was opposed to the German Idealism represented by his younger colleague Frederick Rauch. Clashes with Rauch contributed to his resignation.]

VIII. THE CATECHISM IN AMERICA

A growing sympathy began to appear, in different directions, with the great religious and benevolent movements of the day generally, as they had come to engage the attention of other Christian denominations. Sabbath Schools were formed. Prayer-meetings, special services for the promotion of religion, revivals, and all kindred forms of action, became common at least in a part of the Church; in spite of all the prejudice which continued to be felt towards them in another part.[18] [This was] altogether a great change undoubtedly in the state of the German Reformed Church; a true moral resurrection, we may say, so far as it has gone, in which all good men are bound to rejoice.

Yet it may not be disguised, at the same time, that the influence under which this favorable change took place, was in some respects foreign from the original character of the Church itself; and that it included tendencies also, to say the least, which could not fail, if carried forward, to subvert this character altogether. We have no right to complain of the influence itself on this account; it was in the highest degree seasonable, salutary, necessary. In no other way perhaps, was it possible to reach effectually the wants of the case. But even a salutary reaction may bring with it new dangers of its own; which it would be folly to overlook, because of the good with which they may thus happen to be associated. Methodism, in the last century, was salutary for the Church of England, in the way of provoking spiritual life; but could it be, substituted, without disastrous loss, for the proper constitutional spirit of the Church of England itself, in its own sphere? So in the case before us. The renovation of the German Church required, we may say, that it should be brought into active contact with a church life which had not been originally its own; that the leaven of Puritanism in particular should be made to enter to some extent into its constitution. But it did not follow, for this reason, that its own original and properly constitutional life was in its own nature bad, and worthy only of being forever cast aside, to make room for the genius of Puritanism in full.[19] It might still be fundamentally a better church life than this. The spiritual tendency in the German Church then became itself wrong, when its zeal for practical piety was allowed to run into the character of an actual hostility to the established institutions of the Church; as though *these* were fairly chargeable with the evils which were felt to be at hand; so that the only remedy in the case must needs be, to demolish the old church system entirely, and re-construct all again upon a new and altogether different model.

To this extreme, as we all know, the tendency in question at one time threatened to carry the whole Church. The properly German spirit of the body fell in some measure into the back-ground, as something antiquated and obsolete; while purely English modes of thinking, of the modern Puritan order, came forward to occupy its

18. [The churches of the Free Synod were suspicious of all such ecumenical endeavors, for they threatened local control of finances and programming. The missionary endeavors, the Sunday School movement, the Bible societies, and programs of social amelioration (such as temperance and abolition) were felt to be dominated by the "Puritans" of New England.]

19 [Nevin here was informed by the theme common to Romanticism and Idealism that every culture possesses its own unique "spirit" or "life" that is manifested in its art, religion, and politics.]

Document 1: The History and Genius of the Heidelberg Catechism

place.[20] Catechumen classes became unfashionable; confirmation lost its credit; the old church festivals fell into neglect; liturgical services seemed to savor of formality and superstition. Forms altogether were counted dangerous. The idea of sacramental grace was practically renounced. The entire theory of religion, in a word, was quietly changed into another form. It was no longer the theory embodied in the Catechism, and interwoven throughout with the ancient usages and institutions of the Church.

Such we say was the form in which this new spirit seemed for a time to threaten at least, the very foundations of the old German church life. The case was made worse by the simultaneous working of the same evil precisely, only under a more aggravated character, in the Lutheran Church; where the anxious bench was fast becoming for many a more powerful sacrament than baptism; and Luther's cardinal article of justification by faith seemed well-nigh ready to lose itself forever in the methodistical imagination of justification by feeling.[21]

Happily however this revolutionary tendency in the German Reformed Church has received a check. It has begun to be perceived that it is not necessary to destroy the old, in order to redeem it from abuse; and a better sense than formerly is coming to prevail of the constitutional character of the Church itself, as compared with the spirit of other American denominations. It is felt that it must be an ecclesiastical solecism for the Church to pretend to stand in any other character than that which belongs to her by true historical descent. In all this we have reason to rejoice. It augurs well for the prosperity and importance of the body, in time to come. Let us trust then that the process of church resurrection, years ago commenced, will be carried out happily to its proper completion in the direction now taken; not by parting with any truly valuable acquisition already made, on the opposite side; but by so fastening the new life of the Church on its own original root and trunk that it may rise towards the future, vigorous and rich always with the full wealth of the past.

The German Reformed Church in the United States includes in her connection, at this time, about 240 ministers, and upwards of 700 congregations, embracing not less probably than 75,000 members. A vast population besides of course is comprehended by outward connection, in her proper ecclesiastical charge. The organization falls into two Synods; one in the west, with six Classes; the other east of the Alleghany Mountains, with eleven Classes.

The only symbolical book which the Church acknowledges is the Heidelberg Catechism.

A feeling of more than common ecclesiastical relationship has subsisted from the first between the Reformed Dutch and German Reformed Churches in this country.

---

20. [Following Rauch, Nevin assumed that English culture is more pragmatic and action-oriented than is the speculative and mystical culture of the Germans. That activist sensibility, according to the Mercersburg theologians, manifested itself in the Puritan passion for constructing "godly commonwealths." See Rauch, *Psychology*.]

21 [Nevin feared that the Methodist movement, like all forms of Pietism, gave the impression that individuals are justified by the strength and sincerity of their faith,]

Steps were taken a few years since however, to bring them still closer together, in the way of something like a formal union. The result was the formation of what has been styled the *Triennial Convention;* in which the two German Synods, and the General Synod of the Dutch Church, are brought together by special delegates, once in three years, to transact in an advisory way such business as may be found to be of common concern. A praiseworthy experiment certainly, in the cause of Protestant catholicity; but not likely after all, it may be feared, to issue in any solid permanent advantage to this cause.[22] It is not easy to see indeed how, under any circumstances, a connection so loose and general could amount to anything more than the friendly correspondence previously established between the two Churches; while it is very plain that it must be attended with some dangers altogether its own. It has begun to appear already in fact that the arrangement is on, which is very liable to become a source of difficulty and distrust; and many in both Churches are coming to believe that the sooner it is brought to an amicable and quiet close the better.

For with all their ecclesiastical affinity, the two Churches are by no means prepared to unite. The genius of the German Church has always been more free theologically than that of the Dutch; too much so altogether, in the view of this last, to be thoroughly orthodox. Both hold the Heidelberg Catechism; but the Dutch Church binds it to a given sense by the Belgic Confession and the Articles of Dort; while the German Church significantly refuses to acknowledge any such rule. She will have no symbol but the free, untrammeled Catechism itself. The Dutch Church again includes in its constitution more of the Puritan element than has yet come to prevail in the German Church. So we may say, in some sense, from the first; in Holland, as compared with Germany; although we meet with much here in the beginning, the old Calvinistic theory of the sacraments for instance, that belongs to a different system. But the fact noticed characterizes more particularly, of course, the state of the Church in this country. Here, hemmed in and surrounded on all sides by Puritan forms of thinking, it was hardly possible that, with the loss of her own tongue and cut off from all correspondence with the mother country, she should *not* give way largely to the power of this widely predominant system. It is well known besides, that the Church has received, into its ministry particularly, a considerable amount of *Scotch* life;[23] which in the nature of the case may be supposed to have exerted a modifying influence upon its character, in the same general direction. The German Church, on the other hand, has less original affinity with Puritanism, and

---

22. [Although Nevin hoped that the German Reformed and the Dutch Reformed churches in America would recognize and appreciate their common rootage in the Heidelberg Catechism, and although he saw them as allies in supporting catechetical instruction, he feared that the scholastic and speculative spirit encoded in the decrees of the Synod of Dort made any closer intimacy between the German and Dutch Reformed unwise. Nevin did not want the Catechism to be interpreted through the lens of predestinarian theory. He was also suspicious of the seeming Zwinglian tendencies in many Dutch Reformed Church ministers' understanding of the Lord's Supper.]

23. [Nevin's nemesis John Williams Proudfit was an example of the influx of scholastic Scottish-descended Presbyterians into the Dutch Reformed Church. See the following essays.]

Document 1: The History and Genius of the Heidelberg Catechism

her circumstances have been more favorable to the preservation of her own distinctive character; though full of spiritual disadvantage in other respects. It is only of late, we may say, that a different tendency has shown itself to some extent in her communion; in connection with the revival of a more active religious life, and in the way of opposition to the dead formality that prevailed before. But as we have just now seen, this tendency is already losing itself again in the perception that the constitutional life of the Church is after all itself the best form in which to seek her spiritual renovation; and her effort is now accordingly to understand and carry out practically her own original spirit, rather than to fly from it as something false and bad. This she finds is likely to prove in the end the true secret of her strength and prosperity; as it has already served indeed to make her more united and harmonious within herself, than she ever was before. Her relations moreover to the old world, now brought so near by constant correspondence and emigration, indicate more and more clearly every year, that no other course than this would be answerable at all to her ecclesiastical vocation. Never was it more reasonable and important than it is just at this time, in that as a *German* Church she should remain true to her German character, and *not* renounce it in favor of any other. This is coming to be felt apparently more and more on all sides; so that the question may be considered as now fully settled indeed, not without something of a crisis—especially within the last two years—that the Church will adhere still to the genius of her own historical life, as having clearly no call or right to persist in her separate organization at all, under any other character. She will be German, and not Puritan; Catholic, as well as Protestant; historical, no less than biblical; bound, and at the same time free; in opposition to all mechanical tradition, all lifeless stability, whether in theology or church life; cherishing childlike reverence for the past, only to look beyond the present always, with youthful faith and hope, to a more perfect future.

In these circumstances, the Dutch and German Churches might still walk happily together in the bonds of the Triennial Convention, (since the connection after all is very loose) if only full allowance were made on each side for the distinctive character of the other. But this is more perhaps, than the case as the world now stands can reasonably be expected to admit; and if so, it must be plain of course that the two bodies are not yet prepared for union, even under this loose and imperfect form. It may be doubted whether either branch of the German Church in this country can enter into any very close connection with a body of different origin and constitution, without being required to sacrifice for the purpose all its own nature. Such a sacrifice, involving as it must a total divorce from the rich church life of Germany itself, ought not to be thought of at this juncture. The most natural alliance after all in this case would be one between the two German bodies themselves, as in Germany; on the basis of their common nationality and substantially common faith. If such a union *could* be consummated, in an inward solid way, it would open at once, in the relations now coming to exist, between the old world and the new, a long vista of results, vast and momentous, to the end of which no human vision could reach.

IX. Theology of the Catechism

Seal of general approbation. Ecumenical character. Objectiveness. Earnest practical spirit. Doctrinal reserve. Opposed to all Pelagianism. Theory of sin and redemption. Relations to high Calvinism on the subject of the decrees. Theory of the sacraments, and of good works.

The high estimation in which the Heidelberg Catechism has always been held in the Church forms in itself an argument of its great worth. When we consider the circumstances under which it appeared, and then take into view the reputation and authority which it so soon acquired in every direction, we are made to feel that it must have been pre-eminently adapted to meet and satisfy the ends embraced in its design. Its authors were as theologians comparatively young; not in the rank properly of the *Reformers* technically so called; without any particular ecclesiastical weight for the Church at large. The Palatinate was just introduced into the sisterhood of the Reformed Churches, with large participation still in the old Lutheran life with which it was on all sides surrounded. The Catechism was wholly a provincial interest; intended to serve the wants of a single country, without reference to any broader use. And yet it was received almost at once, throughout the entire Reformed Church, with admiration and respect, as the best formulary of its kind which had yet been produced within the communion. The church had other valuable catechisms already in use; and it might have been expected that the one framed by Calvin in particular would have been more likely than any other to assert a general permanent supremacy within her borders. But all gave way in this respect to the new Catechism of the Palatinate. The authority of others continued to be at best provincial or national only, and not general. So also [it was] with the different Confessions of Faith. Each country had its own, formed for itself and limited to its own use. Only the Heidelberg Catechism might be said to carry a truly ecumenical character as the acknowledged symbol of the Church as a whole. It was welcomed and applauded in Switzerland, France, England, Scotland, and Holland, as well as by all who were favorably disposed towards the Reformed faith in Germany itself. Nor was this praise transient; an ephemeral burst of applause, succeeded again by general neglect. On the contrary, the authority of the Catechism grew with its age. It became *the* Catechism emphatically of the Reformed Church; the counterpart in full of Luther's Catechism, in its central relation to the other great Protestant confession, as distinguished by Luther's name. In this character, we find the Heidelberg Catechism quoted and appealed to, on all sides, by both friends and foes. It formed the text book of theology in learned universities. Profound divines, (*Ursinus, Alting, Piscator, Cocceius, A. Schultens,*[1] *&c.*) have made it the basis of their dogmatic systems, in this way. Innumerable pulpits and schools have lent their aid to give it voice and power in the world. It has been as the daily bread of the sanctuary to millions, generation after generation. Never was a catechism more honored, in the way of translations, commentaries and expositions.

All this implies an extraordinary merit in the Catechism itself. We may allow indeed that the terms in which some of the old divines have spoken of its excellence are carried beyond due measure. But this general testimony of the whole Reformed Church in its favor must even be of force to show that they had good reason to speak loudly on this point. Such wide-spread and long continued symbolical authority, admitted in so free a way, could not be the result of mere accident. To command such favor the Catechism must have been undoubtedly *worthy* of it in its own constitution.

The fact of its meeting such general favor is important in another view. It shows that the Catechism was the product, truly and fully, of the religious life of the Reformed Church at the time. No creed or confession can be of genuine force that has not this character. The life must go before the creed, and pour itself into it as its proper form.[2] The creed may come to its utterance in the first place, through the medium of a single mind; but the single mind, in such case, must ever be the bearer of the general life in whose name it speaks; otherwise its voice will not be heard nor felt.[3] Here is

---

1. [Albert Schultens (1686–1750) was a Dutch theologian and philologist who pioneered the comparative study of Semitic languages.]

2. [This concept of "life" as something prior to doctrine and creed was partly acquired by Nevin through his early engagement with the works of the English poet Samuel Taylor Coleridge (1772–1834). He often included excerpts of Coleridge's writings in a journal, *The Friend*, that he published during his early years at Western Seminary. An American edition of Coleridge's *Aids to Reflection* had appeared in 1829, two years before Nevin began using Coleridge-like vocabulary. For a presentation of Nevin's concept of "life" in this early period, see David Layman, editor's introduction to *Born of Water and the Spirit*, The Mercersburg Theology Study Series, vol. 6, 16–19. The centrality of "life" in Nevin's thought continued unabated. In the mid-1840's he attached an abridged translation of one of the German theologian Carl Ullmann's (1796–1865) essays describing Christianity as a "life" to his own *The Mystical Presence*. (See Ullmann, "Preliminary Essay," in Nevin, *The Mystical Presence*. This can be found in Nevin, *The Mystical Presence and the Doctrine of the Reformed Church on the Lord's Supper*, ed. Linden J. DeBie, 15–39. Ullmann's German original was *Über den unterscheiden charakter oder das Wesen Christenthums*.) Nevin later recalled that diverse appropriations of vitalistic language by German scholars such as Neander (1796–1850) and Isaak Dorner (1809–84) had nourished his theological development.]

3. [Nevin rejected theories such as that held by the British essayist and historian Thomas Carlyle (1795–1881) who argued that "great men" are the principal dynamic factors in historical movements. Nevin was familiar with Carlyle's understanding of Luther through his colleague Philip

the proper criterion of a true church confession, whether it be in the character of a liturgy, catechism, or hymn book. It must be the life of the Church itself, embodied through some proper organ in such form of speech, as is at once recognized and responded to by the Church at large as its own word. This relation between word and life is happily exhibited in the case of the Heidelberg Catechism. Though in one sense a private work, it was by no means the product of simply individual reflection, on the part either of one or many. Ursinus, in the preparation of it, was the organ of a religious life far more general and comprehensive than his own. The Catechism is the utterance of the Reformed faith, as it stood at the time, and found expression for itself through his person. The evidence of this is found in the free, full response with which it was met, on the part of the Church, not only in the Palatinate, but also in other lands. It was as though the whole Reformed Church heard, and joyfully recognized, her own voice in the Heidelberg Catechism. No product of mere private judgment, or private will, *could* have come thus into such universal favor.

This peculiar virtue of the Catechism reveals itself in its whole constitution and spirit. It is characterized by a sort of priestly solemnity and unction, which all are constrained to reverence and respect. In attending upon its instructions, we seem to listen to the voice of the Church, and not to the words of any single human teacher. It was this feeling, no doubt, which led some formerly to challenge for it a kind of supernatural character, something like inspiration in fact, or at least an extraordinary presence of the Spirit in its composition. Ursinus, with all his abilities, was felt in this work, as Bullinger expresses it, to have fairly transcended himself. He did so in fact; and in a deep and true sense, we may even say that he *was* inspired. He spake not of himself nor from himself simply; but it was the life of the Church, (which is always truly a divine life) that sought, and found expression through his words. It is this preeminently that imparts to the Catechism its power and glory.

It is not merely a form of sound words for the understanding; as though one had sat down and in the way of abstract reflection compiled a scheme or theory of the Christian faith for others to look upon and study. The Catechism is more than mere doctrine. It is doctrine apprehended and represented continually in the form of life. It begins with the misery of man in his natural state; sets forth, in the second place, the glorious plan of redemption; and represents, in the end, the proper practical fruits of this great salvation, in the life of the regenerated man. The method is said to have been borrowed from St. Paul's Epistle to the Romans; which in like manner exhibits first the helplessness of the human race under the law, then the gospel method of righteousness, and finally, from the twelfth chapter to the end, the duties which spring naturally from the principle of Christian gratitude. However this may be, the construction of

---

Schaff's *The Principle of Protestantism*, which Nevin translated from German to English in 1845. See *The Development of the Church*, ed. David Bains and Theodore Trost, 117. Nevin's view was closer to that of G. W. F. Hegel (1770–831) who proposed that great leaders simply instantiated the general dynamics of an historical epoch. Familiarity with Hegel was partly mediated to Nevin by his colleague Frederick Rauch.]

Document 1: The History and Genius of the Heidelberg Catechism

the Catechism as a whole is simple, beautiful and clear; while the freshness of a sacred religious feeling breathes through its whole execution. It is for the heart full as much as for the head. The pathos of a deep toned piety flows like an undercurrent through all its teachings, from beginning to end. This serves to impart a character of dignity and force to its very style, which at times, with all its simplicity, becomes truly eloquent. What can be more fine, for instance, than the question and answer with which the whole system is introduced? Never perhaps have the substance and worth of the Christian salvation, as a whole, been more comprehensively, forcibly, and touchingly presented, in so small a compass. We may refer also to the 27th and 28th Questions, as particular instances in which the same elevation of tone and expression is strikingly displayed. The Catechism of Luther is eminently distinguished for its excellence also, in the whole view now described. It is high praise to say of the Heidelberg Catechism that it can bear a favorable comparison with that symbol in this respect. As it regards popularity and force of expression indeed, the Catechism of Luther is allowed to have the advantage; but the Reformed Catechism excels it, on the other hand, in the richness of its contents, and the order with which they are inwardly digested.

The Catechism is of course throughout decidedly Protestant. Occasionally it assumes even an openly polemical aspect towards the errors of the Church of Rome. It is besides clearly Calvinistic or Reformed, in opposition to the Lutheran confession; particularly in the form in which this last is exhibited, as complete finally in the Form [Formula] of Concord. At the same time however, its character is remarkably broad and free. This results from its practical constitution, as just explained, and from the fact no doubt also in some measure of its German origin. All thorny, dialectic subtleties, of force for the understanding only, and having but little value for the heart and life, are for the most part carefully avoided.[4] The knotty points of Calvinism, as they have been called, are not brought forward as necessary objects of orthodox belief one way or the other. Only in such form could the Catechism have gained such universal credit and authority, as we find allowed to it in fact throughout the entire Reformed Church. For there were material differences in the Church itself, with regard to the way in which certain doctrines were to be carried out theoretically to their last consequences for the understanding. Had the Catechism allowed itself to pronounce a definite decision on such points of divergent opinion, it must necessarily have shrunk in the same proportion into the character of a particular rather than general confession. By avoiding this, it became a mirror for the true life of the Reformed Church as a whole. France, Switzerland, Germany, and Holland were not exactly of one mind,

---

4. [Nevin reveals his indebtedness to authors like Neander and Coleridge, both of whom distinguished "understanding," which Coleridge defined as the faculty of judging according to sense, from a higher form of knowledge, which he often called "reason." Reason, unlike the more empirical understanding, could intuit supersensible realities. The distinction of "understanding" and "reason" was rooted in Kant's critical philosophy, although Kant severely restricted the scope of reason, particularly in regard to metaphysics, and would have vigorously discounted the notion of supersensible intuitions. For Coleridge on reason, see, for example, *Aids to Reflection*.]

as to much that might be comprehended in the details of the Calvinistic system; but they could move hand in hand together, *so far* at least as they were required to go by the Heidelberg Catechism; and on this basis accordingly they were willing to join their common faith and common profession, without regard for the time to such differences as might possibly lie beyond.

It has sometimes been made an objection to the Catechism that it is not sufficiently definite and explicit on some of these hard points of Calvinism.[5] But we should consider this to be rather one of its highest recommendations. For children particularly, such excursions into the territory of metaphysics, in the name of religious instruction, are ever to be deprecated and deplored. But we may go farther, and say that they are wholly out of character in any church confession or creed. No Church has a right to incorporate them in any way into its basis of ecclesiastical communion. In any case an extensive, complicated creed must be regarded as a great evil; and the Church is to be congratulated that can be content to measure its orthodoxy by so simple and general a formulary as the Heidelberg Catechism, to the exclusion of every more narrow standard. No platform of faith should ever be *less* broad. Whether even this be not too narrow, may well be made a question.

Some have pretended indeed that the Catechism carries, occasionally at least, an actually Arminian sense, in the view it takes of the plan of salvation.[6] Arminius himself, as we have seen, appealed to it at times, as being in harmony with his own views; and the same thing was done also by his followers. But the appeal was not felt to carry with it any real weight. The Arminians showed plainly enough that they did not themselves honestly believe the Catechism to be on their side; while the whole Reformed Church, with the Synod of Dort at its head, united in holding it up to the view of the world as a true witness of their common faith. So far as the plan of salvation is concerned, in its relation to human sinfulness on the one hand and God's grace on the other, the system of doctrine contained in the Heidelberg Catechism, as a whole, is clearly the same that was held by the Evangelical Protestant Church in general, in the sixteenth century, in opposition to the pelagianizing errors of Rome.[7]

5. [Nevin is alluding to the Reformed scholasticism that came to expression in the decrees of the Synod of Dort and continued to flourish at Princeton Seminary.]

6. [Jacob Arminius (1560–1609) voiced concerns that Calvinists were interpreting God's sovereignty in regard to salvation in ways that suggested absolute divine determinism. Against this view, Arminius argued that God's grace can be resisted or accepted, which implied some degree of responsible freedom even in sinful humanity. This belief could be taken to suggest that Christians can take some credit for their own salvation by virtue of not resisting grace. The enemies of Arminius regarded this as a subtle form of Pelagianism in that the individual's own efforts contributed decisively to her salvation.]

7. ["Pelagianism" was a term of abuse deployed against Christians influenced by the British monk Pelagius (355–420), whose teachings became popular in Rome. It is not entirely certain what Pelagius himself taught, but his theology seems to have revolved around the convictions that humans are not born with debilitating corruption and that the human will remains free to choose righteous action. Consequently, the term became linked with the concept of self-justification through the performance of good works. In the Reformation era Protestants habitually accused Catholics of being Pelagian.]

It begins accordingly, by asserting in the strongest terms the general depravity and corruption of our nature. Not only the fact that all men are involved in the contradiction of sin is affirmed (Ques. 3–5), but this fact is referred to its true ground as holding in the very life of the race itself (Ques. 6, 7). The evil is deep and broad as humanity itself, and not of a kind therefore to be ever surmounted by the will of the single sinner separately considered. This is a blow at the root of all Pelagianism. An organic ruin needs an organic redemption.[8] That which is born of the flesh, is and must remain flesh; can never leave itself behind; can never transcend its own sphere (Ques. 8). Our spiritual nature is in ruins; inclined to all evil, disabled for all good but still under law, and possessed of a capacity for salvation. If it be asked, *how* this ruin took place, the Catechism pretends not to fathom the full depth of the mystery. It asserts only that it came not from God, but from the free will of man himself. Our first parents were holy, and had power to keep their first estate; but by willful disobedience they fell, and so brought sin and death upon the entire race. The origin of sin, the Catechism seeks not to explain.[9] It rejects Fatalism on the one hand, and Pelagianism on the other; and like the bible itself, takes its course firmly between these two irreligious extremes, leaving the understanding to get along with its own embarrassment in the case as it best can. There are truths that transcend the understanding; to be grasped only by a higher power.

What was lost in Adam, the Catechism teaches in the next place, has been recovered for us again, and more than recovered, in Christ. He is the fountain of the whole Christian salvation, (Ques. 18), having in himself all the qualifications that are needed to constitute a perfect medium of reconciliation between the human nature and the divine (Ques. 12–17); being in his own person in fact the fullest conjunction of both; so that "the same human nature which hath sinned," is brought to make a full satisfaction for sin, and to become thus at the same time the righteousness of God, in Him as the second Adam. To this high benefit the individual sinner is advanced, by union with Christ, through faith; which involves a living apprehension, not simply of an abstract doctrine, but of the whole perennial *fact* of Christianity as embodied in the Apostolic Creed (Ques. 21–59).[10] The great cardinal doctrine of justification by faith

---

8. [Nevin opposed the theory that the guilt and corruption of the original sin of Adam was only imputed to us by God because Adam was the legal representative or "federal head" of the race. Such a view was common among American Presbyterians and some Congregationalists. Against this Nevin insisted that Adam was not only an individual, but also the race, because all individuals are "organically" connected to him. Adam's corruption, and therefore also his guilt, is in us. See Nevin, *The Mystical Presence and the Doctrine of the Reformed Church on the Lord's Supper*, ed. Linden J. DeBie, 15–39.]

9. [Here Nevin was resisting scholastic Reformed speculation that the fall of Adam and Eve had been part of God's eternal plan, so that God would be able to manifest God's glory through the drama of redemption and damnation. This view was suggested by certain portions of the Westminster Confession.]

10. [Nevin is suggesting that the imputation of Christ's righteousness, the basis of the sinner's justification, is a fruit of the believer's union with Christ and consequent participation in Christ's life. Sanctification also is the fruit of union with Christ for it is the blossoming of Christ's life in the

alone, through the imputation of Christ's satisfaction, righteousness and holiness, in opposition to the idea of all merit on the part of the believer himself, is asserted in the strongest language (Ques. 60–64). This threefold imputation itself implies however, that the objective righteousness which is thus set over to our account in Christ involves from the very start the principle of our personal sanctification. Apprehended by faith, it has become already the power of a new divine life in the subject of this faith; "for it is impossible that those who are thus implanted into Christ, should *not* bring forth fruits of thankfulness" (Ques. 64). Faith itself, comprehending thus in itself the whole force of the Christian life, is no product of the human will. The Holy Ghost "works it in our hearts by the preaching of the gospel, and confirms it by the use of the sacraments" (Ques. 65–85).

All is of grace; and the divine sovereignty reigns supreme throughout the whole work. But now when we fall back on the deep questions that concern the relation of this sovereignty to human freedom, the Catechism modestly forbears again to return any answer. Not only does it shrink from asserting the supralapsarian theory of the decrees, the only consistent form of metaphysical Calvinism; but the whole doctrine of the decrees is passed over in silence, except as comprised in the providence of God.[11] The question of predestination is brought no closer than this (Ques. 20), that of Adam's fallen posterity those only are saved by Christ "who are ingrafted into him, and receive all his benefits, by a true faith." Still less of course, do we hear of anything like a decree of absolute reprobation.[12] The Catechism again knows nothing formally of a limited or particular atonement, restricting the intrinsic force and value of Christ's work to a certain portion of the human family, with the exclusion of the rest from all possibility of salvation.[13] On the contrary, regardless of all difficulties and true to all sound religious feeling, it asserts, with the unequivocal sense of the scriptures themselves (Ques. 37), that he "sustained, in body and soul, the wrath of God against the sins *of all mankind*;" which is of course implied also, in the previous

---

believer's heart. See Evans, *Imputation and Impartation*.]

11 [Supralapsarianism was the theory that God's decrees of election and reprobation logically preceded God's decree (or permission) of the fall of Adam and Eve. The doctrine was based on the assumption that God's ultimate purpose must have been the manifestation of God's glorious judgment toward some and God's glorious mercy toward others. Humanity's fall into sin was a means toward that end. Supralapsarianism was proposed by the Reformed theologians Beza and Zanchius. It was not affirmed by the Synod of Dort, but neither was it rejected.]

12. ["Absolute reprobation" was the theory that God not only elected certain individuals for salvation quite apart from any foreseen merit or faith on their parts, but also ordained certain individuals to damnation (or passed them over), quite apart from God's foreknowledge of their specific sins or lack of faith. Of course, in this view, all of fallen humanity was deserving of divine condemnation, so God was not being unjust in not giving the gift of faith to those chosen for reprobation.]

13. ["Limited atonement" was the belief that Christ died for the elect only, and that the benefits of his reconciling acts were never intended to be extended to humanity as a whole. This view was adopted by the Synod of Dort.]

declaration (Ques. 16) that the satisfaction which God's justice requires for sin must be made *by the nature* which hath sinned.

So also if the question be asked, whether God's grace be irresistible in the conversion of men, and incapable of being altogether lost afterwards, the Heidelberg Catechism refuses to give an answer.[14] As it does not teach an unconditional election, so neither does it make salvation to be independent of all contrary motion on the part of the human will. The doctrine of the final perseverance of the saints, as it is called, it leaves in a great measure unsettled.[15] The nearest approach to it is in the first Question. This however places the security of the believer after all, not so much on the absolute purpose of God to save him, as upon the actual relation at the time subsisting between him and his faithful Savior Jesus Christ. The inward assurance of eternal life at least, as we all know, may still fail, through a relapse into sin; and it is not clear, from the Catechism, that along with this loss of the Holy Spirit the regenerate may not in some cases lose also their whole interest in Christ, and so fall back to perdition.

Here then is a material difference between the Heidelberg Catechism and the symbolical books generally of the Reformed Church. It may be said indeed that the Calvinistic points to which we have now referred are at least involved in the system which it teaches. So it must have seemed of course to that part of the Reformed body for which these points had become of confessional authority; otherwise it could not have been endorsed, by the Synod of Dort for instance, as sound and orthodox. But this only shows that the Catechism leaves these points untouched. They lie *beyond* its horizon.[16] The Belgic Church might consider them necessary to complete its system; but there was always a part of the Reformed Church which thought differently. The Catechism is so constructed as to allow this difference; and this not by accident, as we may clearly see, but with deliberate design. The authors of it seem to have held their own theological convictions purposely in abeyance, that they might be true to the objective church life with which they were surrounded. This we all know included much that could never have been satisfied with anything like extreme Calvinism on the subject of the decrees. From all this accordingly the Catechism was made carefully to abstain.

---

14. [The view that the elect could not resist the offer of God's grace was affirmed by the Synod of Dort. According to this doctrine, faith should not in any manner be regarded as the product of a free human response to God's grace or cooperation with it.]

15. [The belief that the elect could not fall from grace but would persevere in grace throughout their lives was adopted by the Synod of Dort.]

16. [Throughout this section Nevin argues that the Heidelberg Catechism refuses to legislate on the abstruse issues of the extent of the atonement, the order of God's decrees, the relation of grace and freewill, the perseverance of the saints, and unconditional election and reprobation. For Nevin, the Catechism's wise reticence on these imponderable matters stood in contrast to the speculative dogmatism of a major strand of the Dutch Reformed tradition.]

IX. THEOLOGY OF THE CATECHISM

Some have even charged it with contradictions on this account; because it appears occasionally to favor in one direction, what it might be thought to oppose again in another. But in this it resembles the Bible itself; which also gives countenance occasionally to views that seem metaphysically to conflict with each other; though no doubt they are capable of full reconciliation, in some deeper ground, which we perhaps may have no power now to fathom.[17] All great truths indeed are polar; [they] comprise in themselves opposite forces or powers, whose very contradiction is found to be necessary at last to the everlasting harmony of their constitution.

The Catechism, like the Bible, is willing to tolerate *such* contradictions; and does so in fact. Its orthodoxy is not necessarily that of the Belgic Confession. It allows this of course, but is does not require it. As a platform of ecclesiastical communion it includes thus much; but we are bound in conscience to say, it includes also a great deal more.

On the sacraments, the Catechism is explicitly Calvinistic; steering throughout a careful middle course, between Lutheranism on the one hand, and Zwinglianism on the other.[18] Here again however, we may observe a certain effort after the widest practicable comprehension in its representations. There was some Zwinglian feeling in the Palatinate, it would seem, along with the predominant Lutheran and Calvinistic; and we find accordingly a sort of irenical condescension in the Catechism even on this side, such as we do not meet with in the Calvinistic symbols commonly. The Gallic, Old Scotch, and Low Dutch Confessions, for instance, are more uncompromisingly strong. The Catechism does not go so far as to say, with the Low Dutch Confession, that what is eaten in the sacrament is the *very natural body of Christ* ("ipsissimum Christi corpus naturale"), and that what is drunk is his *true blood*. Still its general sense is sufficiently clear, as corresponding in full with the sacramental theory of Calvin.[19]

Faith, uniting us in the power of a common life with Christ, is the fountain of all good works. The third part of the Catechism is occupied accordingly with the law of God, as the rule of Christian life, and the duty of prayer. Here the Ten Commandments and the Lord's Prayer are introduced as the basis of all its instructions. In Luther's Catechism the Commandments come first. It has been said that the opposite order as exhibited in the Heidelberg Catechism, (and in Calvin's also) indicates a legal tendency on the side of the Reformed Church. But it is hard to see why. The law is

---

17. [Nevin here is reflecting the Hegelian notion that there may be some truth in each of the two poles of a dialectical tension, which may be reconciled in a higher synthesis.]

18 [Nevin feared that the followers of Zwingli construed the Lord's Supper as a strategy to trigger the remembrance of Christ's passion, while the strict Lutherans believed that Christ's presence was linked to the physical elements of the bread and wine. Neither view, he cautioned, suggested a real mystical presence of Christ.]

19. For a full exhibition of this theory, as embodied in the symbolical books of the Reformed Church generally in the sixteenth century, the reader is referred to the author's work entitled the *Mystical Presence*.

the rule of that new obedience to which the believer is formed in Christ; and this obedience does but carry out and complete the faith from which it springs. As works without faith have no worth, so also faith without works is dead.[20]

20. [Nevin here is appealing to the "third use of the Law," which was a major theme in Reformed theology. The Law is not just a threat that terrifies the conscience and awakens the longing for forgiveness, nor is it only a deterrent that restrains sin through the threat of punishment. Luther had emphasized these "two uses of the Law," and subsequent Lutherans continued to stress them. But in the Heidelberg Catechism the Law has a crucial "third use," for it is also a welcomed guide to direct the lives of the saints. (Although this "third use of the Law" became a hallmark of Reformed theology, Melanchthon and even Luther himself had espoused it, with careful qualifications, and it is affirmed in the Lutheran Formula of Concord.)]

X. Church Spirit of the Catechism

German origin. Relations to Lutheranism and the Augsburg Confession. Prussian Church. Positive and catholic. Historical basis in the Apostles' Creed. Sacramental feeling. Churchly associations. Old Palatinate Liturgy. Baptismal educational religion. Confirmation. Conclusion.

To understand fully the character of the Heidelberg Catechism, regard must be had to the ecclesiastical connections and conditions in the midst of which it had its origin. It cannot be estimated fairly apart from its history. Every genuine spiritual creation, such as we suppose the Catechism to be, includes in itself necessarily a life of its own, which is at the same time the product organically of the general life, with which it is surrounded and from which it springs. Only in view of its birth-soil and native associations can it be at last truly and adequately comprehended.[1]

In the case before us two facts particularly, under this view, need to be kept always in mind. The Catechism is of *German* origin, and we may say also in a certain sense of *Lutheran* extraction. [These are] two most significant considerations truly, in the determination of its church character.

The Catechism, we say, is German; the growth of German soil; the product of German life. Its birth is not to be traced to Switzerland, Scotland, or Holland. Though approved by the Synod of Dort, it is not just such a Catechism as a large part of the Synod of Dort would itself have produced. Still less is it such a Catechism as the spirit of English Puritanism might have been expected to produce, in the days of Cromwell, or at any time since.

It is also closely related, in origin and constitution, to the Lutheran confession. This is shown by its history, and lies involved besides in the fact of its being German. The peculiarities of Lutheranism, as distinguished from the general tendency of the Reformed Church, in their common opposition to the Church of Rome, resolve themselves very much at last, it must be confessed, into the distinctive genius of the

---

1. [Here Nevin's indebtedness to Frederick Rauch is evident. See Rauch, *Psychology*.]

Document 1: The History and Genius of the Heidelberg Catechism

German national mind; of which Luther himself may be taken as a living, personal mirror and type; its most perfect personification in fact, in the sphere of religion. Any *German* Church must be expected then, in the nature of the case, to appear in some affinity with the religious life of this communion. Even the Roman Catholic Church in Germany shows a material difference, in this view, from the character which distinguishes the same faith in Italy or France. So also, in the case of the German *Reformed* Church. With the German nationality for its basis, the German life circulating through all its veins, it could not be the same thing in full with the same confession in Holland or Scotland. With all their opposition, the two creeds in Germany could never fully fly asunder; their mutual repulsion always showing in fact the force of a mutual attraction, as though each were all the time tormented with the secret feeling that it could not be complete without the other. It is only in the German Church indeed, we may say, that the two great divisions of the Protestant evangelical faith have seemed able, to this day, to understand one another at all, in their principal difference, so as to perceive clearly either their own contradiction or agreement in its true ground. The Church of England has sometimes been styled *Ecclesia Lutheranizans*; but the title belongs more properly to the Reformed Church of Germany itself.[2]

The Palatinate, as we have seen, was originally Lutheran. Its transition moreover to the Reformed confession was not intended to be a renunciation of Lutheranism in full; but is to be viewed rather as a protest merely against the form in which it was held by such men as Westphal, Hesshuss, Brentz, Andreæ, &c; the high orthodoxy in short of the Stuttgart Confession, which became triumphant afterwards in the Form [Formula] of Concord.[3] The Lutheran Church of Germany included in itself from the start two diverging tendencies; closely related; but necessarily variant and hostile at the same time, if allowed to assert their claims. It was believed by such men as Melanchthon, that no rupture was required on this account. The orthodoxy of the Church, they supposed, might safely make itself so wide as to embrace both forms of thinking. But this expectation was disappointed. It came, as we have seen, to an open war; deep, earnest, violent, and long; between high Lutheranism and Calvinistic Lutheranism; agitating all Germany. The movement in the Palatinate, and in Bremen, belonged to this great dialectic process; as did also the movement afterwards in Anhalt, Hesse, Brandenburg; the whole development, in one word, of the *German Reformed Church*. All hinged on the eucharistic question; and in the case of this question, on the mode simply, not the fact, of Christ's real presence in the sacrament. The controversy lay not between Lutheranism and Zwinglianism, but between Lutheranism and Calvinism. No rebellion, properly speaking, was intended against the Augsburg Confession.

2. [Nevin is implying that the German Reformed Church had more spiritually in common with moderate Lutheranism than it did with the English, Scottish, Swiss, and Dutch Reformed traditions.]

3. [In 1559, the theologians of Württemberg convened a synod at Stuttgart to compose a confessional document that would distinguish Lutheran orthodoxy from Zwinglian and Calvinist doctrines, particularly in regard to the sacraments. The ubiquity of Christ's body and the "*communicatio idiomatum*" were affirmed as articles of belief.]

X. CHURCH SPIRIT OF THE CATECHISM

In the form in which it had been expounded and defined by Melanchthon himself, all were willing to own its authority.[4] The Heidelberg Catechism was designed to interpret, rather than to contradict, the Augsburg Confession; to explain the sense, in which it was held by the Church in the Palatinate. Frederick the Third had himself signed it, in its unaltered form, at Naumburg, a. 1561, a short time before the Catechism appeared; to which subscription we find him afterwards publicly appealing as still valid, in the year 1566, when called to account by the imperial diet at Augsburg; with such success too, that his right to be recognized as a member politically of the Lutheran confession was formally acknowledged by this august body. Ursinus moreover was the special friend of Melanchthon himself, the author of the Augsburg Confession; to which of course he stood sworn also, in its Melanchthonian sense, as a teacher in Bresslau.[5] How in such circumstances could the Heidelberg Catechism be anything else than simply German Calvinistic, or Semi-Lutheran we may say, in its theological constitution and spirit?

Heidelberg professed indeed, in this case, to make common cause simply with Wittenberg, against the high toned theology of Tübingen and Jena. The theologians of Wittenberg, it is true, hard pressed after the death of Melanchthon to maintain the place, pretended not to acknowledge this connection. But all the world has since allowed that they were chargeable in doing so with disingenuous equivocation, being brought into a snare in the case by the fear of man.

The history of the general German Reformed Church subsequently serves throughout to exemplify still farther its close relationship, as now affirmed, with the Lutheran Church. It was always more or less reserved on the subject of the decrees; particularly in Anhalt and Brandenburg; quite satisfied here in fact, for the most part, with the orthodoxy of the Augsburg Confession. The *Repetitio Anhaltina* proclaims in fact its formal assent to this Confession in full; and on the article of the Lord's Supper goes so far as to say that "along with the bread and wine is truly distributed and received, that very body which was offered for us on the altar of the cross, and the self-same precious blood that flowed from the sacred wounds of Christ, freely shed for

---

4. In this sense, it must have been subscribed by Calvin himself, when he stood in the service of the Church at Strasburg. See Planck's Gesch. d. prot. Theol. book VI, chap. 1. [See Gottlieb Jacob Planck (1751–1833) *Geschichte der protestantischen Theologie* (Göttigen: Banderhoed and Ruprecht, 1831).] Also, Salig's Hist. of the Augsburg Confession, book II, chap. 13. [See Christian August Salig (1692–1738), *Vollständige Historie der Augsburgischen Confession*, 3 volumes (Halle, 1730).] Calvin was both preacher and professor in Strasburg, and stood in high credit at the time with the Lutheran Church generally; taking part in its public transactions. "I do not reject at all the Augsburg Confession," he says in one of his letters, a. 1557, "having long ago very cheerfully subscribed to it, in the sense in which it has been explained by its author." In the year 1539, he presented to the ecclesiastical authorities of Strasburg a particular confession of his doctrine on the Lord's Supper, signed by Farel [1489–1565] and Viret [1511–71] along with himself; in which it is most explicitly declared, that Christ communicates to us, not simply his spirit, but the substance also of his flesh and blood, for our nourishment unto everlasting life.

5. [Ursinus had taught in Bresslau, which was a Lutheran city.]

Document 1: The History and Genius of the Heidelberg Catechism

us for the remission of sins." Specially noticeable is the spirit of the German Reformed Church of Prussia as exhibited to us originally in the electorate of Brandenburg. The celebrated *Confession of Sigismund* [1614] broadly declares its adhesion to the Augsburg Confession, as presented to Charles V in the year 1530; asserts the sacramental presence of Christ's true body and the true blood, in the Lord's Supper; but only in the Calvinistic sense; while, at the same time it distinctly rejects the idea of all unconditional election and reprobation. Along with this Confession the Reformed Church of Brandenburg acknowledged as authoritative for its faith, the Articles of the *Leipsic Conference*, held in the year 1631, and the *Declaration of Thorn,* bearing the date 1645. Both these instruments again do homage to the Augsburg Confession; though refusing to admit of course the high Lutheran positions of the Form [Formula] of Concord as forming any part of its true and proper sense. On the sacramental presence, the language of both is peculiarly strong.[6]

In the end, as we all know, it has come to a formal union of the two confessions, not only in Prussia, but throughout Protestant Germany generally.[7] The confessional differences are not yet indeed fully abolished; but it has been felt that they were no sufficient reason to keep the two Churches asunder. They constitute now (as they ought to do all the world over), one Evangelical Communion; and in such form are at this time actively engaged in working out, as they best may, the difficult theological and ecclesiastical problems that lie in their way.[8]

---

6. These confessions of Leipsic [Leipzig] and Thorn grew out of efforts made to secure a religious union between the Lutheran and Reformed Churches in the first case, and with the Romanists also in the second. They show how far the Reformed theologians were willing to go towards a common rule of faith. The design in both cases failed; but the spirit of the Reformed Church was exemplified at least, with good advantage, in its publicly adhering, as it did subsequently in the kingdom of Prussia, to the irenical platform here proposed. A certain *Dr. J. Berg* [John Bergius, 1587–1658], of orthodox memory, appears particularly prominent, on the Reformed side, in the conference at Leipsic. Here it is said, in plump terms, that in the Lord's Supper, along with the bread and wine, the substantial essence (das Wesen und die Substanz) of the body and blood of Jesus Christ himself, is the object of an actual *present* participation to all worthy communicants, through the power of faith. No less plump and explicit is the Declaration of Thorn. The elements, it tells us, are most certain m[e]dia [trans: thoroughly] and effectual instruments, by which the body and blood of Christ are exhibited or offered to all communicants, and truly given and received, in the case of believers, in the way of salutary, vivific food to the soul; we participate especially in the very substance of his body and blood, that self-same victim that hung upon the cross for the sins of the world; and this, not only as regards the soul, but as regards our body also; for while the act of participation is primarily spiritual, by faith, the force of it extends also to our whole persons, "inserting and uniting our very bones into Christ's body, by the power of his Spirit, unto the hope of the resurrection and eternal life, that we may be flesh of his flesh and bone of his bones." *Niemeyer's Coll. Conf. Ref. pp.* 662, 663, 681–83 [Hermann Agathon Niemeyer, *Collectio Confessionum in Ecclesiis Reformatis* (Leipzig, 1840)].

7 [Nevin is alluding to the fact that in 1817 King Frederick Wilhelm III of Prussia issued a series of decrees that created the United Church of Prussia, the state-sponsored union of Reformed and Lutheran traditions. Several other German states then followed this example.]

8. Much is still wanting to make this union inwardly complete, in the full reconciliation of all confessional contradictions. As it is however, it must be considered a great point gained in the history of the Protestant Church. No wonder that good men in Germany, not understanding our difficulties

X. CHURCH SPIRIT OF THE CATECHISM

In the midst of all this close correspondence with German Lutheranism, the Heidelberg Catechism has always been recognized as the general, distinctive, confessional formulary of the whole German Reformed Church. This single fact reflects great light on its true character and spirit.

The life which it embodies is that of the Reformed Church in Germany in the period of the Reformation; when religion had vigorous hold on the hearts of men as a divine fact, and before the rationalistic tendency involved in Protestantism had become strong enough to make itself felt on the general faith. The Catechism is itself a strikingly impressive monument of the inwardness and fullness that characterized the religious life of the Church at the time when it was formed. Whatever we may think of the theological controversies with which the spirits of men were so actively inflamed on all sides, it is quite plain that the age was filled with the consciousness of a divine reality in the objects of its faith, such as we too often miss in the exhibitions of later history. The Catechism is not cold workmanship merely of the understanding. It is full of feeling and faith. The joyousness of a fresh, simple, childlike trust appears beautifully, touchingly interwoven with all its divinity. It is only here and there that we feel in its pages the presence of the war spirit, with which its origin was on all sides surrounded. As a whole, it is moderate, gentle and soft; an image thus, we may suppose, of the quiet though earnest soul of Ursinus himself. It is positive or affirmative mainly in its teachings, rather than negative. Such was the character of the Protestant faith generally in the sixteenth century. It did not stand in mere contradiction to the faith of Rome. It had large contents of its own, an inward independent life, which it felt bound to assert; and it was the assertion of this life only, which threw it necessarily into the attitude of protest against the errors of the ancient Church. In all this of course, there was no thought of breaking all historical connection with the life of the ancient Church itself. On the contrary, the sense of the objective, the historical, the

---

in this free country, should get out of patience at times with the *American* German Churches, for not consenting to unite in the same way. No wonder that many coming over here, should feel it a sore sacrifice, to be put back once more on an election between *Lutheran* and *Reformed,* after having so happily surmounted all opposition of this sort in their native land. The two German confessions *should* be one, in America as well as Europe. It is a clear case. The Augsburg Confession, as explained by Melanchthon and signed by Calvin, is abundantly broad enough for both Catechisms; and on this platform the *whole* German Church, if still true in any measure to its original life, might well stand shoulder to shoulder, and hand to hand, in the Lord's work. And it deserves to be well considered, whether vast spiritual interests are not coming to be periled by our present position, in its relation particularly to the emigration which is so rapidly accumulating upon us from Germany. It is not saying too much to affirm that as a *United Evangelical Church* our opportunity for acting advantageously on this emigration, from Maine to Texas, would be vastly more large and full of promise than it is at present. Such a United Church may yet force itself forward, under less favorable auspices. For it is hardly to be expected that the emigrant population, so very large as it is and is coming to be, will consent to be ruled permanently by our American view of what is expedient and necessary in this case; while it is not to be desired certainly that it should be left, without ecclesiastical organization, at the mercy of fanaticism and infidelity. As things are at present going, the old German Churches are of very little account religiously, for the ocean of German life that is now rolling in upon us, wave after wave, from the shores of the old world.

Document 1: The History and Genius of the Heidelberg Catechism

catholic, and the always enduring, in the Church, as distinguished from the waywardness of mere private judgment and individual will, wrought powerfully in the whole theology of the age. The grand characteristic of the period was its power to *create*, rather than its power to destroy; unlike the genius of that shallow war which is now too often waged against Rome from the standpoint of mere rationalistic contradiction and denial; strong in its affectation of pulling down, but impotent as water towards all purposes of building up. The sixteenth century was not simply Protestant; it was Catholic, *Reformed* Catholic, at the same time. So especially, we may say, in Germany, the cradle properly of the Reformation life. In this catholic church spirit, the Heidelberg Catechism largely participates. In no other Reformed symbol probably, are the great constituents of the true and proper character of this confession, liberty and reverence for authority—the sense of the individual and the sense of the general—more fairly and happily combined.

A fine illustration of the catholic, historical feeling of the Catechism is found in the fact that so large a part of its instructions are based upon the Apostles' Creed.[9] In this, it is true, it does but show itself conformable to the general spirit of Protestantism in the age in which it was formed. No catechism could be considered complete, no confession sound, in the sixteenth century, without a formal recognition of this ancient ground work of Christian doctrine. The case, we all know, has become lamentably changed in later times. It is not saying too much to affirm that with a large part of our modern Protestantism, the Creed has come to be well-nigh shorn of its credit altogether. Even where it may be allowed theoretically to be of some authority, it is but too common still to make little or no account of it practically. It has become silent, to a fearful extent, in the family, in the school, and in the pulpit. Rationalism and the spirit of sect—the great plague of our present Christianity—can never be expected of course to take any pleasure in the Creed. Puritanism too, though professing to regard it with some favor, cannot be expected to admire it much at heart. It is hard for it to say: *I believe in a holy catholic Church;* even if the article on the descent to Hades, were out of the way. In what Puritan church is the Creed recited? In what Puritan family is it repeated by the children? Is it of any true *symbolical* force, in one word, for Puritanism at all? Puritanism sees nothing divine in the Creed; feels no respect for it, as the first grand outbirth of the Christian life in the form of believing confession. Puritanism in fact holds itself competent in full, to manufacture, on the shortest notice, for the use of Christendom, a *better* creed; or if need be, half a dozen better Creeds; quarrying the whole material fresh from the Bible, in the way of private judgment, without any thanks to this old *Symbolum Apostolicum* whatsoever.[10] Altogether [this is] a very

---

9. [Nevin wrote a series of articles in 1849 on the importance of the Apostles' Creed for *The Mercersburg Review* and then reworked and published the material as *The Apostles' Creed: Its Origin, Constitution, and Plan* (Mercersburg, PA: H. A. Mish), 1849. See *The Early Creeds*, ed. Charles Yrigoyen.]

10. Witness the endless covenants of single Congregational churches in New England and the West. Witness the Confession of Faith, not long since framed by a few New England missionaries at Constantinople, for the organization and control of the new Protestant Armenian Church, whose

curious and significant fact; well worthy of consideration, in any estimate that may be made of the posture and spirit of modern Protestantism, as compared with the Protestantism of the sixteenth century. For in the end it is most certain that this low esteem of the Creed is at once the fruit and evidence of a low conception also of the Church. A sense for the Creed, and a sense for Historical Religion and the Church, must ever go hand in hand together; and where the first is wanting in any measure, we may know assuredly that the second is wanting also to the same extent.

The Heidelberg Catechism reveals its church character in its reverence for the Creed. It not only makes use of it as a text, but enters with hearty interest and affection into its general spirit. Take it altogether, its commentary on "the articles of our Catholic undoubted Christian faith," as here brought into view, must be considered peculiarly happy. We have to regret indeed always the turn given (Ques. 44) to the clause, in the fourth article, *He descended into Hell*.[11] The Catechism asserts, on the topic, what is in itself a most interesting and important truth; but we must shut our eyes to all history, to suppose that it *is the* truth intended in this particular case by the language of the Creed. The doctrine is sound, but the interpretation is bad.

---

foundations have been laid in that city; a work professedly drawn by *original* deduction from the Bible; elaborated in the course of a few days or hours; without one syllable in recognition of the ancient fundamental Creed of Christendom! The greatest marvel of all perhaps, is that this bold way of going to work in so solemn a case should be quietly accepted so generally (by the whole American Board for instance), as nothing out of the way, a mere matter of course. Witness again the articles of our late World's Convention at London. Christendom to be united on *such* a basis! An Evangelical Alliance that might seem never to have heard of the Symbolum Apostolicum!—A much sounder feeling is at work in Germany, with all its errors. At this very moment an active protest is sounding on all sides against a Form of Ordination proposed for the use of the United Evangelical Church in Prussia, by the General Synod which met last summer in Berlin; on the ground that it does not embrace in full the Apostles' Creed. The formula is good as far as it goes; better altogether than the articles of the London Convention. But why should it not give us the Creed? cries all pious Germany, with Hengstenberg and his thunder-toned *Evangelische Kirchen-Zeitung* at its head. [This is] a most wonderful fact, in the present posture of that spiritually tumultuating land. The cry will be heard. No Confession will be permitted now to stand in Germany that shall refuse to do full homage to the Apostles' Creed. So let it be, throughout the universal Church! [Ernst Wilhelm Hengstenberg (1802–69) was a German Lutheran biblical scholar who taught in Berlin. He championed Lutheran orthodoxy in opposition to the spread of rationalism in the Protestant churches and their theological faculties. Although he had initially supported the union church of Prussia, after the mid-1840s he began to sharply critique it and to defend Lutheran confessional orthodoxy against its dilution by Reformed doctrines.]

11. [The meaning of Christ's "descent into Hell" had been hotly debated in the Reformation era. Lutheran and Reformed theologians were divided among themselves on this issue. Calvin had rejected the belief that Christ had liberated the deceased faithful who had lived before Christ and were imprisoned in Hell, and regarded the phrase as pointing to the completion and severity of Christ's earthly sufferings (*Institutes of the Christian Religion*, Book 2, chapter 16). Many subsequent Reformed theologians proposed that the phrase pointed to Christ's spiritual anguish before his death as an aspect of his bearing of the terror of God's judgement upon sin. Nevin sought to recover the older patristic sense of the doctrine, suggesting that the concept indicated Christ's victory over death and separation from God and his pledge to the deceased that they would be raised from their "intermediate state." See Erb, *Nevin's Theology*, 336.]

Document 1: The History and Genius of the Heidelberg Catechism

The church feeling of the Catechism appears again, in the high account which it makes of the sacraments; here also in full harmony with the general Protestant spirit of the sixteenth century, and in noticeable contrast with much at least of the Protestant spirit of the present time. The sacraments are held to carry with them an objective force. Their constitution includes grace, for all who are prepared to turn it to account. Thus Baptism is not only a symbol of the washing of regeneration (Ques. 73), but a solemn authentication of the fact itself—the proper body of its inward soul—in all cases where the requisite conditions of its presence are at hand.[12] Children too, born of believers and so entitled to the privilege, must be admitted into the Church by this ordinance (Ques. 74), as the seal and pledge of their saving relationship to Christ; and should be trained up as Christians, children of God and not children of the devil, accordingly. So again, the Lord's Supper is the actual bearer of a divine life; the mediatorial life of the Son of God, designated as his body and blood; with which he feeds the souls of his people, by the power of the Holy Ghost, unto everlasting salvation (Ques. 75). It is not a token merely of our interest in the atonement of Christ, but serves actually to unite us more and more to his sacred body (Ques. 76) thus helping forward that great mystery by which we are to become fully like him at last in the power of a common life.

In full harmony with the catholic and sacramental character of the Catechism, as now represented, we find it, to be churchly also in all its connections and associations; to an extent indeed, which it is not easy for us now, in the Puritan atmosphere with which we are surrounded, fully to perceive and admit. Its proper historical relations in this view, particularly as they are presented to us in the *German* Church, are far enough removed from that character of spiritualistic baldness in which too many imagine the perfection of Protestantism to consist at the present time. They include the altar, the organ, and the gown; church lessons, and a church year, with its regular cycle of religious festivals; repetitions of the Lord's Prayer and Creed; liturgical services; an entire order of worship in short, which to the nostrils of modern Puritanism, it is to be feared, would carry no small stench of popery itself throughout.[13] Think of the fact however as we may, there it stands; and we must let it go for what it is worth. It shows at least that the original and proper church life of the Heidelberg Catechism was something different from modern Puritanism; and that Puritan associations and

---

12. [Nevin objected to the notion that baptism was a testimony to a grace that was experienced in the general subjective religious life of an individual, quite independently of the ecclesial context of the ritual. Rather, the sacramental rituals, situated in the ongoing life of the church, have the power to certify and accomplish what they promise. For Nevin's writings on baptism, see *Born of Water and the Spirit*, ed. David W. Layman. See especially Layman's introduction to "Noel on Baptism," 80–81 in that volume.]

13. [All of the things that Nevin mentions had been criticized by the Puritans (and other iconoclastic strands of the Reformed tradition) as remnants of Roman Catholic piety. In Nevin's America aversion to the liturgical year, vestments, etc. was still strong in many Congregational, Presbyterian, Baptist, and broadly evangelical circles.]

modes of thought are not exactly the sphere, in all probability, in which this life is likely to be either rightly understood or fully turned to account.

Let us cast our eyes here a moment, on the old German Liturgy of the Palatinate; once used even in this country; now fast sinking into oblivion.[14] It is divided into four parts: I. DOCTRINE; II. PUBLIC PRAYER; III. SACRAMENTS; IV. CHURCH USAGES. *Part First* contains directions for preaching and catechetical exercises; among other things: a form of exhortation and brief prayer introductory to the sermon; how preaching is to be conducted on the Sabbath; on the prescribed week days, viz. Wednesdays and Fridays; on days for humiliation and prayer, (first Wednesday of every month); on festival days, &c.—*Part Second* contains prayers to precede and follow the sermon; special prayer for Christmas, New Year's Day, Good Friday, Easter, Ascension, and Whitsuntide; morning and evening prayer for every day. *Part Third* contains an Admonition on Holy Baptism; Form of Baptism; Preparation for the Holy Supper; Communion service; Use of the keys in ecclesiastical discipline. *Part Fourth* provides for festival and holy days; for church Psalmody and clerical costume; announcements of marriages; visiting the sick; prayer with the sick; with the dying; administration of the sacrament to the sick; visiting prisoners; burial service.—Such are the contents general of this old German Reformed Liturgy.

The sacramental doctrine of the Liturgy corresponds in full with that of the Catechism. In one case it goes so far as to speak of redemption as not only promised, but freely granted, (*versprochen und geschenket*) in holy baptism. All baptisms must be in the church. The service includes a repetition of the Creed. In the case of the Lord's Supper, after the preparation service, all persons intending to commune are required to come forward and take their place round the altar to receive instruction and make confession of their repentance and faith, according to a particular form prescribed for the occasion; then the pastor *shall descend from the pulpit*, and take his place *before the table* or altar, for this service; the form itself includes, 1. an admonition to

---

14. I have no copy of this old Liturgy at hand; but remembering to have met with one some time ago in the possession of the venerable father Pomp of Easton, I took the liberty of requesting the Rev. J. H. A. Bomberger, of that place, to make a special inspection of it for my use, in the present case. This service he has done to good purpose; and it is *through his eyes* accordingly, as Carlyle would say, that it is here made to pass resurrectionally before our vision. An interesting old relic; handed to the Rev. *Nicholas Pomp*, father of our Easton patriarch, on his leaving Germany as a missionary to this country, last century; date 1763; reprint according to the title page of the edition of 1684; which again, as we are informed by the introduction, is substantially the original *Kirchen-Ordnung* of the Reformed Church of the Palatinate, as published by Frederick III, in 1563, and afterwards revived, in 1585, by the prince John Casimir; only "an etlichen wenigen Orten verbessert und erklært" [trans: improved and expanded in a few places]. Are there any other copies of this old Liturgy still in the country? Could it not be deposited from some quarter in our Seminary Library, as a sort of "fossil remain," to let the German Church see hereafter what she was *before the flood?* [John Henry Augustus Bomberger (1817–1890) was a German Reformed minister who graduated from Marshall College (1837) and Mercersburg Seminary (1838) and later went on to become president of Ursinus College. He was a radical abolitionist and is known for his condensed translation of the *Schaff-Herzog Encyclopedia of Religious Knowledge*.]

self-examination; 2. a confession of sin, to be repeated aloud by the people, it would seem, after the pastor ("*sprechet derhalben mit mir*"); and finally, 3. a formal absolution of the truly penitent, with the judgment of God against such as do not repent. It is directed that the Lord's Supper be administered in towns twice a month, in villages and country places four times a year, viz. on Christmas, Easter, Whitsuntide, and the first Sabbath in September; more frequently, if convenient.

It has been already mentioned that the Liturgy of the Reformed Dutch Church in this country is founded on this old Liturgy of the Palatinate. It includes however only a small part of the original work, and this with some modifications. Its first prayer seems to be from some different quarter; the second however is a literal translation, not of the prayer for ordinary Sabbaths, but of that used on the monthly supplication days, ("Bættagen fuer alle Noth und Anliegen der Christenheit"); not quite suitable of course for ordinary occasions. In the Form for Baptism, the German service is plainly followed; some entire passages literally translated; the Creed omitted. In the case of the Lord's Supper, the preparation service, confession, absolution, &c. are *not* found in the Dutch Liturgy. This last uses however the same high sacramental tone in the ordinance itself; true in this respect to the old Reformed doctrine, as presented in the Belgic Confession. The full Burial Service of the German Liturgy is wanting altogether in the Dutch; as also all the prayers for Festival Days, of which this last takes no recognition.

To complete the view now taken of the churchly spirit of the Heidelberg Catechism, as illustrated in these connections and tendencies, it remains only to notice briefly the theory of religion on which its whole meaning and use are found to be constructed. This assumes throughout that the Church is, in a certain sense, the medium and bearer of spiritual life for her own children; that whilst religion is a preeminently individual and subjective interest in one view, it is still, in another, conditioned and upheld, like all life, by an objective ground that lies without and beyond its particular subject altogether. The children of believing parents have a right to baptism; by this holy sacrament they are translated from the world over into the Church, and have a real title thus to all the grace of the new covenant; it is the duty of parents to believe this, and to train them up in the same faith; which in such case is itself the Christian consciousness, while the want of it is baptismal infidelity; all the appliances of Christian education are to be employed to form them to a pious and holy life, with the confidence that what is thus done for them in the Church and through the Church (the family being in this case but a part of the church system), carries along with it a truly divine force; at the proper season, they must be handed over to the Church, to be prepared by catechetical discipline for the other great sacrament; and finally, thus prepared, they must be introduced to all the privileges of their church state, that they may grow up from this point onward by proper use of the means of grace, to the stature of full manhood in Christ. Right or wrong, this is the theory of the Catechism; as it was the theory, indeed of the whole Church in the sixteenth century unless we choose to include under this name the fanaticism of the Anabaptists, and other demonstrations of a kindred kind. Religion, according to this view, is something that rests in the general life of the Church; capable of organic transmission; not by blood, nor by the force of mere natural example and teaching; but by the order of grace, as a divine, historical constitution in the Church itself, including resources, living *capacities* and powers, in its own being, for this very purpose. Men may refuse to believe all this, and act accordingly; but that only shows their natural infidelity for all the realness of Christianity. Faith in a life-bearing Church comes to the same thing at last with faith in a life-giving Christ; for the Church is the Body of Christ, the fullness of Him that filleth all in all [Eph 1:22–23].

The Catechism proceeds throughout on this theory of baptismal, educational religion. It is formed for the baptized children and youth of the Church; who are received and addressed, not as aliens and foreigners from the household of faith, but as church members; who have a full right to all the blessings of the covenant, in this character; and who are now to be prepared for a personal approach accordingly to the sacramental altar. The catechumen, in this view, is addressed from the very start, as a Christian: "What is thy only comfort in life and death?" And the answer put into his mouth is taken in full again from the Christian standpoint, and no other. I belong to Christ, he is taught to say, in soul and body; he is my Savior; hath fully satisfied for my sins, and delivered me from the devil; preserves me; assures me of eternal life. So also onward to the end. The Creed, with its glorious contents, is not for another simply, but for the catechumen himself. All is personal, practical, possessional. "Why art thou called a Christian?" it is asked (Ques. 32); and the answer is at once ready: "Because I am a member of Christ by faith, and thus am partaker of his anointing; that so I may confess his name, and present myself a living sacrifice to him; and that with a free and good conscience, I may fight against sin and Satan, in this life; and afterwards reign with him eternally, over all creatures." But is it not dangerous, it may be asked, to put such language into the mouths of young persons, who may be still unconverted, and enemies in fact to the grace of the gospel?[15] Would it not be wiser and safer to teach what Christianity is in itself, without encouraging them in this way to lay claim to it for themselves? [This is] a plausible suggestion certainly; which however it is not necessary now to answer in full. Our concern here is simply with the fact that the Catechism goes upon this method. We must add at the same time, that in doing so the Catechism does but follow the general practice of the holy catholic Church from the beginning; which has always considered her children sacred to God by baptism, and felt it her duty to train them from childhood into this same consciousness. Hence she

---

15. [While not rejecting ecclesial pedagogy for the young and unconverted (which were part of the ordinary preparatory means of grace), the "New Divinity" Congregational theologians pointed to the severe spiritual dangers of failing to respond faithfully to those means of grace. See Samuel Hopkins, *Enquiry Concerning the Promises of the Gospel* (Boston: McAlpin and Fleming, 1765). The fear of hypocritically espousing orthodox doctrine while remaining unregenerate became common in many strands of the Reformed tradition.]

puts the Creed into their mouth from childhood itself; repeating it with them and before them; not waiting till they can understand and approve it fully for themselves; but seeking rather, with maternal interest, to *breathe* it into them as a portion of her own life; that they may grow up into it, and be filled with the power of it, in all subsequent time. In all this too there is much sound philosophy, as well as sound religion; for faith is life, and it is by life only, and not at all by mere doctrine, that it can ever be exerted in the soul. The Creed subsists properly in the life of the Church. Baptism inserts the infant into this life, objectively considered; and gives him a full right to claim it as his own; and makes it proper and necessary, that he should be engaged to lisp himself into it subjectively also, from the very sides of the cradle. If the Church be dead, this theory, held only *as a theory,* may easily run into practical abuse; and if the Church, whether dead or alive, have no faith in her own divine constitution, the proper fruits of the system cannot be expected of course to appear.

But all this is of no force against the system itself, under its true form. The Catechism owns this churchly process of making Christians. It is not general religious instruction which it proposes in the case of the young. The very thing it designs is to prepare them for an open personal profession of their faith, and an approach to the Lord's Supper, at a certain given time. The catechumens are candidates for *Confirmation.* All looks openly to its proper end in this rite. Confirmation is no sacrament of course; but it is a beautifully significant ordinance, in which the sacrament of baptism may be said to come finally to its natural and necessary completion. Baptism becomes complete only in the personal assumption of its vows on the part of its subject; this calls for *some* rite; and it is certainly hard to conceive of any more appropriate in itself, or less open to the charge of superstition, than the scriptural ceremony which the Church has in fact employed, from the earliest time, for this purpose. Confirmation and the old Catechetical System go properly together.

But enough has now been said, to show the spirit of the Heidelberg Catechism, and along with this the true genius of the German Reformed Church. Many reflections are suggested by the whole subject on which however it would not be proper here to enlarge. The object of this tract is accomplished, if it may serve the purpose simply of a true historical picture. One thing is certain; the German Church is not Puritan; and there is no good reason why she should be required now to succumb absolutely to Puritan forms, and Puritan modes of thought, from whatever quarter they may be presented. She had a life of her own, once at least; which it is still important that she should understand and cherish, with becoming self-respect; if indeed she have yet any vocation to fill at all as a separate independent Church. Not that Puritanism is to be blindly hated and opposed. We owe it much, which we are bound to acknowledge with gratitude and affection. Nor yet either that we should fall back blindly to the past, as it lies behind us in our own history. All sudden outward *reforms* of this sort, that rest upon no interior necessity in the life of the Church itself, are to be deprecated as likely to do more harm than good. But it is much that we should be able to understand and honor the worth that actually belongs to our own life; so as to cherish it, and turn it to account, accordingly, that we may not suffer ourselves to be overwhelmed by foreign influences; but may be watchful rather, to strengthen the things that remain; and to go forward, if not in the very track, yet still in the general spirit and genius at least of those good "old paths," in which our ecclesiastical fathers delighted to walk in the age of the Reformation. Let us not cast away as "relics of popery," in such a time especially as the present, the *churchly elements* that belong of right to our original constitution. If Puritanism and Methodism, with all the excellencies they possess in their own sphere, be palpably unhistorical, unsacramental, unliturgical, and unchurchly altogether, that is no good reason surely why we should be all this too, in the face of the Heidelberg Catechism, and in broad violation of our whole character as a GERMAN CHURCH.

Document 2

"Zacharias Ursinus" (1851)

(by John Williamson Nevin)

Editor's Introduction

In 1852 George W. Williard[1] published *The Commentary of Dr. Zacharias Ursinus on the Heidelberg Catechism*, which was his new English translation of Ursinus' lectures on the Heidelberg Catechism.[2] Williard had been a student at Marshall College and the seminary at Mercersburg, and was a pastor in the German Reformed Church. His at least partial appreciation for the nascent Mercersburg Theology went back to his student days. In 1839 he defended Professor Frederick Rauch from the accusation that Rauch had been responsible for the theological turmoil on campus that had led to the resignation of his more rationalistic colleague, Lewis Mayer. Even then Williard displayed sympathy for the introduction of German Idealism into theological studies. Over a decade later, in 1852 he argued that the *Mercersburg Review*, the principal organ of the Mercersburg Theology, should continue in publication even after Nevin, its star contributor, had resigned from the Mercersburg faculty. In his introduction to the translation, Williard borrowed Nevin's vocabulary, describing the Catechism as the expression of a "life," rather than being a "mechanical" exposition.[3] However, Williard proved to be an independent thinker, for he later expressed doubts about the adequacy of the Provisional Liturgy that had been largely inspired by the Mercersburg theologians. In spite of that, his qualified indebtedness to the Mercersburg Theology was overt, as was his enthusiasm for the Heidelberg Catechism.

These lectures, edited by Ursinus' student David Pareus, had been originally published in Latin. They had already been translated into English in the late sixteenth century by Henry Parry.[4] Williard was afraid that few copies of that translation

---

1. [George Williard (1818–1900) was a minister of the Reformed Church in Pennsylvania and Ohio. He received a classical education at Marshall College in Mercersburg and went on to pursue theological studies at the neighboring seminary. Having strong scholarly proclivities, he became president of Heidelberg College in Triffin, Ohio, in 1866. He is also remembered for heading the publication of the periodical *Western Missionary* for thirteen years (1853–1868).]

2. [See *The Commentary of Dr. Zacharias Ursinus on the Heidelberg Catechism*, trans. George Williard (Columbus: Scott and Bascom, 1851).]

3. Williard, *The Commentary of Dr. Zacharias Ursinus*, v.

4. [Henry Parry (1561–1616) was a moderately Reformed Anglican theologian who eventually became Bishop of Worcester. His translation of Ursinus' lectures was entitled *The Summe of Christian Religion* (Oxford, 1587).]

had survived, and he worried that the Elizabethan diction of Parry's volume now sounded archaic. This was an unfortunate situation, he contended, for Ursinus' lectures were crucially important for the exposition of the theology of the Catechism. Their significance was guaranteed by the fact that they had issued from the mouth of its principal author. Williard opined that such a substantive interpretation of the Heidelberg Catechism should be of value not only to German Reformed churches, but also to Protestants more generally. The Catechism, he suggested, was a profound exposition of biblical teachings, and its meaning should be made as clear as possible to new generations.

Given Williard's pedigree, it is not surprising that he invited Nevin to provide the introduction to his translation of Ursinus' lectures. Obligingly, Nevin furnished a biography of Ursinus, utilizing material from an article on Ursinus that he had already published in *The Mercersburg Review* in 1851.[5] That article had partly functioned as a commercial for Williard's anticipated tome. Nevin had ended that article with a notice that Williard's translation was in the press, and that Nevin had previewed a sampling of it. In all likelihood Nevin wrote the essay in order to generate interest in Williard's upcoming volume. That article and its slight reworking as the introduction to Williard's translation were themselves based on Nevin's earlier book of 1847 on the Catechism. Nevin's recurrent borrowings from his previous authorship show that his assessment of the Catechism remained fairly constant.

Much to Nevin's surprise, that seemingly innocuous introduction to Williard's translation of Ursinus would trigger a bitter controversy with a champion of scholastic Calvinism, John Williams Proudfit (1801–1870). Nevin's article on Ursinus, which was reused as the introduction to Williard's book, is reproduced here.

---

5. [Nevin, "Zacharias Ursinus," *The Mercersburg Review* 3 (1851) 490–512.]

"Zacharias Ursinus"[1]

Among the reformers of the second generation, the race of distinguished men, who, though themselves the children of the reformation, were yet in a certain sense joined with the proper original apostles of that great work in carrying it out to its final settlement and conclusion, no one can be named who is more worthy of honorable recollection, than the learned and amiable author of the far-famed Heidelberg Catechism. In some respects, indeed, the authorship of this symbol must be referred, we know, to different hands. But in its main plan and reigning spirit, it is the genial product, plainly, of a single mind, and to the end of time, accordingly, it will be known and revered as a monument sacred to the memory of *Zacharias Ursinus*.

In one view we may say of the Catechism, that it forms the best history, and clearest picture of the man himself; for the materials of his biography, outwardly considered, are comparatively scanty, and of no very striking interest. He had neither taste nor talent for the field of outward adventure and exploit. His whole nature shrank rather from the arena of public life. In its noise and tumult, he took, comparatively speaking, but little part. The world in which he moved and acted mainly was that of the spirit; and here, his proper home, was the sphere of religion. To understand his history and character, we need not so much to be familiar with the events of his life

---

1. [J. W. N[evin], *Mercersburg Review* 3 (September 1851) 490–512. Reprinted as "The Introduction" to *The Commentary of Dr. Zacharias Ursinus . . .* , vii–xxiii. The latter version does not include the notes in the original.] In the preparation of this article, use has been made of the following works: ALTING'S *Historia de Ecclesiis Palatini*; VAN ALPEN'S *Geschichte und Literatur des Heidelberg'schen Katechismus*; PLANCK'S *Geschichte der protestantischen Theologie*; BAYLE'S *Dict. hist. et crit. art Ursin.*; SEISEN's *Geschichte der Reformation zu Heidelberg*; K. F. VIERORDT'S *Geschichte der Reformation im Grossherzogthum Baden*; EBRARD's *Das Dogma vom heil. Abendmahl und seine Geschichte*. Reference may be made also to the writer's own work on the *History and Genius of the Heidelberg Catechism*. [See Heinrich Alting (1583–1644), *Historia Ecclesiæ Palatinæ* (Groningen, 1728, originally published 1644); Heinrich Simon Van Alpen (1761–1830), *Geschichte und Literatur des Heidelbergischen Katechismus* (Frankfurt, 1800); Gottlieb Jacob Planck (1751–1833, *Geschichte der protestantischen Theologie* (Göttigen: Banderhoed and Ruprecht, 1831); Pierre Bayle (1647–1706), *Historische and Critische Wörterbuch* (Leipzig: Breitkopf, 1740-44); D. Seisen, *Geschichte der Reformation zu Heidelberg* (Heidelberg: J. C. B. Mohr, 1846); Karl F. Vierordt (1790–864), *Geschichte der Reformation im Grossherzogthum Baden* (Karlsruhe: G. Braun, 1847); Johann Heinrich August Ebrard (1818–88) *Das Dogma vom heiligen Abendmahl und seine Geschichte* (Frankfurt: Heinrich Zimmer, 1845).]

Document 2: "Zacharias Ursinus"

outwardly taken, as to know the principles and facts which go to make up its constitution in an inward view; and of this, we can have no more true or honorable representation, perhaps, than the likeness that is still preserved of him in his own Catechism. Here, most emphatically may it be said, that "he being dead, yet speaketh" [Heb 11:4].

Ursinus was a native of Bresslau, the capital of Silesia. He was born on the 18th of July, in the year 1534, of respectable parents, whose circumstances, however, in a worldly view, appear to have been of the most common and moderate order. The proper family name was *Beer*, (Bear) which, according to the fashion of the learned world in that period, was exchanged subsequently, in his case, for the more sonorous corresponding Latin title, *Ursinus*. He discovered at a very early period, a more than usual talent and disposition for acquiring knowledge, and was sent in his sixteenth year accordingly to Wittenberg, for the prosecution of his studies in the celebrated University of that place, then under the auspices mainly of the amiable and excellent Melanchthon. Here he was supported, in part it seems, for a time at least, by foreign assistance, and particularly by an allowance from the Senate of his native city; while he was enabled soon to help himself also, in part, by a certain amount of service in teaching.

He remained in connection with this University, altogether, seven years, though not without some interruption. The breaking out of the plague in Wittenberg was the occasion of his spending a winter in company with Melanchthon, at Torgaw; and for some other reason, the threatening aspect, perhaps, of the political heavens, he left the institution again in 1552, and returned with honorable testimonials to the place of his birth. The year after, however, we find him back once more in his beloved Wittenberg, where his studies were continued now with great diligence and success, on to the year 1557.

During this period, his proficiency in the arts and sciences was such as to win for him general approbation and favor. He is represented as excelling particularly in classical literature, philosophy and theology. He was considered besides quite a master of poetry; and composed himself various productions in Latin and Greek verse, which were much admired. Along with all this intellectual culture too went hand in hand a corresponding culture of the inner spiritual man, which formed the crowning grace of his education, and added new value to every gift besides. Naturally gentle, modest, amiable and sincere, these qualities were refined and improved still farther by the power of religion, which was with him a matter of living sense and inward heart-felt experience, the deepest and most comprehensive habit of the soul. It speaks with special significance to his praise, that Melanchthon, the ornament of the University, conceived a very high regard for his abilities and moral qualities, and continued on terms of intimate personal friendship with him to the end of his own life. The high opinion in which he held his pupil is shown strikingly by the encyclical letter of recommendation which he placed in his hands, when he proposed, at the close of his course in Wittenberg, to go abroad for a time, on a tour of observation and acquaintance in other parts of the learned world as it then stood.

This sort of travel, which served to bring the young apprentice of letters into personal contact with foreign scholars, was considered in that age necessary in some sense to a finished theological training; and it shows the importance attached to it, as well as the honorable relation in which he stood to his native place, in that the Senate of Bresslau saw proper, in the case of Ursinus, to provide for the expenses of his journey out of the public funds. It was on the ground of this municipal generosity mainly, that he felt himself bound subsequently to devote his first professional labors to the service of this city.

Melanchthon describes him in his circular as a young man of respectable extraction, endowed of God with a gift for poetry, of upright and gentle manners, deserving the love and praise of all good men. [2] "He has lived in our Academy," he goes on to say, "about seven years, and has endeared himself to everybody of right feeling among us, by his sound erudition, and his earnest piety towards God." Then follows a notice of his pilgrimage, undertaken to make himself acquainted with the wise and good in other lands; who are affectionately asked, accordingly, to receive him in a spirit answerable to his learning and modesty.

Provided with this high recommendation, he accompanied Melanchthon first to the memorable conference, held in 1557, at Worms, from which place he proceeded afterwards to Heidelberg, Strasburg, Basel, Lausanne and Geneva. This brought him into acquaintance with the leaders generally of the Reformed Church; who seem to have been gained, in a short lime, to as favorable a judgment of his character, as that just quoted from Melanchthon himself. From Switzerland he passed by Lyons and Orleans to the city of Paris, where he spent some time perfecting himself in French and Hebrew. After this, we find him again in Switzerland, making himself at home, especially in Zurich, where he enjoyed the intimate confidence and friendship of Bullinger, Peter Martyr, Gessnerand,[3] and other distinguished men, then belonging to that place.

On his return to Wittenberg, he received a call (Sept., 1558) from the authorities of Bresslau, to take charge of its principal school, the Elizabethan Gymnasium. Here his services gave great satisfaction. But it was not long before a difficulty rose, which brought this first settlement to an abrupt termination. This was nothing less than a charge against him of unsound faith in regard to the sacraments. It was a time when Lutheran Germany was passing into a general hurricane of excitement under the progress of the second great sacramental war, which resulted in its rupture, finally, into two confessions. Ursinus was found to hold the Calvinistic view of Christ's presence in the Lord's supper, as distinguished from the high Lutheran doctrine of such

---

2. [Nevin found this information about Melanchthon and Ursinus in "Ursinus," in Pierre Bayle, *Dictionaire Historique et Critique*, 3rd ed. (Rotterdam: Michel Bohm, 1720), 4, 2850.]

3. [Conrad Gessner (1516–65) was the chief physician of Zürich. He was a true Renaissance polymath who wrote on philology, zoology, botany, and bibliography.]

Document 2: "Zacharias Ursinus"

men as Westphal[4] and Tilemann Hesshuss.[5] An alarm was raised accordingly, by the clergy of the place, on the subject of his orthodoxy. As in the case of the celebrated minister Hardenberg, of Bremen, so here one great ground of suspicion was Melanchthon's friendship and favor. It seemed to be taken for granted, by the zealots for high Lutheranism, that no one could be in close intimacy with Melanchthon, who was not at bottom a Crypto-Calvinist. Ursinus published a small tract in his own justification, setting forth in clear and compact summary his views of the sacramental presence.[6] This was his first theological production. It exhibited what might be regarded as the Melanchthonian doctrine of the eucharist, and was in fact approved and commended by Melanchthon himself in terms of the highest praise. It did not serve, however, to silence the spirit of persecution in Bresslau. The author was still held up to reproach as a *sacramentarian*. In these circumstances, he made up his mind in a short time to withdraw. The magistracy would gladly have retained him, in spite of the industrious clamor of his enemies. But he had a strong constitutional aversion to all strife and commotion; and he retired accordingly, with an honorable dismission, a voluntary martyr to the holy cause of peace, to seek a more quiet sphere of action in some different quarter.

When asked by a friend at this time, whither he would now go, his reply was in keeping with the union of gentleness and firmness that entered so largely into his character. "I am well content to quit my country," he said,

> when it will not tolerate the confession of truth which I cannot with a good conscience renounce. Were my excellent preceptor, Philip, still alive, I would betake myself to no one else than him. As he is dead, however, my mind is made up to turn to the Zurichers, who are in no great credit here, indeed, but whose fame stands so high with other churches, that it cannot be obscured by our preachers. They are pious, learned, great men, in whose society I am disposed, henceforth, to spend my life. As regards the rest, God will provide.

He reached Zurich on the 3rd of October, 1560, and devoted the following winter here to the active prosecution of his studies, under the guidance, more particularly, as it would seem, of the distinguished theologian, Peter Martyr.[7] His relations to this learned and excellent man were in some respects of the same kind, with those

---

4. [Joachim Westphal (1511–74) became the leader of the Gnesio-Lutheran party of Hamburg. He argued against the notion of adiaphora and resisted anything that he feared would compromise belief in the corporeal presence of Christ in the Eucharist. He figures in Nevin's narratives as one of the chief exemplars of narrow dogmatism.]

5. [Tilemann Hesshuss (or Heshusius, 1527–88) was a Gnesio-Lutheran theologian known for his polemical spirit.]

6. [Ursinus, *Gründtliche bericht vom Heilegen Abendmal unsers Herren Jesu Christi* (Heidelberg: Mayer, 1564).]

7. [Peter Martyr Vermigli (1499–1562) was a Reformed theologian who taught in Strasbourg, Oxford, and Zürich. He vehemently denied that Christ was locally present in the Eucharistic elements. He was also known for developing a doctrine of double predestination.]

in which he had stood previously with Melanchthon. Among all the Swiss reformers, there was no one to whom he attached himself so closely, or who exerted over him the same influence, as this may be traced still in his subsequent writings. So far as the Reformed complexion is found to prevail directly in Ursinus, the pupil of Melanchthon, the modification is to be referred mainly to Peter Martyr.

In the meantime God was preparing a proper theatre for his activity in the Church of the Palatinate, for which, also, his whole previous history and training might seem to have been designed and ordered, in the way of special Providence.

This interesting country had hardly become well settled on the side of the Reformation, before it was thrown into violent commotion, in common with other parts of Germany, by the breaking out of the second sacramental war, to which we have already referred, as leading to the rupture of the two confessions. Out of this rupture, and in the midst of these storms of fierce theological debate, grew the *German Reformed Church*, over against the cause of high Lutheranism, as this came to its natural completion finally, in the Form [Formula] of Concord.

The great point at issue in the controversy, as it now stood, was the *mode* simply of Christ's mystical presence in the holy eucharist. The fact of a real communication with his true mediatorial life, the substance of his body and blood, was acknowledged in general terms on both sides. The rigid Lutheran party, however, were not satisfied with this.[8] They insisted on a nearer definition of the manner in which the mystery must be regarded as having place; and contended in particular for the formula, "*In, with and under*," as indispensable to a complete expression of the Savior's sacramental presence. He must be so comprehended in the elements, as to be received along with them by the *mouth*, on the part of all communicants, whether believers or unbelievers. It was for refusing to admit these extreme requisitions only that the other party was branded with the epithet "sacramentarian," and held up to malediction in every direction as the pest of society.[9] The heresy of which it was judged to be guilty stood simply in this, that the presence of Christ was held to be, after the theory of Calvin, not "in, with and under" the bread, but only *with* it; not for the mouth, but only for *faith*; not in the flesh, but only by the *spirit*, as the medium of a higher mode of existence; not for unbelievers, therefore, but only for *believers*. This was the nature of the question that now kindled all Germany into conflagration. It respected altogether the mode or manner of Christ's substantial presence in the Lord's Supper, not the awful fact of the mystery itself as always owned by the Christian Church.

The controversy soon reached the Palatinate. The city of Heidelberg especially, and its University, were thrown by it into complete confusion. It was in the midst

---

8 [By "rigid Lutherans" Nevin usually means the Gnesio-Lutheran faction that arose in the 1540's. These strict adherents of the unaltered Augsburg Confession insisted upon an identification of the body and blood of Christ with the physical bread and wine.]

9. ["Sacramentarian" was used pejoratively to refer to the Eucharistic views of the "Philippist" party in the Lutheran family, and also to the perspectives of many Reformed theologians.]

Document 2: "Zacharias Ursinus"

of this tempestuous agitation that the wise and excellent Prince Frederick the Third, surnamed the Pious,[10] succeeded to the electorate. Under his auspices, as is generally known, the Reformed or Calvinistic tendency became established in the Palatinate. In the first place, the public quiet was restored by the dismission of the two factious spirits, Hesshuss[11] and Klebiz,[12] who, as leaders on different sides, made the pulpit ring with intemperate strife, and were not to be silenced in any more gentle way. It was then felt necessary, in the next place, to have the subject of this controversy brought to some such settlement, if possible, as might preserve the peace of the country in time to come. The Elector conceived the design, accordingly, of establishing a rule of faith for his dominions, which might serve as a common measure to compose and regulate the existing distraction. The Augsburg Confession, plainly, was not enough for this object; for the point to be settled was mainly, in what sense that Confession was to be taken on the question here in debate. Melanchthon was consulted in the case, and one of the last acts he performed is found in the celebrated *Response,* by which he gave his sanction to the general course proposed by the Elector Frederick;[13] although, of course, he could not be supposed to have in view the end to which the movement came finally, as a formal transition to the Reformed Church. Such, however, was in a little time the result. There was no violent revolution in this change. The reigning spirit of the University, and of the land, was already more Reformed than Lutheran. Some alterations were made in the forms of worship. In all new appointments, preference was given to Calvinistic divines, and several were called from abroad to occupy places of trust and power. Finally, the whole work may be said to have become complete by the formation of the Heidelberg Catechism.

Among the new appointments of which we have just spoken, no name deserves to be regarded as more important or conspicuous than that of Zacharias Ursinus. The direct occasion of his call appears to have been an invitation of the same kind addressed in the first place to his friend, Peter Martyr, which this last saw proper to decline on account of his advanced age, while he used his influence afterwards to secure the situation for Ursinus. In this way he was brought to Heidelberg, A. D. 1561, where he became honorably settled as principal of the institution known as the "Collegium Sapientia," in the twenty-eighth year of his age.

---

10. [Elector Frederick III, the Pious (1515–76), was attracted to Protestantism long before he became Elector Palatine of the Rhine in 1559. Shortly after commencing his rule, he established the Reformed faith as the religion of the Palatinate in spite of Lutherna opposition.]

11. [Tilemann Heshusius (1527–88) was a vehement Gnesio-Lutheran controversialist.]

12. [William Klebiz (or Klebitz, 1533–68), was a Lutheran reformer who served as a deacon at the Church of the Holy Spirit in Heidelberg while Hesshuss was the chief minister and superintendent. His Reformed understanding of the nature of Christ's presence in the Lord's Supper catalyzed an ongoing controversy with Hesshuss. The dispute was only terminated when both antagonists were removed from their respective offices.]

13. [Philip Melancthon, *Iudicium de controversis Coena Domini, Responsio* (Geissler, 1560).]

The year following, he was promoted to the degree of Doctor of Divinity, which imposed on him the duty of delivering theological lectures in the University.

It soon became plain, that he was formed to be the ruling spirit of the new movement, which had commenced in the Church of the Palatinate. He gained completely the confidence of the Elector; his learning and piety, and excellent judgment, secured for him the general respect of his colleagues; and from all sides, the eyes of men were turned to him more and more as the best representative and expounder of the cause in whose service he stood, and to whose defense he had cheerfully consecrated his life. In this way, with all the natural quietness of his character, we find him gradually placed in the very heart and center of the great ecclesiastical struggle in which he was called to take part. His settlement at Heidelberg continued till the death of his patron, Frederick, in 1576, a period of fifteen years. During this time, his labors were kept up with the most untiring constancy and diligence; the occasion and demand for them, being still in proportion to their generally acknowledged faithfulness and worth. His regular official services were extensive and heavy; the more especially so, as he could never consent to be loose or superficial in his preparations, but felt himself bound always to bestow on his lectures the most thorough and conscientious care. But in addition to all this, he was called upon continually to conduct a large amount of other business, growing out of the public history of the times, and often of the most arduous and responsible kind. On every emergency, in which it became necessary to vindicate or support the Reformed faith, as it stood in the Palatinate, whether this was to be done in the name of the theological faculty of Heidelberg, or by the authority of the Elector, Ursinus was still looked to as the leading counsellor and spokesman of the transaction. With the high position, moreover, which the Church of the Palatinate very soon won among the Churches generally of the same confession, associated as its distinctive genius and spirit were from the beginning with his name, the representative character now noticed took from year to year a still wider range, extending in time, we might almost say, like that of Calvin himself, to the entire Reformed communion. As the earlier chiefs of this faith were removed by death, there was no one who, by his personal connections, his extensive knowledge, his clear insight into the interior nature of the points in debate, and the admirable qualities of his spirit, could be said to be better fitted to represent the communion in any such general way, and there was no one probably, to whom in truth the confidence of all was so much disposed to turn, as the main prop and pillar, theologically, of the whole Reformed cause.

Among the public ecclesiastical services to which we have just referred, the first place belongs, of course, to the formation of the *Heidelberg Catechism,* which is to be regarded as in some sense, the foundation of his subsequent labors.

To this task he was appointed in 1562, by the Elector Frederick, in association with the distinguished theological professor and court-preacher, Caspar Olevianus. Each of them drew up separately, in the first place, his own scheme or sketch of what was supposed to be required, Olevianus in a popular tract on the Covenant of Grace, and Ursinus in a twofold Catechism, the larger for older persons, and the smaller one for children.[14] Out of these preliminary works was formed, in the first place, the Catechism as it now stands. It has been generally assumed from the first, that the principal agency in its production is to be ascribed to Ursinus; and to be fully convinced of the correctness of this view, it is only necessary to compare the work itself with his larger and smaller Catechisms, previously composed, as well as with his writings upon it in the way of commentary and defense afterwards. Whatever use may have been made of foreign suggestion or help, it is sufficiently plain from the interior structure of the formulary itself that it is no mechanical compilation, but the living product of a single mind; there is an inward unity, harmony, freshness and vitality, pervading it throughout, which show it to be, in this respect, a genuine work of art, the inspiration, in a certain sense, of one representing the life of many.[15] And it is no less plain, we may say, that the one mind in which it has thus been molded and cast, is that emphatically of Ursinus and of no one besides. The Catechism breathes his spirit, reflects his image, and speaks to us in the very tones of his voice, from the first page to the last. It is well known what widely-extended favor this little work soon found in all

14. Olevianus was a decided and strenuous disciple of Calvin. He had less learning than Ursinus, but was more practical and popular. He excelled as a preacher rather than as a professor. He had great influence with the Elector; and to him mainly the Reformed Church of the Palatinate was indebted for its organization and discipline borrowed from the Calvinistic model. It was well that his activity went prevailingly in this direction, and that the Catechism was cast mainly in the mold of a different mind. At the same time it owes something no doubt to his theology. He laid great stress on the idea of the *Covenant of Grace,* as a key to the right understanding of religion, and in this respect may be regarded as the forerunner of Cocceius and Lampe, who afterwards brought the "covenant theology" so widely into fashion in the Reformed Church. His dying hours were full of lively confidence and joy. The last word he spoke, when asked whether he was sure of his own salvation, is said to have been, as he raised his feeble hand and brought it to his breast, "*Certissimus.*" This point of *assurance,* as an element of faith, was held to be an important distinction of Protestantism, over against the Catholic view of justification. Ursinus also insisted upon it with great emphasis; going so far as to say, in one case, that it is blasphemous and devilish to question the fact, and that if a man have not assurance of his salvation before leaving this world, he can never have it in the next. "Faith itself is this assurance, which is the beginning of eternal life . . . It makes my hair stand on end to hear it denied . . . Not for a hundred thousand worlds would I be so far from my Christ, as not to know certainly whether I were his or not. That is true heathenism and the very sill of hell." Hence the peculiar form which the definition of faith takes in the 21st Question of the Catechism. With Olevianus all terminated, as with Calvin, on God's absolute predestination, as the fountain of the covenant and so the principle of redemption. Ursinus was a believer too in predestination; he read over the whole Bible at one time, from beginning to end, just to satisfy himself on this point, and it remained a settled article for him ever after. But it was controlled practically by the Melanchthonian or proper German habit previously established in his soul. He could not make the decree of election, which is by its very conception partial and abstract, to be the *principium* or root of the new creation. No such election accordingly appears in the Catechism. It moves in harmony with the old Apostles Creed. It teaches (Quest. 37) not a limited, but a universal atonement, an incarnation for the race, not a Gnostic or Baptistic phantasmagoria for only a part of it.

15. [The theme that a literary work should be an organic, unified harmony of diverse parts, expressing the cohesive spirit of the author, was a commonplace of Romantic and Idealist aesthetic theory, which Nevin taught to students at Marshall College in 1840, and later at Franklin and Marshall College. (See Appel, *Life and Works*, 668–69.) The theme was powerfully articulated in Friedrich Schlegel's (1772–1829) lectures on transcendental philosophy in 1801.]

parts of the Reformed Church. In every direction, it was welcomed as the best popular summary of religious doctrine that had yet appeared on the side of this confession. Distinguished divines in other lands united in bearing testimony to its merits. It was considered the glory of the Palatinate to have presented it to the world. Some went so far, as to make it the fruit of a special and extraordinary influence of God's spirit, approaching even to inspiration. It rose rapidly into the character of a general symbol, answerable in such view to what Luther's Catechism had already become as a popular standard for the other confession. Far and wide, it became the basis on which systems of religious instruction were formed, by the most excellent and learned divines. In the course of time, commentaries, paraphrases, and courses of sermons, were written upon it almost without number. Few works have passed into as many different versions. It was translated into Hebrew, ancient and modern Greek, Latin, Low Dutch, Spanish, French, English, Italian, Bohemian, Polish, Hungarian, Arabic and Malay. In all this, we have at once an argument of its great worth. It must have been admirably adapted to meet the wants of the Church at large, as well as admirably true to the inmost sense of its general life, to come in this way so easily and so soon to such wide reputation and credit. Originally a provincial interest merely, it yet grew rapidly into the character of a general or universal symbol; while other older catechisms and confessions of faith had force, at best, only for the particular countries that gave them birth. It was owned with applause in Switzerland, France, England, Scotland and Holland, as well as by all who were favorably disposed towards the Reformed faith, in Germany itself. Nor was this praise transient, an ephemeral burst of applause, succeeded again by general indifference and neglect. On the contrary, the authority of the symbol grew with its age. It became for the Reformed body, as we have just seen, the counterpart in full of the similar text book held by the Lutheran body from the hand of Luther himself.[16] In this character, we find it quoted and appealed to on all sides, by both friends and foes. Such vast popularity, we say, of itself implies vast merit. We may allow, indeed, that the terms in which some of the old divines have spoken of its excellence are carried beyond due measure. But this general testimony of the whole Reformed Church in its favor must ever be of force to show that they had good reason to speak here with a certain amount of enthusiasm.

The fact of its wide-spread and long continued popularity is important, also, in another view; it goes to show that the formulary was the product, truly and fully, of the religious life of the Reformed Church, in the full bloom of its historical development, as this was reached at the time when the work made its appearance. No creed or confession can be of genuine force that has not this inwardly organic connection with the life it represents.[17] This must go before the symbol, creating it for its own use. The

---

16. [Nevin is referring to Luther's popular Small Catechism.]

17. [The notion that every culture or historical movement has a unique spirit or "life" that exists prior to its cultursl productions was common to most forms of Romanticism and to Hegelianism. Nevin was probably influenced here by Rauch (1806–41), his German émigré colleague at Mercersburg

creed so produced, may come to its utterance, indeed, in the first place, through the medium of a single mind; but the single mind, in such case, must ever be the organ and bearer of the general life in whose name it speaks; otherwise it will not be heard nor felt. Here is the proper criterion of any true Church confession, whether it be in the character of a liturgy, catechism or hymn-book. It must be the life of the Church itself, embodied through some proper organ, in such form of speech, as is at once recognized and responded to by the Church at large, as its own word. This relation between word and life is happily exhibited in the case now under consideration. Though in one sense a private work, the formulary before us was by no means the product of simply individual reflection on the part either of one or of several. Ursinus, in the preparation of it, was the organ of a religious life, far more general and comprehensive than his own. It is the utterance of the Reformed faith, as this stood at the time, and found expression for itself through his person. The evidence of this we have in the free, full response with which it was met, on the part of the Church, not only in the Palatinate, but also in other lands. It was as though the entire Reformed Church heard, and joyfully recognized, her own voice in the Heidelberg Catechism. No product of mere private judgment or private will *could* have come thus into such universal favor.

The great merit which may be fairly inferred from this great reputation is amply verified when we come to consider the actual character of the work itself. The more it is carefully studied and examined, the more is it likely to be admired. Among all Protestant symbols, whether of earlier or later date, we hold it to be decidedly the best. It is pervaded throughout by a thoroughly scientific spirit, far beyond what is common in formularies of this sort. But its science is always earnestly and solemnly practical. It is doctrine apprehended and represented continually in the form of life. The construction of the whole is uncommonly simple, beautiful and clear, while the freshness of a sacred religious feeling breathes through its entire execution. It is for the heart, full as much as for the head. The pathos of a deep toned piety flows like an undercurrent, through all its teaching, from beginning to end. This serves to impart a peculiar character of dignity and force to its very style, which at times, with all its simplicity, becomes truly eloquent, and moves with a sort of priestly solemnity which all are constrained to reverence and respect. Among its characteristic perfections deserves to be noted particularly its *catholic* spirit, and the rich *mystical* element, that is found to enter so largely into its composition.[18] No other Reformed symbolical book can compare with it in these respects.

---

for one year who had been immersed in Hegelian thought. In his *Psychology* (the second edition of which Nevin edited and for which he wrote the introduction) Rauch used organic, collective, and developmental language to describe the way that the life of a culture comes to expression in individual and literary works.]

18. [The use of the term "mystical," especially because it occurred in proximity to "catholic," alarmed Nevin's critics, who feared that it was a justification of Roman Catholic "superstition." See the following essay in this volume by John Williams Proudfit as an example of this hostile response.]

Its catholicity appears in its sympathy with the religious life of the old Catholic Church, in its care to avoid the thorny dialectic subtleties of Calvinism, in the preference it shows for the positive in religion as opposed to the merely negative and controversial, and in the broad and free character generally, which marks the tone of its instructions. Considering the temper of the times, and the relations out of which it grew, it is remarkably free from polemical and party prejudices. A fine illustration of the catholic, historical feeling now noticed is found in the fact that so large a part of the work is based directly upon the Apostles' Creed.[19] It not only makes use of this as a text, but enters with evidently hearty interest and affection also into its general spirit; with the sound, and most certainly right feeling that no Protestant doctrine can ever be held in a safe form, which is not so held as to be in truth a living branch from the trunk of this primitive symbol in the consciousness of faith. We have to regret indeed always, the turn given (Q. 44) to the clause in the fourth article, *He descended into hell;* where the authority of Calvin is followed, in giving to the words a signification which is good in its own nature, but at the same time notoriously at war with the historical sense of the clause itself.[20] A great deal of offence too, as is generally known, has been taken with the unfortunate declaration by which the Roman mass is denounced, at the close of the 80th Question, as being "nothing else than a denial of the one sacrifice and sufferings of Jesus Christ, and an accursed idolatry." But it should never be forgotten, that this harsh anathema, so foreign from the spirit of Melanchthon and Ursinus, and from the reigning tone also of the Heidelberg Catechism, forms no part of the original work as published under the hand of Ursinus himself. It is wanting in the first edition; and was afterwards foisted in, only by the authority of the Elector Frederick, in the way of angry retort and counterblast, we are told, for certain severe declarations the other way, which had been passed a short time before by the Council of Trent.[21]

19 [Nevin wrote a series of articles in 1849 on the importance of the Apostles' Creed for *The Mercersburg Review* and then rewrote and published them as *The Apostles' Creed: Its Origin, Constitution, and Plan*. See Charles Yrigoyen and Lee Barrett, ed., *The Early Creeds* (2020).]

20 [Nevin objected to interpreting Christ's descent into hell as deliverance from hellish torments in general, and preferred to see it as Christ's entering the sphere of the dead in order to triumph over death.]

21. "Frederick by no means followed passively and blindly the counsel of his theologians; but the Reformed doctrine, and along with it the most determined dislike towards the Roman worship, and towards all that was still retained from it in the Lutheran church, were for him a matter of strong inward and personal religious conviction, which he well knew himself how to uphold and defend from his own diligent and careful study of the Scriptures. From these, particularly from the *Old* Testament, he deduced his duty, to tolerate no idolatry in his land, though it should be in never so mild and plausible a form. Hence in the *second* and *third* editions of the Heidelberg Catechism, the 80th Question, by his positive order alone, and *against* the counsel and will of its authors, was made to receive the addition, then, highly offensive and dangerous: 'So that the mass, at bottom, is nothing else than a denial of the one sacrifice and sufferings of Jesus Christ, and an accursed idolatry'; and he obstinately refused afterwards to give up the clause, in spite of all intimidations from the emperor and the empire set before him for the purpose."—*Goebel, Churches of the Rhine*, p. 365. [See Max Goebel, *Geschichte des christlichen Lebens in der rheinisch-westphälischen evangelischen Kirche* (Coblenz: Baedeker, 1849).] That same writer, p. 391, attributes the few polemical bristles generally of the Catechism

Document 2: "Zacharias Ursinus"

The mystical element of the Catechism is closely connected with the catholic spirit, of which we have just spoken. It is that quality in religion, by which it goes beyond all simply logical or intellectual apprehension, and addresses itself directly to the soul, as something to be felt and believed even where it is too deep to be explained.[22] The Bible abounds with such mysticism. It prevails, especially, in every page of the Apostle John. We find it largely in Luther. It has been often said that the Reformed faith, as distinguished from the Catholic and the Lutheran, is unfriendly to this element, that it moves supremely in the sphere of the understanding, and so is ever prone to run into rationalism; and it must be confessed, that there is some show of reason for the serious charge. Zwingli's great fault, as well as his chief strength, lay in the clear intellectuality of his nature. Calvin had a deeper sense of the mystical, but at the same time a still vaster power of logic also, which made it very difficult for such sense to come steadily to its proper rights. His theory of the decrees, for instance, does violence continually to his theory of the sacraments. It is only in its last and best form, as we find this brought out in the German Palatinate, that the Reformed system can be said fairly to have surmounted the force of the objection now noticed. The Heidelberg Catechism has regard throughout to the lawful claims of the understanding; its author was thoroughly versed in all the dialectic subtleties of the age, and an uncommonly fine logic, in truth, distinguishes its whole composition. But along with this runs, at the same time, a continual appeal to the interior sense of the soul, a sort of solemn undertone, sounding from the depths of the invisible world, which only an unction from the Holy One, can enable any fully to hear and understand. The words are often

---

to the same zealous interference of the Elector, who had no hesitation about thrusting his hand in this way, where it seemed necessary, into what he considered emphatically his own work. He had, it seems, a truly theocratic sense of his vocation to act as a nursing father to the church. When certain preachers afterwards fell into the Arian apostasy of Adam Neuser (who subsequently turned Mohammedan and died at last an atheist in Constantinople), and were convicted by the theological faculty of blasphemy, the jurists still hesitated about condemning them to capital punishment; but Frederick promptly took the matter into his own hands, with the remark, "that he had the Holy Ghost also in the business as a master and teacher of truth," deposing and banishing two of the offenders, and in the course of a few months actually depriving the Hollander Sylvanus of his head, by public execution in Heidelberg. [Adam Neuser (1530–576) was a pastor in Heidelberg who entertained doubts about the doctrine of the Trinity and leaned toward the Arian view that the "Son" was a being created by God at some point in time. John Sylvan (died 1572) was a Reformed pastor and theologian who clashed with Olevianus on the issue of church discipline, which Sylvan did not want to be enforced by the civic magistrates. Sylvan became convinced that the doctrine of the Trinity was not implied by the Bible. Convicted of heresy, he was executed in 1572. The Elector probably felt that because the orthodoxy of the Palatinate was already under suspicion because of its eucharistic teachings, his territory could not tolerate beliefs that were even more unsettling. Nevin got this account from Heinrich Alting, *Historia Ecclesiæ Palatinæ*, in *Monumenta Pietatis & Literaria*, ed. Ludwig Christian Mieg (Franfurt am Main: Johann Maximilian, 1701), 208–9.]

22. [For Nevin "mystical" suggested the identification of religious knowledge with a primal, foundational, intuitive dimension of experience that was prior to conceptualization. This theme was common among the German Romantics. For a hostile analysis of this use of "mystical," see Charles Hodge's lengthy critique of mysticism, including the views of Schleiermacher, in *Systematic Theology*, I:61–69.]

felt in this way to mean much more than they logically express. The Catechism is no cold workmanship merely of the rationalizing intellect. It is full of feeling and faith. The joyousness of a fresh, simple, childlike trust appears beautifully and touchingly interwoven with all its divinity. A rich vein of mysticism runs everywhere through its doctrinal statements. A strain of heavenly music seems to flow around us at all times, while we listen to its voice. It is moderate, gentle, soft, in one word, *Melanchthonian*, in its whole cadence; the fit echo and image thus, we may fairly suppose, of the quiet, though profoundly earnest soul of Ursinus himself.

It carries the palm, very decidedly, in our view, as we have before said, over all other Protestant symbols, whether formed before it or since.

But notwithstanding all that has now been said, the Catechism was received far and wide in Germany itself, at the time of its appearance, as a loud declaration of war; and became at once the signal for an angry, violent onset, in the way of contradiction and reproach, from all parts of the Lutheran Church. The high toned party which was now filling the whole empire with its alarm of heresy could not be expected of course to tolerate patiently any religious formulary that might be felt to fall short at all of its own rigorous measure of orthodoxy. From this quarter, accordingly, the Catechism was assaulted, more fiercely than even from the Church of Rome itself. Its very moderation, indeed, seemed to magnify the front of its offence. Had there been more of the lion or tiger in its mien, and less of the lamb, its presence might have proved possibly less irritating to the polemical humor of the times. As it was, there was felt to be provocation in its very meekness. Its outward carriage was held to be deceitful and treacherous; and its heresy was counted all the worse for being hard to find, and shy of coming to the light. The winds of strife were let loose upon it accordingly, from all points of the compass.

Not only the unity and quiet of the German Church, but the peace also of the German empire, seemed in the eyes of the high Lutheran party to be brought into jeopardy, by the new Confession.[23] It was held to be not only heresy in religion, but treason also in politics. Both the Elector and his theologians found their faith severely tried by the general outcry which was raised at their expense. But they were men of faith, and they stood the trial nobly and well.

The attack was opened by Tilemann Hesshuss[24] and the celebrated Flaccius Illyricus,[25] each of whom came out with an angry publication against the Calvinistic Catechism, as they called it, full of the most intolerant invective and abuse, and grossly misrepresenting at different points, the religious change which had taken place in the

---

23. [The "high Lutheran party" refers to the Gnesio-Lutherans.]

24. [Tilemann Heshusius, *Verae et Sanae confessionis de praesentia corpus Christiin Coena Domini* (Kirchener, 1562).]

25. [See Matthias Flacius Illyricus, *Widerlegung Eines Klienen Deutschen/Calvinischen Catechismi* (Heinrich Geissler, 1563). Illyricus (1520–75) was a theologian, church historian, philosopher, and Lutheran zealot.]

Document 2: "Zacharias Ursinus"

Palatinate. Among other calumnies, the new faith was charged with turning the Lord's Supper into a profane meal, with undervaluing the necessity of infant baptism, with iconomachy, and with an attempt to alter the decalogue in departing from the old order of its precepts. Other blasts of warning and alarm were soon heard, in much the same tone, from different quarters. Wirtemberg [Württemberg] in particular, issued a solemn censure, drawn up by her two best divines, in which eighteen questions of the Catechism were taxed with serious heresy, and no effort spared to bring into discredit especially its doctrine of the holy eucharist. It was necessary to meet this multitudinous outcry with a prompt and vigorous answer; and such an answer accordingly soon appeared, with all due solemnity, in the name of the united theological faculty of Heidelberg. The task of preparing it, however, fell on Ursinus, who showed himself at the same time well able to discharge the service in a truly efficient and becoming way. The honor of the Catechism was fully vindicated, and the effect of the whole controversy was only to render its authority in the Palatinate more firm than before.

Meanwhile the Elector was taken solemnly to account, in a more private way, by several of his brother princes, who seemed to think the whole empire scandalized by his unorthodox conduct. This led to the celebrated conference or debate of Maulbronn; in which the leading theologians of Wirtemberg [Württemberg] and the Palatinate came together for the purpose of bringing the whole difficulty, if possible, to a proper resolution and settlement. The Heidelberg divines were not themselves in favor of the measure; apprehending more evil from it than good. But they allowed their objections to be overruled, not caring to show what might be construed in any quarter, into a want of confidence in their own cause. The conference took place in the month of April, 1564, and lasted we are told, a whole week, from the tenth day of the month to the sixteenth. Among the disputants from Heidelberg were the Professors, Bocquin,[26] Olevianus and Ursinus. On the other side appeared Brentius,[27] two of the Tübingen Professors, and other distinguished divines. The burden of the debate, however, was thrown mainly upon Ursinus in the one case, and wholly upon James Andreæ,[28] the great and good chancellor of the University of Tübingen, in the other.

The acts of this *colloquy of Maulbronn* are of the highest value for the history of the German Reformed Church, and serve at the same time to throw a most honorable light on the whole character of Ursinus. They furnish throughout a lively image of his keen penetration, his comprehensive science, and his clear doctrinal precision, as

---

26. [Peter Bocquin (d. 1582) had been influenced by Calvin, and was regarded as the premier Reformed theologian of Heidelberg before the advent of Ursinus.]

27 [Johann Brenz (1499–1570) was the leading Reformer of Württemberg, where he became the chief religious adviser to the Duke. He eventually became an opponent of the "Calvinizing" tendencies within Lutheranism.]

28. [James Andreæ (1529–90) was an allegedly moderate Lutheran theologian who sought to reconcile the Gnesio-Lutherans and the Philippists. Nevertheless, he sided with Westphal in the controversy with Calvin over the Lord's Supper, thereby showing that he leaned toward the conservative position. He was the principal German editor of the *Formula of Concord* (1580).]

well as a brilliant exemplification of the firmness with which he adhered to his own convictions of truth and right. His distinctions and determinations, especially on the question of the *Ubiquity*,[29] may be regarded as carrying with them a sort of truly classical authority for the Reformed theology in all subsequent times.

The colloquy itself, however, only led afterwards to new controversy. It ended with a compact, indeed, to abstain from public strife, but, unhappily, this was soon forgotten and broken. Both sides, as a matter of course, claimed the victory; and it was not long till an effort was made, on the part of the Wirtemberg [Württemberg] divines, to establish this claim in their own favor, by publishing what they called an epitome of the debate in a form to suit themselves; placing the whole discussion, with no small ingenuity and address, in a light by no means fair or satisfactory to the other side. To meet this misrepresentation, the divines of the Palatinate published, in the first place, a copy in full of the proceedings of the colloquy from the official record made at the time; and then added a clear and distinct reply to the Wirtemberg [Württemberg] epitome, exposing what they conceived to be its grave offences against truth. This called forth, in the year 1565, the great "*Declaration and Confession of the Theologians of Tübingen on the Majesty of the Man Christ, and the Presence of his Body and Blood in the Holy Supper.*"[30] Then came in reply again from the side of the Palatinate, in 1566, a "*Solid Refutation of the Sophisms and Cavils of the Wirtemberg Divines*"[31] designed to make clean ground once more of the whole field. The controversy was renewed and continued thus in its full strength; and the author of the Catechism was still required to hold a weapon for its defense in one hand, while he labored on its proper exposition with the other. Both services were well fulfilled.

Among his various apologetic tracts, the chief place is due to the *Exegesis verae doctrinae de Sacramentis et Eucharistia*, published in the name of the Heidelberg Faculty and by order of the Consistory, whose sanction gave it at the same time the force of a public confession. It was translated also into the vernacular tongue, and in a short time went through several editions. It is still a work of great interest and value, as it furnishes the most authentic interpretation, which is anywhere to he found, of the real

---

29. [The doctrine of the ubiquity of Christ's body was intended to explain how Christ could be present in, with, and under the physical elements in many different locations at the same time when the Lord's Supper was celebrated concurrently. The theory was that the divine quality of omnipresence was communicated to Christ's human nature, so that even his corporality could share in the divine ubiquity. This belief would become a litmus test of orthodoxy for doctrinally conservative Lutherans. Most Reformed theologians would counter this with the claim that the body of Christ is not omnipresent on earth, but is seated at the right hand of the Father in heaven. In general, the Lutherans tended to gravitate toward a more Alexandrian Christology that emphasized the unity of Christ's person, while the Reformed moved toward a more Antiochene Christology that stressed the distinction of the two natures.]

30. [For a similar text, see *Confessio et Sententiae Ministorum Verbi in Comitatu Mansfeldensi* (Gaubisius, 1565).]

31. [*Verantwortung Wider die ungegründten auflagen und verkerungen* (Heidelberg: Maier, 1564).]

sacramental doctrine of the Catechism, in the sense which it had in the beginning for Ursinus himself, as well as for the whole theological faculty of Heidelberg.

As just intimated, however, the business of such public apology and defense, by no means exhausted the labors of Ursinus in regard to this truly admirable symbol. The Catechism was fully enthroned in the Palatinate, from the beginning, as the rule and measure of the public faith. It was made the basis of theological instruction in the University. It was introduced into all the churches and schools, under a regulation which required the whole of it to be gone over in course, in the way of familiar repetition and explanation, once every year. A regular system of catechization was established in the churches, to which the afternoon of every Lord's Day was devoted, and which was so conducted as to include grown persons as well as children. Ursinus, in his capacity of professor, accommodated himself also to the general rule, and made it a point to go over the text of the Catechism once a year with his theological lectures. This custom he is said to have kept up regularly onto the year 1577. Notes of his lectures were taken down by the students, which were allowed soon after his death, at three different places, to make their appearance in print. As much injustice was done to him, however, by the defective character of these publications, his particular friend and favorite disciple, David Pareus, who possessed besides all necessary qualifications for the task, was called upon to revise the whole, and to put the work into a form that should be more faithful to the name and spirit of its illustrious author. This service of duty and love could not have fallen into better hands, and no pains were spared now to render the publication complete. Under such properly authentic form, it appeared first in the year 1591, at Heidelberg, in four parts, each furnished with a separate preface by Pareus;[32] since which time, it has gone through numerous editions, in different countries. The Heidelberg Catechism has been honored with an almost countless number of commentaries of later date; but this first one, derived from Ursinus himself through David Pareus, has been generally allowed to be the best that has been written. No other at all events can have the same weight as an exposition of its true meaning.

In the midst of other agitations in the year 1564, the plague broke out with great violence in Heidelberg, causing both the court and the university to consult their own safety by withdrawing for a time from the place. During this solemn recess, Ursinus wrote and published a small work on Preparation for Death. It appeared first in German, but was translated afterwards into Latin, in which form it is found in the general collection of his Works, under the title of *Pia Meditatio Mortis*.[33]

In the year 1571, he received an urgent call to Lausanne, which he seems to have been somewhat inclined to accept, in view chiefly of the undue burden of his labors at Heidelberg, which was found to be greater than his physical constitution, naturally

---

32. [See *Explicationum catecheticarum D. Zachariae Ursini Silesii* (Heidelberg: Harnish, 1591).]

33. [See Zacharias Ursinus, *D. Zacheriae Ursini theology celeberrimi, Opera theological*, ed. David Pareus and Quirinius Reuter, 3 vols. (Heidelberg: Johannis Lancelotti, 1612), 1:910–23.]

weak, could well support. To retain him in his place the Elector allowed him to transfer a portion of his college service to an assistant.

His marriage with Margaret Trautwein followed the year after, and is represented as having added materially to his comfort and rest. He was at the time nearly forty years of age.

This domestic settlement, however, was not of long duration. With the death of his patron Frederick, in October 1576, the whole religious state of the Palatinate fell once more into disorder. He was succeeded in the electorate by his eldest son, *Louis*,[34] whose previous connections had inspired him with a strong zeal for Lutheranism, in full opposition to the entire course of his father. Before his death the old prince had sought an interview with his son, wishing to bring him under an engagement, if possible, to respect his views in regard to the church, as expressed in his last will and testament. Louis, however, thought proper to decline the interview, and subsequently showed no regard whatever to his father's directions. On the contrary, he made it his business, from the start, to turn all things into an entirely different train. The clergy, together with the mayor and citizens of Heidelberg, addressed a petition to him, praying for liberty of conscience, and offering one of the churches for the particular use of those who belonged to his confession. His brother, *Duke Casimir*,[35] lent his intercession also, to sustain the request. But it answered no purpose; Louis declared that *his* conscience would not suffer him to receive the petition. The following year, accordingly, he came with his court to Heidelberg, dismissed the preachers, filled all places with Lutheran incumbents, caused a new church service to be introduced, and in one word, changed the public religion into quite another scheme and form. The more prominent theologians were soon compelled to leave their places; among whom, of course, were the authors of the Heidelberg Catechism, Olevianus and Ursinus.

Ursinus found an honorable refuge with Prince Casimir, second son of the late Elector, who exercised a small sovereignty of his own at Neustadt, and made it his business to succor and encourage there, as far as he could, the cause now persecuted by his Lutheran brother. The distinguished divine was constituted professor of theology in the Neustadt Gymnasium, which the prince now proposed to raise to the character of something like a substitute for what the University of Heidelberg had been previously for the Reformed Church. The new institution, under the title of the *Casimirianum*, soon became quite important. It could hardly be otherwise, with such

---

34. [Elector Louis (or Ludwig) VI (1539–83) was a devout Lutheran who supported the unaltered Augsburg Confession. Raised by his Lutheran mother, he had long disapproved of his father's Reformed proclivities.]

35. [Duke John Casimir (1543–92), the younger son of Frederick III, remained staunchly Reformed after his father's death, unlike his Lutheran older brother. He led troops from the Palatinate in the Dutch revolt against the Catholic Hapsburgs and kept the German Reformed academic tradition alive in his small territory after Louis had purged the University of Heidelberg of Calvinists.]

Document 2: "Zacharias Ursinus"

names as Ursinus, Jerome Zanchius,[36] Francis Junius,[37] Daniel Tossanus,[38] John Piscator[39] in its theological faculty, and others of the like order in other departments. Here Ursinus continued to labor, true to the faith of his own dishonored Catechism, till the day of his death.

His last publication of any importance was a work of some size, undertaken by order of Prince Casimir, and issued in the name of the Neustadt clergy, in 1581, in review and censure of the celebrated Form [Formula] of Concord.[40] This was executed with his usual ability, and did good service at the time to the cause of the Reformed Church.

The triumph of Lutheranism in the Palatinate proved in the end to be short. Before the plan could be fully executed, by which it was proposed to extend the revolution of the capital over the entire province, Prince Louis died, in the midst of his days; and now at once the whole face of things was brought to assume again a new aspect. The administration of the government fell into the hands of Duke Casimir, who soon after took measures to restore the Reformed faith to its former power and credit. As far as possible, the old professors were once more brought back to the University. The Casimirianum of Neustadt saw itself shorn by degrees of its transient glory. The Form [Formula] of Concord sank into disgrace, while its rival standard, the Heidelberg Catechism, rose gloriously into view again as the ecclesiastical banner of the Palatinate. In due time, the whole order of the church was restored as it had stood at the death of Frederick the Pious.

But there was one among the banished theologians of Neustadt who did *not* return at this time with his colleagues, to the scene of his former labors. The author of the Catechism himself, the learned and pious Ursinus, was not permitted to have part in the triumph to which it was now advanced. His feeble constitution, which had been for some time sinking more and more under the untiring labors of his profession, gave way finally altogether; and on the 6th of March, 1583, the very year in which Prince Casimir came into power, he was quietly translated to a higher and better world. The event took place in the 49th year of his age.

---

36 [Jerome Zanchius (1516–90) was an Italian-born Reformed theologian who used a scholastic method reminiscent of Aquinas to organize and elaborate Reformed doctrine. Although Nevin appreciated Zanchius' intellectual stature, he was not sympathetic to his theological method.]

37. [Francis Junius (1545–1602), who had studied under Calvin and Beza, also helped pioneer Reformed scholasticism.]

38. [Daniel Tossanus (1541–1602) was a French Reformed theologian who fled from the St. Bartholomew's Day massacre of Protestants in Paris and Orleans. He pastored French refugees in Basel, and later moved to Heidelberg, where he eventually taught theology.]

39. [John Piscator (1546–1625) was a prolific and somewhat mercurial German Reformed theologian, active in Heidelberg and Herborn, who transitioned from being a double predestinarian to being an Arminian.]

40. [Ursinus, *De Libro Concordiae quem vocant* (Neustadt: Harnisch, 1581).]

He was buried in the choir of the church at Neustadt, where his colleagues erected also a suitable monument to his memory. The inscription describes him as a sincere theologian, distinguished for resisting heresies on the person and supper of Christ, an acute philosopher, a prudent man, and an excellent instructor of youth. A funeral oration was pronounced on the occasion in Latin, by Francis Junius,[41] which is still important for the picture it preserves of his mind and character. Its representations, of course, are somewhat rhetorical, and some allowance must be made for the colorings of friendship and grief; but after all proper abatement on this score, it is such a glowing eulogy, as coming from one so intimately familiar with the man, must be allowed to tell greatly to his praise.

His works were published collectively, sometime after his death, in three folio volumes, by his friend and disciple David Pareus.[42]

The leading traits of his character have been already brought into view in some measure, in the sketch now given of his life. An enduring witness of his theological learning, and of his intellectual abilities in general, is found in his works. The best monument of his virtues and moral merits is the influence he exerted while living, and the good name he left behind him throughout the whole Reformed Church at his death, the odor of which has come down to our own time. He was at once a great and a good man.

He seems to have excelled as an academic lecturer. His friend, Francis Junius, speaks with high commendation also of his talent for preaching; but his own estimate of himself here was probably more sound, which led him to withdraw from the pulpit in a great measure, as not being his proper sphere. His style and manner were too didactic for its use. For the ends of the lecture room, however, they were all that could be desired. At once full, calm, methodical and clear, his mind flowed here without noise or pomp, in a continuously rich stream, both gentle and profound, that was felt to diffuse the most wholesome instruction on all sides. He spared no pains to prepare himself fully for his work, and laid himself out to serve as much as possible the wants of his pupils; throwing his soul with living interest into the task in hand, and encouraging them to do so too by presenting difficulties or risking questions at the close of each exercise; which it was his habit then, however, not to answer on the spot, but to hold in reserve for a well-studied judgment on the following day.

His diligence seemed to have no bounds. Of this we have the best evidence in the vast amount of the labors and services he performed in the course of his public life. His parsimony of time, always as gold to the true student, is illustrated by the inscription which he is said to have had in full view, for the benefit of all impertinent visitors, over the door of his study: "*Amice, quisquis huc venis, aut agito paucis, aut abi, aut me*

---

41. [Francis Junius (1545–1602), a French-born Heidelberg theologian who had studied under Calvin and Beza, helped pioneer Reformed scholasticism.]

42. [See Ursinus, *D. Zacheriae Ursini theology celeberrimi, Opera theological*, ed. David Pareus and Quirinius Reuter, 3 vol. (Heidelberg: Johannis Lancelotti, 1612).]

laborantem adjuva." That is, "Friend, entering here, be short, or go, or else assist me in my work."[43]

This regard for time was with him a sense of duty, and flowed from the general feeling he had, that his powers and his talents were not his own, but belonged to his faithful Savior, Jesus Christ, and that he had no right to divert them from his service. Altogether his conscientiousness was of the highest order. His funeral orator says of him, that he had never heard an idle word fall from his lips; so careful was he with the government of his thoughts and the regulation of his tongue. He may be said indeed to have fallen a martyr, in some sense, to his own faithfulness; for it was the hard service to which he put himself in the discharge of his professional engagements that wore out his strength and brought him down finally to the grave.

The modesty and humility of the man were in full keeping with his general integrity, and contributed much to the pleasing effect of his other virtues. His manners were perfectly unassuming, as his spirit also was free from everything that savored of pride or pretension. He seemed to court obscurity, rather than notoriety. Such of his works as appeared in his own lifetime were published anonymously, or in the name of the Heidelberg faculty; while the greater part of them never saw the light at all in any such form, till after his death.

Altogether, as we have before seen, he was of a reserved, retiring nature; formed for meditation and self-communion; averse from all noise and strife; mystical as well as logical, and no less contemplative than intelligent and acute; a true heir in this respect to Melanchthon's spirit, as well as a true follower of his faith. For theological controversy, though doomed to live in it all his days, he had just as little taste as his illustrious preceptor himself; and when forced to take part in it, one might say of him that scarce the smell of its usual fire was allowed to pass on his garments; so equal was he still, and calm and mild, in the conduct of his own cause, avoiding as far as possible all offensive personalities, and bending his whole force only to the actual merits of the question in debate. On the other hand, however, no one could be more decided and firm in this calm way when it was necessary to withstand error or maintain truth. In this respect he was superior to Melanchthon, less yielding and more steadily true to the chart and compass of his own creed.

He was charged by some with being sour and morose. But this was nothing more, probably, than the construction which his reserved and earnest character naturally carried with it for those who were not able to sympathize with such a spirit, or who saw him only as it were from a distance and not near at hand. It is characteristic of such a soft and quiet nature, to be at the same time ardent and excitable on occasions even to passion; and it is not unlikely that in the case of Ursinus this natural tendency may have been strengthened at times by the morbid habit of his body, disturbing and

---

43. [This information is found in "Ursinus," in *Dictionaire Historique et Critique*, Pierre Bayle, 3rd ed. (Rotterdam: Michel Bohm, 1720), 4:2850. Ursinus seems to have gotten the motto from Aldus Manutius (1449–1515) who was a Venetian humanist and director of a celebrated publishing house.]

clouding the proper serenity of his mind. Francis Junius describes him as just the reverse of the charges now noticed, and as made up of self-forgetting condescension and kindness towards all who came in his way.

The same witness, than whom we could have no better, bears the most honorable testimony also to his habits of devotion and personal piety. Religion with him was not a theory merely, but a business of life. He walked with God, and showed himself thus a worthy follower of those who through faith and patience have entered into the rewards of his kingdom.

On the whole, we may say, it is a great honor for the German Reformed Church to be represented in the beginning by so excellent a man; and it is not going too far perhaps to add that the type of his character has entered powerfully into the true historical spirit of this communion, as distinguished from all other branches of the same faith. Such is the prerogative of genius, and such its high and lofty commission in the world. It stamps its own image, for ages, on what it has power to create.

J. W. N.

Williard's Ursinus.—It is extensively known that the Rev. George W. Williard of Columbus, Ohio, has undertaken to bring out a new translation of the celebrated lectures of Ursinus on the Heidelberg Catechism, as published by David Pareus. The old English translation by Parry[44] is out of date, and at the same time not easy to be obtained. From our general knowledge of Mr. Williard's ability, as well as from a very small specimen we have seen of the forthcoming work itself, we doubt not but his task will be found to be well performed. We are glad to learn, that the work is already nearly through the press and may be expected to make its appearance in the course of a few weeks. The enterprise deserves patronage and favor, and we trust it may not fail to meet in this way its proper reward. All branches of the Reformed Church ought to take an interest in it; but especially may this be expected of the German Reformed Church, whose distinctive glory it is to have produced the Catechism, and to have in it the clearest mirror of its own life. To speak of the value of the Commentary itself would be superfluous. Its merits are universally acknowledged.[45]

---

44. [Henry Parry (1561–1616) was a moderately Reformed Anglican theologian who eventually became Bishop of Worcester. His translation of Ursinus' lectures was entitled *The Summe of Christian Religion* (Oxford, 1587).]

45. [This advertisement was not reprinted in the "Introduction" to the *Commentary*.]

Document 3

"The Heidelberg Catechism and Dr. Nevin" (1852)

(by John Williams Proudfit)

Editor's Introduction

John Williams Proudfit (1801–1870) was much agitated by Williard's translation of Ursinus' lectures on the Heidelberg Catechism and even more by Nevin's introduction to the new volume. His consternation sparked an acrimonious exchange between himself and Nevin that evolved into a critique and a defense of the Mercersburg Theology as a whole.

Proudfit was an offspring of the "anti-burgher" segment of the secession faction that split off from the established Church of Scotland. In 1733 the original "seceders" had exited the Church over the issue of who had the right to nominate ministerial candidates to ecclesial vacancies. Frustration with doctrinal laxity, alarm over the erosion of church discipline, and unhappiness with liturgical extravagance also contributed to their discontent. In 1747 the anti-burghers faction objected to the requirement that holders of public office take an oath asserting their approval of "the religion professed in this kingdom." To the anti-burghers this seemed like an improper assertion of civil authority over religious matters. The dissident party developed a fierce concern for doctrinal rectitude and a habit of resistance to any efforts to compromise their beliefs. This legacy would partly fuel Proudfit's allergic reaction to Nevin in particular and the Mercersburg Theology in general.

Proudfit's ancestors, tired of being persecuted in Scotland, eventually immigrated to North America. In the United States this transplanted heritage evolved into the Associate Presbyterian Church in the United States. Proudfit himself graduated from Union College in 1821, a somewhat revival-friendly Presbyterian school, where he was a classmate of John Nevin. From 1823–24 he attended Princeton Seminary, where he again overlapped with Nevin. As a pastor he served Old Federal Street Presbyterian Church, Newbury Massachusetts, and then shifted his career to the teaching of classical languages. He taught Latin at New York University from 1841–59, and then Greek at Rutgers. Because of the strength of the Dutch Reformed Church in the New Brunswick area, Proudfit began to teach and preach in Dutch Reformed congregations, and in 1854 even started a denominational journal, *The New Brunswick Review*. It was, however, a short-lived venture and was discontinued after only one year. Proudfit found the Dutch Reformed theological heritage, which held the Heidelberg

Document 3: "The Heidelberg Catechism and Dr. Nevin"

Catechism and the Canons of Dort as authoritative, to be very congenial to his own conservative Scottish Presbyterian legacy. The confluence of those Reformed streams would reinforce his antipathy to the perceived Mercersburg innovations.

Proudfit shared at least one characteristic with Nevin. Proudfit highly valued catechisms and catechetical instruction. Like Nevin, he had been reared on the Westminster Confession and its accompanying catechisms. He approvingly recalled that when his father's health was declining, "He employed in recollecting and revolving the whole of the [Westminster] Assembly's catechism, whose lucid and comprehensive definitions of divine truths he always greatly admired."[1]

In spite of his frequent displays of ire, Proudfit was much more than an acerbic polemicist, for his academic prowess with the two classical languages is abundantly clear in the text and footnotes of this essay. In recognition of his linguistic skills, in 1841 he was awarded an honorary Doctor of Divinity degree by Union College.

Proudfit's theological production demonstrated that he harbored a particular animus toward the Mercersburg theologians, attacking not only the works of Nevin, but also those of Schaff. After reading Nevin's three 1849 articles on the Apostles' Creed, Proudfit penned a lengthy essay which appeared in *The Biblical Repertory and Princeton Review* in October 1852 (vol. 24. no. 4, 662–77) challenging Nevin's views on the Creed. Against Nevin he argued that the Creed was not authored by the Apostles (Nevin of course agreed with him) and did not represent a consensus of the church during the apostolic era. Its late origin, he contended, undermined its authority. The Reformers, he claimed, recognized the Bible alone as being authoritative, and not the Creed. Moreover, Proudfit dismissed the notion of a development of doctrine as a dangerous concession to Roman Catholicism. For him the Creed was not the eventual blossoming of theological seeds that had been planted in the soil of the New Testament.

Proudfit and Nevin also disagreed in print on the meaning and significance of the Heidelberg Catechism. The publication of Williard's new translation of Ursinus' lectures on the Catechism provided Proudfit with the occasion to renew his attacks on the Mercersburg Theology. He published a review of Williard's volume in the January 1852 issue of *The Biblical Repertory and Princeton Review*[2] and Nevin responded with an article on the Catechism in *The Mercersburg Review* in the March 1852 publication.[3] According to Proudfit, Nevin's publications on both the Creed and the Heidelberg Catechism were part of his implicit attempt to paint Catholicism in a favorable light. Proudfit's roots in the Scottish seceder tradition and his new affiliation with the Dutch Reformed tradition combined to reinforce a virulent anti-Catholic prejudice.

---

1. Proudfit and John Forsyth, *Memoire of the Late Rev. Alexander Proudfit*, 358.

2. John Williams Proudfit, "The Heidelberg Catechism and Dr. Nevin," *The Biblical Repertory and Princeton Review* 24 (January 1852) 91–134.

3. John Williamson Nevin, "The Heidelberg Catechism," *The Mercersburg Review* 4 (March 1852) 155–86.

The rhetoric exchanged between the two became increasingly combative as they interpreted the Catechism itself in their respective articles. Proudfit accused Nevin of Catholic mystification, and Nevin denounced Proudfit as a "Puritan." The clash became so rancorous that Nevin began to fear that it was damaging the relationship between the Dutch and German branches of the Reformed family in the United States.

At first Proudfit seems to parallel Nevin's enthusiasm for catechetical instruction. He begins his essay by pointing to the primacy of oral proclamation in Christianity, claiming that the power of the written word is derivative from the potency of the spoken word. For this reason he then lauds the oral question-and-answer format of many catechisms. The use of the Heidelberg Catechism for confirmation purposes, he asserts, is to be praised for exemplifying that dialogical method. Like Nevin, Proudfit praises the Heidelberg Catechism in particular for encapsulating the reverential mood appropriate for a confession of faith.

But then the critique begins. First, Proudfit sought to discredit Williard by maligning his abiltites as a translator. Williard, in his view, did not consult the most authoritative editions of Ursinus' lectures. Moreover, in his assessment, Williard simply mistranslated certain key words. To reinforce this point, Proudfit tried to demonstrate his own linguistic superiority by spicing his pages with lengthy Greek and Latin quotations, often without translating them. He thereby displayed his own facility and flattered his implied audience with the implication that his readers were accomplished classicists, even more accomplished than the theologically compromised Williard.

After the attack on Williard's competence, Proudfit then reveals the ultimate reason for his disdain for the book. Williard is guilty not so much of ineptitude, but of his association with Nevin, the author of the introduction. It is the theological content of Nevin's introduction that really raises Proudfit's hackles. Nevin, according to Proudfit, has entirely misinterpreted Ursinus' lectures (and the Heidelberg Catechism) in order to pursue his own agenda of rapprochement with Rome.

Proudfit's criticism of Nevin partly revolved around the Catechism's condemnation of the Roman mass as "idolatry" in question 80. Nevin had suggested (probably accurately) that the phrase had been added in later editions by Frederick the Pious, and had not been part of Ursinus and Olevianus' original intention. Nevin proposed that the more volatile Frederick had been incensed by the eucharistic theology articulated by the Council of Trent and had seized the opportunity to deliver a counterblow. Nevin argued for this point about the authorship of question 80 in order to draw attention to the conciliatory dimension of the Catechism as conceived by Ursinus and Olevianus. The irenic thrust was so strong, Nevin claimed, that it even sought to avoid giving undue offense to Catholics. Proudfit saw this contention as an initial step on the road to Rome. Part of his counter-argument was to defend question 80, with its anti-idolatry clause, as an essential and original component of the Heidelberg Catechism's anti-Roman animus.

"The Heidelberg Catechism and Dr. Nevin."

[A book review by John Williams Proudfit on *The Commentary of Dr. Zacharias Ursinus on the Heidelberg Catechism*. Translated from the original Latin by the Rev. G. W. Williard, A. M. (With an Introduction by Dr. Nevin.) First American Edition. Columbus: Scott & Bascom, Printers. 1851.]

The great instrument by which God has chosen to diffuse and perpetuate his truth among men is the living voice. John Bunyan, as usual, clothes a great truth in a quaint conceit when he represents "Ear-Gate" as the principal entrance to the town of Mansoul, through which Diabolus first carried the city, and against which those valiant soldiers of the great King Shaddai, Captain Boanerges and Captain Conviction "did bend their main force."[1] The pen and the press, powerful as they are, are mostly powerful in seconding, extending, and perpetuating the impressions of the living voice. They are utterly inadequate to the first publication of truth as to the making immediate, profound, and general impressions on the minds of men. They could never have called the world to repentance and preparation for the coming of the Son of God as did "the voice" of John the Baptist. They could never have sent out the "line" of the gospel "into all the earth, and its words unto the ends of the world" within the space of a quarter of a century, as it was "sounded forth" by the preaching of the apostles and primitive Christians. They could never have rolled up the population of Europe in one vast surge, and precipitated it upon Asia, as did the preaching of Peter the Hermit.[2] They could never have made nor begun the Reformation, though they had a mighty and indispensable agency in extending and completing it. They could never have awakened the slumbering churches of England and America as did the

---

1. [See John Bunyan, *The Holy War Made by King Shaddai upon Diabolus, to Regain the Metropolis of the World.* John Bunyan (1628–1688) was an English writer and Non-Conformist preacher best remembered for authoring *The Pilgrim's Progress* (1678). *The Holy War* is an allegory of the fall and redemption of humanity ("Mansoul"), in which humanity's crucial vulnerability to temptation is the faculty of hearing ("Ear-Gate").]

2. [Peter the Hermit (1050–1115) was a priest of Amiens whose popular preaching helped inspire the First Crusade.]

preaching of Whitefield[3] and Wesley.[4] They could never have agitated the general mind of Britain and of this country, as we have recently seen it done by the presence and the voice of one man. The pen and the press have done and are doing great things, and will do greater still. But they cannot transcend their office. They cannot pass out of their sphere. Their power must be exerted, for the most part, upon minds and communities already attentive, thoughtful, and mature. To arouse the soul, to pour into it the vivifying power of new truth, is the peculiar work of the living voice, trembling under the vast emotions which that truth has already awaked, and transmitting those emotions, by the mysterious and irresistible power of sympathy, to other souls.

If this truth has, in any case, a special and peculiar force, it is in its application to the training of the young. Then especially is "Ear-Gate" the main avenue, and the voice the most effective, in fact the only effective instrument when truth is to be adapted to the ever changing moods of the young mind—all eager as it is for knowledge, yet impatient of protracted attention; curious of facts, yet easily wearied of abstractions; earnest and tender, yet prone to levity; deeply and keenly susceptible at once to the things of the spiritual and the sensible world.

Oral instruction was the great ordinance of God for perpetuating religion in the ancient Church. "I know Abraham that he will *command* his children and his household after him, and they shall keep the way of the Lord." Gen. xviii. 19. "These words which I command thee this day—thou shalt teach them diligently unto thy children, and shalt *talk* of them when thou sittest in thine house, and when thou walkest by the way, and when thou liest down, and when thou risest up." Deut. vi. 6, 7. "*Tell* ye your children of it, and let your children *tell* their children, and their children another generation." Joel i. 3. "The priest's lips should keep knowledge, and they should seek the law *at his mouth.*" Mal. ii. 7. Thus the whole historical and spiritual life of the Church was to be borne along from generation to generation by the living voice of parent, priest, and prophet. In what precise form this oral instruction was administered, cannot now, we believe, be determined. The religious instruction of Theophilus (Luke i. 4), of Apollos (Acts xviii. 25), and of the Jew addressed by Paul as the representative of his Church and nation (Rom. ii. 18) are all alluded to under the term. All had been "catechized," whatever sense was then attached to the word, in the first principles of religion. The Greek commentators of the early Church appear to have generally understood the word in these passages as implying a system of early oral instruction

---

3. [George Whitefield (1714–70) was an Anglican minister who itinerated throughout England, Wales, and the American colonies, preaching fervently to huge and very responsive crowds. Even worldly and skeptical Benjamin Franklin was moved by his rhetorical abilities, and the two became unlikely friends.]

4. [John Wesley (1703–1791) was an English cleric, theologian, and evangelist who founded the Methodist movement within the Church of England and emphasized such Arminian theological doctrines as imparted righteousness and entire sanctification as a culminating work of grace. He focused on the development of intensive personal accountability, discipleship and religious instruction through the formation of small prayer groups.]

Document 3: "The Heidelberg Catechism and Dr. Nevin"

and religious truth. The Hebrew words (one of which signifies to *narrate*, or *rehearse*; the other to *inculcate*, literally to *sharpen*,) denote a constant and earnest oral teaching, but imply nothing as to the recipient of the instruction. Κατηχεω, [Trans. "to instruct"] if we look at its derivation, sees to include more, and to denote a process vocal and audible on both sides (κατ'ηχω διδασκειν) [Trans. "catechetical teaching"] in which the thought and the voice of the pupil give back an *echo* to that of the teacher. Such a meaning must, however, we think, rest on the *vis etymi* [Trans. "the force of an early form of a word"] and not on the *usus loquendi* [Trans. "the use of a word in current parlance"]; though such great names as D'Outrein[5] and Melanchthon have claimed even the latter in its support. "Κατηχειν [Trans. "to teach"] (says Melanchthon) signifies not simply to teach, but carries with it the idea of reading or lecturing and hearing the pupils recite what has been said and again," that method of teaching in which the utterances of the master are called forth by questions is properly denoted by. That it was not restricted by the early Christian writers to its modern signification, i.e. instruction by question and answer, is evident from the fact that some of their writings of this sort, for example the κατηχειν of Cyril of Jerusalem[6] are composed in a continuous style, without question and answer. The communication of instruction, however, by ερωτησεις [Trans. "questions"] and αποχρισεις [Trans. "answers"] dates from a very early period, as we find a specimen of it in Justin Martyr,[7] and it became thereafter a favorite method of solving difficult questions in religion and ethics, and of conveying Christian knowledge to the young and ignorant.

Oral instruction, at least, in a familiar way, which is the proper and universal idea expressed whether by question and answer or otherwise,[8] was held in the highest estimation in the early Church, not only as a means of holy nurture to her own children, but of recovery to the lapsed, and of conversion to pagans and others who were yet without. The fathers of the Church were general and firm in the belief that they had direct scriptural and apostolic sanction for the practice. They looked upon the γαλα [Trans. "milk"] of Paul, 1 Cor. iii. 2 ; Heb. v. 12, 13; and the λογικον αδολον γαλα [Trans. "pure spiritual milk"] of Peter, 1 Pet. ii. 2, as referring distinctly to familiar oral instruction[9] in Christian truth adapted to young and simple minds, and interpreted

---

5. [Johannes D'Outrien (1662–1722) was a Dutch preacher and author of devotional works.]

6 [Cyril of Jerusalem (c 313--336) was a theologian of the early church whose theological views were in alignment with the Nicene orthodoxy. He is most remembered for his preparation of twenty-three lectures for catechumens in Jerusalem in which he stressed themes of healing and regeneration.]

7. [Justin Martyr was a second-century apologist who defended the moral ethos of Christianity, comparing it to Stoicism, and used the concept "Logos" (Word) to interpret the person of Christ.]

8. Κατηχησις est familiaris per vivam vocem facta institutio in elementis Christianæ religionis. [Trans. "Catechesis by the living voice is the familiar way to instruct in the elements of the Christian religion."] Suicer. Thes. Ecc. e. Pat. Græc. Catechesis proprie est elementaris institutio Christianæ religionis, viva docentis voce tradita, et a discentibus reddita. [Trans. "Catechesis is properly elementary instruction in the Christian religion, handed on by a teacher's living voice and returned by the learners."] Henr. Altingius in explic. Cat. Pal. p. m. 2.

9. Ταλαή κατήχησις. Clem. Alex. Strom, on 1 Cor. iii. 2.

the στοιχεια της αρχης των λογιων του θεου [Trans. "basic elements of the oracles of God"], Heb. v. 12, and the λογος της αρχης του Χριστου [Trans. "basic teaching about Christ"], Heb. vi. 1, as denoting the elements of Christian doctrine imparted in the same form. Those who were under this kind of "instruction" (κατηχουμενοι) were regarded as εν προθυροις της ευσεβιας;[10] "in the vestibule of piety." One class of Christian ministers was specially devoted to this sort of instruction, and were called κατηχηται, "Catechists." It has been thought by some that this was a distinct office. It might have been so in particular cases, but was, we think, generally attached to the office of pastor, and Jerome[11] and Augustine[12] have observed that while the apostle Paul has in other cases separated the functions of Christian ministers, he has spoken of these two together—"Pastors and Teachers." It is altogether probable that in some of the larger and wealthier churches the office of Catechist was distinct. Some of the most venerable names of the ancient Church are enrolled among the catechists of Alexandria. Pantænus,[13] Clemens [Clement] Alexandrinus[14] and Origen[15] head the list. Pantænus was the teacher of Clemens, as Clemens was of Origen, and in both cases the pupil succeeded his master in the office of catechist. Jerome entitles Clemens κατηχησεων magister,[16] and Origen[17] adjutor κατηχησεως, which renders it probable that in the church of Alexandria that office was a distinct one, and formed the proper occupation of those eminent men. Jerome says[18] that Origen availed himself of the great concourse of youth that came to him for literary instruction, to teach them in the Christian faith. According to Eusebius,[19] when the entire charge of catechetical

10. Greg. Naz. Or. 40.

11. [Jerome (c. 347–420) was an historian and theologian best known for his translation of the Bible into Latin. His version became known as the *Vulgate* and was eventually adopted as the authoritative version of the Bible by the Roman Catholic Church.]

12. [Augustine (354–430) was a teacher of rhetoric from North Africa who became Bishop of Hippo Regius. One of the most influential theologians in the history of Christianity, he pioneered Western reflection on grace, election, original sin, the Trinity, the relation of sacred and secular history, and almost every other doctrinal topic.]

13. [Pantaenus (c. 120–c. 216) was a Stoic philosopher who converted to Christianity and organized the famous catechetical school in Alexandria, which became influential in the development of Christian theology. His most celebrated student was Clement of Alexandria.]

14. [Clement (c. 150–215) was a Christian middle Platonist philosophical theologian who taught in the catechetical school of Alexandria.]

15. [Origen (c. 182–c. 251) was an important theologian and teacher of the early church, who was influential in the Greek-speaking East, particularly in Alexandria. Borrowing from Platonic thought, he engaged in allegorical exegesis, speculative theology, and reflection on spiritual practices.]

16. Alexandriae ecclesiasticam scholam tenuit κατηχηεοων magister fait. Catal. Scrip. Ecc. Cap. 48.

17. Ibid. Cap. 64.

18. Concursus ad eum miri facti sunt, quos ille propteræ recipiebat, ut sub occasione secularis literaturæ, in fide Christi eos institueret. Ibid.

19. Ecc. Hist. Lib. VI. Cap. 3. [Eusebius (c. 260–c. 340) was a Roman ecclesial historian and Bishop of Caesarea Maritima. His *The Ecclesiastic History* is one of the earliest histories of the Christian

instruction was devolved upon him by Demetrius, then bishop of that church, he immediately forsook his profession of literary teacher, to devote himself wholly to that work. In such high estimation was the business of catechetical instruction then held, as to command the whole time and labor of the greatest minds of the Church.

And in the like estimation it continued to be held so long as truth was looked upon as the proper glory and power of Christianity, and *the teaching of truth* as the great means of converting souls and rearing up a holy posterity to perpetuate the Church. But when the *ecclesiastical* spirit overcame the evangelical, and the Church grew more and more worldly and material in all her institutions and instrumentalities, relying on the secular arm rather than the sword of the Spirit,[20] and adopting the usages of paganism in order to convert pagans, and making more of a splendid ritual than of a pure faith, and magnifying church orthodoxy above vital piety, and addressing the senses by shows and music and incense, rather than the soul by the vivifying light of truth, catechetical instruction of course declined. During the proper period of Roman domination, it was almost extinct and forgotten. The peril of awakening intellect and stimulating thought is an *arcanum imperii* [Trans. "secret government"] of all despotisms, and pre-eminently of that, the most enormous and inexorable despotism under which the prostrate intellect and soul of man ever groaned. There were occasional attempts in councils held for ecclesiastical discipline, to revive the practice of catechetical instruction. It was enjoined on the clergy in the Canons of the Council of Braques, A. D. 572, of Tourain 813, and of Mentz 1347. The Capitularia of Charlemagne also required it. But the spirit of the dominant Church was too strong for the edicts of princes or the canons of councils. Rubrics, breviaries, rosaries, and agendas were much more to the mind of Rome than Catechisms. They amused and tranquillized the minds of men with a semblance of religion,[21] but did not implant those fructifying germs of thought and irrepressible aspirations which always accompany truth. Images were, in her esteem, a much safer medium of instruction than books.[22]

Few and meagre, however, as were the catechetical productions of that dark period, they are never to be forgotten. There is a curious specimen still extant of a German Catechism composed by an unknown monk of Weissenburg, in the ninth century, containing an explanation of the Lord's Prayer and the Apostles' Creed, and,

---

church, and partly functioned as an apology for Constantine's revolution in the relation of the church and the empire.]

20. [Here Proudfit's rootage in the Scottish Seceder tradition is evident.]

21. [Throughout the essay Proudfit associates ecclesial despotism with the denigration of critical thought, and attributes both vices to the Roman Catholic Church.]

22. "Gregorius Papa idola et imagines in templis collocavit, *ut essent pro libris imperitæ multitudini.*" [trans: Pope Grgeory put idols and images in rhe churches in order to be books for the ignorant multitude."] Sibelius, quoted by Van Alphen, Prol. ad Cat. Heid. p. 17—as if idolatry were a refuge from ignorance! This was, indeed, throwing the blind man into the ditch instead of attempting to restore his sight.

(instead of the ten commandments) *a list of the deadly sins*.[23] This substitution was not infrequent during that period. The Papal Church has never faltered in her policy to abrogate the law of God that she may keep her own traditions.

As the spirit of life began to stir in the Church and resistance to Rome waxed stronger, Catechisms were multiplied. The Waldenses, in their Confession of Faith presented to Francis I,[24] allude to catechetical instruction as in use among them.[25] John Wickliffe composed in English several tracts under the title of *Pauper Rusticus*, intended to teach the poor the principal truths of Christianity, "without an apparatus of many books."[26] Among these were an exposition of the Creed, the Lord's Prayer, and the Ten Commandments;[27] Huss wrote a catechism in his prison at Constance, which is still extant among his works.[28] And, (stirred up, it is said, by these examples) Gerson, the learned and excellent Chancellor of Paris, wrote a tract, (how sweet the title!) "*de parvulis ad Christum trahendis*" [Trans. "*On Bringing Children to Christ*"] and spent the last days of a life distinguished by the highest honors of genius and learning, in *catechizing little children*.[29]

One of the first evidences of re-awakened Christian life at the era of the Reformation was the restoration, and that in tenfold glory and efficacy, of the noble art of catechizing. More catechisms were produced within fifty years after 1517 than in ten centuries before. Luther, in his "*brevis formula decalogi, symboli apostolici et orationis*

---

23 Augusti, Versuch einer Einleit, &c., p. 33.

24. [Francis I (1494-1547) was the King of France from 1515-1547 who helped stimulate the French Renaissance by patronizing Italian scholars, artists and writers, including Leonardo da Vinci. His reign witnessed the rise of centralized monarchy in France, the promulgation of humanism, and the beginnings of Protestantism.]

25 [The Waldensians were a Christian group that arose in France in the twelfth century. Because they embraced apostolic poverty they were declared to be heretical. Surviving in the Alpine valleys of France and Italy, most of the Waldensians were absorbed by various Reformed churches during the Reformation era.]

26. [John Wycliffe (1320-84) was an English theologian, Oxford professor, and outspoken critic of many of the practices of the Roman Catholic Church. He led a team of scholars who translated the Vulgate into Middle English (1384). In Proudfit's religious culture Wycliffe was regarded as a voice of dissent within the Roman Catholic Church and therefore as a forerunner of the Reformation and a crucial link connecting Protestantism with the faithful remnant in the medieval church. His writings had a profound impact on the theology of the early Czech reformer, John Huss.]

27. From the decrees of the Councils of Braques, Tourain and Mentz, it appears that these were of old considered the heads of catechetical instruction.

28. [Jan Huss (1369-1415) was a dissident Bohemian theologian, philosopher, and reformer who was executed as a heretic. His opposition to the theological views of the Catholic Church in Bohemia, especially on ecclesiology, simony, and the Eucharist, were closely aligned with those of John Wycliffe. Huss' controversial opinions were articulated most fully in his *De Ecclesia* (1413). His understanding of the sacraments anticipated the views of some early Protestants. The Hussite movement that he inspired has been seen as a harbinger of the Reformation.]

29. [Jean Gerson (1363-1429) was a French theologian, educator, and poet who absorbed and disseminated some of the teachings of the medieval mystics. He was also Chancellor of the University of Paris, a leader of the conciliar movement, one of the most significant theologians at the Council of Constance, and an early pioneer of natural rights theory.]

Document 3: "The Heidelberg Catechism and Dr. Nevin"

dominicæ" [Trans. "Brief Sum of the Decalogue, the Apostles' Creed, and the Lord's Prayer"] (1518 and 1520) and in his "Larger" and "Lesser Catechisms" (1529) led the way. His example led to the composition of a multitude of catechisms by his followers. Buddæus[30] enumerates no less than twenty by the Lutherans alone; and his list is by no means complete. The Romanists, alarmed by the rapid spread of the new doctrines in this form, were compelled in self-defense to resort to the same method. This is candidly admitted by the Jesuit Possevin while urging on his own church the importance of catechetical instruction.[31] "Some object, 'the heretics use this sort of teaching. Do you think it right to imitate them? At least, you will not deny that the word *catechizing* ought not to be used, for that savors too strongly of heretical practice.' Who can bear such trifling? Ought not a Christian rather to acknowledge his own fault than to screen his individual sin to the general peril and disadvantage?"[32] Fleury composed a "*Catechismus historicus*," which, baring the Romish errors and superstitions it contains, is an admirable model, as it uses the *events* of Scripture as a means of impressing its truths and precepts on the young mind—a method which might undoubtedly be used so as to render this kind of tuition more interesting and attractive to the young.[33]

Loyola and his disciples pressed with great ardor into the career of catechetical instruction.[34] Catechisms were extensively used not only in the educational institutions of the Jesuits, but in their foreign missions. The Council of Trent[35] ordered the preparation of a Catechism, which, under the direction of the Pope, was composed, or at least completed and arranged by Cardinal Sirlet,[36] and was of course proclaimed as the "*lydius lapis, certissima et infallibilis norma, ad quam examinanda est omnis doctrina*"—("the touchstone, the unquestionable and infallible model whereby all doctrine is to he tried") whereas the Protestant Catechisms followed each answer with an array of *proofs* from the Bible, implying the duty of searching the Scriptures, whether those things were so. (A striking exemplification of the genius of the Protestant and Roman

---

30. Isag. Hist. Theo. l. Lib Post. Cap. I. § 12. [Johann Franz Buddaeus (1667–1729) was a Lutheran philosopher, theologian, and historian.]

31. [Antonion Possevino (1533–1611) was a Jesuit controversialist, encyclopedist, and papal envoy. He was a master of anti-Protestant polemics.]

32. 1 Epist. de necessitate, utilitate ac ratione Cath. Cat. cited by Van Alphen and Augusti.

33. [Andre-Hercule de Fleury (1653–1743) was a French Catholic cardinal. A person of enormous political power, he was chaplain to Louis XIV and the tutor of Louis XV.]

34. [Ignatius Loyola (1491–1556) was a Basque priest who co-founded the Jesuit order and developed a simple regimen of spiritual exercises. The Jesuits became known for their missionary endeavors, their educational institutions, and their loyalty to the pope.]

35. Father Paul. Lib. 8.

36. Moreri. Sirlet. [Cardinal Sirleti (1514–1585) was an Italian ecclesiast, theologian, and linguist. He played a major role in the Council of Trent and oversaw the production of the Roman catechism.]

Churches!) In brief, the Socinians,[37] Remonstrants,[38] Anabaptists, Catabaptists,[39] and Quakers, in fact all the sects and subdivisions of religious opinion, in which the boundless and lawless mental activity of that age manifested itself, expounded their several doctrines in Catechisms. Even the Turks are reported to have felt the general impulse of Christendom, and to have reduced the doctrines of Islamism into this form.[40]

The Reformed Church, properly so called in distinction from the Lutheran, contributed its full share to the catechetical symbols of which the age was so prolific. Besides many "Confessiones," "Articuli," "Theses," "Rationes," and "Expositiones Fidei" (various titles and forms indeed, but all exhibiting a harmonious system of the Reformed doctrine), the sixteenth century gave birth, within that Church, to the Catechism of Geneva (by Calvin, 1536), that of Zurich (by Bullinger, 1559), and that of the Palatinate (by Ursinus, 1563).

None of these enjoyed a higher repute, or exerted a wider or more enduring influence among the Reformed churches, than the last. It was composed by order of Frederic III, Palatine of the Rhine, Elector of the Empire, and Duke of Bavaria, in 1562. The work of preparing it was committed to Caspar Olevianus, Court-Preacher of the Elector, and Zacharias Ursinus, Professor of the Collegium Sapientiæ, assisted, as some affirm, by Peter Boquin[41] and Immanuel Tremellius.[42] The finishing and arranging hand was undoubtedly that of Ursinus, and it has, therefore, been regarded as his work. In the Electoral diploma, which accompanied its publication and ordered it to be introduced in the churches and schools of the Palatinate, Frederic declares his intention, in causing it to be prepared, to have been "that his people might be led to the right knowledge of God, their Creator and Redeemer, from his own word." He expresses his conviction that "there can be no well-established order, either in church, state, or families, unless the youth are instructed from their earliest years, in true and pure religion, and constantly exercised in it." He states that he has caused

---

37. [Socinianism was a cluster of nontrinitarian movements that arose in the sixteen and seventeenth centuries, often associated with the work of Faustus Socinus (1539–1604). Strong in Poland and Transylvania, Socinians were identified with the denial of the pre-existence of Christ, original sin, and Christ's substitutionary atonement. As a term of abuse, eventually "Socinian" was used almost interchangeably with "Unitarian."]

38 ["Remonstrants" were followers of the theologian Jacob Arminius (1560–1609). Arminius had voiced concerns that the hyper-Calvinists were interpreting God's sovereignty in regard to salvation in ways that suggested absolute divine determinism. The Remonstrants also objected to the use of state power to enforce a particular vision of orthodox doctrine. Proudfit shared the conservative Dutch Calvinist disdain for Arminianism's moderate view of election.]

39. ["Catabaptist" was a term used in the sixteenth century for Christian groups that experimented with non-traditional modes of baptism, ranging from dripping to immersion. Because baptism in their view was an outward sign, some factions regarded it as optional.]

40. Hoornbeek in Van Alphen. Prol.

41 [Peter Bocquin (d. 1582) had been influenced by Calvin, and was regarded as the premier Reformed theologian of Heidelberg before the advent of Ursinus.]

42. [Immanuel Tremellius (1510–89) was an Italian Jewish convert to Christianity who became a leading translator of the Old Testament.]

Document 3: "The Heidelberg Catechism and Dr. Nevin"

this Catechism to be prepared, that the pastors and schoolmasters, throughout his estates, may have a fixed and definite form by which to conduct such instruction, and earnestly enjoins upon them to be diligent and faithful in using it to that end. We should be glad to transfer this admirable document to our pages entire. It breathes the spirit of a wise and pious prince, "ruling over men in the fear of God," and "watching for their souls as one that must give an account." That such was the true character of Frederic, the testimony even of those who were by no means friendly to him places beyond a doubt. The diploma is dated January 19th, 1563.[43]

Ursinus, in rapid progress and early maturity in learning, wisdom, and piety, was one of the wonders of that wonderful age. He was born at Breslau, July 18th, 1534, of a respectable family, but so far from being *pecunious* (we borrow the quaint term from Bayle)[44] that he was assisted in obtaining his education both by public and private liberality: another noble son whom the Church has raised for her own service and the glory of her Lord, and an illustrious example of the wise economy of such liberality! He entered, in his eighteenth year, the University of Wittenberg, where he passed five years, the beloved pupil and intimate friend of Melanchthon. He afterwards visited several foreign cities and universities, among the rest, Geneva (where he formed a friendship with Calvin, who gave him his books, inscribed with his autograph), and Paris, where he resided a short time to perfect himself in French and in Hebrew under the tuition of Mercier.[45] When about twenty-four years of age, he was called to preside over the Elizabethan school in his native town of Breslau. But his "Theses de Sacramentis,"[46] which showed his opinions to be of the Reformed stamp, caused so much disturbance that he voluntarily resigned his office and left his country, "*honestissimo cum testimonio Senatus*," [Trans. "most honorably with the testimony of the Senate"] declaring that exile was a welcome discharge from the intolerable labor of keeping school.[47] From Breslau he went to Zurich, where he resided for a while in the

---

43. It is given entire by Van den Honert, Schat-Boek der Verklasingen over den Nederlandschen Catechismus, Voorreede, p. 9, &c., and by Niemeyer Coll. Conf. in Ecc. Ref. publ. p. 428, &c. [See Johannes Van den Honert, ed., *Schat-Boek der Verklasingen over den Nederlandschen Catechismus* (Gortinchen: Nicolas Goetzee, 1763).]

44. [See Pierre Bayle (1647–1706), *Historische and Critische Wörterbuch* (Leipzig: Breitkopf, 1740–44). Bayle (1647–1706) was a French philosopher, writer and Reformed thinker best known for his *Historical and Critical Dictionary* (1697), which was one of the first encyclopedias of ideas and their authors. He was a champion of the principle of religious toleration, opposed the use of scripture to justify coercion, and influenced the development of the Enlightenment.]

45. [Pierre Le Mercier taught in the theology faculty of the Sorbonne from the early to the mid-sixteenth century.]

46. [See Ursinus, *De Sacramentis* (Neustadt: Harnish, 1564).]

47. Moreri. *Dav. Pareus.*—"fatigues si terribles (i. e. de conduire la jeunesse au Collège de Sapience) que le bon Zacharie Ursin l'estimoit heureux d'avoir éte exilé par les Lutheriens, puisque cet exilé delivroit de cette terrible carrière." [trans: ". . . fatigues so terrible (leading the youth at the Collège de Sapience), that the good Zachary Ursinus counted himself happy to have been exiled by the Lutherans, because this exile delivered him from this terrible career."] We find this mentioned only by Moreri. But *sympathy* prompts us to insert it—the only joke we have met with of "le bon Zacharie Ursin." That he

society of Peter Martyr[48] and Gesner.[49] Thus did his wanderings lead him, Θεου ὑπ' ἀμυμονι πομπῃ [Trans. "God blessing him on the way"], to intimate communion with the master minds of the Reformation, and ripened him for the great work of his life.

Just after he had completed his twenty-seventh year, he was invited to the University of Heidelberg, and in the following year, was appointed to the professorship of *Loci Communes.*

In the faculty of that renowned University, he was associated with Boquin and Tremellius, and with these eminent and pious men, *una manu, concordibus votis* [Trans. "one band, a concord of devotion"], labored in the tuition of youth and edification of the Church of God. Many eminent preachers and theologians were formed under their care. In the year 1562, he was employed, as we have stated above, by order of the Elector, in the preparation of the Heidelberg Catechism. In 1571 he was invited to the chair of Theology in the University of Lausanne, whither he was inclined to go, as his health was suffering severely under his multiplied labors; but the urgent wishes of the Elector, who at the same time permitted him to choose one or more colleagues to lighten his toil, induced him to remain at Heidelberg. He thereupon took a colleague, and shortly after, a wife, being married to Margaret Trautwein, in 1572—"and yet" (apologetically subjoins Melchior Adam,)[50] "he was none the less diligent" (why should he be?) "in the education of youth and the composition of useful works." By this marriage he had one son, who was *hæres paternæ virtutis* [Trans. "heir of the father's virtue"].

In 1577 the death of the great and good Elector and the accession of his son Louis,[51] who brought Lutheranism into the Palatinate with a high hand, were followed by a sweeping revolution in the University, and Ursinus, dismissed from his professorship, and once more an exile, betook himself to Neustadt, whither he was invited by Casimir,[52] a younger son of Frederic, who inherited his father's attach-

---

continued in this "terrible carrière" to the last "egregie omnes partes implens præceptoris et magistri fidelis" (Mel. Adam,) is a proof of the *vis indefessa* [trans: motive force] of his principles and character.

48. [Peter Martyr Vermigli (1499–1562) was a Reformed theologian who taught in Strasbourg, Oxford, and Zürich. He vehemently denied that Christ was locally present in the eucharistic elements and developed a doctrine of double predestination.]

49. [Conrad Gessner (1516–65) was the chief physician of Zürich. He was a true Renaissance polymath who wrote on philology, zoology, botany, and bibliography.]

50. [See Melchior Adam, *Dignorum Laude Virorum* (Frankfurt: Johann à Sande, 1705), 255. Melchior Adam (1575–1622) was a German Calvinist literary historian who is remembered for writing a five-volume collection of literary biographies.]

51. [Elector Louis (or Ludwig) VI (1539–83) was a devout Lutheran who supported the unaltered Augsburg Confession. Raised by his Lutheran mother, he had long disapproved of his father's Reformed proclivities.]

52. [Duke John Casimir (1543–92), the younger son of Frederick III, remained staunchly Reformed after his father's death, unlike his Lutheran older brother. He led troops from the Palatinate in the Dutch revolt against the Catholic Hapsburgs and kept the German Reformed academic tradition alive in his small territory after Louis had purged the University of Heidelberg of Calvinists. He created the Collegium Casimirianum in Neustadt in 1578 as a substitute university for the Reformed

ment to the Reformed faith. This prince founded at Neustadt, the principal town of his own estates, a college named after himself *Casimirianum*, in the faculty of which Ursinus was once more associated with some of his former friends and colleagues of the University of Heidelberg. There, in the various labors of a professor and an author, he spent the last five years of his life, manfully combatting the various infirmities of an over-worked system, and even from the bed to which sickness at last confined him, dictating not only a multitude of letters, but several works of considerable size, among which was his "Refutatio Jesuitarum." At last, "having fought a good fight and finished his course, he received from the heavenly Arbiter and Rewarder that amaranthine crown. For he died in the Lord, as if falling into a sweet sleep, with his friends around him, on the sixth of March, 1583, and in the forty-ninth year of his age." He left behind him a request that as he had lived without pomp, so he might be carried to his grave without it, and interred nowhere else but in the common and public cemetery. This wish was complied with, and a monument erected to his memory by the *Schola Casimiriana*, bearing an epitaph which presents a glowing, but not more than just picture of his great talents and virtues.

His writings were collected after his death and published in three folio volumes by his grateful pupils, Pareus[53] and Quirinus.[54] But by far the most important work of his life and most durable monument to his memory is his immortal Catechism. Over what a multitude of young minds has it scattered the seeds of truth! How many, while repeating its "form of sound words," have "with the heart believed unto righteousness, and with the mouth made confession unto salvation!" [Rom 10:10].

His other voluminous works have been comparatively neglected. But the Catechism, translated into fourteen languages,[55] expounded in innumerable churches,

---

theologians who had been dismissed.]

53. [David Pareus (1548–1622) was a student of Ursinus who became a major theologian in his own right. Like his mentor, he sought to find common ground between the Lutherans and the Reformed traditions. His irenic overtures to the Lutherans did not bear lasting fruit. See *Corpus doctrinae Orthodoxae Sive Catecheticarum Explicationum D. Zachariae Ursini Opus absolutum*, ed. David Pareus (Rhodin, 1612). *Explicationum catecheticarum D. Zachariae Ursini Silesii* (Neustadt, 1593).]

54. [Quirinus Reuter was a Heidelberg theologian who published an interpretation of the Catechism in 1585.]

55. Niemeyer (Coll. Conf. Ref. Præf. p. 62,) enumerates them. Besides the original German and the immediately subsequent Latin version by Lagus and Pithopceus, it was translated into Dutch, Greek, Modern Greek, Spanish, Polish, Hungarian, Arabic, Cingalese, French, English, Italian, Bohemian, and Hebrew. Henry Ailing (Explic. Cat. p. 6,) adds "the lingua Indica," by which he may mean the Cingalese. The same writer says, "*Sed authentica est sola editio Germanica in qua omnia non rotundiora modo, sed etiam* εμφατικωτερα." "The German edition alone is of authority, in which everything is not only more fully but more energetically expressed," (ibid.) It is an interesting fact, which deserves to be mentioned, that many, if not most of the above translations into the languages of distant races were made under the auspices of the United States of Holland, who sent missions along with their colonies to the ends of the earth. A copy of the noble edition in Modern Greek, translated and published by order of the States General (1648) is now before us. A just monument has yet to be erected to the liberality and Christian zeal of that heroic Republic.

and repeated by innumerable youth, has entered into the life-blood and circulated through all the veins of Reformed Christendom.

In no way, perhaps, has its influence been more profoundly and permanently diffused than by the unparalleled extent to which it has been used as a text book of theological instruction. Van Alphen gives a list of no less than ninety Commentaries and illustrative works of various kinds, which had been written upon it by eminent divines before his time, (1729).[56] A very large portion of these were originally delivered in the shape of lectures in the universities and theological schools.

The ascendency of the Catechism in the Palatinate, the country of its birth, was, it is true, subjected to many and severe interruptions and reverses. First, by the accession of Louis and the forcible reinstating of Lutheranism, (1577,) afterwards by the disasters of Frederick, the titular and transient king of Bohemia (1620),[57] shortly after and yet more terribly by the Thirty Years War in which Popery was brought into the Palatinate by the merciless Tilly at the point of the bayonet; and finally, by the accession of a prince of the Romish faith, (1686).[58] But the same storms which expelled it from its native seats, wafts its imperishable seeds across the sea to this western continent, to find a far wider field, and to yield, we hope, far richer harvests in the German Reformed Church of the United States.

But no church of the Reformed family has imbibed the doctrine of the Heidelberg Catechism more deeply, adhered to it more steadily, or brought a larger share of sacred learning to its defense and illustration, than the venerable Reformed Dutch Church. Her princes and fathers were the first (of foreign countries)[59] to adopt it as a symbol of their faith, in the Synod of Wesel,[60] 1568, and solemnly re-affirmed this act at the Synod of Embden, 1571, of Dort, 1578, of Middleburg, 1581, of Gravenhagen, 1586, and finally, in the National Synod of Dort,[61] 1618-19, where the foreign as well

---

56. [See Heinrich Simon van Alpen, *Geschichte und Literatur des Heidelbergischen Katechismus* (Frankfurt am Main: Hermannischen Buchhandlung, 1800).]

57. [Elector Frederick V (1596-1632) was elected to be King of Bohemia by the Czechs who were revolting against the Hapsburgs. Frederick saw himself as the military leader of a Protestant coalition and accepted the crown. He was defeated in less than a year by the largely Catholic forces of the Empire at the battle of White Mountain. This triggered the vicious Thirty Years' War and led to the occupation of the Palatinate by the Catholic armies. Frederick fled to the Netherlands.]

58 [Johann Tserclaes, Count von Tilly (1559-1632) was one of the most brutal leaders of the forces of the Catholic League during the first half of the Thirty Years' War.]

59 In varias easque florentissimas orbis Christiani provincias magno piorum gaudio et fructu introducta est, atque etiamnum obtinet: cujus primum exemplum dedere Ecclesiae Belgicas, Anno 1571, H. Alting, Explic. Cat. p. 6.

60. Van den Honert. Schat-Boek der Verk. over den Ned. Cat. Voorreede, p. 12.

61. Bishops Hall [Joseph Hall, 1574-1656] and Davenant [John Davenant, 1572-1641] were the delegates of the Church of England. "I well remember," says Trigland, "that the divines of Great Britain highly extolled that little book, and said that neither their churches, nor the French, had such a suitable catechism; that the men who had composed it had been unusually assisted by the Spirit of God at the time; that they had, in sundry other matters, excelled several divines, but in composing that catechism they had excelled themselves." Ecc. Hist. p. 1145, quoted by Vanderkemp on the Cat. Pref. p. 25.

as the native divines expressed their cordial and entire approbation of its doctrines. Her temples have resounded with its exposition, and her children have been imbued with its truth for nearly three centuries. The solid bulwarks which the learning of her Altinges and Hoornbeeks, and Hommiuses, and Van Tyls, and a host of other eminent divines has thrown up around the Protestant faith, were erected, even to the outermost buttress and escarpment, on the outline of the Catechism. The heartiness with which she adopted it, and the predominance which her free institutions and her vast opulence and power, as well as the learning of her divines and schools, gave her, in the seventeenth century, contributed largely to the unparalleled prominence and diffusion of this, her favorite symbol. Holland was indebted to a pure and living faith for strength to stand up against the most fearful odds ever perhaps successfully encountered by a nation, and ultimately to wrest her liberties from the iron grasp of Philip II;[62] and she sought, with grateful ardor, to repay the debt. She poured it into the minds of the youth who resorted from far to her Universities and Schools of Theology; she taught it to the exiles from England, Scotland, France, and Germany, whom her heroic arm sheltered from persecution; she sent it to her colonies in the East and West Indies; and, in fine, she, too, transmitted it with her emigrant children to America, to experience a freer and wider diffusion after the decay of her own liberties, and (it must be added) the decline of her own piety in the Old World.

Of the numerous commentaries on the Catechism, which we have above alluded to, that of Ursinus himself has, of course, taken precedence,[63] being the author's exposition of his own work. Ursinus, while occupying the chair of Theology in the "*Collegium Sapientiæ*," "regularly went through an annual course of lectures on the Catechism down to the year 1577."[64] These lectures, taken down at the time of delivery, were published after his death by his friend and pupil, David Pareus. It would appear, from a letter of Sibrand Lubbert[65] to Pareus (dated 1591), that someone had already published Commentaries on the Catechism, which did him great injustice. He expresses much satisfaction that Pareus had given them to the world in a correct form.

---

62. [Philip II (1527–98) was King of Spain, Portugal, and Naples and Sicily, as well as Duke of Milan and Lord of the Netherlands. A staunch Roman Catholic, his repressive religious policies in the Netherlands helped spark the Dutch Revolt. For the Dutch Reformed population Philip was the personification of intolerance and persecution. The folk memory of Catholic brutality was brought with the Dutch immigrants to North America.]

63 Innumeris commentariis, Germanicis, Latinis, et aliarum linguarum illustrate est: quos inter Ursiniani, Explicationum Catecheticarum titulo evulgati, primas facile tenent. H. Altingi, Exp. Cat. p. 6.

64. Henr. Altingi Mon. lit. et piet. cited by Van Alphen, Prol. p. 32.

65. An eminent theologian of that day and Professor of Theology at Franeker. He had been a pupil of Ursinus, and was so highly esteemed by him that when the Elector allowed him to choose an associate in his professorship, he nominated Lubbert; who, says Moreri, "répondit modestement qu'il ne se sentoit assez habile pour bien remplir une place, où ce Professeur illustre avait acquis tant de gloire." [Trans. "responded modestly that he did not feel accomplished enough to fill a position where this professor had acquired so much glory."] Moreri adds that Ursinus could find no other whom he was willing to recommend. Lubbert himself composed a Commentary on the Catechism.

The work received, also, the fullest authentication from other disciples and friends of Ursinus, among whom were Quirinus Reuterus (one of the editors of Ursinus), and Bartholomew Keckermann,[66] afterwards Professor of Theology at Dantzic. Where Pareus inserts observations of his own, he does so separately and under his own name. The only instance of this we have observed is the "Additio Davidis Parei de Transubstantiatione et Consubstantiatione," appended to the exposition of the 78th Question.

This "Opus Catecheticum," originally published in Latin, was translated into various languages, passed through a multitude of editions, and was held in high repute in all the churches of the Reformation. Pareus was (as well as Ursinus,) a voluminous writer. His Critical Commentaries on the New Testament have ranked with the best productions of that class.[67] But none of his works have reached a circulation at all to be compared with this compilation of the lectures of Ursinus. Many wondered, he tells us,[68] that with such pressing occupations of his own, he should bestow so much time and labor on the work of another, whence no reward or reputation would accrue to himself. But, he adds, "I shall have fruit enough, if others derive rich fruit from hence; glory enough, if the glory, that is, the truth and purity of heavenly doctrine, be by any labor of mine, transmitted unimpaired to posterity."

There is extant a beautiful and deeply touching letter from the editor, David Pareus, to his accomplished and eminent son, Philip Pareus, from which we learn that the work had been under his hand for many years, and had been subjected to frequent and severe revision. "Even as a precious gem," he says,

> is never so perfectly shapen and polished by the hands of the jeweler, but he desires to render it still more lustrous, and at every glance sees some new charm which may be added to it; so I never take this CATECHETICAL TREASURE into my hands, but I seem to hear the living voice of my preceptor again, and to learn something which had before escaped me; and I never lay it aside, but something here or there occurs to my mind which I wish to render more exact and explicit.

Along with this letter, he commits to the hands of his son a copy of the work which had received his "*ultima cura*" [trans: ultimate care] his "*postrema recognition*" [trans: final attention] and solemnly charges him, in the event of his death, (*si quid humanitùs mihi accidat* [trans: if anything should happen to me]) to give it to the world in that form. This letter is dated from his "Patmos," as he terms it (a retreat to which he had fled from the war then raging in the Palatinate), the 30th December, 1621, in the seventy-fourth year of his age, and about four months before his death.

---

66. [Bartholomäus Keckermann (1572–1608) was a Reformed theologian and professor of rhetoric.]

67. [See, for example, David Pareus, *In Divinam ad Romanos S. Pauli Apostoli Epistolam Commentarius* (Franfurt: Johannes Lancelloti, 1608).]

68. Pref. and Ded. 1598

Document 3: "The Heidelberg Catechism and Dr. Nevin"

Any additions or modifications after the above date must, of course, be looked upon as corruptions. The great popularity of the work caused many surreptitious editions of it to be issued, which as Philip Pareus tells us were often interpolated and otherwise corrupted. The only editions to be relied upon as genuine are those which were published before the death of David Pareus by himself, or after it, by Philip. We have before us three editions: that of Heidelberg in 1612;[69] that of Geneva, 1622;[70] and that of Hanover, 1634.[71]

Such is the work which Mr. Williard has just presented to the world in an English translation, and which we have reached by a much longer *détour* than we expected. But these introductory and explanatory remarks, will not, we think, be deemed amiss in reference to a work, the wide circulation of which in a pure form would be an immense benefit to our churches and community, and in fact, to the great and daily increasing portion of mankind who read the English language. It is a vast and various treasure of sacred knowledge, in which profound learning and logical acuteness have contributed their maturest and noblest efforts towards the defense and illustration of Christian truth. It has other and still higher excellencies. It is not only profound but deeply practical, not only exact but warm with the breath and pulse of Christian life. It solves a multitude of doubts and difficulties which are ever afloat in the popular mind in reference to the higher and harder points (the δυσνοητα) [trans: difficult to understand points] of Christian theology. The lectures which form this commentary were delivered, be it remembered, to theological classes, from which came forth not a few of the eminent professors, preachers, and authors of that day, among whom were Kimedontius, Keckermann, Lubbert, Pareus, and Quirinus. We should rejoice to see a translation which would do full justice to it, placed in the hands of every minister and theological student, and in fact, in every reading family through our country. We do not know a system of divinity which combines more (generally uncombined) excellencies, or better suited to furnish Christians of every profession and grade of acquirement with "a reason of the hope that is in them" [1 Peter 3:15]. It breathes, moreover, that fiducial and joyful spirit in which all, we think, will allow that the European cast of piety has greatly the advantage of our own, and resembles much more the scriptural and primitive model. It is as rare to hear the language of *doubt* there, as of *assurance* here. Doubt in fact, seems to have attained, with us, to a rank among the Christian graces, as if it were an evidence of humility and sincerity; instead of being, as it certainly is, a dishonor to our Lord, a reflection on his truth, and a violation of the plain precepts to trust and rejoice in him at all times, and to offer unto him the sacrifices of praise continually.[72] We have often been struck with the contrast at this point between

---

69. [Ursinus, *Corpus doctrinae Orthodoxae sive Catechetarium Explicationum D. Zachariae Ursini* (Heidelberg: Johannes Lancelloti, 1612).]

70. [Ursinus, *Corpus doctrinae Christianae Ecclesiarum* (Geneva: Tornaesium, 1622).]

71. [Ursinus, *Corpus doctrinae Christianae Ecclesiarum* (Hanover, 1634).]

72. [Like Nevin, Proudfit was disturbed by the prevalence of Enlightenment inspired skepticism

the piety of undoubted Christians in Europe and our own country, and have been puzzled for an adequate cause of it. But since we have been led to look more narrowly into the genius of this Catechism, we are inclined to think that its extensive use among the Swiss, Dutch and German Churches has had not a little to do with it. One of its principal beauties is that many of the answers[73] are in the form of an act of faith.[74] This, whenever faith is vital and sincere, would naturally tend to give it a confident and *appropriative* character. The same cheerful spirit pervades, as might be expected, the commentary which is the author's expansion of his own work. We would gladly welcome it to general circulation as a probable corrective to an acknowledged defect (accompanied, we gratefully own, with many admirable peculiarities) in Christian life and piety as it has been developed in our highly favored country. Why should not the characteristic activity and liberality of American Christians be accompanied, as these qualities were in the first age, with the fullness of Christian joy?

The old English translation of this work, we may add, by Parry[75] (which passed through repeated editions in its day), is a very unskillful performance, and besides, is now antiquated and extremely scarce. We heartily wish that we could speak of Mr. Williard's work, in its concrete form, with as cordial approbation as we can and do of the project which gave birth to it. But we are speaking of an authoritative exposition of the most widely received perhaps of all the symbols of the Reformed Faith; and we shall speak candidly, though not, we hope, unkindly. We feel compelled to express at once, our earnest hope and firm conviction that *the work, in its present form, can never go into general circulation in any of the Reformed Churches.*

The editorial and typographical execution of the work are, *ultra spem veniæ* [trans: beyond hope of pardon], negligent and inaccurate. The *errata* in spelling, pointing and numbering are so frequent and material as to be a serious blemish. The classics and fathers quoted in the exposition are sometimes cruelly handled. But more and worse than all this, *the 84th, 85th, and 95th questions of the Catechism, with the Scriptural proofs thereto pertaining, are omitted entire*; the exposition, meanwhile, jogging on as if quite unconscious that it had parted company with the text. This must, we think, be regarded as a *peccatum mortale* [trans: mortal sin] as it regards the present impression.

It is greatly to be regretted that Mr. Williard entered on his work with so meagre an apparatus. "The Latin copy" he says

---

in the United States.]

73. E.g., 1, 2, 21, 32, 52, 53, and many others.

74. [Nevin would agree with this assessment of the Catechism's rhetorical mood and force.]

75 [Henry Parry (1561–1616) was a moderately Reformed Anglican theologian who eventually became Bishop of Worcester. His translation of Ursinus' lectures was entitled *The Summe of Christian Religion* (Oxford, 1587).]

Document 3: "The Heidelberg Catechism and Dr. Nevin"

> from which we have made the present translation, was published in Geneva in the year 1616,[76] and is, without doubt, a copy of the best and most complete edition made by Dr. David Pareus, the intimate friend and disciple of Ursinus. It is, in every respect, greatly superior to another copy, the use of which we secured from the Rev. Dr. Hendron, of the Presbyterian Church, *after having made very considerable progress in the work of translation.*

Why Mr. Williard considers his own and only copy "without doubt the best and most complete," and "in every respect greatly superior" to the (not very graciously acknowledged) copy of Dr. Hendron does not appear. We are sorry to abate his good opinion of it. But, by turning back to the letter we have quoted above (p. 105) from Pareus himself, the reader will perceive that he pronounces the copy which he then sent to his son (Dec. 30th, 1621) the one which had received his *ultima cura* and the final form in which he wished his compilation of his master's lectures to go down to future ages. That edition could not, of course, have been published till 1622, about six years later than that possessed by Mr. Williard. He had, it seems, but two copies, and "secured the use" of the second, only "after having made very considerable progress in the work." He ought, we think, as we are sure he *might,* have obtained larger materials for collation.

He had, it seems, also, "the old English translation by Parry," "printed in the year 1645," "which," says he, "we constantly consulted in making the present translation." He did more, however, than "consult" it. "The old English translation," he tells us, (Pref. p. iv,) "contains considerable matter which is not to be found in either of the Latin copies now in our possession. We have, in several instances, taken the liberty of inserting short extracts, changing the style and construction of many of the sentences so as to adapt it to the taste of the modern reader. Whenever this is done, it is marked by the word 'addenda.'" In this practice (which Mr. Williard acknowledges with a praise-worthy frankness), we must remind him that he has departed from all the just principles which ought to guide a translator. We cannot well conceive a larger "liberty," than for a translator to "insert short extracts" from unknown sources (Parry is, we believe, unknown, save by this translation), "changing the style and construction so as to adapt it to the *taste* of the modern reader." Especially are such "liberties" to be censured, when taken with the writings of a man who poised and pondered every word in which he spoke God's truth, with such a *religiosa diligentia* [trans: religious diligence] as did Ursinus.[77]

---

76. [See Ursinus, *Corpus doctrinae Orthodoxae sive Catechetarium Explicationum D. Zachariae Ursini* (Geneva: Crispini, 1616). Actually this is a republication of the 1612 Heidelberg edition.]

77 "If any of his pupils imperfectly comprehended anything that was said in his lectures, or had any other doubt or difficulty to submit to him, he directed them to lay the same before him in writing, saying that he would reflect on the subject at home, and give the solution at the opening of the next day's lecture. He thus relieved himself from extemporaneous responses, and furnished his students with *well-premeditated* solutions of their doubts."—Mel. Adam, vit. Urs.

The instances are neither few nor unimportant in which Mr. Williard has failed to present the meaning of his author with fidelity and precision. On p. 9, Ursinus, speaking of "the testimony of the Holy Ghost," says that it is *"renatorum proprium"* which Mr. Williard renders as *"being also applicable to the unregenerate*, does not only convince their consciences, &c., but also *moves and inclines their hearts* to assent to this doctrine and to *receive it as the truth of God."* Here "the testimony of the Holy Ghost," by which, says Ursinus, "we mean a strong and lively faith, wrought in the hearts of the faithful by the Holy Spirit," &c., by an erroneous translation, which precisely reverses the *protasis* of the proposition, is predicated of "the unregenerate!"[78]

On p. 230, *"dum aduc vivebant,"* is translated "when he hitherto existed," which transfers to Christ what is affirmed of "the disobedient" (1 Pet. iii. 19).[79] Mr. Williard was betrayed into this mistake, we doubt not, by an inaccurate copy. But, if it were so, it shows the importance (hinted at above) of larger means of collation.

In the Exp. of 2. 66, Ursinus speaking of the application of the word *sacramentum* to Christian ordinances, says, *"ista quidem satis concinna est metaphora,"* which Mr. Williard (p. 341) renders, "this is, indeed, beautiful and significant!"

On p. 379, we have the words of our Lord, *do this in remembrance of me*, expounded as follows: "This remembrance or commemoration of Christ, precedes and is taken for faith in the heart; after which, we make public confession, and acknowledgments of our thankfulness." In what possible sense can the commemoration of Christ *"precede* and *be taken for* faith in the heart?" The Latin is perfectly simple, thus, *"Haec recordatio et commemoratio est primum ipsa fides in corde: deinde publica confessio et gratiarum actio"* [trans: This remembrance and reminder is at first faith in the heart; then a public confession and grateful action].

In the farther treatment of the Lord's Supper, p. 395, we have the following unfathomable statement: "There is, therefore, no invisible thing or action that brings to view the nature or thing signified by the sacrament." The Latin reads, *"nulla igitur res sive actio invisibilis rationem sive appellationem sacramenti tueri potest."* This is distinct enough. Ursinus is reasoning to prove that "the sacraments were instituted to be *visible testimonies* and pledges of grace;" against the Romish doctrine that the body of Christ, *invisible under the bread*, is the sacrament. He therefore affirms, directly in point, that "no invisible thing or action can have the nature or the name of a sacrament;" because, as he says, in the same connection, "Sacraments or signs ought to be visible; and that does not deserve to be called a sacrament (as Erasmus says) which is not accomplished by an external sign."

But we will not fatigue the reader with farther specimens, though they might easily be multiplied.

---

78 [Here Proudfit is disturbed by the suggestion that the Holy Spirit works on the hearts of the unregenerate in a manner similar to the way that it works on the hearts of the regenerate.]

79. [Proudfit is objecting to the translation suggesting that the pre-existent Christ preached to the disobedient sinners who lived before the flood.]

Document 3: "The Heidelberg Catechism and Dr. Nevin"

Mr. Williard has committed a much graver error than any of those we have noticed, in ushering his work to the Christian public under the auspices of Dr. Nevin. The Heidelberg Catechism surely needed no "Introduction" to the Reformed Churches; as little did the name and commentary of its author. And in introducing these, Dr. Nevin has availed himself of the opportunity to "introduce" a good many other things besides, forming, on the whole, very uncongenial company, to say the least, both for the author and the book. Besides, the damage which Mr. Williard has thus incurred is uncompensated, as far as we can see, by the slightest gain of any sort. For, in relation to Mr. Williard himself, and the execution of his work, Dr. Nevin[80] maintains a profound silence, which is even more killing than *faint praise*.

But though Dr. Nevin carefully abstains from praising Mr. Williard or his translation, Mr. Williard abundantly praises "the excellent 'Introduction,' from the pen of Dr. Nevin," which, he tells us, "will be read with much interest, and throw much light upon the life and character of the author of these Lectures." Mr. Williard has thus fully endorsed the statements of Dr. Nevin, and compelled us to look upon the "translation" and "Introduction," as part and parcel of the same work.

While, in fact, Mr. Williard gives whatever weight his full commendation may carry with it, to the "excellent Introduction," he cautiously limits his adhesion to the doctrines of the Commentary. "We do not, of course, intend," he says, "to be understood as giving an unqualified approval of every view and sentiment contained in these Lectures." As he has not thought it necessary thus to "qualify" his "approval" of the Introduction, the reader is, of course, left to conclude that he is entirely identified with it.

What sort of "light" is thrown by Dr. Nevin's Introduction on the Catechism and Commentary of Ursinus, as well as on his "life and character," we propose, by a brief analysis, to show.

Dr. Nevin has certainly found no lack of "characteristic perfections" in the Heidelberg Catechism. "Its very style," he tells us, "moves with a sort of priestly solemnity which all are constrained to reverence and respect;" there "runs" in it "a continual appeal to the interior sense of the soul, a sort of solemn undertone, sounding from the depths of the invisible world."[81] "A strain of heavenly music seems to flow around us at all times, while we listen to its voice."[82] We cannot object to these encomiums, though we are far from aspiring to understand them. If they be indeed *peculiarities* of this Catechism, to Dr. Nevin must, we think, be conceded the merit of having first discovered and brought them to light. The Catechism has been lauded by learned divines and venerable Synods, from Bullinger down to the Westminster Assembly, with commendation quite as strong and various as may safely be awarded to any merely human composition. It has been pronounced "solid, clear, logical, scriptural;" "*vix alia,*" they have assured us, "*dari poterit solidior, concinnior, perfectior et ad captum*

---

80. Translator's Pref. p. iv.
81. [See Nevin, this volume, 168.]
82. [See Nevin, this volume, 169.]

adultiorum pariter et juniorum accommodatior" [trans: "scarcely any other can present something more solid, more elegant, more perfect and more closely adapted to the apprehension of the adult as well as the young"].[83] But for Dr. Nevin it has been reserved to apprehend and disclose "the priestly solemnity" of its movement and "the heavenly music which flows around" it. If these epithets, reduced to pedestrian style, mean simply the full, rich and harmonious exhibition of truth, the matter comes then within the range of our humble consciousness; and we must say, that in our plain way, we have been profoundly sensible to the same qualities in the Westminster Catechism, whose luminous and comprehensive statements have often penetrated and charmed our very soul.

Dr. Nevin commends the Catechism for "its care to avoid the thorny, dialectic subtleties of Calvinism."[84] And again in his "History of the Catechism," he tells us that "the knotty points of Calvinism are not brought forward in it as necessary objects of belief, one way or the other."[85] Among these "knotty points" and thorny dialectic subtleties of Calvinism," he enumerates the doctrines of " predestination,[86] "a limited or particular atonement,"[87] "irresistible grace,"[88] "the perseverance of the saints," and more faintly, the relations of the human will to conversion and salvation. These are the "knotty" and "hard points," "the thorny dialectic subtleties of Calvinism" which the Catechism has taken "care to avoid," and in relation to which it maintains, if we are to believe Dr. Nevin, a cautiously guarded non-committal. An astonishing statement truly! Why then was it called by way of eminence "the Calvinistic Catechism?" Why attacked as such, by Romanists, Lutherans, Socinians, and Remonstrants? Why adopted by all the branches of the Reformed Church as an embodiment of Calvinism? Why was its author banished from Breslau as a Calvinist? How totally must *he* have misapprehended the character of his own work![89] How must the Dutch, German, and

83. See the "Judicia Theologorum, &.C., de Catechizandi ratione," among the Acta Syn. Dord. Sess. XV.

84. [See Nevin, this volume, 167.]

85. History and Genius of the Heid. Catechism, p. 131. The "Introduction" so largely consists of extracts from that work, that we are justified in viewing them as a connected exposition of Dr. Nevin's sentiments; especially, as at the close of the "Introduction," he refers his readers to the "History." [See Nevin, *History and Genius of the Heidelberg Catechism*, this volume, 156.]

86. Hist, and Gen. of the Heid. Cat. p. 135. [See Nevin, *History and Genius of the Heidelberg Catechism*, this volume, 135.]

87. Hist, and Gen. of the Heid. Cat. p. 135. [See Nevin, *History and Genius of the Heidelberg Catechism*, this volume, 135.]

88. p. 136. [See Nevin, *History and Genius of the Heidelberg Catechism*, this volume, 136.]

89. See his [Ursinus'] Exposition and "Miscellanea Catechetica" passim; from the latter of which might be compiled an elaborate demonstration of the Five ("knotty") Points of Calvinism. We would particularly refer the reader to No. 4 of that collection, consisting of a long letter on Predestination and the questions involved in it, addressed to a friend who was perplexed on these points. He assures his troubled friend that it is as clearly revealed as any other truth in the Bible, and that it is attended with no difficulty, "provided only we read the Holy Scripture without prejudice and without bias, and with the sincere desire not of reforming God after our own fancies (*non reformandi Deum ad nostras*

Document 3: "The Heidelberg Catechism and Dr. Nevin"

Swiss Reformed Churches be amazed to find that they have been expounding from their pulpits, and teaching to their children, for almost three centuries, a Catechism in which doctrines which they have ever deemed vital and precious forms of evangelical truth are "avoided" and "not brought forward as necessary objects of orthodox belief!" How incredibly strange that the Westminster Assembly never detected this Laodicean latitudinarianism, but blindly gave it their earnest commendation! How superfluous the labor of Coppenstein in "*ex-calvinizing*" it, since it contained no Calvinism at all![90] How utterly, in fact, has it been misunderstood, by friends and foes, in that age and in all succeeding times, till the "light" has been "thrown upon it" by the Introduction of Dr. Nevin![91]

The reader has but to take this work into his hand and read over Questions 1st, 2nd, 7th, 8th, (but if we would complete the enumeration, we must include by far the greater portion of the Catechism; we will only add, therefore, the 21st) with the author's own exposition, and he will see these same "hard, knotty points" unfolded as rich life-germs of truth to all the uses of Christian comfort and sanctification; aye, and guarded too, by the author, in armor of proof against all assailants. We will promise him from our own experience, not only a full satisfaction of his doubts (if he has any), on this particular question, but a most edifying and delightful improvement of his time. The Heidelberg Catechism "avoiding" Calvinism! Verily, the temerity of mere assertion "can no farther go." If its Calvinism was strong enough to satisfy the Calvinists of that day, and the "hard-handed Puritans"[92] of England, a hundred years later, we certainly think it may satisfy us.

Dr. Nevin commends "the broad, free character which marks the tone of its instructions. It is, he says, "moderate, gentle, *soft*."[93] Rather questionable praise, we think, for "a form of sound words"—and certainly not more questionable in itself than in its application to the Heidelberg Catechism, which, after all Dr. Nevin has said of its "freedom from controversial," "polemical" and "party prejudices," really wears a more

---

φαντασιας) but of learning of him from himself, and of ascribing all glory to him and transferring it from ourselves to him. Thus," he adds, "have those things become easy to me which appeared difficult, so long as I depended on the authority of men, who neither profited themselves nor me." He clearly presents the doctrine with its adjuncts in that aspect in which it is so beautifully expressed in the XVII. Article of the Ch. of England; "The godly consideration of predestination and our election in Christ is full of sweet, pleasant, and unspeakable comfort." All the Five Points of (what is called) Calvinism protrude themselves in this long and admirable letter. The author tells his friend at the close, "*totam noctem impendi huic scriptioni, summa cum difficultate*" [Trans. "spent the whole night writing this, most great with difficulty"]. It is dated Sept. 11, 1573.

90. [See Johann Andreas Coppenstein, *Uncalvinisch Heydelbergische Catechismus, Veruncalvinisiert* (Heidelberg: Leonhart Neander, 1624).]

91. [Proudfit is contending that the Catechism does teach, at least implicitly, the doctrines of the Synod of Dort.]

92. "Early Christianity," No. II. [Nevin, "Early Christianity," *Mercersburg Review* (1851) 461–90; 513–62; repr. *Catholic and Reformed*, ed. Yrigoyen and Bricker, 177–256. The phrase cannot be located.]

93. [See Nevin, in this volume, 169.]

hostile and warlike front towards error and errorists than other Reformed symbols. For example, the Westminster Catechism confines itself to the simple and direct statement of truth,[94] whereas the Heidelberg Catechism repeatedly connects with such statement, a specification of the opposite error.

Prominent among its "characteristic perfections" is "the mystical element," "the rich, mystical element that is found to enter so largely into its composition," "the rich vein of mysticism which runs everywhere through its doctrinal statements."[95] Here is another occult quality of which its author and his early expounders never appear to have dreamed. Ursinus himself makes short work with μυστηριον [trans: mystery] by a very brief explanation of its classic derivation and use, and its scriptural and theological application, in his exposition of the 66th Question. He nowhere else uses the word, as far as we remember, even in reference to the Lord's Supper. But Dr. Nevin has found a "rich vein of mysticism entering largely into its composition," "running everywhere through its doctrinal statements." What is this? Dr. Nevin has thought proper to enlighten us. "The mystical element," he says,[96]

> is that quality in religion, by which it goes beyond all simply logical or intellectual apprehension, and addresses itself directly to the soul, as something to be felt and believed, even where it is too deep to be explained. The Bible abounds with such mysticism. It prevails, especially, in every page of the Apostle John. We find it largely in Luther. It has been often said that the Reformed faith, as distinguished from the Catholic and the Lutheran, is unfriendly to this element ... and so is ever prone to run into rationalism. And it must be confessed that there is some show of reason for the serious charge.

A very serious charge indeed! That "the Reformed faith as distinguished from the *Catholic* and the Lutheran, is unfriendly to an element" with which "the Bible abounds," and which "prevails in every page of the Apostle John!" But it is satisfactory to know that the Heidelberg Catechism being "the product of the Reformed Church in the full bloom of its historical development" has eliminated this hostile quality and thus "surmounted the force of the objection now mentioned;" in other words, has approximated to "*the Catholic* and Lutheran" systems. It seems difficult to conceive again why it was then so "fiercely assaulted" at once from Lutheranism and "from the Church of Rome itself!"[97]

But as for the existence of this "mystical element," this "quality which goes beyond all intellectual apprehension" in the Heidelberg Catechism, it is sufficient to

---

94. So does the Catechismus Genevensis (by Calvin.) The nearest approach which it makes to a hostile demonstration in any direction, is where it declares any departure from the command of Christ, in the doctrine and celebration of the Sacraments, to be *summum nefas* [Trans. "monstrous crime"].

95. Intro. p. 15 and 16. [See Nevin, in this volume, 169.]

96. Intro. p. 15. [See Nevin, in this volume, 168.]

97. Int. p. 16. [See Nevin, in this volume, 169.]

oppose to the assertion one plain declaration of Ursinus himself from innumerable others. It occurs in the Prolegomena to the Catechism No. IV. § 7—"Instruction must be *short, simple,* and *perspicuous,*" ("*brevis, simplex et perspicua*") on account of the ignorance and infirmity of learners." And *herein,* he says, *lies the great necessity and value of catechetical instruction.* How totally then must the worthy author have failed of his own aim and conception of a good Catechism, if he has made one which is pervaded "through all its doctrinal statements" with "that quality which goes beyond all intellectual apprehension!" How ill adapted would such a Catechism be to impart that "true *knowledge* of God and of his Son Jesus Christ, without which" (Ursinus tells us in § 3 of the same chapter) "no one that has attained to years of discretion and understanding can be saved" (sustaining the assertion by John xvii. 3). This whole No. of the Prolegomena is occupied with the demonstration of the necessity of a clear, solid and intelligible communication of the doctrines of Christianity. It has ever been deemed an extraordinary merit of this Catechism, that it was "*ad captum tam juniorum quam adultiorum accommodatus*" [trans: suited to the capacities of both the young and the adult]. Hear what Bullinger says of it,[98] after stating that he had read it with great eagerness and many thanks to God. "*Ordo libelli dilucidus est, et res ipsæ sincere verissimeque propositæ. Plana sunt omnia, piissima, fructuosissima, succincta brevitate comprehendentia magnas res et copiosas.*" [Trans: The order of the book is clearly outlined, and the matter itself is sincerely and correctly pursued. All things everywhere are most fruitful, succinct and brief, covering great and copious things.] So far were the ablest men of that day from detecting "the rich mystical element, going beyond all intellectual apprehension" which Dr. Nevin has discovered, "running everywhere through its doctrinal statements."

That it "addresses itself directly to the soul" is perfectly true. So do all the Reformed symbols; because they speak that "word of God which *pierceth* even to the dividing asunder of the soul and spirit" [Hebrews 4:12]. But they "address the soul" none the less "directly" because they address it *through* the intellect. "How many things are necessary for thee to *know*?" (says the Heidelberg Catechism (Q. 2). Again, "Whence knowest thou thy misery?" (Q. 3). "What is true Faith? (Q. 21); Ans. True Faith is not only a certain knowledge, whereby I hold for truth all that God has revealed to us in his word, but also an assured confidence, which the Holy Ghost works by the gospel in my heart," &c. Here everything is rational, (in the true sense,) manly, intelligent, and eminently free from the "mystical element," by Dr. Nevin's own exposition of it.[99] The Reformed creeds, and those who ministered them, sought not to stupefy and overcloud the human intellect with "mysticism," but to quicken and invigorate its faculties by the vital beams of truth, and to call them forth to their highest and noblest exercise, in the contemplation of the sublime verities of revelation. They therefore opened wide

98. In a letter written 1563, the same year in which the Catechism was published. It is quoted by Van Alphen. Oec. Cat. Pal. Prol. p. 40.

99. [Proudfit is assuming that "knowledge" always involves propositional cognition.]

to them the Bible. Their first and most earnest labor was to make it speak in the vulgar tongue of every race. They invited all men to come to its light, and to search into its truths, in a spirit at once reverential and free. In a word, they "fed the souls of men with *knowledge* and *understanding*,"[100] not with "doctrinal statements going beyond all intellectual apprehension!"

We dismiss this point with simply marking that these words, "mystery," "mysticism," "*mystical*" (Rev. xvii. 5), have been great favorites with the Papal Church. In fact, there have been wise and good men not a few (and the Reformers among them) who thought they could read on her brow, written by the finger of God, the name of "MYSTERY."[101] For that very reason, the Reformers eschewed both the word and the thing. They looked upon it as a sort of bandage which Rome tied over the eyes of men, when she wanted to put her hand into their pockets, or her "hook into their noses." When they spoke of "mysteries," it was of "the mysteries of God" and "of the kingdom of God;" the "deep things of God," and not the inventions and impostures which men have covered over with the veil of *mystery*. Nor do we know any sense in which any of them (and Ursinus as little as the rest) would have accepted the compliment which Dr. Nevin has here paid to the Heidelberg Catechism. With historical "mysticism" they certainly had little sympathy; and as little, we believe, with that "quality" in a certain school of modern German philosophy, which "goes beyond all intellectual apprehension."[102] The independence of the logical and intuitional consciousness was not yet brought to light. They speak as if they thought it necessary (in all things intelligible) to be understood in order to be "felt and believed."

But it soon becomes apparent in what direction this deep current of "mysticism" is wafting us. "The mystical element of the Catechism" (says Dr. Nevin, p. 15) "is closely connected with the Catholic spirit," "its sympathy with the religious life of the old Catholic Church."[103] This too, is numbered "among its characteristic perfections!" If by "the old Catholic Church" Dr. Nevin means the old (Roman) Catholic Church (and we can understand the author of "Early Christianity"[104] in no other sense), what are we to make of its direct antagonism to the Papal Church and doctrine, in every

---

100. [See Jer 3:15.]

101. It is painful to observe Dr. Nevin's fondness for this word; to hear him for example, frequently (even in the course of this Introduction) allude to the sacrament under the name of "the awful mystery." It brings to one's mind Bellarmine's "*tremenda mysteria missa*" [Trans. "tremendous mystery of the mass"] and the like Romish misnomers of "the Lord's Supper." Robert Bellarmine (or Bellarmini, 1542–1621) was an Italian cardinal and Jesuit theologian who enumerated and analyzed the disputed points that divided Catholics and Protestants.]

102. [Proudfit is ridiculing the strands of Idealism and Romanticism that posited a mode of apprehension that was prior to induction, conceptualization, and analytic reflection. For a parallel critique of mysticism see Charles Hodge, *Systematic Theology*, I, 64.]

103. [See Nevin, in this volume, 167.]

104. [Nevin, "Early Christianity," *Mercersburg Review* (1851) 461–90; 513–62; repr. *Catholic and Reformed*, ed. Yrigoyen and Bricker, 177–256.]

Document 3: "The Heidelberg Catechism and Dr. Nevin"

one of the "*præcipui articuli*" [trans: principal articles][105] in which the fathers of the Protestant Church made the "controversy" with Rome to consist. To select a few examples;—see its pointed condemnation of the claim of Rome to be "the only true Church, out of which there is no salvation," in Q. 54; of the Romish doctrine of good works in Q. 91, and in its whole treatment of the doctrine of justification; of the mass, Q. 80; of the power of the keys, Q. 83, 84, 85; of the use of images, Q. 96, 97, 98; of the invocation of saints, Q. 30, 99, 100, 102; and of enforced celibacy,[106] in the treatment of "marriage" in connection with Q. 109. This compliment of "sympathy with the old Catholic Church" appears simply ludicrous when we pass out of the Catechism into this "exposition of its true meaning,"[107] and see the author, with the whip of small cords in his hand, laying about him vigorously and with a will, at "schoolmen," "Papists," "monks," and "mass-mongers." A strange manifestation of sympathy, indeed! And still the question recurs, how came it that the Catechism was so "fiercely assaulted at the time of its appearance (as Dr. Nevin tells us it was, p. 16) from the Church of Rome?" She generally knows her friends, even her secret friends, too well to make them the objects of her "assaults."

Dr. Nevin, however, is determined to divest the Catechism, not only of all the "knotty" "hard points of Calvinism," but of all bristling manifestations of hostility towards Rome. He therefore sets himself to dismantle one of the *propugnacula* of the Reformed faith, in the following style:

> A great deal of offence, as is generally known, has been taken with the unfortunate declaration, by which the Roman mass is denounced, at the close of the 80th question, as being "nothing else than a denial of the one sacrifice and sufferings of Jesus Christ, and an accursed idolatry." But it should never be forgotten, that this harsh anathema, so foreign from the spirit of Melanchthon and Ursinus, and from the reigning tone also of the Heidelberg Catechism, forms no part of the original work as published under the hand of Ursinus himself. It is wanting in the first two editions; and was afterwards foisted in, only by the authority of the Elector Frederick, in the way of angry retort and counterblast, we are told, for certain severe declarations the other way, which had been passed a short time before by the council of Trent.[108]

We have here given Dr. Nevin's statement on this subject *entire*, without omitting or italicizing a word, that there may be no possibility of unfairness. We now beg the reader to compare it, statement by statement, with the following passage from his "History and Genius of the Heidelberg Catechism" (p. 54, 1847), which we transfer from his pages to our own with the same scrupulosity.

105. See the "Epilogus" to the Confess. Augustana. Hase, Libri Symbol. Ecc. Evang. p. 45. [See Karl Hase, ed., *Libri symbolici Ecclesiae evangelicae, sive, Concordia*, 2nd ed. (Leipzig. 1837).]

106. And of "penance" and "extreme unction" in the Expos. of Q[uestion]. 68th.

107. Dr. Nevin's Intro. p. 19.

108. [See Nevin, in this volume, 167.]

One remarkable distinction characterized the first edition, as compared with all which have been published since. The 80th Question, in which the Roman mass is denounced as an 'accursed idolatry,' was not suffered to make its appearance. In the second edition, it is found in its place, only the *accursed idolatry* is still suppressed. Finally, however, as in this same year the decrees of the Council of Trent came out anathematizing all who would not own the mass to be divine, the Elector took pains to have the question restored in full to the form in which it was originally composed, while the previous text was allowed to go out of use as defective and incorrect. This gave rise, subsequently, to no small controversy and reproach.[109]

The comparison of these passages brings to light two entirely irreconcilable discrepancies.

1. The "Introduction" states that the passage in question "is *wanting in the first two editions.*" The "History," that "in the second edition it is found in its place, only the 'accursed idolatry' is suppressed."
2. The "Introduction" affirms that it "*forms no part of the original work as published under the hand of Ursinus himself.*" The "History" states that in the first edition, the whole 80th Question *was not suffered to make its appearance*; in the second it is *found in its place, only* the "accursed idolatry is *still suppressed*, but that, finally, the Elector took pains to have the Question RESTORED *in full to* THE FORM *in which it was* ORIGINALLY COMPOSED, while the previous text was allowed to go out of use as *defective* and *incorrect.*"

How widely then, has Dr. Nevin changed ground between 1847 and 1851! We shall convince the reader presently, that his *progress*, in this respect, (we fear in others too,) has been in the direction of *error* and not of *truth*. We might quote him against himself, for he has given us the right to do so, by referring us to the "History" at the close of the "Introduction." But a "historian" who makes opposite statements of facts in the space of four years, without a syllable of retraction or explanation, is an *authority* so precarious that we cannot bring ourselves to rely upon it. Nor need we. A brief statement of unquestionable *facts* will put this matter in its true light.

The Catechism was first published in German (as we have seen) in January, 1563. Three successive editions were issued during that year. The first did not contain the 80th Question. The second contained it, with the exception of the last clause, "and an accursed idolatry." The third contained it *entire as it now stands*, closing with the declaration—"Und ist also die Mess im grund nichts anders, denn ein Verläugnung des einigen opffers un leidens Jesu Christi, und ein vermaledeite Abgötterey." [Trans: Consequently the Mass is basically nothing else than a denial of the once and for all passion of Jesus Christ, and a condemnable idolatry.]

To this third edition was appended the following notice,

109. [See Nevin, in this volume, 85.]

Document 3: "The Heidelberg Catechism and Dr. Nevin"

"*An den Christlichen Leser.*
 Was im ersten truck übersehen, als furnemlich folio 55, ist jetzunder auss befebl Churfüstlicher Gnaden addiert worden, 1563."

"To the Christian reader.
 What was overlooked (or omitted) in the former edition, as, especially, fol. 55, has now been added by order of his Electoral Grace, 1563."

On the 55th folio stood the 80th Question.[110] The Catechism *containing the 80th Question in this complete form*, was translated, the same year, 1563, into Latin, and shortly afterwards, successively, into the numerous European and Asiatic languages we have mentioned above, all carrying with them the 80th question, *precisely as it now stands* in the popular editions in use in the Reformed Churches.

These are the *facts* in the case which no man will contest.[111] Now for the charge of Dr. Nevin, that "the unfortunate declaration, by which the Roman Mass is denounced, at the close of the 80th Question, *forms no part of the original work* as published under the hand of Ursinus himself, but was *afterwards foisted in, only by the authority of the Elector Frederick.*"[112]

"To foist. To insert by forgery." Such is the whole definition of Dr. Johnson.[113] Have then the Reformed Churches been teaching, preaching and expounding for nearly three centuries a *forgery* under the belief that it was a truth of God? Such is the heavy charge brought against them by Dr. Nevin. Blessed be God, there is no truth in it.

We will take the phrase in its largest latitude. It can bear but three interpretations, viz., that the clause in question was inserted *after the death of Ursinus, without his knowledge, or against his consent and convictions.*

It was not inserted *after the death* of Ursinus. The whole question stands precisely in its present form in Niemeyer's copies, both German and Latin, printed from editions of 1563.[114] Ursinus died in 1583, twenty years afterward. It was not, therefore, inserted *after his death*.

It was not inserted *without his knowledge*. He expounded his own catechism throughout, year by year from 1563 to 1577 (fourteen years). The work before us consists of these "Expositions." It could not have been inserted therefore, *without his knowledge*.

---

110. Koecher, Cat. Gesch., p. 250.

111. The reader is referred to the following authorities:—Van Alphen Oec. Cat. Pal. Prologus, p. 29, &c., Koecher Cat. Geschichle der Ref. Kir. p. 250. Augusti. Versuch einer hist. krit. Ein. in die beyden Haupt. Kat. p. 115, Ac., Niemeyer Coll. Conf. in Ecc. Ref. Praef. p. 57, Ac. The latter presents the historical argument in its fullest and at the same time its briefest form. He printed both the German and Latin copies in his collection from the editions of 1563.

112. [See Nevin, in this volume, 167.]

113. [See Samuel Johnson, *A Dictionary of the English Language*, 2 vols (London: Knapton and Longman, 1827).]

114. Collectio, &c. p. 411 and 448, Kæcher says too, that he had *before his eyes*, while writing his "Catechetische Geschichte," a copy of the edition of 1563, in which the 80th Q. stood entire. Sec Cat. Gesch. des Ref. Kir. p. 251. 1756.

It was not inserted *against his consent and conviction*. Let the reader but look through his "Explicatio" of this question, and of the whole subject from Q. 75th to 80th, and see how he sustains every position and clause in it, *and this among the rest*, from the nature of things, from Scripture, and from the fathers, and he will be satisfied that not only his mind but his heart was in it. Let him read his "Theses de Sacramentis"[115] and he will receive yet more abundant proof.[116] We will not tire him with citations, but content ourselves with *one* which of itself will banish all doubt. In the year 1569 (six years after the publication of the Catechism), Ursinus *added* to the exposition of this 80th Q. eight "discrimina" in support of its doctrine, in which he reasserts and proves it, *clause by clause*, and deduces from the whole the following conclusion. "*Haec discrimina ostendunt, missam Papisticam in fundamento nihil esse aliud, quam abnegationem unici sacrificii Christi et horribilem idololatriam.*" "These *discrimina* show that the Popish Mass, at bottom, is nothing else than a denial of the one sacrifice of Christ and a horrible idolatry." A repetition, almost word for word, of the passage in question! It could not, therefore, have been inserted *without his consent and against his conviction*.[117]

But we will go further. *It was contained in the original draft as written by Ursinus.* Else why was it said to have been "*omitted*" (übersehen), in the *notula* appended to the third impression? Can anything be said to be *omitted* in the printing which was not *contained* in the manuscript copy? This very inscription substantiates beyond a doubt the statement of Dr. Nevin (1847) that, in the third edition, "it was *restored* to the form in which it was *originally composed*."

What shall we say then of Dr. Nevin's charge—in contradiction to all history (his own "History" included), that it was "*foisted in afterwards*, only by the authority of the Elector Frederick?" We have no disposition to find a name for it. It is sufficient for us to have demonstrated "the innocence of the Heidelberg Catechism."

Having thus far dealt with facts, shall we offer a probable conjecture as to this *gradual* insertion of the 80th question? It was a bold declaration of the truth of God. The previous questions (75 to 79) had contained a full statement of the doctrine of the Lord's Supper. This ("What is the *difference* between the Lord's Supper and the Popish Mass?") merely presented it *in contrast* with the corrupt and idolatrous substitute of the Papal Church. The Elector had to encounter the hostility of the imperial throne and of the Popish princes. Even his Lutheran brethren were disaffected by the Calvinistic features of the Catechism. He was overawed for a moment by the manifold perils of his position, and thought perhaps that the positive statement of the *truth* was

---

115. Bound up with the edition of 1622.

116. We have not the entire works of Ursinus within our reach, but Van Alphen says (Oec. Cat. Pal. Prol. p. 30) in reference to this 80th Q.—"In operibus Ursini *non tantum legitur integra*, sed etiam quod ad singulas partes explicatur et asseritur. Vide ilia Tom. I. p. 285." [Trans. "Ursinus read not only the entire work, but also explicated and acknowledged the individual parts." See Ursinus, *De Sacramentis* (Neustadt: Harnish, 1564).]

117. See these "discrimina," Lat. ed. of 1622, p. 541. Williard's Tr. p. 421.

enough, without holding up the opposite *error*. In the first edition, therefore, "the 80th question was not suffered to appear." In the second, he gathered more courage, and "it is found in its place, only the *accursed idolatry* is still suppressed." In the third, he *encouraged himself in the Lord his God* [1 Sam 30:6], and let the whole truth come out; in fact, "took pains" (ashamed it may be of having so far yielded to the fear of man) "to have the question restored in full to the form in which it was originally composed," saying, that "even if it should come to the shedding of blood, it would be an honor for which, if my God and Father should so please to use me, I could never be sufficiently thankful in this world or the next."

For the words of this noble confession, we are indebted to Dr. Nevin[118] (the Dr. Nevin, we mean, of 1847) as well as for the picture of his calm heroism at the Diet shortly after, where he was called to account for his Catechism, and "witnessed a good confession" before the Emperor and Princes, saying "in conclusion, he would still comfort himself in the sure promise of his Lord and Savior Jesus Christ, made to him as well as to all saints, that whatever he might lose for his name in this life, should be restored to him a hundred fold in the next."[119]

"The unfortunate declaration," Dr. Nevin tells us, gave "a great deal of offence." To whom? Not to the Reformed Church. "The evidence of this, we have in the free, full response with which it (the Catechism) was met, on the part of the Church, not only in the Palatinate, but also, in other lands. It was, as though the entire Reformed Church heard and joyfully recognized her own voice in the Heidelberg Catechism." We are indebted to Dr. Nevin ("Introduction," p. 14)[120] for this glowing description of its hearty and general approval; which is fully sustained by other authorities. Buddeus, (himself a Lutheran) tells us that even the Lutherans praised it.[121]

To the Papal Court and Hierarchy, the whole symbol, and pre-eminently this declaration "gave" no doubt "a great deal of offence;" for it fell upon them with the awful force and majesty of truth. To them it was, indeed, "an unfortunate declaration," for it and other like utterances of God's truth by the preachers, writers, and creeds of

---

118. History, &c. p. 65. Nevin, in this volume, 93.]

119. Hist. & Gen. of the Heid. Cat. p. 66, 7. See also the account of his truly blessed death in this same work, p. 69. [Nevin, in this volume, 93.]

120. [Nevin, in this volume, 166.]

121. Isag. Hist. Theol. p. 541. "Catechismus Heidelbergensis . . . magna non tantum a reformatæ Ecclesiæ addictis, *consensione* receptus, sed et a *nostratibus interdum laudatus est*." [Trans. "The Heidelberg Catechism . . . great not only by the devoted Reformed churches, consensus having been received, but also is sometimes praised by us." See Johann Franz Buddeus (1667–1729), *Isagoge Historico-Theologica* (Leipzig: Thomas Fritch, 1727–30).] The Catechism was libelled, he adds, by a Jesuit of the Palatinate, and defended by the illustrious James Lenfant, in a book entitled "L'innocence du Catechisme de Heidelberg demontrée contre deux libelles d'un Jesuite." [Jacques Lenfant, *L'innocence du Catechisme de Heidelberg* (Amsterdam: Pierre Humbert, 1723); (originally published 1688). Lenfant (1661–1728) was a French Reformed theologian who fled from France after the revocation of the Edict of Nantes and eventually settled in Berlin. Throughout his career he polemicized against the Jesuits and defended the Heidelberg Catechism against their criticisms that it departed from the teachings of the early church.]

the Reformation, broke the spell by which Rome had long held the nations entranced in her "strong delusions," and was at least "the beginning of the end" of her power.

It was "so foreign from the spirit of Melanchthon," says Dr. Nevin.[122] Now, Melanchthon understood his own "spirit" as well as most men. Let him express it for himself. In an address from the University of Wittenberg to the Elector Frederic, Duke of Saxony, we meet with the following expressions, and more like them. "*Missarum perniciosus et impius abusus*" [trans: Masses are pernicious and impious abuses]. They are numbered "*inter gravissima omnium et maxime horribilia peccata*" [trans: among all the gravest and most horrible sins]. "*Meræ imposturæ ad fraudem et fallaciam propter quæstum excogitatæ;—unde impuri sacrificuli occasione corradendæ pecuniæ*," &c. (Mere tricks, devised to deceive and ensnare for the sake of gain—whence impure priests take occasion to scrape up money," &c.) The profanation of the Lord's Supper by the Corinthian Church is called to mind, and the judgments which followed it, and it is added, "Wherefore, since we far more unworthily, and by utterly abominable practices, pollute a most holy ordinance, there is no doubt but we are yet more dreadfully punished with wars, pestilence, and infinite disasters, the greatness of which is before our eyes; and not only so, but (what is still more sad and more to be dreaded) with that blindness, and as it were frenzy, of a reprobate mind, which are daily observed in the ministers and defenders of the *Mass*."

To this document stands subscribed the name (*clarum et venerabile!*) of "Philippus Melanchthon."[123]

"So foreign" adds Dr. Nevin, "from the spirit of Ursinus." Now we may suppose the reader pretty well satisfied by this time "what manner of spirit" Ursinus "was of" in this matter. However, we will give him one more manifestation of it.

In his exposition of the 78th Question, he says of the worship of Christ's body in the bread as performed in the mass, "this is that fearful idolatry which is practiced in the Popish mass, which, without doubt, is so detestable to God that it would be better to suffer death a thousand times than once to commit it." *Hæc est ipsa illa horrenda idololatria, quæ in missa Papistica exercetur, quæ haud dubie tam est detestabilis*[124] *Deo, ut satius sit mille mortes oppetere, quam semel eam committere.* Lat. Ed. p. 431. Cf. Williard, p. 399.

We are sorry to strip the brow of Ursinus of one of the laurels with which the eloquent and somewhat poetic eulogium of Dr. Nevin has adorned it. But the truth must be told. We fear he is hardly entitled to all the μαλθακοι λογοι [trans: soft words], the epithets of "moderate," "gentle," "soft," "quiet soul," (Int. p. 16,)[125] with which Dr. Nevin

---

122. [See Nevin, in this volume, 167.]

123. Sententia Academiae Wittenbergensis ad Principem Frider. Duc. Sax. Elect. (Luth. Op. Tom. II.)

124. Mr. Williard translates "detestabilis" "displeasing." *Displeasing* is not a *translation* of *detestabilis*.

125. [Nevin, in this volume, 169.]

Document 3: "The Heidelberg Catechism and Dr. Nevin"

has somewhat profusely bepraised him. There is reason to fear that he regarded the abominations of Popery with even more than a *holy* indignation. We commend him to the charitable judgment of the reader in this matter, while we subjoin a single passage for his consideration. But he will excuse us for dropping it into a footnote, and leaving it modestly covered over with the veil (however thin to learned eyes) of its original Latinity. It may dissipate some of the saintly hues in which Dr. Nevin has drawn him; but, one thing is certain: it will leave him no longer entitled, either to praise or censure, on the score of "sympathy with the old (Roman) Catholic Church." The letter below was addressed "to a gentleman of Breslau who had just come back from Italy."[126]

In fact, if Dr. Nevin is looking for "sympathy with the religious life of the old Catholic Church" in any such sense[127] as he means, we do not know "to which of the saints" (in the Protestant calendar at least) he "will turn." "In Luther," he says above, (Int. p. 16,) "we find largely" that "mystical element" which "is closely connected with the Catholic spirit of which we have just spoken." Luther too, we insist, must have the privilege of speaking for himself. Hear then his voice: "*Quid ergo sequitur?—Missas quas sacrificia vocant, esse summam idololatriam et impietatem.*" [Trans: What follows, then? Calling the masses "sacrifices" is the height of idolatry and impiety.] And shortly after, "*Quare concludimus, constanti fiducia, Missarum usum sacrificiorum idem esse quod negare Christum.*"[128] "What then follows? That the masses which they call sacrifices are the height of idolatry and impiety. Wherefore, we conclude with unshaken confidence that the use of the sacrifices of the masses is nothing else than to *deny Christ*." A startling approximation that, to the "harsh anathema" in the 80th Question! The next page completes the resemblance—"*tanta impietatis novissimsæ execramenta*" [trans: such impiety of the worst excrement].[129]

Luther too shakes off Dr. Nevin's compliment of "sympathy" &c., in the same rude way as Ursinus: "That dragon's tail," (the mass) "hath drawn after it many abominations and idolatries."[130]

Calvin declares that "if all the angels of heaven should come to the mass, they could not purify it from its pollutions by their holy presence."[131]

---

126. Zach. Ursini Epistola ad amicum (Patricium Vratislaviensem) *ex Italia reversum. Gratulor tibi felicem reditum ex cloaca Diabolorum*, et precor, ut prosit tibi *balneum* quod *post illam* ingressus es. Quod si opus est, etiam *pumicem* huic schedæ inclusum tibi maitto, quo *fricatus* redeas nobis *lautus sat commode,*" &.c.

127. For the exposition of that sense, we refer the reader again to "Early Christianity" in the September and November numbers of the Mercersburg Review [*Mercersburg Review* (1851) 461–90; 513–62; repr. *Catholic and Reformed*, ed. Yrigoyen and Bricker, 177–256].

128. Luther de abroganda Missa priv. Op. Tom. II. p. 260.

129. Luther de abroganda Missa priv. Op. Tom. II. p. 261.

130. "Cauda ista draconis traxit multas abominationes et idololatrias."

131. "Ne omnes quidem Angelos, si Missae intersint, posse eluere ejus sordes sua sanctitate." Epist. qui liceat participate cultui Romanos Synagogae. Op. Calv. Tom. IX. p. 205.

This feeling and conviction then, and the severity with which it is expressed, were common to all the Reformers. It was this that made them Reformers. It was not with them a matter of temperament, but of faith. The stern soul of Calvin, the fiery vehemence of Luther, the tranquil Ursinus, the serene and philosophic Melanchthon, were all equally terrible in denouncing the impieties of the mass. They thought and spoke of it differently from what we do, because they knew more of it. They had emerged from the unfathomable pit of Romish corruption, and they fled, and called other men to flee for their lives. Luther said at his table, "I would not take a thousand florins for the advantage of having gone to Rome. If I had not been there, I should always have thought that I was speaking too strongly . . . I confess that I have often been too violent, but *never towards the Papacy*. To speak against that, a man ought to have a tongue on purpose, whose words should be thunderbolts. "[132]

A milder age followed the stormy period of the actual Reformation, abounding in "Irenica" and "conditions of peace." The works and lives of such men as Junius,[133] Parseus,[134] John Turretine[135] and Werenfels,[136] form a most interesting feature in the church history of that period. The various branches of the Protestant Church felt a strong affinity towards each other. The Churches of England and Holland held across the channel "*junctas manus, pignus amicitiæ*" [trans: joined hands, a pledge of friendship]. Good and great men in the several Protestant communions earnestly sought to bring about a "Christian alliance." But the works written by men of this stamp (and even for this express object) uniformly maintain "that there can be no sound agreement betwixt Popery and the profession of the Gospel, no more than betwixt light and darkness, falsehood and truth, God and Belial; and therefore no reconciliation can be devised betwixt them." We cite the exact words of Archbishop Ussher.[137] The

---

132. Michelet. Vie de Luther, Tome II. p. 103. [Proudfit is referring to Jules Michelet, *Mémoires de Luther* (Paris: L. Hachette, 1835).]

133. Polyander asked Junius shortly before his death which of his numerous works was his own favorite. "My Irenicon," said the good man, "for in all the rest I wrote as a theologian, in that as a Christian." [Francis Junius (1545–1602), who had studied under Calvin and Beza, helped pioneer Reformed scholasticism.]

134. [David Paraeus (1548–1622) was a professor at Heidelberg who argued against the Lutheran doctrine of ubiquity and against Bellarmini's view of the Eucharist.]

135. [François Turrettini (or Francis Turretine, 1623–87) was a Genevan-Italian Reformed theologian who defended the decisions of the Synod of Dort and articulated the theory of the plenary verbal inspiration of the Bible. His three-part *Institutio Theologiae Elencticae* (1679–85) was widely used as a textbook of conservative scholastic Reformed theology, and shaped many early-nineteenth century Reformed theologians in America.]

136. [Samuel Warenfels (1657–1740) was an orthodox but tolerant Swiss Reformed theologian who promoted the historical study of the Bible as a strategy for combatting narrowly doctrinal interpretations.]

137. Sum and Substance of Chris. Rel. p. 413, fol. 167S. [James Ussher (or Usher, 1581–1656) was the Church of Ireland Archbishop of Armagh, Primate of Ireland (1626–56), and a prolific writer about biblical history and the early church. He is most famous for his attempt to precisely date the creation of the universe. Well-versed in Patristic scholarship, he also identified the authentic letters of

Document 3: "The Heidelberg Catechism and Dr. Nevin"

meek and pacific Bishop Davenant goes still farther. "The Roman Church" ("being," as he elsewhere says in the same letter, "in doctrine a false, and in practice an *idolatrous* Church") "is no more a true Church in respect of Christ, or those due qualities and proper actions which Christ requires, than an arrant whore is a true and lawful wife unto her husband. You would not think, I am sure, in that sense, of calling that strumpet a true Church."[138] "*Sane non possumus, salva conscientia, cum iis consociari*" [trans: of course we can, in good conscience, along with those associating], says John Turretine,[139] the very embodiment of the pacific and comprehensive spirit. And all these peace-makers spoke the same language.[140] Without exception, however, they admitted (as did also the earlier and sterner Reformers,) that there were persons of sincere piety within the communion of the Church of Rome.[141] Why, then, do they, with one voice, proclaim the impossibility of a reconciliation with the Papal Church, consistently with a good conscience? One, from their many reasons, and generally the first and foremost was the perpetual sacrilege and idolatry of "the Roman Mass."

What, then, is the Roman Mass? To answer this question, we shall not go to "Morse & Co.[142] (albeit with us a decidedly respectable authority,) but ascend, at once, to a source of information which Dr. Nevin at least will admit to be august and indisputable—the Council of Trent.

The nine "Canons of the Mass" (passed by the Council of Trent, at its 22d Session, Sept. 17, 1562) ordain the following among other "Capita doctrinæ Missæ;"[143]

Ignatius of Antioch. See Ussher, *The Summe and Substance of Christian Religion* (London: Ranew and Robinson, 1670).]

138. Letter to the Bp. of Exon. Life, pref. to Comm. on Col. p. 36, 37. [John Davenant (1572–1641) was an Anglican bishop and moderate Reformed theologian. He served as one of the English delegates to the Synod of Dort, where he advocated the position that Christ died for all human beings in opposition to the theory of limited atonement. See Davenant, *An Exposition of the Epistle of St. Paul to the Colossians*, trans. Josiah Allport (London: Adams, Hamilton, and Co, 1832).]

139. De Artie. Fundamentalibus. Dilucid. Job. Alpli. Turretine. Vol. III. p. 63. [Jean-Alphonse Turrettini (1671–1737), the son of François Turrettini, was a Genevan theologian who sought to dispense with the requirement that ministers subscribe to the Helvetic Consensus. He also labored to promote a rapprochement between the Lutheran and Reformed communions.]

140. Even the Romanists admired these men. See Moreri's eloquent tribute to "l'illustre Alph. Turretin" and Werenfels (Sam.) whom he pronounces "Théologiens du premier ordre et animes à l'envi d'un esprit de prudence, de charité et de Concorde" [trans: theologians of the first order and animated by the envy of a spirit of prudence, charity, and concord], Diet. Hist. "Werenfels."

141. Arch. Ussher thinks that "even a Pope may be saved. For some, (in likelihood) have entered into and continued in that See ignorantly. Wherefore, they may possibly find place for repentance," etc. He is remarkably cautious in handling that point. Sum and Subst. &c. ibid.

142. "Early Christianity," Merc. Rev. Sept. 1851 [479]; [repr., *Catholic and Reformed*, ed. Yrigoyen and Bricker, 195. In that article Nevin was critiquing the virulent anti-Catholic "fanaticism" of Rev. Sydney E. Morse (1794–1871) who was the chief editor of the *New York Observer*. Sydney Morse was the younger brother of the inventor Samuel F. B. Morse.]

143. Pet. Soav. Pol. Hist. Conc. Trident. 1. VI. p. 520, 1. [Although there is a closing quotation mark at the end of this paragraph in the original, it does not appear to be a direct quote. One English version of the Canons can be found at *The Canons and Decrees of the Sacred and Œcumenical Council*

that the Mass is not a commemoration of a sacrifice, but a true and proper sacrifice of Jesus Christ, offered up to the Father by the hands of the priest; that Christ instituted the apostles and their successors as priests, thus to offer up his body and blood; that this offering up of the body and blood of Christ is a propitiation for sins not only of the living, but of the dead; that this sacrifice is rightly performed to the memory and honor of the saints; that it is rightly performed with such ceremonies, vestments and outward signs as the Church ordains; that it is rightly performed when the priest sacramentally communicates alone; that it is rightly performed when the words of consecration are uttered in an unknown tongue, and in a low voice.

The nine Anathemas corresponding to the Canons ordain that whosoever shall speak in opposition to any doctrine or usage contained in any one of these Canons is anathematized and damned. ("*Anathemate fulminari*, lit. thunderstricken with a curse, *et damnandum esse.*")

Here then, a mortal and a sinner clad in vestments and muttering (in a low voice and an unknown tongue) formulae of purely human (and most of them of heathen) invention, pretends to offer up to God the person of his beloved, and now glorified Son; the overpowering splendor of whose presence is such that his own beloved Apostle at the first glance, "fell at his feet as it were dead," (Rev. i.); who saith of himself, "I live for evermore!"—of whom his inspired Apostle testifies, "he hath by *one* offering *perfected forever* them that are sanctified" [Hebrews 10:14]. A sinful creature offers up in sacrifice his CREATOR: in the face of his own words, "No man taketh my life from me. I lay it down of myself." And this horrible mockery is gone through, not only to make a propitiation for the sins of the living, but to reverse the doom and alter the eternal state of the dead; nay more, and (if possible) worse, that human nature which "the Mighty God" (Is. ix. 6,) assumed into an unspeakable union with his own, is offered up in sacrifice "*to the memory and honor*"[144] of dead men whom Rome is pleased to call *saints*; some of them persons under whose crimes the very earth trembled while they lived upon it—men who would have been hanged in any country under the government of laws: and this unutterable rite is what Rome has made out of "the Lord's Supper;" that sweet and happy festival of grateful commemoration and holy communion in which the Redeemer, to *bring to mind himself*, and *to show forth his death*, took bread and blessed it and said, This is my body, and took the cup saying, This is my blood, his actual person being then before their eyes, and within the reach of their hands, his breast supporting the beloved disciple, his voice speaking to them, his mouth eating and drinking along with them. And Rome has not only thus turned the table into an altar, and the feast into a sacrifice, and the blessing into a muttered and unintelligible *consecration*,[145] and the affectionate memorial into a fearful immolation, and "the broken bread" into a wafer, and taken away the "cup of blessing" from

---

of Trent . . . , trans. Rev. J. Waterworth (London: C. Dolman, 1848), 158–59.]

144. "In memoriam et honorem sanctorum."—Hist. Concil. Trident.

145. "Summissa voce," "non lingua vulgari."—Ibid.

Document 3: "The Heidelberg Catechism and Dr. Nevin"

those to whom Christ gave it, saying, Drink ye *all* of it, and changed the words which Christ *spake to* his disciples that his *peace might abide in them*, and that their *joy might be full*—words, O how full of kind explanation even of their unexpressed doubts and difficulties, (John xiv. 8, 9 ; xvi. 19,) and clear, deep revelations of truth and grace, into words of which they cannot understand a syllable, doubly concealed as they are by *an unknown language and a low tone*; but when she has thus changed "the Lord's Supper" into her own "Mass," if any man speak a word[146] against jot or tittle of the new rite which she has thus brought into the place of that which Christ bequeathed to us, she excommunicates him from the Church on earth (*her* Church, blessed be God!), and dooms him to eternal fire in hell—aye, and gives him a foretaste of it too, in present and material fire, *wherever she has the power*.

This, reader, is "the Roman Mass."[147] To see how desperately many, even of the Roman bishops and clergy, struggled step by step, against the *horribile decretum* [trans: awful decree], you have but to look into the debates which preceded its passage in the Council. But the Pope, through his legates, was inexorable. The canons (curses and all) were at last passed by a *plurality of votes*; and Rome, on that day, branded on her own brow the mark of an idolatrous and apostate Church, which will cleave to her in the sight of God and man till she is herself "consumed by the breath of the Lord, and destroyed by the brightness of his coming" [2 Thess 2:8].

Will it be believed that Dr. Nevin has, within a few weeks, applied to this mixture of "abominable idolatries" the title of "the tremendous sacrament of the altar;" and in reference to the Papal Church and power in general, has held the following language: "The Papacy itself is a wonder of wonders.[148] There is nothing like it in all history besides." (That is undoubtedly true.)

> So all men will feel who stop to *think* about it in more than a fool's way. History, too, *even in Protestant hands*,[149] is coming more and more to do justice to the vast and mighty merits of the system in past times . . . Think of the theology of this old Catholic Church,[150] of its body of ethics,[151] of its canon

146. "Si quis dixerit" is the sole prefix to every anathema.—Ibid.

147. Can we wonder that Luther said of it, "It is incomprehensible that such an impious abuse is daily endured by God." ("Inæstimabile est tanturn impietatis abusum quotidie a Deo ferri."—Op. II. p. 250.) Or that Melancthon ascribes to it the "wars, pestilence, and infinite disasters" which afflicted Germany in his day? It seems, even now, that no country in which it is performed *by authority* can have either liberty or peace.

148. Cf. Rev. xiii. 3; "all the world wondered after the beast."

149. These italics are ours.

150. "The old Catholic Church" *is*, then, "the Papacy." Cf. above, p. 58.

151. This "body of ethics" has been admirably expounded by one of her own most gifted members, Pascal. See his "Lettres Provinciales." [Blaise Pascal (1623–1662) was a French Catholic mathematician and religious philosopher who appealed to existential motivations to defend Christianity. He adhered to the Jansenist theological party, which was suspected by the Jesuits of being too sympathetic to certain Protestant doctrines. He wrote in such a way as to evoke confusion and despair in readers so that they would be receptive to the offer of God's grace.]

law. The Cathedral of Cologne is no such work as this last. The dome of St. Peter is less sublimely grand than the first . . . However much of rubbish the Reformation found occasion to remove, it was still compelled *to do homage to the main body of the Roman theology as orthodox and right*; and to this day, *Protestantism has no valid mission in the world any farther than it is willing to build on this old foundation!!*"[152]

When Dr. Nevin chooses to expatiate in this strain from his theological chair at Mercersburg, and in contrast with "the vast and mighty merits of the Papacy," to discourse of "Protestant myths," and dilate on the "vast errors and monstrous diseases" of Protestantism nay, even to indulge in bitter sneers at "plenty of Bibles" as the means of reforming and saving the world, while he extols "the Papacy" as "the power of order and law, the fountain of a new civilization," &c., &c.; much as we may wonder and grieve at the strange and sad spectacle, it is not for us to interfere. But we cannot permit him, on the plea of "introducing" a Catechism which we all revere, and an exposition which bears the stamp of long and wide approval, to come, in his *mystical presence*,[153] into the sacred arcanum of theology, and, by a few quiet postulates, unlock the very citadel of the Reformed faith, and deliver up the key to the Romanists.

We do not hesitate to say that by the process through which he has made the Heidelberg Catechism to pass in this "Introduction,"[154] the strongest contrapositions which can be framed in words must speedily blend into each other. A man may reason that

"Black's not *so* black, nor white *so very* white,"[155]

till he has lost the power of distinguishing them. He may eventually persuade himself that "darkness *is* light, and light darkness." He may even bring his understanding to embrace the monstrous absurdity, that Popery is "early Christianity." But, while we deplore that he should thus bewilder himself, it would be treason to Christian truth to allow him voluntarily an opportunity of extensively bewildering and misleading others by misrepresenting and (we must use the right word) *calumniating* a manual so clear in the doctrine and so instinct with the life of Protestant Christianity as the venerable Heidelberg Catechism. It is, says Dr. Nevin, "a Calvinistic Catechism," yet it "avoids" Calvinism; it is "throughout decidedly Protestant,[156] yet it manifests great "sympathy for the old Catholic Church;" it does indeed contain one "harsh anathema,"

---

152. Mercersburg Rev., Nov. 1851. "Early Christianity," over Dr. Nevin's initials [532–33; repr. *Catholic and Reformed*, ed. Yrigoyen and Bricker, 226–27.]. See also the previous No.

153. [Proudfit scoffingly alludes to the title of Nevin's book on the Eucharist, *The Mystical Presence*.]

154. The reader may see the same process applied to the Thirty-Nine Articles of the Church of England in Tract No. 90, of the Oxford series.

155. [The quote is from George Canning (1770–827), the British Tory Prime Minister. See his poem "The New Morality," in his weekly journal *The Anti-Jacobin*, no. 36, July 9, 1798.]

156. "Hist. and Gen." &c. p. 130 [See Nevin, *History and Genius*, in this volume, 132.]

Document 3: "The Heidelberg Catechism and Dr. Nevin"

but that, "it should ever be remembered," is a forgery! Suffer Dr. Nevin thus to "go about the bulwarks" of this ancient creed, knock off the "hard, knotty points of Calvinism," and spike the tremendous ordnance that utters its thunders from the 80th Question—and he will soon make the Catechism what he *calls* it, "moderate, gentle, *soft*"—quite harmless towards Popery and every other error; itself in fact, "a city broken down and without walls."

But we forbear. *Adstat Typographus.* [trans: Printer, attend.] The reader, no doubt, is weary, and so are we. Enough we think, has been said to convince him that Mr. Williard's work, executed, and especially "introduced" as it is, cannot hope to be received with affection and confidence by the Reformed Churches; with some measure of which they would surely have welcomed it, even with its present imperfections, if it had come before them unattended by the "Introduction" and the "Translator's Preface."

An adequate translation of this noble "Body of Divinity" must therefore be still considered a *desideratum.* Can we look to Mr. Williard to supply it? If he will return, affectionately and cordially, to the faith which shed such unfading glory over the early annals of the German Reformed Church; if he will look more to Heidelberg and less to Mercersburg; and, taking this "Opus Catecheticum" in that final and condensed form in which Pareus bequeathed the Lectures of his venerated teacher to future times, "consulting" meanwhile the Latin much more constantly than "the old English translation," above all, retrenching inexorably, all "addenda" and "extracts" whether "short" or long from apocryphal sources—will reproduce the work in English with as close an imitation as possible, of the terse and elegant conciseness of the original—he will perform a work,

Οψιμον, οψιτελεστον, ὅου κλεος ουποτ ολειται[157];—

a service for which (long after the crotchets of Dr. Nevin have passed into oblivion), future generations of enlightened Christians will "rise up and call him blessed."

---

157. [Trans. "Late, late of fulfillment, which glory will never destroy".]

DOCUMENT 4

"The Heidelberg Catechism" (1852)

(by John Williamson Nevin)

Editor's Introduction

Nevin responded to Proudfit's criticisms with no little venom. The sarcasm and irony in his essay are thick.

First Nevin asserted with vehemence that Proudfit's concern about discrepancy between Nevin's 1847 and 1851 accounts of the evolution of Question 80 of the Heidelberg Catechism through its first three editions did not affect the substance of Nevin's argument. Nevin's change of mind about some minor matters (particularly the inclusion of anything like Question 80 in the first edition) did not invalidate his consistent conclusion that the inclusion of the "idolatry of the Mass" theme had not originally been intended by Ursinus, but was rather the product of Frederick's intervention. Nevin claimed that any modification of his earlier opinion that Question 80 had been entirely absent in the first edition were due to his more recent access to more secondary sources and his reconsideration of his earlier construal of some of the texts. His change of mind was not due to any nefarious motivation. Moreover, his failure to draw attention to his reinterpretation of the genesis of Question 80 in 1851 was simply the result of his desire to avoid a display of pedantry in a context where it was not appropriate. Nevin concludes that his contention that Elector Frederick had the "idolatry" clause inserted into the third edition was still valid, and that by doing so Frederick was unrighteously exercising civil authority in theological matters (even though the constitutional arrangements in Heidelberg allowed him to do this).

What is at stake for Nevin is the irenic spirit of the Catechism, especially as intended by Ursinus. He rejects Proudfit's argument that all of the Reformers objected to the Roman Mass and that therefore the Heidelberg theologians must have shared their antipathy. Nevin admits that it is obvious that all Protestant theologians, including Ursinus, condemned the eucharistic theology of the Roman Church. But, Nevin adds, that critique does not mean that the condemnation must be included in a confessional document. For Nevin the purpose of a confessional document is to affirm essential convictions and not to engage in divisive polemics.

Nevin then objects to Proudfit's assertion that his positive use of the terms "mystery" and "catholic" necessarily indicates a fondness for those aspects of the Roman Church to which the Reformers had so strenuously objected. Nevin points out that

Document 4: "The Heidelberg Catechism"

the concept "Reformed" actually denotes a spectrum of theological positions, some of which veer off into rationalism. The "Puritan" spirit may be allergic to "mystery," but that does not mean that all strands of the Reformed tradition share that sensibility. Moreover, Nevin accuses Proudfit of failing to appreciate what "mystery" signifies in this context. Nevin was relying on the distinction drawn by many German "mediating" theologians between "understanding," which was defined as the faculty of judging according to perceived data, from a higher form of knowledge, which was often called "reason." Reason, unlike the more empirical understanding, could intuit non-empirical phenomena like goodness and beauty and even apprehend supersensible realities. This was crucial for Nevin, for he employed the concept "mystery" to describe the objective presence of sacramental grace in the celebration of the Eucharist.

Nevin also objected that Proudfit was using "Reformed" and "Calvinist" as if those concepts essentially referred to a precise doctrine of election. But, Nevin countered, that identification of Calvinism with the five points of the Synod of Dort was a post-Reformation habit; it was not the essence of the original meaning of "Reformed." Not only was predestination not the defining characteristic of the Reformed tradition historically speaking, but it also should never be regarded as such, for the issue transcends human understanding. By elaborating this argument Nevin was defending his interpretation of the Catechism from the accusation that he was advocating an unhealthy and un-Reformed doctrinal vagueness. He was also declaring that the Catechism need not be read through the lens of the Synod of Dort, and actually had more in common with Melanchthonian Lutheranism than with Dutch hyper-Calvinism. While being careful to avoid insinuating that the "Dutch" interpretation of the Catechism was invalid, he did describe it scornfully. Clearly Nevin was nudging the German Reformed Church away from a more intimate alliance with the Dutch Reformed Church and toward cooperation with the Lutherans.

In conclusion Nevin dismissed Proudfit's critique of the translation, declaring his criticisms to be captious and trivial. At this point Nevin's contempt for Proudfit's essay becomes overt and edges toward a critique of Proudfit's character.

"The Heidelberg Catechism"[1]

We find in the last number of the Princeton Repertory a long article on Ursinus and the Heidelberg Catechism (attributed to the pen of the Rev. Dr. Proudfit of New Brunswick) in which we are called to account, not in the sweetest tone imaginable, for our article on the distinguished author of this formulary, which appears as an Introduction to Williard's translation of his Commentary on the Catechism, and which was published also in a late number of the Mercersburg Review.[2] To make out a more full and ample case, reference is had also to our small volume, published some years since, under the title of the "History and Genius of the Heidelberg Catechism,"[3] as well as to the first and second of our recent articles on "Early Christianity."[4]

First comes the unfortunate tail of the 80th question; a point, hardly entitled in our opinion, to half a dozen pages of grave discussion in an ostensibly scientific review, and of which in the end just nothing at all is made for the reviewer's main purpose. The only show of advantage he may seem to have against us (and it is but a thin show at best), is found in some slight discrepancy there is between our statement of the matter in 1847 and the representation we have made of it in 1851; this too concerning a single doubtful historical particular merely, and not changing the substance of the principal fact. In 1851 we say, of the tail of the 80th question, that it formed no part of the original Catechism as published under the hand of Ursinus himself; that it is wanting in the first two editions; and that it "was afterwards foisted in, only by the authority of the Elector Frederick, in the way of angry retort and counterblast, we are told, for certain severe declarations the other way, which had been passed a short time before by the Council of Trent."[5] Dr. Proudfit has no historical authority to urge in opposition to this statement. But on turning to our own book published in 1847, he finds the same statement in relation to the tail of the question, namely that it did not appear before the

1. [J. W. N[evin], *Mercersburg Review* 4 (March 1852) 155–86.]

2. [Nevin, "Zacharias Ursinus," *Mercersburg Review* 3 (September 1851) 490–512; in this volume, 157.]

3. [John Nevin, *The History and Genius of the Heidelberg Catechism*.]

4. [John Nevin, "Early Christianity," *Mercersburg Review* (1851) 461–90; 513–62; repr. *Catholic and Reformed*, eds. Yrigoyen and Bricker, 177–256.]

5. [See Nevin, in this volume, 167.]

third edition, but along with this an intimation that the whole question was wanting in the first edition; while it is added, that the Elector took pains afterwards, in view of the decrees passed by the Council of Trent, "to have the question restored in full to *the form in which it was originally composed,*" allowing the previous text to go out of use as "*defective and incorrect.*"[6] That this representation differs some from the other, is at once evident enough. The reviewer allows, that it may be accounted for by a change of view in regard to what was the actual state of the case, between the dates of the two statements; but goes on immediately to say, that the progress from the statement of 1847 to that of 1851 has been in the direction of error and not of truth; mumbling something about our having failed to explain the variation in the later version, and with no small indelicacy insinuating a charge of direct dishonesty in the whole business. The man who talks in this way may well be held somewhat sternly to the strict proof of what he says. "We shall convince the reader," writes Dr. Proudfit, "that his progress in this respect, (we fear in others too) has been in the direction of error and not of truth."[7] This means, if it mean anything at all, that the light in which the point in hand is presented by us in 1847 is nearer the truth than the view taken of it in 1851. But now what is the evidence brought to uphold this assertion? We have looked for it with some interest; and at first expected indeed (from the confident tone of the critic), that our own former impression was about to be justified again by some proof, better than any we had been able to find for it when writing our later sketch. But we are constrained to say, that we have been altogether disappointed. Not a word is quoted from any authority which is of any real force to show that the 80th question "was contained in the original draft as written by Ursinus," or that the third edition restored here simply what had been omitted in the first and second. The only show of evidence for any such supposition (beyond our own mistaken statement in 1847), is found in a single word of the notice to the Christian Reader appended, as Niemeyer says, to both the second and third editions: "*Was im ersten truck übersehen wird, als fürnemlich folio 55, ist jetzunder auss befelch Churfürstlicher Gnaden addiert worden.*"[8] The proof is made to lie in the word "übersehen" which Dr. Proudfit chooses to translate in the sense of "*omitted.*" This implies that it belonged to the first draft. "Can anything be said to be omitted in the printing," asks our censor triumphantly, "which was not contained in the manuscript copy? This very inscription substantiates, beyond a doubt, the statement of Dr. N. (1847), that in the third edition it was restored to the form in which it was originally composed. What shall we say then of Dr. N's. charge, in contradiction to all history, &c.—? We have no disposition to find a name for it."[9] All this proof, however, is mere smoke. The first

---

6. [See Nevin, in this volume, 85.]

7. [See Proudfit, in this volume, 209.]

8. What was *overlooked* in the first edition, as especially fol. 55, has now been added by order of his Electoral Grace, 1562. [See Hermann Agathon Niemeyer, *Collectio Confessionum in Ecclesiis Reformatis* (Leipzig, 1840), preface, lviii.]

9. [See Proudfit, in this volume, 211.]

sense of the word "übersehen," as Dr. P. himself very well knows, is "overlooked." To overlook *may* signify to omit; an oversight is an omission; but no such term would be used to express a deliberate suppression, like that which is imagined in the case now before us. Had the addition thus accounted for been in truth part of the text as it first stood, the fact would have been stated in plain terms. Besides, the note was appended to the second edition as well as to the third; which however gave this question differently. The second then, according to this view, pretended to make good the overseen omission of copy in the first, but overlooked also itself the last clause, making room thus for still farther correction in the third. But again, the note refers to this novelty as one only, though the main one (*fürnemlich folio* 55) among several alterations found in this third edition; for as Van Alpen informs us, "the first edition was in many things different from those that followed."[10] These other differences seem not indeed to have touched the substance of the text, but to have been confined to the form in which it was printed, the division into sabbaths, and the citations of scriptural proof. But the word "übersehen" extends to them all; and if Dr. Proudfit's exegesis is good, it must follow that the whole of these later emendations belonged in truth to the original copy as drawn up by Ursinus, and had been omitted by over sight when it was first printed— a tough hypothesis, which even the Brunswick Professor himself, we presume, will hardly care to swallow. Altogether it is clear, that "*übersehen*" here is *not* to be forced into the meaning of "*omitted*;" but that it is to be taken in its proper secondary sense of "*missed*" or as we say, "*wanting*;" and simply informs the reader, that the additions, or new things, found in the 2nd and 3rd editions as compared with the first were brought in to complete the Catechism by order of his Grace the Elector, who was the head at once of both Church and State, so far as the Palatinate was then concerned. This implies, that the want of the 80th question in the first edition, as well as the other matters now corrected, might be considered a defect or oversight, a sort of chasm in the text that needed to be filled in order that it might be properly complete; but it implies nothing beyond this, and instead of substantiating the point for which it is urged by Dr. Proudfit, goes very decidedly, we think, to substantiate precisely the contrary.

Dr. Proudfit's conjectural construction, then, to explain the "gradual insertion of the 80th question," falls to the ground with the airy bottom on which it is made to rest. It is at best not very honorable to Frederick and his theologians. Their zeal for truth gave birth in the first place to this question just as it now stands; but when ready, it was held most politic to keep it back, fear prevailing over faith in the Elector's mind. Gradually, however, the pious prince mustered courage to bring it out; first, all but the tail; and then the whole figure, tail and all; cunningly accounting for its tardy appearance, at the same time, by the transparent lie that it had been "over looked" in the first edition, left out by accident rather than design. A pretty exemplification truly of Frederick's piety and good sense. Happily for his memory, however, the apology

---

10. [Heinrich Simon van Alpen, *Geschichte und Literatur des Heidelbergischen Katechismus* (Frankfurt am Main: Hermannischen Buchhandlung, 1800).]

regards a case which is as purely hypothetical as itself. The entire "*fact*," of which it pretends to be the historical construction, resolves itself, as we have said before, into sheer smoke.

Still, the blunder itself is one towards which we at least are bound to exercise some indulgence; for it is one into which our own book of 1847 somehow fell, as we have already seen; and our " precarious" example in the case, we are much inclined to suspect, has gone farther than any other appearance of authority to throw our brother of New Brunswick out of the right track. We certainly had some ground before us in 1847, which seemed at the time to justify the shape into which our statement was thrown in writing the "History and Genius of the Heidelberg Catechism," but what it was exactly, we are now wholly at a loss to say; perhaps some expression in Van Alpen,[11] whose work we have not had latterly within reach; most probably however, in any case, just some such misconstrued phrase or word, as we have now had under consideration from the note preserved by Niemeyer. At all events, when we came to speak of the point again in 1851, we found it impossible to verify what we said before of the original manuscript text. On the contrary, our authorities were plainly against it. Witnesses of the most respectable order, not before at hand, convinced us that our former statement was without proper foundation; a conclusion, which we saw to be required also by the inward evidence of the whole case. So we quietly receded from our earlier representation, making our statement in 1851 conformable to what we then believed, and now believe, to be the simple truth of history. The statement is given purposely in the most general terms. It does not say that the 80th question was wanting altogether in the first edition; for the authorities are ambiguous as to that point also, (Niemeyer has it, following Van Alpen, "*vel prorsus omnissa vel mutilata*" [trans: either totally omitted or mutilated]); and it decides not how or whence the question came, when finally introduced into the text. The statement looks only to the tail of the thing. That, at any rate, belonged neither to the first nor second edition. The harsh anathema formed no part of the original work, "as published under the hand of Ursinus himself;" even had it been in the manuscript draft, this would remain true; it was not *published* under his hand; his judgment, in that case, must be regarded as having gone against its publication. So much latitude our statement was purposely framed to include. But the latitude need not have been put so wide. The supposition of any such keeping back of the 80th question, and more especially the anathema which forms the tail of it, is purely gratuitous, and rests so far as we are able to see on no proof whatever.

But why was there no retraction then in 1851 of what had been said four years before in 1847, no explanation of the discrepancy between the earlier statement and the last? Dr. P. affects to find this very suspicious. But we beg leave to say that it would have savored of pedantry, to go out of our way, in such an article as our Introduction to Williard's *Ursinus*, to clear up a circumstantial point of this sort, to show how we

11. [Van Alpen, *Geschichte und Literatur des Heidelbergischen Katechismus*.]

had been led to take a different view of the circumstance in question at different times. The object of our last article required no such digression; it was enough to state in general terms the historical fact as it appeared to us at the time. What historian does not find occasion, in successive editions even of the same work (if he be not himself a scientific automaton), to correct himself in many more serious respects? But what historian is bound, in every instance of doing so, to parade an officious explanation of the acknowledged discrepancy? The case calls for no such anxious and tedious pedantry.

We have said that the circumstance thus brought into small dispute is of no conclusive account, at any rate, for the reviewer's main object. Had the 80th question been prepared in full before the issue of the first edition of the Catechism (whether from the pen of Ursinus or from that of Olevianus) it would be still certain that it was deliberately stricken out, so far as it failed to appear in the *original publication*, and that the concluding anathema at least, "so foreign from the reigning spirit of Melanchthon and Ursinus," formed no part of this publication, but was "wanting in the first two editions" altogether. The case, however, is made stronger, when we know that they now boldly appeal to it as abundantly bearing us out in all that we have said. It is a simple matter of historical fact, that the last clause of the 80th question formed no part of the Catechism as first published; that it was wanting in the second edition as well as the first; and that it "was afterwards foisted in only by the authority of the Elector Frederick, in the way of angry retort and counterblast,"[12] over against certain corresponding fulminations of the Council of Trent.

We have lately furnished a series of historical authorities and quotations in proof of this general fact in reply to the challenge of some unknown minister of the Reformed Dutch Church, through the columns of the *Christian Intelligencer*.[13] It is not necessary to repeat them in this place. Their weight is not impaired in the least by anything in Dr. Proudfit's article. Rather we may say, he himself grants in truth the whole fact which he makes a show of calling in question; only trying to break the force of it, as we have seen, by foisting in (*pax verbo* [trans: a word of peace]) a perfectly untenable hypothesis for its explanation. The case is one, indeed, which allows of no dispute, and in reference to which we never dreamed of being called upon to make any defense. All writers on the Catechism agree that the last clause of the 80th question did not belong to it as originally published, but was added to the third edition "*aus Churfürstlicher Gnaden*" [trans: out of Electoral grace].

But granting this, as he has to do, our Brunswick critic still labors to mark out his charge of historical falsification, by raising small issues in his own way, for which there is no real ground in anything we have actually said, just for the purpose, as it might seem, of diverting attention from the only question that is really in debate. Thus the word "foist," he tells us, must mean "to insert by *forgery*" because it is so defined by Dr.

---

12. [See Nevin, in this volume, 167.]

13. [*The Christian Intelligencer* was a periodical of the Protestant Reformed Dutch Church published in New York City from 1830 to 1920.]

DOCUMENT 4: "THE HEIDELBERG CATECHISM"

Johnson;[14] as if every man of common education did not know, that the reigning *usus loquendi* [trans: use of the word] of this country at least allows it a much wider signification. We never thought of forgery, in applying it to the Elector Frederick. Webster defines it, "to insert surreptitiously, wrongfully, or without warrant." This the good old Elector did. When the Catechism was first ready for publication, it was submitted to a synod of the superintendents and leading pastors of the Palatinate for examination and review; and thus approved, it came out under the sanction of proper ecclesiastical authority, as well as by order of the civil power. It was the work, not simply of Ursinus nor of Frederick, but of the Church. But the addition now before us was not in that first text. It was introduced afterwards, without any action of the church, by the sole authority of the temporal prince. That he had full political right to do this, under the Erastian[15] order of the Palatinate, we are perfectly well aware. But had he any true church right to exercise such power? We believe not. It is not for any secular prince to make articles of faith for the church within his realm, however pious may be his intentions. Frederick then acted without proper religious warrant, when he undertook to mend the Catechism from his own will. The liberty may have been sanctioned by the subsequent acquiescence of the church. But still in itself it was arbitrary, temerarious, and wrong; and this is just what we meant to imply, when we applied to his conduct the disparaging word now under consideration. The malediction of the 80th question *was* "foisted" into the Catechism, after its first formal publication, by the sole authority of the Elector Frederick.[16]

But now, according to Dr. Proudfit, this can bear but three interpretations, namely, "that the clause in question was inserted after the death of Ursinus, without his knowledge, or against his consent and convictions." We say, it calls not necessarily for any of these suppositions. Certainly Ursinus, who outlived Frederick, knew of this addition made to the Catechism before it was a year old, acquiesced in it with the rest of the church, and considered it doctrinally correct. But it does not follow from this, that it was not brought in without warrant by the Elector, or that the judgment of Ursinus went in favor of the supposed improvement. He might consider the clause theologically sound, and yet not wish to see it in the Catechism. Or, even if we suppose him fully reconciled to the thing, when it took place, the general nature of the fact, as we have

---

14. Hereupon the Professor grows tragic, with solemn mien, and deep sepulchral tone, delivering himself as follows: "Have then the Reformed Churches been teaching, preaching and expounding for nearly three centuries, a forgery, under the belief that it was a truth of God? Such is the heavy charge brought against them by Dr. Nevin. Blessed be God, there is no truth in it"—A very *affecting* stroke of rhetoric certainly. [See Proudfit, in this volume, 210.]

15. [Thomas Erastus (1524–1583) was a Swiss theologian who argued that the state, and not the church through excommunication, should punish crimes. His view became extended to the general theory that the state had the authority to govern the church, which he actually never maintained.]

16. [Nevin is criticizing Frederick, whom he usually lionized, for using his civil authority to interfere in ecclesial and theological matters. Like most Americans, Nevin had a strong commitment to the church's independence from the state. Of course Nevin also disliked the overtly anti-catholic content of Frederick's intervention.]

stated it, remains the same. It is still certain, at all events, that the clause was not from the will of Ursinus, as this appears in the first publication of the Catechism; and also, that it was added afterwards, however publicly, on the sole responsibility of the Elector.

The following passage, quoted before on the point here in consideration as a note to our article in its [Mercersburg] Review form (not seen probably, or at least not heeded, by our present critic), it may be worthwhile here to quote again:

> Frederick by no means followed passively and blindly the counsel of his theologians; but the Reformed doctrine, and along with it the most determined dislike towards the Roman worship, and towards all that was still retained from it in the Lutheran church, were for him a matter of strong inward and personal religious conviction, which he well knew himself how to uphold and defend from his own diligent and careful study of the Scriptures. From these, particularly from the *Old* Testament, he deduced his duty to tolerate no idolatry in his land, though it should be in never so mild and plausible a form. Hence in the *second* and *third* editions of the Heidelberg Catechism, the 80th question, by his positive order alone, and *against* the counsel and will of its authors, was made to receive the addition, then highly offensive and dangerous, "So that the mass, at bottom, is nothing else than a denial of the one sacrifice and sufferings of Jesus Christ, and an accursed idolatry;" and he obstinately refused afterwards to give up the clause, in spite of all intimidations from the emperor and the empire set before him[17] for the purpose."—*Goebel, Churches of the Rhine*, p. 365.[18]

This writer, it will be seen, does not hesitate to say that the addition to the 80th question was brought in against the counsel and will positively of Ursinus and Olevianus. Our language has been much more reserved and guarded. We have said merely that it was wanting in the Catechism as they first gave it to the world, and that it was foisted in afterwards by another will.

So says *Seisen* also, in his late *Denkschrift* (p. 201) devoted specially to the History of the Reformation in Heidelberg.[19] *Vierordt*, in his History of the Reformation in Baden, (p. 466) has the same testimony.[20] So the article on the Heidelberg Cat-

---

17. Ebrard, in his work on the Lord's Supper (Vol. II. p. 609), also takes occasion to tell his readers, that "the last clause of the celebrated 80th question is *not original*, but was added first in the *third* edition, *most arbitrarily* (höchst eigenhändig), by the Elector," language quite as strong, we think, as the "*foisted in*" of our own article. [See Johann Heinrich August Ebrard (1818–88) *Das Dogma vom heiligen Abendmahl und seine Geschichte* (Frankfurt: Heinrich Zimmer, 1845), 2:609.]

18. [See Max Goebel, *Geschichte des christlichen Lebens in der rheinisch-westphälischen evangelischen Kirche* (Coblenz: Baedeker, 1849), 365.]

19. [See D. Seisen, *Geschichte der Reformation zu Heidelberg* (Heidelberg: J. C. B. Mohr, 1846).]

20. [See Karl F. Vierordt, *Geschichte der Reformation im Grossherzogthum Baden* (Karlsruhe: G. Braun, 1847), vol. 1. Karl Friedrich Vierordt (1790–864) was a German theologian, professor, and historian.]

DOCUMENT 4: "THE HEIDELBERG CATECHISM"

echism in the Encyclopedia of *Ersch* and *Gruber*;[21] so *Niemeyer*,[22] as we have just seen (p. 57, 58); so *Böckel* (p. 398);[23] and so *Henry Alting*, in his Hist. Eccl, Pal. (c. 44),[24] who says the addition was made "ex speciali Electoris mandate [trans: by the Elector's special mandate]."

Dr. Proudfit takes pains, in his characteristic style, to show that Melanchthon and Ursinus had a bad opinion of the mass, as well as of Romanism generally, and that it is therefore false to say that the anathema of the Catechism was "foreign from their spirit." This is small criticism, and when all is done is mere quibble. We know very well that all the Reformers were enemies to the Church of Rome and denounced the Roman mass. But what then? Will it follow, that all of them were alike prepared and disposed to insert this sweeping clause of the 80th question, in a standing church symbol? Or supposing even they were so, through stress of controversial zeal, might not this itself be still, for some of them at least, a thing foreign from their own reigning spirit? Luther could be violent enough against the mass, when it suited; but for all this, we know very well that *his* spirit here was not the same with that of Zwingli; as altogether the *animus* of Lutheranism, we may say, was materially different from that of the Reformed confession. So Melanchthon may say very hard things of Romanism; but it is gross wrong to argue from this, that he was not any more mild and irenical in his spirit than Luther and the other Reformers generally. We know that he was. His character is, in this respect, well settled in history, and not to be overthrown by any special pleading or quibbling in Dr. Proudfit's peculiar vein. It is notorious too, that Ursinus, with all his constitutional earnestness, partook largely of the same quiet and pacific spirit. Dr. P. indeed allows himself to question his title to the praise we have bestowed upon him on this score; but with no good reason that we can see, in the face of our own remark, that "it is characteristic of such a soft and quiet nature to be at the same lime ardent, and excitable on occasions even to passion."[25] Then again, the reigning spirit of the Heidelberg Catechism is not a point that can be said to be now open for contradiction or debate. No one questions its decidedly Protestant character, its general opposition to the Church of Rome, its Reformed or Calvinistic complexion as distinguished from high Lutheranism. But with all this, its predominant character is truly like that of Melanchthon himself, full of moderation and peace, rich in gentleness and love throughout. Altogether then, we had a perfect right to characterize the harsh anathema attached to the 80th question, as "foreign from the spirit of Melanchthon

21. [See Johann Samuel Ersch and Johann Gottfried Gruber, *Encyclopädie der Wissenschaften und Künste* (Leipzig, 1818–42).]

22. [See Hermann Agathon Niemeyer, *Collectio Confessionum in Ecclesiis Reformatis* (Leipzig, 1840).]

23. [See E. G. Adolf Böckel, *Die Bekenntniss-Schriften der Evangelisch-Reformirten Kirche* (Leipzig, 1847).]

24 [See Heinrich Alting, *Historia Ecclesiæ Palatinæ* (Groningen, 1728; originally published 1644).]

25. [See Nevin, in this volume, 176.]

and Ursinus, and from the *reigning* tone also of the Heidelberg Catechism."[26] It is not in fair keeping with the proper ecclesiastical genius of these great men; and it forms a marked exception to the method and manner of the Catechism, to its general bearing, as it comes before us at all other points.

Another specimen of our critic's special pleading, equally sophistical and unfair, is presented to us in the way he deals with certain leading features attributed by our article to the Heidelberg Catechism, particularly its mystical element and its sympathy with the old catholic life of the church. His remarks on "mysticism," which he takes as of one sense simply with "mystery," and as the exclusion of intelligibility, are sufficiently illogical, not to say ridiculously absurd. And it is if possible still more absurd to deny what we have said of the "catholic" spirit of the Catechism, by just assuming at once that this must mean sympathy with the distinguishing features of Romanism at the time of the Reformation, and then going on gravely to show that the formulary is plainly antagonistic to this system on all proper Protestant points. As if anyone in his senses could ever think otherwise of a *Reformed* symbol! This however is the very "art and mystery," on which the reviewer mainly relies, for giving effect to his whole attack. He sees in all a covert league with Romanism, a design even to Romanize the Reformed church, by making it appear that the Heidelberg Catechism is after all more Roman than Protestant. To such end looks and runs the word "catholic;" and this again is the key to the changes rung on that other word "mystical." It is all to seduce Protestants into the arms of the "Great Harlot." But Dr. Proudfit can see through the mill-stone of this awful "gun powder plot,"[27] and he will set the world right. If it be too late to save the German Reformed church from being swallowed up alive by the horrible snare, (without knowing it,) he will see to it at least that the Reformed Dutch church, and all other branches of the Reformed church, be properly warned and kept out of harm's way. So we have the cry, *Romanism! Romanism!* lustily shouted for effect. That is always sure, in such a case, to carry the popular ear. For the popular mind too, it is able to cover a multitude of sins, offences we mean against logic as well as charity and truth. "But is it really so?" asks the fanatical jealousy thus roused, rubbing its owlish eyes, and peering into the dark inane.—"Certainly," our alarmist replies, "you may see it in this picture of the Catechism and Ursinus, as plain as the nose on your own face."—"Where? Do in pity tell."—"Why *there*, in what is said of the catholic and mystical spirit of the work. Do not these terms point straight towards Rome? Is she not 'MYSTERY,' by apocalyptic seal? And is not she also the '*Catholic*' church? But the Catechism has always been praised for its simplicity and perspicuity. It is notoriously at war moreover with Romanism; else why should it have been so fiercely assaulted by the Papists, when it first appeared? Does Rome not know her own friends? *Ergo*, this picture of the Heidelberg Catechism, both as given in 1847 and now as we have it here

---

26. [See Nevin, in this volume, 167.]

27. [An allusion to a failed assassination plot against King James I by Catholics in 1605. The scheme involved the use of gunpowder to blow up the House of Lords.]

again in 1851, we are bound to consider insidious and false."—So runs the argument; lame enough in all conscience; made up of *ad captandum* [trans: designed to please the crowd] clap-trap mainly; but for this very reason also, we may add, but too sure of its own currency with the popular prejudice to which it makes its appeal.

All this however does not disturb in the least the truth of our picture, taken in its own fair and proper sense. The Catechism remains still truly *Melanchthonian* in its constitution; and carries in it accordingly both a catholic spirit and a rich mystical vein, beyond all that is to be found of this sort in any other symbolical book of the Reformed confession.

It breathes, we say, a *catholic* spirit. This does not mean, that it is either Roman or Lutheran in its theological mind; we know that it is neither; we speak of it always as a Reformed symbol, and judge it from the standpoint and standard of its own class. The Reformed confession includes various types of thought, receding more or less from Lutheranism and Catholicism in the Roman form. Modern Puritanism forms the extreme left of this prismatic spectrum, the greatest possible refraction, where the light of Christianity shades off finally, through the faint violet of Baptistic Independency, into clear Unitarian negation. The Heidelberg Catechism, on the other hand, represent just the other side of the Reformed scheme, that namely by which it lies next to the original Lutheran confession, and so in felt organic connection also with the past life of the church in its universal character.[28] This grew in some measure necessarily out of the circumstances of its formation; the fact was felt and acknowledged when the symbol first made its appearance; and the evidence of it is still open to all in the work itself. It has found more favor even in the Lutheran church than any other symbol belonging to the Reformed interest; and for this latter interest itself, as we all know, it was exalted at once to a sort of ecumenical authority; a fact of itself sufficient to attest its catholic character. This character here, however, implies more than mere liberality. Unitarianism is liberal; all indifferentism, all negative rationalism, is liberal in its own way; carries in itself just because it is negative, no positive contents for faith and life. Catholicity, on the contrary, supposes faith, truth, concrete reality, a given substance in the form of religion, a divine historical fact to be submitted to by all men, and found to be commensurate with the universal wants of the world. Such is the old force of the term, as employed to express a characteristic attribute of the church from the beginning. So understood, it carries in it necessarily the idea of sympathy and correspondence with the old life of Christianity, as this has formed the historical identity of the church through all ages, before the Reformation as well as since; for surely this life must have comprehended in it the true and proper substance of Christianity all along (however overlaid with corruptions and errors), from which

---

28. [Again Nevin suggests that the type of Reformed theology represented by the Heidelberg Catechism may have more in common with moderate Lutheranism than it does with the "modern Puritanism" that he associates with the neglect of historical confessions, creeds, catechisms, liturgies, and ecclesial practices. Here Nevin's sense of the organic development of the church through the ages is evident, including Protestantism's rootage in Roman Catholicism.]

to be disunited, must be held to be one and the same thing with ecclesiastical death. The catholicity of the Heidelberg Catechism then involves certainly, as it ought to do, "sympathy with the religious life of the old Catholic Church." In this trait, it goes beyond all other Reformed symbols; though it is in contrast with the later forms of Puritanism mainly that its significance comes fully into view. The Reformed faith generally in the beginning, though not just of one type here, owned the necessity of such fellowship in spirit with the historical substance of Catholicism as it had come down from other ages; and for this very reason fell in easily with the catholic soul and voice of the Heidelberg Catechism. But no such mind belongs to modern Puritanism. This has almost no sympathy whatever with the old church faith. All really churchly and catholic ideas are for it a perfect abomination. It disowns the sacraments in their ancient sense, and scouts the obligation of the creed. In contradistinction to this system that now affects to be not only the whole sense of the Reformed confession, (which notoriously it is not), but the whole sense also of whole Protestantism, (which is a still greater falsehood), we have characterized the Catechism as being in its reigning spirit historical and catholic. It is not Puritan. Modern Puritanism could not use it with hearty freedom and good-will; and those who try to bend it to this standard are always guilty of doing it gross violence and wrong. Its veneration for the creed, its doctrine of the holy sacraments, at once place it in a different order of religious faith. It does not go on the assumption, that the truths of Christianity may be put together in any and every way to suit the private judgment of modern times;[29] but holds the form and order of the creed to be the necessary type, and indispensable condition, of all sound doctrine; a true *regula fidei* [trans: rule of faith], the force of which must extend with real plastic power[30] to every other article of evangelical belief to make it really orthodox and right. "No Protestant doctrine can ever be held in a safe form, which is not so held as to be in truth a living branch from the trunk of this primitive symbol, in the consciousness of faith."[31]

29. "Protestantism takes the doctrines of the Bible into its creed, in just such an order as it thinks *to be natural*. But the other system holds itself bound to the order of the Apostles' Creed." Thus speaks the Puritan Recorder, in its caricature not long since of our second article on Early Christianity; not aware seemingly of the abyss of rationalism, which such a confession involves. For "Protestantism" however in this case, we should read "Puritanism." This last does indeed pretend to reconstruct Christianity from the bottom, putting its parts together as to itself seems natural; but original Protestantism was guilty of no such presumption. It felt itself bound to follow the Apostles' Creed and the decisions of the first general councils. [*The Puritan Recorder*, published in Boston, Massachusetts between 1849 and 1858, was a weekly newspaper that carried religious news and opinion pieces that would be of interest to the Congregationalists of New England. The first article in *The Puritan Recorder* series on the Apostles' Creed was "The Mercersburg Theology," July 24, 1849.]

30. [A "plastic power," according to Frederick Rauch (Nevin's predecessor at Mercersburg Seminary) "is the principle of individual life and its preservation, which . . . will confine the form of each individual to its species" (*Psychology*, 28–29). In more Aristotelian language, Nevin is saying that the creed has an "essence" that manifests itself in and is operative throughout all the articles of belief.]

31. Dr. Proudfit puts on a show of surprise over the following declaration, found in one of our late articles: 'However much of rubbish the Reformation found occasion to remove, it was still compelled

DOCUMENT 4: "The Heidelberg Catechism"

The Catechism, we say again, makes room largely for the *mystical* interest in religion, as well as for that which is merely logical and intellectual. We doubt whether Dr. Proudfit has the idea at all which this term is employed to express, by such writers for instance as Neander[32] or Ullmann,[33] when applied to the subject of the religious life under the opposition now stated; for it is not easy to understand otherwise, how it could be so grossly caricatured as we find it to be in his hands. The Catechism is not made up of riddles certainly, transcendentalisms or far-fetched Delphic oracles. Its "*mystik*" is not mystification, mysticism in the bad sense. But what then? We may say the same thing, with just as much force, of the Bible. Is there then no mystical element here? Are its propositions of so much force only, in general, as may be felt through the medium of the logical understanding? The Old Testament is throughout mystical, the letter symbolizing the spirit, the face of Moses covered with a veil "which is done away in Christ." Christ's parables are mystical, resting on real and not simply notional

---

to do homage to the main body of the Roman theology as orthodox and right; and to this day Protestantism has no valid mission in the world, any farther than it is willing to build on this old foundation." [See Proudfit, in this volume, 219.] If he can really think that the truth of this statement is set aside by a couple of exclamation points, we have only to say that we pity his theological and historical knowledge. Let anyone take the trouble merely to read the *Summa* of Thomas Aquinas, or even the Catechism only of the Council of Trent, and if he has a spark of ingenuous feeling in him, he will be heartily ashamed of the ignorance and prejudice that too commonly reign among Protestants with regard to this point. The great body of our divinity, God be praised, is not of yesterday, but has come down to us as a rich legacy from former times, *through the Roman Catholic Church*. The same may be said of the ethical wealth, which is embodied in our modern civilization. How much of all, pray, do we owe to the Waldenses, Albigenses, and Paulicians? [The Waldensians were a Christian movement that arose in France in the twelfth century. Because they embraced apostolic poverty they were declared to be heretical. Surviving in the Alpine valleys of France and Italy, most of the Waldensians were absorbed by various Reformed churches during the Reformation era. The Paulicians were a dualistic Christian sect that arose in Armenia in the seventh century. Some Protestants regarded all these dissident groups as possible precursors of Protestantism, as a faithful remnant that preserved authentic religion during the period of alleged papal apostasy.] Take away the old Catholic trunk, and there can be no worth nor life in any Protestant doctrine. The mission of Protestantism most certainly, if it be from heaven and not as its enemies tell us from hell, is to build on the foundation already laid, and not to lay a new one for its own use. The article of justification by faith, for instance, is sound and good, if it be rooted in a heartfelt submission to the objective mysteries of the Apostles' Creed; whereas without this, as among our more unsacramental sects generally, it must be regarded as only a pestiferous delusion.

32. [Johann August Neander (1789–1850) was a German theologian and church historian whose view of history was profoundly influenced by his studies with Friedrich Schleiermacher while at Halle. He is best remembered for his *General History of the Christian Religion and Church* (*Allgemeine Geschichte der christlichen Religion und Kirche*).]

33. [Nevin reveals his indebtedness to authors like Neander (1789–1850), Karl Ullmann (1796–1865), and other "mediating" theologians who had been influenced by Schleiermacher and other post-Kantians. Many of these German theologians distinguished "understanding," which was defined as the faculty of judging according to sense, from a higher form of knowledge, which was often called "reason." Reason, unlike the more empirical understanding, could intuit supersensible realities. The distinction of "understanding" and "reason" was rooted in Kant's critical philosophy, although Kant severely restricted the scope of reason, particularly in regard to metaphysics, and would have discounted the notion of supersensible intuitions.]

analogies between the world of nature and the world of grace, which neither thought nor language can fully fathom, which can be felt only in the profoundest depths of the soul. The same may be said of his miracles. To a truly contemplative faith, they mean immeasurably more than they at once outwardly express. His teaching partook largely of the same character. "The words that I speak unto you," he said himself, "they are spirit and they are life" [John 6:63]. They are pregnant with a sense which goes far beyond either grammar or logic; missing which altogether, having no organ for it indeed, our rational exegesis too often turns them into mere "flesh that profiteth nothing" [John 6:63]. The sacred writers of the New Testament generally show more or less of the same quality; but most of all he who leaned on Jesus' bosom, and whom the ancients compare with the eagle soaring towards the sun. Without some sense for the mystical, no interpreter can understand or expound St. John. Who has not felt the force and beauty of the celebrated picture applied to him by Claudius: "Twilight and night; and through them the quick gleaming lightning. A soft evening cloud, and behind it the big full moon bodily!"[34] Does this imply unintelligibleness, or the opposite of clear simplicity? According to Dr. Proudfit's scheme of thinking, it does; but listen to Olshausen,[35] to say the least quite as competent a judge:

> The thoughts of John have the greatest simplicity, and along with this a metaphysical spirituality, they carry in them logical sharpness, without having proceeded from the standpoint of mere reflection. Born from the depth of intuition, they are still far from the cloudiness and confusion of mysticism; expressed in the plainest language, they unite in themselves the depth of genuine *mystik* with the clearness and precision of genuine *scholastik*. Where indeed the intuitive powers are wanting, or lie still undeveloped, the depth of John however clear must appear to be darkness; but for such standpoint also the Gospel of John was not written.[36]

34. [The quoted statement is by Matthias Claudius (1740–815), a German poet and journalist. It is contained in his review of Salomo Semler's *Paraphrasi Evangelii Johannis* contained in his journal *Wandsbecker Bote* (*The Wandsbeck Messenger*), vol. 1, 9.]

35. [Hermann Olshausen (1796–1839) was a German theologian and New Testament exegete who had been influenced by Schleiermacher and Neander during his studies at the universities of Kiel (1814) and Berlin (1816). He is remembered for his influential *Kommentar über sämmtliche Schriften des Neuen Testaments* (1830).

36. *Bib. Comm.* Vol. II. p. 24. [Hermann Olshausen, *Biblical Commentary on the Gospels*, trans. Thomas Brown (Edinburgh: T & T Clark, 1848), 2:24.]—Take the following passage also to the same point from Schaff's *Geschichte der Christlichen Kirche*, p. 344: "With, Paul, John possesses in common depth of knowledge. They are the two apostles who have left for us the fullest and most developed schemes of doctrine. But their knowledge is of different sort. Paul, trained in the school learning of the Pharisees, is an uncommonly sharp thinker and skillful dialectician, exhibiting the Christian doctrines for intellectual comprehension, proceeding from ground to consequence, from cause to effect, from the general to the particular, from propositions to conclusions, with true logical evidence and precision—a representative thus of genuine scholasticism (*Scholastik*) in the best sense of the word. The knowledge of John is intuition and contemplation. He sees his object with the soul (*Gemüth*), he takes in all as a single picture, and represents thus the deepest truths without proof, as an eye-witness, in their immediate originality. His knowledge of divine things is the deep reaching gaze of love, which

DOCUMENT 4: "The Heidelberg Catechism"

Now we do not pretend to make the Heidelberg Catechism of one character here with this sacred composition; we only make use of the example to show the absurdity of the criticism that has been so pompously paraded against the whole idea of a mystical element in the Catechism, as well as to illustrate in what general sense we and others have attributed to it such a quality, and are disposed to vindicate for it the same honorable distinction still.

Let it be kept in mind that we speak of it relatively to its own class. It is a *Reformed* symbol and must be judged of from the bosom of this confession. What we have said before of the genius of the Reformed confession, as being naturally unfavorable to the mystical element and disposed to move rather in the line of mere logical reflection, is too well established as a fact to be unsettled at all by the flimsy dialectics brought to bear upon it by Dr. Proudfit. It is acknowledged by all respectable writers on comparative symbolism. Not to speak of Zwingli, we find in Calvin here a spiritual nature very different from that of Luther. He is more rigorously rational and dialectic. This does not of itself imply reproach; for if the Bible abounds in one of the elements now contrasted, it abounds in the other likewise. If John is mystical, Paul is no less logical, with the same title to inspiration. There is a sound rationalism in religion, as well as a sound mysticism; though both terms, nakedly taken, carry in our language commonly a bad sense. This very fact, however, shows how possible it is for the right in either case to run into wrong; and we are reminded by it, at the same time, that each tendency is exposed naturally to its own abuse, and not to that of the other. Thus it is that the logical interest in religion, as we find it represented by the Reformed confession since the days of Zwingli and Calvin, though in itself a very good and necessary side of our common Christianity, carries in itself always notwithstanding a dangerous liability to become rationalistic. Not as if danger lay only on this side, and all was security on the other. But the danger of one side is not just that of the other. The constitutional leaning of the Reformed church is not towards bad mysticism, but towards bad rationalism. Now what we have said in relation to the Heidelberg Catechism is simply this, that it goes beyond all other symbols of its own confession in a proper combination of the mystical element with the merely rational, in the business of religious instruction. This by no means denies to it the common quality of the Reformed theology, logical clearness and precision; but on the contrary assumes this rather to be the reigning character of the work. "The Heidelberg Catechism," we expressly say,

> has regard throughout to the lawful claims of the understanding; its author was thoroughly versed in all the dialectic subtleties of the age, and an uncommonly fine logic in truth distinguishes its whole composition. But *along with this* runs, at the same time, a continual appeal to the interior sense of the soul, a sort of solemn undertone, sounding from the depths of the invisible world, which only an unction from the Holy One can enable any fully to hear and

---

always directs itself to the center, and from this outwards embraces all points of the periphery at one glance. He is the representative of all genuine mysticism (*Mystik*)."

understand. The words are *often* felt, in this way, to mean much more than they logically express. The Catechism is no cold workmanship merely of the rationalizing intellect. It is full of feeling and faith.[37]

It is not easy, of course, to prove or exemplify for the merely logical understanding the presence of a quality which addresses itself wholly to a different organ. To be apprehended at all, it must be felt. We may appeal again, however, to the sympathy in which the Catechism stands with the theory of religion embodied in the Apostles' Creed, and its palpable disagreement here with the spirit and genius of modern Puritanism. In the view of the creed, all religion rests in the acknowledgment of the mystery of the incarnation and its necessary consequences, historically considered, in the felt living sense of these supernatural realities, submitted to as actually at hand in the world by faith.[38] The system includes the idea of the church, as the medium of salvation, and of divine sacraments carrying in them objective force and power. But this churchly and sacramental side of religion involves of itself the force of what we now speak of as the mystical interest in proper conjunction with the merely intellectual or rational. Puritanism, in its modern shape, may be said to lack it altogether. It deals with religion as a matter of purely individual opinion and private experience. It turns it objectively into a mere abstraction. With the Heidelberg Catechism, on the contrary, it is regarded as a living concrete power. The catechumen is set down in the bosom as it were of the new creation, as a divine supernatural fact, and is taught to give his responses accordingly, not simply from the standpoint of outward reflection (as in the case for instance of the excellent Westminster Catechism), but from the condition of faith; the things being treated as of actual validity for him, as a member of the church by baptism, in virtue of what the church is for all the purposes of salvation by the constitution of its own glorious Head. Some have made this very feature an objection to the Catechism. But it agrees with all ecclesiastical antiquity, and falls in too with the general tone and style of the New Testament.

Look only at the sacramental doctrine of the Heidelberg Catechism, the light especially in which it presents the mystery of the Savior's presence in the holy eucharist. Dr. Proudfit, for some reason, avoids this point, only transiently touching on what he takes to be our disposition to lay too much stress on the mystical view of this sacrament. We have been a little surprised indeed, that in undertaking to vindicate the *innocence* of the Catechism against our representations, he should have taken no notice of what we have said of its differing from the Lutheran doctrine of the sacramental presence, on the question of mode only, and not at all on the question of fact. Some have pretended heretofore to deny this, and to make us out guilty of a serious error for asserting in favor of the old Reformed faith anything better than the rationalistic

---

37. [See Nevin, in this volume, 169.]

38. [Here Nevin accentuates the centrality of the Incarnation as a supernatural mystery in his understanding of Christianity. His high valuation of the church and its sacraments as the conduits of Christ's life follow from this emphasis.]

conception so common in modern times. We take it to be of some account, so far as this point is concerned, that Dr. Proudfit does not venture to make any open capital of the matter, however well suited it might seem at first view for his general purpose. This amounts in the circumstances to a sort of quiet acknowledgment that here at least we have the advantage of the cause he represents; that the participation of Christ's glorified body in the sacrament, through the mystical intervention of the Spirit, was held by the Reformed church generally in the sixteenth century; and that it is plainly taught, over and over again, in the Heidelberg Catechism. Dr. Proudfit knows too, that it is taught in the Confession of the Reformed Dutch church, in terms that shut out every sort of ambiguity. Does the Dutch church, at the present time, still hold fast to this part of her proper hereditary faith? Does our critic, Dr. Proudfit himself, regard it as anything more than a figure of rhetoric? We presume not to answer either of these questions. One thing is certain however; namely, that the sacramental doctrine of the Heidelberg Catechism is not in conformity with the present reigning *Puritan* standard, and that it is distinguished from this precisely by its mystical element, by its acknowledgment of a real mystery of grace in the holy sacrament, which was universally owned by the ancient church, but which Puritanism now sees fit to reject.[39] This distinction, however, implies a great deal more than itself nakedly considered. It may suit a certain style of theology, to conceive of the sacramental doctrine of the old Reformed faith as a sort of outward accident only, in no organic connection with its general system, and capable of being dissevered from it with gain rather than loss. But in its own nature, as we may easily enough see, the case is of a very different character. The doctrine in question must of necessity condition materially the whole system or scheme to which it belongs; and nothing therefore can be more precarious, than to think of measuring and trying this by another system that is not conditioned in its constitution by any such doctrine whatever. It is in vain to affect little or no regard for the point here brought into view, as though it were after all a small matter that the old idea of sacramental grace has been so widely lost in the religious thinking of the

---

39. Dr. Proudfit dislikes our use of the word "mystery." It is painful, he says, to hear it brought forward so much, in connection with the church and the sacraments. It is a favorite term with Romanists, the proper badge indeed of the Papacy; "for which very reason," if we take his word for it, "the Reformers eschewed both the word and the thing." Could we well have however, we ask in return, a more palpable apology for laying stress on the word, at the present time, than just such a barefaced attempt in the bosom, not of New England Congregationalism, but of the Reformed Dutch church, to kill and root out from Protestantism the whole glorious idea which the word represents? It is not true, that the Reformers eschewed either the word or the thing. Will it be pretended, that Luther made no account of the *mystery* of the holy eucharist, that he looked upon it as a mere "supper," in the low rationalistic sense insinuated (note p. 117) by Dr. Proudfit? [See Proudfit, in this volume, 207.] And is it not just this unmystical view that Calvin stigmatizes as profane? The sacraments have always been mysteries for the faith of the church, and must remain so as long as there is any true faith in the world. The church itself is a mystery. All the articles of the creed are mysteries; not simply in the sense of unfathomable doctrines, but in the sense of gloriously awful supernatural realities, historically present for faith in the bosom of the world under its natural form. Of all this, Puritanism, we are sorry to say, seems now to have almost no sense whatever.

present time. Unless we take the ground that the universal ancient church was out of its senses on this subject, and that original Protestantism labored also with regard to it under the most perfect delusion, we must see and feel that the modern error is something more than a single dead *fly* merely, causing the ointment of the apothecary to stink. It reaches far into the very life of faith and piety; and it is hard to say which class of persons most deserves indignant reprehension and rebuke; those who wantonly discard the mystery of the sacrament altogether, as it was once universally received, or those who condescendingly profess to make still some account of it, and yet the next moment turn round and shake hands with the first openly unbelieving class, as being after all of one mind with it mainly in its virulent opposition to every churchly idea, and as having no power apparently to see any danger whatever in the contrary direction. Only think of the distinction between Pedobaptists and Anti-pedobaptists,[40] the whole significance of which turns on the old idea of sacramental grace, sinking in the estimation of the first into the character of a mere secondary circumstance; or of American Lutheranism betaking itself for support and backing, in its unsacramental tendencies, to a tribunal which holds the mystery of the holy catholic church for a figment, and charges the Apostles' creed with wholesale heresy![41]

But our critic finds another string to play his *ad captandum* [trans: designed to please the crowd] strain upon, for the ear of popular prejudice particularly in his own church. We have made it a merit of the Heidelberg formulary, that it takes care "to avoid the thorny, dialectic subtle ties of Calvinism." This statement he affects to find "truly astonishing." Was it not called by way of eminence the Calvinistic Catechism; and so attacked by its enemies; and so received by all branches of the Reformed church? "Why was its author banished from Bresslau as a Calvinist?"[42] Nay is it not called by Dr. N himself a *Calvinistic* symbol? This and much more we have to like declamatory purpose; on the strength of which then the ground is boldly taken, that there is no truth in our assertion, that the hard knotty points in question are all brought out with marked prominence in the Catechism, and that it is the very height of temerity to represent it as avoiding them in any way whatever.

Now of all this we must be allowed to say in plain terms, that it is either very ignorant or else very dishonest. In the first place, does Dr. Proudfit really need to be informed, like the merest tyro in church history, that the term *Calvinistic*, as used in the sixteenth century, in opposition to the term "Lutheran," and as of one sense frequently with "Reformed," is not just of the same signification with this term as now popularly

---

40. [The distinction refers to those who baptize infants and those who are opposed to that practice.]

41. [The Lutheran theologian Samuel Schmucker had denied that baptism communicated regenerating grace and saw the practice as a symbol of initiation into the church. See Schmucker, *Elements of Popular Theology*, 2nd ed. (New York: Leavitt, Lord, and Co., 1834).]

42. [See Proudfit, in this volume, 203.]

DOCUMENT 4: "THE HEIDELBERG CATECHISM"

understood in its relation to Arminianism?[43] In our time, it carries in it at once a reference to the doctrine of the divine decrees, and is taken for the most part in no other sense; whereas, in the age of the Reformation, its reference was most immediately to the doctrine of the holy sacraments. As distinguished from Lutheran, it had regard mainly to the proper Reformed view of the Lord's Supper, as classically explained and defended by the great Genevan Reformer in his *Institutes* and other writing. In this sense only Melanchthon, in the latter part of his life, was looked upon as a sort of *Calvinist*. In this sense it was notoriously that Ursinus came under the reproach of *Calvinism*, in his native city Bresslau. In this sense the Palatinate became *Calvinistic* or Reformed in the year 1562; and in this sense mainly the Heidelberg Catechism was afterwards known and spoken of as a *Calvinist* symbol.[44] It was not Lutheran. It went with Calvin, in opposition to Luther, on the mode of the eucharistic mystery.

In the next place, we ask again, does Dr. Proudfit really need to be informed that the confessional distinction expressed by the title "*Reformed*" as opposed to Lutheranism, was not originally by any means synonymous with a formally professed allegiance to Calvin's theory of the decrees, much less with a full acknowledgment of all the knotty points of this theory as it was first published in his name? "The Protestants in Holland, Bremen, Poland, Hungary, and the Palatinate," says the historian Mosheim,[45] speaking of the Reformed church in the sixteenth century,

> followed indeed the French and Helvetic churches in their sentiments concerning the eucharist, in the simplicity of their worship, and in their principles of ecclesiastical polity; but *not* in their notions of predestination, which intricate doctrine they left undefined, and submitted to the free examination and private judgment of every individual. It may farther be affirmed that before the Synod of Dort, no Reformed church had obliged its members, by any special law, or

---

43. ["Arminianism" was a term applied to the followers of the theologian Jacob Arminius (1560–1609). Arminius had voiced concerns that the more doctrinaire Reformed leaders were interpreting God's sovereignty in ways that suggested absolute divine determinism. The Arminians typically denied the doctrines of total depravity, unconditional grace, limited atonement, irresistible grace, and the perseverance of the saints. Nevin was pointing out that after this dispute "Calvinist" was often used narrowly as a contrast term to "Arminian," focusing on the issue of God's decrees, whereas originally it had suggested Calvin's theology in general, particularly his views on the Eucharist. There the real contrast was with conservative Lutheranism.]

44. We have heard of cases in which advantage has been taken of this very amphibology, to draw both the members and the property of German congregations into the fold of Presbyterianism. "You are *Calvinistic*; that is the very title by which you hold your corporate rights; this however is our title; so you belong to us, the only distinction between us being that you are German and we are English; which is at an end, of course, as soon as you pass from the use of one language to the other." Many an honest German has been puzzled out of his own ecclesiastical identity by this logic; which possibly his English neighbor also no wiser than himself, has used upon him with perfectly good faith.

45. [Johann Lorenz Mosheim (1693–1755) was a German Lutheran church historian and chancellor of the University of Göttingen (1747–55) who is remembered for authoring the *Institutionum historiae ecclesiasticae libri* (1726).]

article of faith, to adhere to the doctrine of the church of Geneva relating to the primary causes of the salvation of the elect or the ruin of the reprobate.[46]

It is admitted by Mosheim, at the same time, that the greatest part of the Reformed doctors, in the countries now mentioned, fell by degrees of their own accord into the Genevan system; a fact "principally owing, no doubt, to the great reputation of the academy of Geneva, which was generally frequented, in this century, by those among the Reformed who were candidates for the ministry."[47] Along with this tendency, however, went from the beginning also an endeavor in different quarters to qualify the rigors of the original system; whilst in some branches of the church at least, it was distinctly understood and avowed that this side of Calvinism formed no part of the public faith whatever. Such particularly was the case with the German Reformed church. *The Confession of Sigismund* (Niemeyer, p. 650, 651) expressly rejects the idea of unconditional decrees.[48] The *Repetitio Anhaltina* (Niemeyer, p. 638, 639) carefully refuses to acknowledge any other cause or principle of election than what we find in the express word of the Gospel itself; according to which the preaching of repentance and grace is universal or for all, and the number of the saved is determined only by the fact of their obedience and faith; the predestination referring mainly to Christ, and God's immutable purpose to save in him, and by him, *sine prosopolepsia*, all that fly to him for redemption and cleave to him perseveringly to the end.[49] The *Declaration of Cassel*, issued by the General Synod of Hessia, a. 1607, professes (art. 6) to believe and teach on the high mystery of election all that is written of it in the Bible; "and beyond this," it adds,

> we believe and teach nothing; but refrain rather from the hard terms employed by some others, that might be an occasion to the simple either of despair or of carnal security, and hold ourselves to such terms as may serve with men the purposes of firm consolation and true godly living: And to be more explicit, our confession here is just the same with what Mr. Luther has drawn out from God's word in his Preface to the Epistle to the Romans.[50]

46. Eccles. Hist, Cent. XVI, Sect. Ill, Part II, Chap. II, (Maclaine's Translation). [See John Mosheim, *An Ecclesiastical History from the Birth of Christ to the Beginning of the Eighteenth Century*, trans. Archibald Maclaine (London: Thomas Tegg & Son, 1838), 2:191–92.]

47. [Mosheim, *Ecclesiastical History . . . to the Beginning of the Eighteenth Century*, 2:191–92.]

48. [See Hermann Agathon Niemeyer, *Collectio Confessionum in Ecclesiis Reformatis* (Leipzig, 1840), 650–51). The "Confession of Sigismund" (1614) was composed under the auspices of John Sigismund, Elector of Brandenburg, (1572–1619), who had converted from Lutheranism to Calvinism and hoped to accommodate both communions.]

49. [Niemeyer, *Collectio Confessionum in Ecclesiis Reformatis*, 638–39. "The Repetitio" was a confession of faith produced in the Duchy of Anhalt in 1581. The Duchy contained both Lutheran and Reformed populations; the confession, intended to "repeat" the Augsburg Confession, was Melanchthonian on most issues.]

50. See Heppe's late work "*Die Einführing der Verbesserungspunkte in Hessen von 1601–1610*," (a contribution to the history of the German Reformed church from original documents,) p. 74, 78. Here we have, according to Heppe, the doctrine of Luther and Melanchthon in regard to predestination, "*as*

DOCUMENT 4: "THE HEIDELBERG CATECHISM"

Universally, we may say, the relation of the German Reformed church to the Lutheran was such as to involve, almost as a matter of course, this moderate view of predestination and its kindred points. It was not here in any special sense, that the two confessions in Germany felt themselves divided. Both professed to rest on the same basis of the original Augsburg Confession. It was only when it came to the mode of the mystery, which both acknowledged in the Lord's Supper, that they could not agree.

This explains the general character and posture of the Heidelberg Catechism. It is primarily the leading standard symbol of the German Reformed church. It is Calvinistic; but the force of this distinction lies mainly in its doctrine of the sacraments; while on the subject of the divine decrees, it falls in rather, as far as it goes, with the Melanchthonian view, avoiding however the more knotty points of the matter altogether. This does not imply certainly, that it goes for Arminianism or Pelagianism, or that it expressly contradicts the points it refuses to teach.[51] Dr Proudfit appeals to its universal reception among the Reformed churches, to prove that it must have contained all that the Synod of Dort, for instance, or the Westminster Assembly, held to be essential here to full orthodox belief.[52] But this is absurd. Such universal reception shows just the contrary; namely, that it did not contain all that might be exacted by the more rigorous Predestinarians; since in that case, how could it have suited the more moderate class, the Melanchthonian spirit in particular of the German church from which it took its rise. It suited all, just *because* it stopped short of determinations in regard to which all were not of the same mind. In this view, it is not to be measured by the full theological system even of its own authors. It was not by any means necessary, that they should put into such a formulary, intended for public and general use, all the details of their own belief, as they might see fit to bring them forward in the lecture

---

the same is found also in the Heidelberg Catechism," while on the sacraments the Declaration gives us Melanchthonian Calvinism. [See Heinrich Heppe, *Die Einführung der Verbesserungspunkte in Hessen von 1601–1610* (Kassel: J. C. Kruger, 1849). Heppe (1820–879) was a German Calvinist theologian and professor of theology at the University of Marburg whose scholarship included dogmatics and the history of the Hessian church. His most influential work was the textbook, *Reformierte Dogmatik* (1861).]

51. ["Pelagianism" was a term of disapproval deployed against Christians influenced by the British monk Pelagius (355–420), whose teachings became popular in Rome. It is not entirely certain what Pelagius himself taught, but his theology seems to have revolved around the convictions that humans are not born with debilitating corruption and that the human will remains free to choose righteous action. Consequently, the term became linked with the concept of self-justification through the performance of good works. In the Reformation era Protestants habitually accused Catholics of being implicitly Pelagian.]

52. "How must the Dutch, German, and Swiss Reformed churches be amazed to find that they have been expounding from their pulpits, and teaching to their children, for almost three centuries, a Catechism in which doctrines which they have ever deemed vital and precious forms of evangelical truth, are 'avoided' and 'not brought forward as necessary objects of orthodox belief!' How incredibly strange that the Westminster Assembly never detected this Laodicean latitudinarianism, but blindly gave it their earnest commendation." [See Proudfit, in this volume, 204.] Why not go into hysterics at once over the deplorable thought that all Christendom has been using for many more centuries the creed and the Lord's Prayer, which yet labor here under still more dismal *latitudinarianism*.

room or pulpit. It is evident, on the contrary, that this was avoided with deliberate purpose and design. The authors of the work have taken pains to hold their own theological convictions as it were in check, in order that the text might be more general, and in this way true to the objective church life with which they were surrounded. This we know was not by any means prepared, in the Palatinate, to accept what may be called extreme Calvinism on the subject of the decrees; and from everything of that sort, accordingly, the Heidelberg symbol was made carefully to abstain.

"The Catechism," says *Ebrard*,[53]

> ... is known to follow the course of the Epistle to the Romans (with omission of Rom. ix- xi). The misery of man, redemption, and thankfulness, form the three main divisions. The disposition is throughout anthropological and soteriological, not speculative. If it has been rightly observed, that the Reformed theology rests on one speculative principle, that of dependence upon God in the predestinarian sense, let us take good care not to confound theology and the church; let us bear in mind, how just this Heidelberg Catechism, with its wholly anthropologic soteriological view of the material principle of faith, has found such vast circulation in the Reformed church as a book of instruction, and wrought with so much effect on the practical church life. The predestinarian theory was tolerated in the Reformed church, and taken up as an organic member into her spiritual life; but it is one of the essential peculiarities precisely of this church, that with genuine catholicity she has tolerated side by side different schools and modes of apprehension. One who should identify the predestinarian system with the spirit of the Reformed church, would deal with her as the Flaccian party[54] have done with the Lutheran. Along with Calvinism in the strict sense, is found in the Reformed church the more lax Zwinglianism (I speak not now of the sacramental doctrine, but of church life generally), and thirdly the Palatine or German Reformed churchdom. Here breathed Melanchthon's spirit. Predestination, as all know, is nowhere taught in the Heidelberg Catechism with so much as a single word; the whole view has proceeded as it were out of Melanchthon's heart.[55]

---

53. [Johannes Ebrard (1818–1888) was a German Protestant theologian, writer, and literary critic who served as professor and pastor in Zürich. His most influential works include his two volume *Christliche Dogmatik* (1851) and his commentary on John's Gospel, *Das Evangelium Johannis und die neueste Hypothese über seine Entstehung* (1845).]

54. [Matthias Flacius Illyricus (1520–75), born in Croatia, was a theologian, church historian, philosopher, and Lutheran zealot. He opposed Melanchthon's efforts in the 1550's to find a way to coexist with the Catholics who had just emerged victorious from the Schmalkaldic war. Illyricus rejected the notion that many Lutheran practices were not necessary for salvation, supported the doctrine of total depravity, claimed that the image of God in humanity had been totally destroyed, and insisted upon the physical presence of Christ in the eucharistic elements. His often extreme views were the cause of much opposition from many of his fellow Lutherans.]

55. Dogma vom h. Abendm. Vol. II. p. 603, 604. [Johann Heinrich August Ebrard (1818–88), *Das Dogma vom heiligen Abendmahl und seine Geschichte* (Frankfurt: Heinrich Zimmer, 1845).]

DOCUMENT 4: "THE HEIDELBERG CATECHISM"

Seisen, in his History of the Reformation in Heidelberg, takes the same view of Melanchthon's relation to the church of the Palatinate, and to the Catechism; and says of this last expressly (p. 205) that the Calvinistic doctrine of predestination enters not formally into its teaching.[56]

Vierordt, (Hist, of the Reformation in Baden, p. 467), disposes of the matter in the same way with the somewhat dry and curt remark: "The doctrine of absolute election is not expressed in the Heidelberg Catechism; and only in later times have some tried to extract it artificially out of the 32nd question."[57]

But a truce with authorities. The Catechism is before us, and may safely enough be allowed to speak for itself. What is the amount of our representation? Not that the general idea of election is wanting in its religious scheme; much less that it is excluded or contradicted. Not that it refuses absolutely to serve as a basis for the theology of Dort or Westminster, if any think it necessary to carry out the Reformed doctrine in that way. Nothing at all of this sort; but only that it does not bring into view the more knotty points of Calvinism, that it takes care to avoid its thorny dialectic subtleties, that it stops short of certain hard positions in regard to which the Reformed church itself has not been of one mind, not urging them as "necessary objects of belief." And can there be any intelligent doubt on this subject? Dr. Proudfit does indeed make a show of triumphantly proving the contrary. But it is at best a very empty show, as any child may easily see that will take the trouble of examining his references.

> The reader has but to take this work into his hand," he tells us, "and read over questions 1st, 2nd, 7th, 8th, (but if we would complete the enumeration, we must include by far the greater portion of the Catechism—we will only add therefore the 21st,) with the author's own exposition, and he will see these same 'hard, knotty points,' unfolded as rich life-germs of truth to all the uses of Christian comfort and sanctification.[58]

This is so very loose and wide as at once to convict itself of being totally without force. Strange indeed, if the Catechism should so teem with the character here in question, and the best theological eyes have failed to see it for so long a time! The questions here referred to say not a word in form of any of the hard points now under consideration. The exposition of Ursinus goes occasionally farther than the text explained; but this by no means authorizes the idea that the text in every such instance formally teaches what is thus brought in by the lecturer; for what we have asserted is that the formulary itself has not been carried out by the authors here to the full length even of their own convictions, that these were held in check rather for the purpose of making it more true to the general objective life it was formed to represent. It is not

---

56. [D. Seisen, *Geschichte der Reformation zu Heidelberg* (Heidelberg: J. C. B. Mohr, 1846).]

57. [Karl F. Vierordt, *Geschichte der Reformation im Grossherzogthum Baden* (Karlsruhe: G. Braun, 1847).]

58. [See Proudfit, in this volume, 204.]

true indeed, that Ursinus does commit himself in his exposition to the hard extremes of Calvinism, in the way intimated by Dr. Proudfit. The references given in support of the assertion prove nothing of the sort, and can hardly be said to have any relevancy whatever to the question in hand.[59] But we look not now to this. What we have to do with is the explicit formal teaching of the Catechism itself. Were there a question as to the actual sense of any part of its text, as in the case for instance of what is said of the mystical side of the Lord's Supper, all would depend on the author's own commentary. But where no part of the text is brought forward for interpretation, it is idle to fetch in any such help. The most that can be made of the author's exposition in that case is that he considered the text a fair and fit basis for the use made of it in this way. We have not questioned the practicability of building on the Catechism a rigorous scheme of the divine decrees; nay, we have expressly said that it could not have been endorsed by the Synod of Dort, if this body had not supposed its own theological system to be fairly involved in it so far as it went. But for all this, it would be ridiculous to pretend that all the determinations of the Synod of Dort are formally taught in the Heidelberg Catechism. And so we say, the hard points generally of metaphysical Calvinism are not there. To prove the contrary, it is not enough to get at them by derivation and round about construction. We must be pointed to some plain and direct teaching of the text itself. Where is the formal and explicit enunciation of these hard points to be found? In what terms are they made to challenge attention and regard? What questions bring them distinctly into view? Not the 1st, 2nd, 7th, 8th, or 21st certainly, to which we are referred by Dr. Proudfit; nor any others, we presume, on which he is likely soon to lay his discriminating finger.

To bring the case down to particulars. Where do we find the supralapsarian scheme presented in the Catechism?[60] Where is the election of a certain number of mankind to everlasting life set forth as the root and principle of redemption, preceding in the order of nature the predestination of Him by whom it was to be accomplished? Which question is it that limits the atonement to the range of this election, making it to have no reference to others, in spite of what is said of the Savior's sufferings in Quest. 37, as being of vicarious force, in body and soul, for "the sins of *all mankind?*"

---

59. The topic of Predestination he handles in form under the 54th question, as a sort of appendix "naturally growing out of the doctrine of the church." This of itself is enough to show that it is nowhere to be found directly and explicitly in the Catechism itself; for no one will pretend that it lies in this question, otherwise at best than by remote theological involution, or that the question is not easily capable of being so taken as to avoid entirely the idea of absolutely unconditional decrees. On the fall of man, question 7, he distinctly rejects the supralapsarian view, making Adam's sin to have been the object only of God's foreknowledge, which did not involve the necessity of what actually took place.

60 [Supralapsarianism was the theory that God's decrees of election and reprobation logically preceded God's decree (or permission) of the fall of Adam and Eve. The doctrine was based on the assumption that God's ultimate purpose must have been the manifestation of God's glorious judgment toward some and God's glorious mercy toward others. Humanity's fall into sin was a means toward that end. Supralapsarianism was proposed by the Reformed theologians Beza and Zanchius. It was not affirmed by the Synod of Dort, but neither was it rejected.]

DOCUMENT 4: "THE HEIDELBERG CATECHISM"

Where is it taught that grace is irresistible, or that the issue of it is not conditioned by the human will? What question affirms the absolute predestination of a given portion of the human race to perdition? Where is the doctrine of the decrees directly defined or asserted in any shape?

These are some of the *hard points* which we say the Heidelberg Catechism has taken care to avoid; and Dr. Proudfit's rhodomontade to the contrary is worth just nothing at all, till he shall condescend to come to the written text of the formulary itself, and quote question and line in proof of his bold contradictions. His course, in the whole matter, is by no means honorable and fair. It is very well known, that these hard points of Calvinism have been of more or less fluctuating authority for the general system so called, from the beginning. In the Synod of Dort itself, the supralapsarian hypothesis could not stand.[61] And what a tendency there is with our Calvinistic bodies generally in these latter days to mollify greatly, if not absolutely to throw away, much that belongs to the system in its full metaphysical glory, is on all sides sufficiently clear and well understood. We seriously question, indeed, whether even Dr. Proudfit himself is prepared deliberately to subscribe to all the "thorny dialectic subtleties" now in consideration—supralapsarianism for instance, and an atonement for a part of the human family only and not for the whole. And yet he falls upon our assertion that the Heidelberg Catechism avoids these subtleties and knotty points, as though it were tantamount at once to saying, that it has nothing to do with the Calvinistic system in any shape; over against which false accusation (a mere man of straw thus set up by himself) he then proceeds to fight lustily, with notes of admiration and other such artillery, till he has to his own satisfaction fairly demolished it, proving effectually that Ursinus was no Pelagian, and that his Catechism is not guilty of "Laodicean latitudinarianism" on the doctrines of grace! As if there were no intermediate ground to be thought of now in the case, between the formal teaching of the extreme points of Calvinism, and a lukewarm indifference to the proper evangelical substance of the system! What then are we to make of the Augsburg Confession? What must we think of Melanchthon, not to speak of Luther himself the great coryphaeus of the Reformation? Must the whole Lutheran theology be branded as Pelagian and Laodicean,

---

61. Speaking of the beginning of the 17th century, (Eccl. Hist. sect. II, part II, chap. II), Mosheim tells us: "There was not any public law or confession of faith that obliged the pastors of the Reformed churches, in any part of the world to conform their sentiments to the theological doctrines that were adopted and taught at Geneva. And accordingly there were many who either rejected entirely the doctrine of that academy on these intricate points, or received it with certain restrictions and modifications. Nay, even those who were in general attached to the theological system of Geneva were not perfectly agreed about the manner of explaining the doctrine relating to the divine decrees. The greatest part were of opinion that God had only permitted the first man to fall into transgression, without positively predetermining his fall. But others went much farther, and presumptuously forgetting their own ignorance on the one hand and the wisdom and equity of the divine counsels on the other, maintained that God. in order to exercise and display his awful justice and his free mercy had decreed from all eternity the transgression of Adam; and so ordered the course of events that our first parents could not possibly avoid their unhappy fall." [Mosheim, *Ecclesiastical History . . . to the Beginning of the Eighteenth Century*, 2:424.]

because it refuses the hard points of Geneva? So it would seem, with *a fortiori* consequence, from Dr. Proudfit's logic; for this theology positively disowns, in the case of some of these intricate knots, what the Heidelberg Catechism at worst but passes over with modest and discreet silence.

We cherish all proper regard for the Reformed Dutch church, and have no wish to abridge in the least its right to carry out the Calvinistic scheme in its own way; but we must earnestly protest, at the same time, against every attempt to convert this liberty into a yoke for the neck of the German church, such as from the beginning it has never yet been willing to accept or bear. The two bodies are closely related in their past history, and have much of a common genius, the kindly sense of which may not soon be extinguished, we sincerely trust, on either side.[62] But with all this they are not now, and never have been of just the same theological constitution and complexion. On the high points of Calvinism, in particular, the German Reformed church has always refused to go even so far as the Belgic Confession or the Decrees of the Synod of Dort, and much less to the *ultima thule* [trans: the ultimate place beyond the borders of the known world] of supralapsarian predestination.[63] The platform of our faith

---

62. This ecclesiastical consanguinity is often recognized, and pleasingly acknowledged, in the peculiar sort of home feeling, which the delegates of one body experience when taking part in the synodical sessions and proceedings of the other. On the Dutch side the relationship is best understood, in the nature of the case, by the true Dutch element still found in that church; as distinguished from the large infusion of foreign life (more or less Puritanic), which has already gone far to undermine the old spirit.

63. See on the character of the German Reformed church, and its relation to Lutheranism and Calvinism, an interesting article by Dr. H. HEPPE, published in Ullmann's *Studien und Kritiken*, July 1850. [See Heinrich Heppe, "Der charakter der deutsch-reformiten kirche," *Studien and Kirtiken*, ed. Carl Ullmann, July, 1850, 1:669–706.] With Calvin, the absolute decree forms the generative principle of all theology. His system turns on it as a pivot, from beginning to end, in a way intrinsically fatal at last even to his own doctrine of the sacraments. The Reformed Confessions generally, as we have before seen, were not willing to follow it out to its proper metaphysical end. "Almost all of them," according to Heppe, "take the *infralapsarian* view, (which cuts the life-nerve of Calvin's system,) and at the Synod of Dort, Gomar [Franciscus Gomarus (1563–1641), a strict Calvinistic Dutch theologian and an implacable critic of Arminianism] found himself, with his supralapsarian theory, in the position almost of a separatist. Only three Confessions present Calvin's dogma in its pure grain, the *Consensus of Geneva*, the *Helvetic Formula* of 1675, and the *Westminster Confession* of the Puritans. The first was not subscribed probably even by Zurich, among all the other Swiss churches. The second must be regarded as a posthumous work of the schools, which in a very short time passed into practical oblivion. So that neither the one nor the other document is of any force in evidence of what was the reigning consciousness of the Reformed church; and the Westminster Confession remains thus the only symbol of full predestinarianism—proof enough, that such Calvinism, arraying itself against the idea of a historical and sacramental church and resolving all into the *decretum Dei absolutum* [trans: God's absolute decree], carries in it no proper power of life." But now in direct opposition to the abstract principle of Calvinism, the German Reformation roots itself from the start in the historical and objective idea of the church. Out of this grew the Melanchthonian tendency as one side of the general movement, over against high Lutheranism as we have it in the Form [Formula] of Concord: the result of which was the German Reformed church, established as a common interest in the Palatinate, in Hesse, and in Brandenburg. This was Calvinistic in its sacramental doctrine, and fell in more or less with Calvinism also at other points; but it never gave up its distinctively German construction of theology. The Elector Frederick most distinctly professed to abide always by the Augsburg Confession,

here is wide and free. If any choose to be extreme predestinationists, they have full liberty to follow their particular inclination. But they are not allowed to narrow the platform itself to any such tight measure. Any attempt to do so, would be met at once by an overwhelming protest, from all parts of the church. There is a difference here between the Dutch and German churches, with all their close historical relationship, which it is very important always to bear in mind; a difference that grows mainly out of another relationship on the German side; that namely which this bears at the same time to confessional Lutheranism. It is not easy to understand or feel the full force of this, (as we have learned experimentally) without being in the bosom of the German Reformed church itself, and sharing in its actual theological life. No other branch of the Reformed church in this country can be said to understand Lutheranism, or to have any natural ecclesiastical sympathy with its proper genius and soul.[64] Now this affinity we have just as little right to ignore or forget, as we have to lose sight of the other. When the sense of it is lost, the constitutional life of the German Reformed church will be also at an end. Let the Dutch church understand this. Our Calvinism is not just that of the Synod of Dort; and we are not willing to admit of course, in the face of all past history, that the Heidelberg Catechism must be rigorously construed by any such rule. In all this however we quarrel not with the Dutch church, which has full right certainly, as we have said before, to carry out her confessional system in her own way; all we ask is, that the German church may be considered free also to stop short here, as she has ever done, with the simple text of the Catechism itself, leaving the hard points that lie beyond without symbolical determination for theology to solve and settle afterwards as it best can.

It only remains to notice briefly the criticism bestowed by Dr. Proudfit on Mr. Williard's translation itself. We have had no opportunity to compare this with the original text, and can therefore say nothing positively as to the ability and fidelity with which it has been executed. But it is easy enough to see, from the face of such evidence as we have before us, that the general criticism of the Brunswick Professor is exceedingly unfair.

He affects to call in question the worth and sufficiency of Mr. Williard's Latin text, (the Geneva edition of 1616) without any good reason that we can see whatever. He takes the translator solemnly to task, at the same time, for venturing out of his copy, in a few instances, to bring in short extracts from the "old English translation by Parry;"

---

and the doctrinal views of Melanchthon. The Heidelberg Catechism is *soteriologically* constructed, and follows Melanchthon's method and spirit throughout. Of predestination in the Calvinistic sense, we hear not a word. Such, we say, is the view taken of the whole case, in this article by Heppe.

64. It is remarkable, that no other Reformed church, (if we are rightly informed,) keeps up any ecclesiastical correspondence with any part of the Lutheran body in this country. A high wall of separation is made thus to shut out this whole confessional interest, which is yet glorified again in history, when it suits, as the main wing of the Reformation. What is thus excluded too is especially the idea of Lutheranism in its true original shape. By giving up its own glorious confessional life, the system (then known as "*American* Lutheranism") propitiates indeed some Puritan favor; but it falls at the same time into the predicament of a characterless Pelagian sect, with which no church fellowship is to be desired.

although these extracts (three in number, we believe, and amounting in all to perhaps two pages of matter) are carefully noted in the text itself as *addenda*, with due warning given of the fact besides in the Preface. In these extracts some alterations are made in Parry's antiquated style "to adapt it to the taste," Mr. Williard says, "of the modern reader." Now only hear Professor Proudfit on this point: "In this practice, we must remind him that he has departed from all the just principles which ought to guide a translator. We cannot well conceive a larger 'liberty,' than for a translator to 'insert short extracts' from unknown sources, changing the style and construction so as to adapt it to the *taste* of the modern reader!"[65] The word *taste* italicised to convey the perfectly gratuitous and we will add *ungentlemanly* insinuation, that the case may include some theological accommodation, instead of the mere fashion of language, the actual "foisting in" of a new sense with sinister purpose and regard.[66] Miserable balderdash!

But there are instances not a few of bad translation in the book, according to our critic. We can only say, not having the original at hand, that the book does not read like a bad translation; on the contrary it runs very clearly and smoothly, more so than translations do commonly, and makes at all events very good sense. Dr. Proudfit quotes a few specimens in proof of his charge; but they are after all of no very considerable account; and we know not how far they may be attributable to variations in the original text. We pretend not however to say that the translation is exempt from errors. That could hardly be expected in the first edition of so large a work. All we wish to say is that Dr. Proudfit's criticism here is chargeable with gross exaggeration.

So as regards the typographical and general editorial execution of the work. It is declared to be unpardonably negligent and inaccurate! This accusation at least, we feel at liberty bluntly to contradict. Typographical errors may indeed be found; but they certainly need some hunting. They are not at once patent. Pages need to be gone over, somewhat microscopically too in many cases, to find them. Then as for the general style of the book, it may easily enough be left to speak for itself; as it has already in truth won in its own favor, on all sides, the highest commendation and praise. Seldom do we meet with a religious work of like size, for common popular use, in the case of which the outward costume both of paper and type is less open to any fair reproach.

But three whole questions, the 84th, 85th and 95th, are left out altogether; "the exposition meanwhile jogging on, as if quite unconscious that it had parted company with the text."[67] Nine readers out of ten, we presume, would infer from the way in which this is brought forward by Dr. Proudfit, that these questions were dropped, commentary and all (the fault perhaps of Mr. Williard's bad Latin copy), while the

---

65. [See Proudfit, in this volume, 200.]

66. It is a little queer that one ground of offence with Williard's work at first in a certain quarter, we are told, was that it did not contain a portion of matter found in Parry's book, which is not from Ursinus at all. The omission was set down for a willful *suppressio veri* [Trans. "suppression of truth"] and evidence of a dreadful conspiracy with Mercersburg to murder the proper life of the Heidelberg Catechism!

67. [See Proudfit, in this volume, 199.]

worthy translator nevertheless went straight ahead with his work, having no sense seemingly of the *hiatus valde deflendus* [trans: a deficiency greatly to be deplored], by which these parts of the catechetical text were thus summarily annihilated! But what is the actual amount of the ominous omission in the end? Why this simply, that these three questions themselves do not appear in their proper place at the head of the sections or chapters of exposition to which they belong; while in truth no part whatever of the exposition itself is broken or wanting in any way. It all comes thus to an easily intelligible oversight of the press, which is a blemish certainly for this first impression of the work, but by no means such a damning sin as it might appear to be from the ambiguous form of Dr. Proudfit's charge.

It is plain enough after all, however, that the criticism of Mr. Williard's work forms but a small part of the real object of Dr. Proudfit's article; the main purpose of it is to assail the Mordecai sitting at the gate, our Introduction namely on the life and character of Ursinus. In what spirit, and with what sort of effect, this has been done, we have now tried to make in some measure apparent. The article is sufficiently ostentatious and ambitious; it is ushered in with quite a historical dissertation on the subject of catechetical instruction, abounds in sophomorical scraps of Latin (the author being a professor of the dead languages), and makes a wonderful parade throughout of doing up its work in a smashing wholesale way. But in all this there is a great deal more show than substance. The historical introduction is but little to the point; the sophomorical scraps of Latin prove nothing; and what affects to be smashing argument resolves itself, on near inspection, into empty smoke or something worse. The argument consists for the most part in creating false issues, by pushing qualified statements out to an extreme sense, by exaggerating and caricaturing points of controversy, in one word by setting up men of straw over whom an easy victory is gained, the weight of which is then pompously employed to crush what has been thus misrepresented and abused. Dr. Proudfit finds it an easy task to show that the Heidelberg Catechism has no sympathy with Romanism, is not made up of unintelligible mystification, and falls in with the general Augustinian theory of salvation in opposition to every sort of Pelagianism; and this he plays off as an overwhelming contradiction to our statement that the Catechism stands pre-eminent among Reformed or Calvinistic symbols for its catholic historical spirit, for its sense of the mystical interest in religion in connection with the intellectual, and for its moderation and reserve in not urging the Calvinistic system to its metaphysical extremes. The logic certainly is both easy and cheap.

We are glad to understand, that the first edition of Mr. Williard's book is already off his hands, and that the demand for it is such as to call for a second. The circulation is of course so far mainly within the German church. It would be a pity if the present *Introduction* merely should stand in the way of its being favorably received in the Reformed Dutch church, as Dr. Proudfit seems to think it should and must do. We beg leave therefore to suggest a simple remedy for the evil. Let a separate edition be engaged for the special use of this venerable sister denomination, carefully revised and with the Introduction left out. Or if preferred, let *another* Introduction be drawn up, either by Dr. Proudfit himself or by somebody else, calculated for the meridian of New Brunswick, and conformed in all respects theologically to the reigning Puritan standard of the present time. Let it roundly affirm that on the subject of the decrees the formal teaching of the Heidelberg Catechism falls not a whit behind the determinations of the Synod of Dort, that it owns no sympathy whatever with the catholic ideas of the ancient church, that it eschews religiously the whole mystical interest in religion and moves only in the sphere of the logical understanding, that it has in it no inward relationship whatever to Lutheranism, that the true key to its sense and spirit should be sought rather in New England Puritanism, that it is unchurchly and unsacramental throughout, acknowledging no objective grace, no mystery at all (just as little, be it whispered, as Art. XXXV of the Belgic Confession[68]) in the holy sacraments, on a full par thus with the universal sectarian rationalism of the day. Let this be the standpoint, we say, of the new Introduction, got up for the special use and benefit of the Reformed Dutch church; and if the Dutch church generally should choose to be satisfied with it, the world at large, we presume, will not feel it necessary to make any objection.

J. W. N.

68. [On "The Holy Supper of our Lord Jesus Christ."]

Document 5

"Historical Introduction" to the Heidelberg Catechism in German, Latin, and English: Tercentenary Edition (1863)

(by John Williamson Nevin)

Editor's Introduction

During a meeting of the Mercersburg Classis in 1859 Nevin's former colleague Philip Schaff proposed that the denomination should celebrate the tercentennial of the adoption of the Heidelberg Catechism in the Palatinate.[1] He also proposed that a critical edition of the Catechism should be prepared for the occasion, including both the Latin and the German texts complemented by an English translation. His proposals elicited enthusiastic agreement, and the Classis' resolutions were subsequently adopted by the Synod. When the planning for the 1863 celebration began, John Nevin was invited to serve on the committee responsible for producing the critical edition. Moreover, he agreed to write the introduction to the volume. When the convention was held in Philadelphia, Nevin was chosen to preside. In the midst of a brutal civil war, for three days scholars from Germany, the Netherlands, and the United States read papers on the history and theology of the Heidelberg Catechism to an audience that filled the sanctuary of Race Street Reformed Church. Nevin's efforts for two decades to raise the profile of the Catechism had evidently born fruit.

For the introduction to the critical edition of the Catechism Nevin once again reworked material that he had previously published, including material from *The Mystical Presence*. He repeated many of his central contentions about the Confession, all of which pointed to its inestimable worth. Nevin again praised Ursinus and Olevianus for generally avoiding the temptation to engage in metaphysical speculation. Other catechisms, he observed critically, had a didactic organization, so that "Christianity comes to appear as a theory, rather than a living fact."[2] Instead of vainly trying to probe inscrutable mysteries, the authors of the Heidelberg Catechism sought to illumine the meaning of Christian doctrines by exhibiting the roles that they play in the living of the Christian life. In the Catechism, Nevin enthused, divisive scholastic disputes were shunned and the unifying practice of piety was foregrounded. Even more than he had done in the past, Nevin emphasized the fact that the Catechism was designed to nurture Christianly appropriate hopes, sorrows, joys, and longing. Using his preferred terminology he characterized the Catechism as being more confessional

1. Appel, *Life and Work*, 605–27.
2. See Nevin, in this volume, 282.]

than didactic. Nevin also described this self-involving force as the Catechism's "anthropological" quality. Unlike Calvin's catechism or the Westminster catechisms, he claimed, the Heidelberg document is not based on God's abstract metaphysical perfections or on the general relation of God to the world. Nevin summarizes, "It is not a system of knowledge merely for the understanding, in which the truths of religion are set forth in the character of abstract thought and general theological doctrine; it is a representation rather of the great facts of religion in their own living and concrete form, so ordered as to address itself continually to the believing contemplation of the heart and soul."[3] It was this existential focus on the passions of the Christian life that had attracted Nevin to the Catechism twenty-three years earlier.

According to Nevin the natural sequence of Christian passions, the "law of its own inward order and progress," determined the Catechism's unique structure.[4] The logic of the heart dictated the sequence of topics, including the sequential arrangement of the Apostles' Creed, the Lord's Prayer, and the Ten Commandments. The underlying flow of guilt, grace, and gratitude pointed to the centrality of the theme of new life through Jesus Christ, rather than to the abstract nature of God. Nevin concluded that like the Apostles' Creed, the Heidelberg Catechism is a testimony to the Incarnation.[5]

Nevin insisted that the Catechism is intended for believers and those who are being formed into believers. It is not an apologetic treatise designed to justify the faith to the unchurched. The Catechism implicitly assumes that those who are in the church are in Christ, and therefore the purpose of the Catechism is to strengthen and deepen that relationship. Nevin associated the decline of interest in infant baptism, understood as incorporation into the life of Christ, with the decline of interest in catechesis. He frequently asserted that catechetical education was not based on the presence of any putative natural endowment in the learner. Rather, according to Nevin catechesis presupposes that grace, the power of a new life, is present as a condition. Catechesis assumes that a higher birth is continuing through the nurture of the church. For Nevin, catechetical instruction is part of the supernatural economy of the Spirit. The practice necessarily belongs to the church, for it completes and perfects the process of sanctification that began with baptism. Because of this conviction Nevin argued vehemently that baptized children are members of the church and are included in God's covenant. As such, they must be sustained by the church's educational efforts. Of course Nevin adds the caveat that catechetical instruction does not bear fruit automatically, but requires the proper ecclesial environment and inward appropriation by the individual believers in order to stimulate spiritual growth.

In this essay Nevin did interject more substantial theological analyses of portions of the Catechism than he had done in his earlier pieces. In general, he contrasted

---

3. See Nevin, in this volume, 283.]
4. See Nevin, in this volume, 282.]
5. See Nevin, in this volume, 285.]

some of Heidelberg's more controversial questions and answers with the speculative treatment of those issues in other Reformed and Lutheran documents. This was a juxtaposition that he had developed more briefly in his earlier writings on the Catechism. As he had done in his response to Proudfit, here he singled out two "knotty" doctrinal loci for special attention: election and the Eucharist.

The speculative extravagances of many Reformed theologies in regard to the topic of election served as a premier example of the perils of intruding metaphysics into an exposition of the Christian faith. Nevin described in detail some of the disturbing variations in order to prove his point.[6] All of them involved inquiries into God's ultimate purposes, and the relation of God's ordaining will to seemingly contingent events and human actions. As Nevin noted, the seventeenth century was unusually obsessed with the relationship between divine omnipotence and human freedom. During that era no major Christian theologian would have denied divine foreknowledge of events or challenged the concept of divine sovereignty. But the question that vexed theological minds was whether this notion of sovereignty entailed God's complete determination of everything that happens in the created order, including the actions, lives, and destinies of human beings, or not. Some Reformed theologians, the sublapsarians, assumed that God had not ordained the fall of Adam and Eve, but had merely allowed it to happen. But then they quickly added that once the Fall had freely happened, God used it as an opportunity to display God's mercy by electing some individuals to salvation, quite independently from God's foreknowledge of any merit on their part, and displaying God's righteous judgment by passing over individuals (who therefore were subject to the full force of God's retributive justice). The issue of whether God deliberately chose these individuals for damnation, or whether they simply ended up damned because God had passed them over, separated the "double predestinarians" from the "single predestinarians." In opposition to this view, the "supralapsarians" balked at the notion that anything could happen apart from God's preordination. Certainly, they reasoned, something as monumental as the Fall of humanity could not be the result of a contingent creaturely act. Therefore, they concluded that the Fall into sin must have been part of God's original intention, so that God could display God's glorious judgment and God's glorious redemption. This faction advocated many of the celebrated tenets of Synod of Dort, that God's election of individuals to salvation was unconditional, that God's grace was irresistible, that Christ's atonement was only intended for the elect, not for humanity in general, and that the elect would persevere in grace. Opposed to both these factions, the Arminians claimed that the salvation or damnation of particular individuals was not purely a function of God's ordination, but partly due to the individual's free response to the divine offer of grace. This opened the door to the view that God had granted a significant amount of freedom to the creaturely realm, and that some degree of spiritual freedom was still intact after the Fall.

---

6. See Nevin, in this volume, 275.]

Document 5: "Historical Introduction"

Over against these positions Nevin praised the Heidelberg Catechism for sticking to the existential significance of the teachings about God's sovereign will; namely, that Christians should trust God both in good fortune and in adversity. On the one hand, at times Nevin seemed to support the anti-Arminian position. For example, Nevin enthused, "All is of grace, and the divine sovereignty reigns supreme throughout the entire work."[7] He rejected the notion that the Catechism supports the Arminian position, for throughout it resists any Pelagian notion of self-salvation by an act of will. Nevin applauds its teachings about the fatal extent of human disability and the corporate corruption of the race.

On the other hand, Nevin at times seemed to be equally critical of the hyper-Calvinists. He argues at length that the Catechism rejects the theory of supralapsarianism, which he criticizes as an example of "metaphysical Calvinism." The Catechism, Nevin notes, asserts emphatically that sin arose from the misuse of human freedom and not from the intentions of God. In passing he opines that supralapsarianism is the only logically consistent form of any doctrine of predestination. By so saying Nevin was implicitly rejecting all theories of foreordination. In his reflections on his early years, Nevin decried the "scheme of transcendental necessity (God's decrees)," lamenting that he had "sucked it in from the Westminster Shorter Catechism."[8] Nevin paraded the fact that he endorsed neither Arminianism nor hyper-Calvinism, and found the whole controversy to be pointless. He approvingly discerned a similar reluctance to speculate about arcane matters in the Catechism. He suggested that the Catechism presupposed that "All great truths indeed, it has been said, are polar; carry in themselves opposing forces or powers, whose very contradiction is found to be necessary at last to the true harmony of their constitution." Nevin had no zeal for the effort to resolve the dialectical tension between divine sovereignty and human responsibility, and his hostility to any such project was becoming more overt.

About the issue of the irresistibility of grace Nevin notes that the Catechism is silent. It avoids philosophizing about the interaction of divine grace and human agency. The Catechism wisely restricts itself to the edifying theme that Christians should absolutely rely upon God's grace, be thankful for God's grace, and take no credit for their own salvation. Believers should be assured that in Christ they are saved. Unwisely the Belgic Confession ventured beyond this uplifting conviction into the realm of metaphysics, as did the canons of Dort. Nevin adds that shifting attention from the objectivity of salvation in Christ to one's own subjective experience of faith is dangerous because the feeling of assurance can fluctuate and can even be lost.

Nevin also denied that the Catechism teaches a doctrine of limited atonement, as conservative Reformed theologians had maintained. In regard to this issue he went beyond the argument that the Catechism eschewed metaphysical speculation and asserted that such a doctrine was incompatible with its explicit affirmations. He wrote,

---

7. Nevin, in this volume, 281.]
8. Nevin, *My Own Life*, 50.

"The Catechism knows nothing of any such particular redemption, offered to all, but intended only for some, and carrying in it for others no possibility of salvation." Nevin pointed out that it clearly proclaims that Christ bore the wrath of God against the whole human race (question 37). He also claimed that the Catechism was a precursor of his own view that humanity is more than an aggregate of individuals; it is from the corporate life of humanity that individuals derive their existence. This, he claimed, was implied by the Catechism's assertion that it was in the same human nature that had sinned that sin must be paid for, based on the parallelism of Adam and Christ in Romans 5: 12–15 (question 16). Christ assumed human nature as a corporate reality and thereby revivified it. Consequently the power of the atonement, as a function of Christ's theanthropic personhood, extends to human nature as a collective reality. In light of this, the notion of an atonement that is restricted to specific individuals makes no sense. (Nevin did add that this transformation of human nature only becomes efficacious for an individual if they are united to Christ in faith.)

Much of Nevin's opposition to the resort to the decrees of God to explain the ground of salvation was due to the fact that such a theory undermines confidence in the efficacy of the sacraments for all who appropriately avail themselves of them. For Nevin, salvation is based on union with Christ through faith, and such faith is available to all who partake in the sacramental and nurturing life of the church. The invitation to come to the Lord's Table is extended to all members of Christ's body, the church, and the benefits of Christ's life, death, and resurrection are intended for all people, not just for the allegedly select company of the elect. Given that sacramental orientation, Nevin could not countenance any claim that the Heidelberg Catechism was compatible with a doctrine of limited atonement.

The discussion of the Eucharist in the Heidelberg Catechism was a matter of special importance to Nevin. In this introduction he paid more attention than he had in the past to such events as the Stuttgard Conference of 1559 involving Ursinus and his Lutheran critics, and to such documents as *Gründlicher bericht* in which Ursinus argued that the Catechism was in accord with the Augsburg Confession.[9] As we have seen, it was this issue that had divided Lutherans and Reformed Protestants during the Reformation era, and continued to do so in nineteenth century America. In 1529 at the Marburg Colloquy Luther's exclamation "This is my body" had clashed with Zwingli's retort "Do this in remembrance of me." In 1577 the reciprocal suspicion of the two large branches of Protestantism had motivated the Lutheran Formula of Concord's condemnation of the "false, erroneous, and deceiving" opinions of the "crass Sacramentarians" (including Zwinglians) and the "subtle Sacramentarians" (including Calvinists, and possibly many followers of Melanchthon). Continuing the denunciations, in 1646 the Reformed Westminster Confession explicitly condemned the Lutheran view that even the wicked receive the body and blood of Christ.

---

9. See Ursinus, *Gründlicher bericht Vom heiligen Abendmal unsers Herren Jesu Christi* (Heidelberg: Johannes Mayer, 1564).

Document 5: "Historical Introduction"

Nevin was discontent with the alternatives advocated by his contemporary Zwinglians and Gnesio-Lutherans. Whatever Zwingli's elusive and complex Eucharist theology may have been, by the nineteenth century he was identified with memorialism, the view that the celebration of the Supper can awaken the recollection of Christ's redemptive work in the minds of the communicants. The ability of the ritual to make Christ present was dependent upon receptivity of the believer to being spiritually moved. Consequently, Nevin critiqued Zwingli for being a "subjectivist" and a "rationalist."[10] Nevin realized that much of Reformed eucharistic theology in the United States had been mostly shaped by the Zwinglian heritage. In so far as Calvin was considered, he was interpreted in the light of Zwinglian principles. In most Reformed communities, including Congregationalists, Presbyterians, and German Reformed people, the sacraments were regarded as signs and seals of grace, but not as means of grace. Nevin knew that the "signs and seals" language was being used to suggest a spiritual phenomenon that could take place apart from the sacramental ritual. Throughout his career Nevin continued to find the Zwinglian sensibility to be spiritually anemic and contrary to the spirit of the Heidelberg Catechism. Nevin wanted to shift the eucharistic focus of the Reformed tradition away from Zwingli and toward Calvin, Melancthon, and the Heidelberg Catechism.

Nevin found the Gnesio-Lutheran position to be equally unsatisfactory. The moderate Lutherans in 1541 had altered the Augsburg Confession in order to accommodate a wider latitude of understandings concerning the mode of Christ's presence in the Lord's Supper.[11] Calvin himself could affirm the altered version (as could Nevin). However, a stricter Lutheran party quickly emerged in opposition. This Lutheran faction insisted upon the bodily presence of Christ "in, with, and under" the bread and the wine, the ubiquity of Christ's body, the oral reception of Christ's body and blood, and the "eating by the unworthy." Such physicalist language greatly disturbed Nevin.

Nevin's discomfort arose from the fact that his central spiritual concerns were not those of the more conservative Lutherans. Their eucharistic language was designed to proclaim the promise of justification in order to stimulate and reinforce trust in God's grace. The emphasis fell on the "presentation" of the salvation accomplished by Christ on the cross, for that was what timid and terrified consciences needed to encounter. The distinctives of conservative Lutheran eucharistic theology followed from this emphasis. For the Lutherans, the purpose of comfort and reassurance requires a vocabulary and syntax that reflects the language of the Incarnation. The continuity of the historical saving work of Christ with the contemporary eucharistic presentation of salvation is attested by the corporeal reality of Christ's body in both of the two

---

10. See Nevin, in this volume, 269.]

11. The Gnesio-Lutherans followed the *Invariata* which described the body and blood of Christ as being "under" the form of bread and wine, while the Philippists (adherents to the view of Melanchthon) adhered to the *Variata* which stated that the body and blood "are truly exhibited" with the bread and wine.

instances. In both the life of Christ and in the eucharistic celebration the "body" is the "pledge" that God adds to the promise. In some sense, the bread and wine "are" the body and blood of Christ, or at least the body and blood of Christ are "in, with, and under" the elements. The discussion of this "sacramental" union echoes the language of Christ's hypostatic union. For the conservative Lutherans, talk of the undivided divine/human reality in the bread and the wine parallels and reinforces the availability of the divine in the earthly life of Jesus of Nazareth. Because it was in the "flesh" that God chose to accomplish salvation, and in the "flesh" that Christ suffered, it is still in a "bodily" mode that Christ remains with us.

For these Lutherans the purpose of nurturing faith in the promises of God requires the insistence that the reality of the presence of Christ in the Eucharist is not caused by faith but is only acknowledged by faith. God's saving presence is real even if it is not received. The presence of Christ depends only on the power of God and is not rendered false by unbelief. The Lutherans emphasized the objectivity of Christ's presence by using the language of "eating" and "oral reception" encoded in the doctrine of the *manducatio impiorum* (or *indignorum*)—the eating of the unfaithful (or the unworthy). Even those who lack any faith partake of the true body and blood of Christ, although, of course, they eat to their own damnation.

Similarly, the Lutheran theory of the "ubiquity" of the body of Christ was important in insisting that God's own self is available in the Incarnation. The Lutherans who adhered to the Formula of Concord reasoned that if God is everywhere, and if Christ's humanity is united to God, then Christ's human nature is everywhere. Where God is, there also is Christ and his identifying body. The theory of ubiquity was a way of stressing the personal union of the two natures and the consequent communication of divine and human attributes *(communicatio idiomatum)*.[12] God cannot be without humanity; there can be no "*Logos asarkos*."[13] In Lutheran discourse, the omnipresent body was intended to safeguard the thorough solidarity of God with humanity. But to Nevin's ears this sounded like such an extreme spiritualization of the humanity of Christ that it no longer bore any semblance to our own.

---

12. The doctrine of the ubiquity of Christ's body was intended to explain how Christ could be present in, with, and under the physical elements in many different locations at the same time, whenever the Lord's Supper was celebrated concurrently. The theory was that the divine quality of omnipresence was communicated to Christ's human nature, so that even his corporality could share in the divine ubiquity. This belief would become a litmus test of orthodoxy for doctrinally conservative Lutherans. Most Reformed theologians would counter this with the claim that the body of Christ is not omnipresent on earth, but is seated at the right hand of the Father in heaven. In general, the Lutherans tended to gravitate toward a more Alexandrian Christology that emphasized the unity of Christ's person, while the Reformed were attracted to a more Antiochene Christology that stressed the distinction of the two natures.

13. "*Logos asarkos*" (Trans. "Word without flesh"), often used perjoratively, suggests that some dimensions of the Second Person of the Trinity exist beyond the enfleshment of the divine nature in the Incarnation. The rejection of that view became a major feature of Lutheranism's criticism of the Reformed tradition.

Document 5: "Historical Introduction"

Nevin embraced an alternative supplied by Calvin and the Heidelberg Catechism. He also approved of Melanchthon's explanation of the Augsburg Confession, and the altered version of that document. According to Nevin, the eucharistic language of the Catechism, while it does echo many Lutheran concerns, serves a somewhat different purpose: to "awaken, arouse, and stimulate" gratitude and thanksgiving for God's paternal nurture, and catalyze a response of loving service. Nevin suggested that the Catechism subtly shifts attention from trust in the mercy of God to the broader theme of participation in Christ's life. According to Nevin's interpretation of the Catechism, the central purpose of the Lord's Supper is to foster the internalization of the revivifying life of Jesus of Nazareth necessary for the growth of true piety. Nevin highlights the Catechism's "food," "growth," and "strengthening" imagery, describing the Supper as the ongoing nourishment that the Father provides for His children. The sacrament is spiritual energy fueling the new life that is already incipiently present in the believer and that will ultimately blossom into immortality. As a consequence, Nevin tended to regard the presence of Christ in the Lord's Supper as an essential channel of the life-giving power of God. Believers communicate with the glorified Christ's life-giving flesh and blood (*caro vivifica*). The Christ made present in the sacrament is humanity's access to the fountain of God's goodness, from which flows life, virtue, righteousness, and wisdom. The effect of the Eucharist is the communication of the benefits of Christ (*beneficia Christi*), including righteousness and eternal life.

In Nevin's reading of the Catechism, the Lutheran language emphasizing the physical elements, pointing to Christ's body being "here" on earth with us, is displaced by the language of "spiritual union." Metaphors of interpersonal communion and organic union are better suited than corporeal terms to express the power of the Lord's Supper to transform the personhood of the believer. This language is in accord with Nevin's view of the church as a nurturing mother and a school, engrafting believers into Christ so that they might be transformed in his image. Nevin notes that the Catechism's talk of union with Christ's flesh does not imply the communicant's proximity to the physical matter of Jesus' body on earth. As he observes, the Heidelberg Catechism states that, "Although he is in heaven and we are on earth, we are nevertheless flesh of his flesh and bone of his bone." For the Catechism and for Nevin, "body" does not mean material particles, but rather points to the animating and organizing principle of a unique life. "Body" does not mean materiality, but the "organic law," the principle of unique personal growth, that accounts for the individual's identity.[14]

Nevin's concentration on eucharistic participation in Christ's life also led him to criticize the Luther doctrine of the "eating of the unworthy." According to Nevin, the Catechism's rhetoric focuses attention on the impact of Christ upon the spirituality of those who believe, making irrelevant Christ's presence irrespective of a faithful response. In this context talk of the eating of the unworthy makes no sense. The reality of the transformation of passions, attitudes, and dispositions renders the language

---

14. Nevin, *The Mystical Presence*, ed. Linden DeBie, 153.

of physicality or "local presence" and "oral" reception unhelpful. Consequently, for Nevin it does not make sense to talk about the unfaithful receiving the body and blood of Christ. Of course, this does not mean that faith "causes" the presence of Christ in the sacramental act; the presence of Christ is due to the objective initiative of God, not the agency of the communicant.

Nevin preferred the Catechism's assertion that the body of Christ is in heaven. He critiqued what he took to be the Lutheran view on the grounds that it dragged the presence of Christ down to the sphere of nature rather than helping individuals to see through the natural medium to the supernatural realm of heavenly glory. The Lutheran concentration on the physical elements frustrates the movement from the physical to the spiritual, and from the outward to the inward. For Nevin, the focus of the Eucharistic celebration should fall on the elevation of the soul. It is God's plan to lift believers up to God's self. The purpose of Christ's descent to earth was to enable humanity to ascend to heaven. Consequently the location of Christ's body in heaven, a theme present in the Catechism, functions as a way of talking about the reality of the human elevation. This elevation requires two emphases: Christ must have a real human nature with which we can identify, and this nature must exist in the glory which we are promised. In this regard the Lutheran concept of the "ubiquity" of Christ's human nature was misleading, for it suggested a pantheistic dissolution of Christ's unique glorified personhood into the consciousness of the race. Rather, according to the Catechism Christ's unsubstitutable glorified personhood is the root of a new creation.[15] In short, Nevin was worried that the Lutheran language of ubiquity fails to indicate adequately the heavenly exaltation of Christ's body and the consequent exaltation of human nature. In a transcendent dimension Christ's body, complete with "organized parts and outward form," enjoys unimaginable attributes and powers which believers shall eschatologically share.[16] For Nevin, Christ must have a real body with a real location, and that location must be heaven. (Of course Nevin added that "heaven" is not literally a geographic place to be conceptualized in terms of earthly spatial dimensions, and the glorified body is not a reassemblage of physical particles.) In Nevin's reading of the Catechism, the main point of the Eucharist is that Christ has ascended to a more perfect realm in order to draw us there. Christ lifts us to himself and therefore we must withdraw our eyes and senses from this earth and raise them to heaven. Nevin concludes that Christ quickens our flesh with his spiritual flesh so that we might become immortal. The appropriate context for talk of the "heavenly location of Christ's body" is the assurance of immortality and the perfection of human nature.

In spite of Nevin's objections to many aspects of Lutheran eucharistic theology, his sense of the objectivity of God's grace in the Lord's Supper was just as strong as any Lutheran's. He insisted that the Heidelberg Catechism asserted that the sacramental signs are efficacious; the spiritual feeding is brought about through the use

15. Nevin, *The Mystical Presence*, ed. Linden DeBie, 154.
16. Nevin, *The Mystical Presence*, ed. Linden DeBie, 153.

Document 5: "Historical Introduction"

of the signs. For Nevin, the union of the Christian with Christ through the Eucharist is unlike anything else in Christian devotion. The promise of God assures the Christian that the signified spiritual reality is truly present when the physical sign is used. This schema, employing the contrasts of "visible/invisible" and "physical/spiritual," is rooted in Nevin's general view that finite phenomena are the visible garments of the invisible God.

These theological themes emerged with new vigor and clarity in Nevin's introduction to the tricentennial polyglot edition of the Catechism. In spite of some oscillations in his theology, including a flirtation with Roman Catholicism, these convictions, which he detected in the Catechism, remained remarkably constant. The opening sections of his introduction have been omitted here, because they mainly reiterated his earlier histories of the Reformation and the genesis of the Catechism, adding very little new material.

"Historical Introduction" to The Heidelberg Catechism in German, Latin, and English: Tercentenary Edition[1]

... So far we have been looking only at the countries of Europe. The Heidelberg Catechism, however, has not held itself to these bounds. With the Dutch colonies, it has gone of course into Asia and Africa; but what is of far more account, it has crossed the Atlantic, and found in America also a new history and a new home. More than two centuries have now passed since it was first erected as a standard of evangelical orthodoxy on the island of Manhattan, where the city of New York has since grown to such vast importance. Around it rallied the faith of thousands, transplanted through successive years from the old world to the shores of the new. In the midst of ecclesiastical convulsions and rude political storms, the *Reformed Dutch Church* of America, clinging fast to her hereditary creed, has since struck her roots deep into the soil, and spread forth her boughs luxuriantly to the face of heaven, till she has become known and honored throughout the whole Christian world.[2] A century later in origin, the American *German Reformed Church*—sprung indeed, in a certain sense, from the same womb, or at least nursed in the beginning by the same maternal arms—comes forward also to claim our attention.

She too has had her deep waters to pass through, whose billows had well-nigh swallowed her up. But the favor of "Him who dwelt in the bush" [Deut 33:16] has accompanied her, notwithstanding, in the midst of her most gloomy seasons of trial. Though sorely tossed, during a long night of desolation, on dark tumultuous seas, with little notice and less sympathy, she has not abandoned still the martyr faith of her fathers.

No force has yet proved sufficient to wrest from her grasp the precious legacy bequeathed to her in the Heidelberg Catechism. At this hour, she clings to it with an

---

1. ["Historical Introduction" to *The Heidelberg Catechism in German, Latin, and English: Tercentenary Edition* (New York: Charles Scribner, 1863), 68–127.]

2. [Although he was critical of the hyper-Calvinism of many of the Dutch Reformed congregations, Nevin nevertheless was appreciative and even envious of the vitality and influence of that denomination, in spite of its small size. He attributed its surprising health to its adherence to the Heidelberg Catechism, and used this point to goad the German Reformed churches to emulate their Dutch siblings.]

attachment that promises to grow stronger only as it becomes more intelligent; rejoicing and glorying in it, as at once the true key to her ecclesiastical life, and the bond by which she is to grow and become fully compacted together, in all coming time, as "a holy temple unto the Lord" [Eph 2:21].

Catholic Constitution of the Symbol

The high estimation in which, as we have now seen, the Heidelberg Catechism has always been held throughout the entire Reformed Church is at once in itself an argument of its great worth. For it was by its inward merits wholly that it came to such general honor and regard. Its authors, we have seen, were as theologians comparatively young; not in the rank of the Reformers properly so-called, and without any particular ecclesiastical weight for the Church at large. The Catechism was wholly a provincial interest in the beginning, intended to serve the wants of a single country, just entering the sisterhood of older Reformed Churches, without reference at all to any broader use. No sooner had it appeared, however, than it began to fix upon itself the attention and admiration also of other lands. It might have been supposed that Calvin's Catechism would be more likely, than any other, to become of classical authority for the Church at large.[3] But this, with all others, gave way in such view to the new Catechism of the Palatinate. While other Catechisms continued to be provincial only, or national, this assumed more and more the character of a catholic or general symbol. So while each country had also its own confession of faith, Helvetic, Gallic, Belgic, or otherwise, the Heidelberg Catechism seemed to move among them all with entire ease and freedom, as a common bond of union for the whole Church. It was welcomed and applauded in Switzerland, France, England, Scotland, and Holland, as well as by all who were friendly to the Reformed faith in Germany itself. Nor was this praise transient, an ephemeral burst of favor, followed again by general neglect. On the contrary, the authority of the Catechism grew with its age. It became the Catechism distinctively of the general Reformed Church; the counterpart in full thus to Luther's Catechism, in its central relation to the Lutheran Church. In this character, we find it quoted and appealed to, on all sides, by both friends and foes. It formed the text book of theology in learned universities. Profound divines (Ursinus, Alting,[4]

---

3. [Nevin is alluding to the Geneva Catechism, composed by Calvin in 1542 to replace his early catechism of 1537, which was deemed to have been too complicated.]

4. [Heinrich Alting (1583–1644) was a German Reformed theologian who taught at Heidelberg until he had to flee from the sack of the city by the Imperialists. In the Netherlands he served as a tutor to the son of the disposed Elector Palatine and resumed his teaching of theology. While not endorsing the Arminian party, he expressed reservations about some of the extreme doctrines of the hyper-Calvinists.]

Piscator,[5] Cocceius,[6] Schultens,[7] and others) have made it in this way the basis of their dogmatic systems. Innumerable pulpits and schools have lent their aid to give it voice and power in the world. It has been as the daily bread of the sanctuary to millions, generation after generation. Never has a Catechism been more honored, in the way of translations, commentaries, and expositions. Never was any work of the sort so scattered, like leaves of the forest, in countless editions from the press.

Such vast popularity creates at once a powerful presumption in favor of the book, as it goes also to show us something of its peculiar character and constitution. The different national branches of the Reformed Church, though forming together one general communion in distinction from the Lutheran, have yet never been wholly of one mind in their confessional views. There was a material difference, in the beginning, between the Zwinglian and the Calvinistic types of doctrine. Calvin's doctrine of the decrees again was not received everywhere in the same form; and with the course of time, especially, the relation between this and the doctrine of the sacraments became the occasion for differences of apprehension, which affected seriously the whole form and structure of theological thought. We can easily see that there was a difference in this way between the Helvetic Church and the Gallican; that neither of these were just the same with the Belgic; and that the Scotch Church again had its own national peculiarities, distinguishing it in a very marked manner from all the rest. It lay in the nature of circumstances, at the same time, that the Reformed Church in Germany, conditioned from the first by other elements and relations, should also have a character of its own, and not be simply the transcript of some other church life brought in passively from abroad. Now that the Heidelberg Catechism should have been able, in the midst of all these differences, to gain such wide acceptance and common favor, can be accounted for only by supposing it to be so constructed that we have in it what may be called the proper substance of the Reformed faith in its most general view. The fact is an argument at once for its broad, irenical, catholic spirit, and yet no less, at the same time, for its faithfulness to the common belief of the Church. Its catholicity, in other words, as regards its own confessional system, is not that of indifference and negation simply; it is eminently active and positive; in this respect like the Apostles' Creed, in its relation to the whole profession of Christianity, than which, as there is no symbol more largely catholic, so is there none also more positive and vitally fundamental to all true Christian faith. Only so can we understand how it should have happened to the Heidelberg Catechism, above all other Catechisms and

---

5. [John Piscator (1546–1625) was a prolific and somewhat mercurial German Reformed theologian, active in Heidelberg and Herborn, who transitioned from being a double predestinarian to being an Arminian.]

6. [Johannes Cocceius (1603–1669) was a Dutch Reformed theologian who emphasized the distinction of the "covenant of works" and the "covenant of grace."]

7. [Albert Schultens (1686–1750) was a Dutch theologian and philologist who pioneered the comparative study of Semitic languages.]

Document 5: "Historical Introduction"

Confessions, to acquire and keep for itself as it has done the ecumenical credit, which has all along been allowed to it in the history of the Reformed Church.

It is one great merit of the Catechism that it is not offensively polemical or controversial in any direction. Its object is in general to affirm, more than to contradict and deny. It is of course Protestant throughout, in opposition to Romanism; and Reformed also throughout, in opposition to Lutheranism; and it was not possible, as the world then stood, that this opposition in both cases should not assert itself, indirectly at least, in strong terms. Such theological thrusts were naturally singled out as occasions for odium and reproach in the beginning, by the parties toward whom they were directed; but looking at the matter now, in the calm light of history, we have reason to be surprised, on the whole, that it is so free from provocation in this form. Even its antagonism to the Roman Catholic Church, if we except the unfortunate and somewhat apocryphal appendix to the 80th question, is managed in a general spirit of moderation, which it was by no means easy to maintain in the middle of the sixteenth century.[8]

Sacramental Doctrine

The controversial relations of the Catechism with the Lutheran Church were determined mainly of course by the sacramental question, and look continually to that order of Lutheran thinking which came to its culmination finally, as the true and proper orthodoxy of the Church, in the Form [Formula] of Concord. This brand of discord, as it proved to be afterward, had not yet indeed made its appearance; but such men as Brentz[9] and Andreae[10] were busily engaged in preparing the way for its advent; and the course of things in the Palatinate had much to do, undoubtedly, with the theological movement which was thus in their hands. Near the close of the year 1559, the superintendents and theologians of the province of Wirtemberg [Württemberg] had met in Synod at Stuttgart, and adopted a new confession of faith, which was intended especially to fortify the orthodoxy of the land against the irruption of such errors as were supposed to be at work in the neighboring kingdom of Frederick the Third. In this Stuttgard Confession, as it was called, the peculiar distinctions of full-toned Lutheranism, as distinguished not simply from the Zwinglian, but also from the Calvinistic and Melanchthonian sacramental theories, were formally proclaimed as the only true faith of the Church; and in particular, the last consequence of the system,

---

8. [The issue of the authorship and significance of the 80th question had been a major component of Nevin's controversy with John Williamson Proudfit.]

9. [Johann Brenz (1499–1570) was the leading Reformer of Württemberg, where he became the chief religious adviser to the Duke. He eventually became an opponent of the "Calvinizing" tendencies within Lutheranism.]

10. [James Andreæ (1529–90) was an allegedly moderate Lutheran theologian who sought to reconcile the Gnesio-Lutherans and the Philippists. Nevertheless, he sided with Westphal in the controversy with Calvin over the Lord's Supper, thereby showing that he leaned toward the conservative position. He was the principal German editor of the *Formula of Concord* (1580).]

the transcendental ubiquity or omnipresence of Christ's glorified body, as a result of the so-called *communicatio idiomatum* [trans: communication of properties] was for the first time unshrinkingly declared to be a necessary part of the Lutheran creed. It was in truth an embryonic anticipation of the Form [Formula] of Concord itself, and opened the way for the general ubiquitarian controversy of which this was finally the grand confessional outgrowth and birth.

Coming out now in the midst of this controversy, the Heidelberg Catechism took ground quietly against all such spiritualization of Christ's body, by simply affirming, on the subject of His ascension and glorification (questions 46–48), that He "was taken up from the earth into heaven, and in our behalf there continues until He shall come again to judge the living and the dead"—"that according to His human nature, He is now not upon earth, but according to His Godhead, majesty, grace, and Spirit, He is at no time absent from us;" which, however, involves no disjunction of His two natures, "for since the Godhead is incomprehensible and everywhere present, it must follow that it is indeed beyond the bounds of the Manhood which it has assumed, but is yet none the less in the same also, and remains personally united to it." This of course, then, conditions again the view that is taken of our communion with the Savior in the Lord's Supper; which holds good, we are told (question 76), "though Christ is in heaven and we on the earth;" the Lord's Supper being an assurance (question 80) "that by the Holy Ghost we are ingrafted into Christ, who with His true body is now in heaven, at the right hand of God His Father, and is to be there worshipped"—whereas the Roman Mass teaches "that Christ is bodily under the form of bread and wine, and is therefore to be worshipped in them."

It was here mainly that the Suabian theologians[11] found occasion for assailing the Catechism with those strictures, which drew forth Ursinus again so vigorously in its defense. In the Maulbron Conference of 1564, which proved so severe a trial to his morbid spirit, the discussion was occupied for five days with the subject of Christ's glorification and omnipresence in the world, coming only on the sixth and last day to the question of His presence in the Holy Eucharist. Then we have the same controversy—"infelix bellum ubiquitarium et sacramentarium" [trans: the unhappy war of ubiquity and sacramentarianism]—kept up for years through the press. Finally, the Form [Formula] of Concord came out; and the last great publication of Ursinus, as we have seen, was his Christian Admonition in reply, which was held by many to be the ablest work that the whole controversy had produced.[12]

There is no room for any mistake, thus, with regard to the sacramental and Christological teaching of the Heidelberg Catechism, so far as antagonism to Lutheran theology in this form is concerned. But we need to have this main issue, as it stood at the time, distinctly and clearly before our minds, in order that we may not fall into the

---

11. ["Suabia" is "Swabia"; it included Württemberg, where Brenz defended pristine Lutheranism from any Reformed infection.]

12 [Ursinus, *Admonitio Christiana De Libri Concordiae* (Neustadt, 1581).]

mistake, on the other side, of lowering its sense to the measure of wholly different relations. To deny the *allenthalhenheit* (everywhereness) of Christ's glorified body, and so to reject the notion of its local comprehension in the sacramental elements, did not amount by any means, in the sixteenth century, as for many it might seem to do now, to a denial of the objective working of His human bodily life in the sacrament, in any and every way. Clearly the Catechism could mean no such radical negation as that; for this would have been to turn into something worse than folly its professed relations to the Lutheran Church, as well as the whole ubiquitarian controversy itself, so earnestly carried on by its friends, for years, with the theologians of Tübingen. As we have seen before, the Catechism was not intended, in the beginning, to be a rupture in full with the German Lutheran Church. It was supposed to be in harmony with the Confession of Augsburg, as explained by Melancthon himself. In its sacramental doctrine, therefore, it was held to come fairly within the range of the tenth article of that Confession in its changed form; which, it will be remembered, differs from its original form only in not making the communication of Christ's body and blood in the sacrament to be in and under the elements, while it is still declared to go along with them, as part of the transaction, in the most real way. The mystery of the fact itself remains as a necessary article of faith; only the question of the mode or manner of it is left without any sort of determination. In this view, unquestionably, the doctrine of Melanchthon here must be considered [to be] the doctrine also of the Heidelberg Catechism. So far as the fact of the sacramental mystery is concerned, the last was supposed at least to mean all that was required by the first. We can have no better authority or evidence on this subject than the formal defense of the sacramental doctrine of the Catechism, which was drawn up by Ursinus himself, at the request of the Elector Frederick, and published March, 1564, in the name of the whole theological faculty of Heidelberg, for the very purpose of setting before the world the true position of the Palatinate with regard to this whole subject. The work to which we refer is the famous "*Gründlicher Bericht*,"[13] the same which in Latin bears the title: "*Vera doctrina de sacra Jesu Christi coena*" [trans: the true doctrine of the sacred meal of Jesus Christ]. Here we have the points urged, as a matter of course, that the body of Christ is in heaven; that it cannot be, therefore, in the sacramental bread; that the elements are signs and seals of the things they represent, and not the things themselves; that these require a different kind of giving and receiving, and are enjoyed only through the right use of the sacrament; that they become ours then, not by the mouth, but only by faith; and that unbelievers, consequently, receive in the sacrament its outward signs only, and nothing more. All this is abundantly plain. But the very object of the vindication is to show, that all this is by no means the whole of the Heidelberg doctrine, as it was the fashion of its calumniators to misrepresent. The signs, we are told, are not void signs, figures only of something which has taken place without them. Where the sacrament

---

13. [Ursinus, *Gründtliche bericht vom Heilegen Abendmal unsers Herren Jesu Christi* (Heidelberg: Mayer, 1564).]

is rightly used, that is, where faith is at hand, the proper organ for the reception of the heavenly gift, this gift goes along with the outward exhibition which is made of it by the signs, really and truly; so that they are in very deed, through the power of the Holy Ghost, the medium and organ of its communication at the time. They are not themselves the gift; they have no power in themselves to produce it; but still they are so bound to it in the way of certification and pledge, by the wonder-working power of God's Spirit, that they become in their right outward use actual vehicles of it to the inward appropriation of faith. What is thus communicated to the believer, moreover, is not simply the merits of Christ, the benefits He has procured for us by His death, but Christ Himself, His "person, substance, and being," through which alone, it is said, we can have any part in such benefits and merits. This mystical union forms the general law of the Christian life; which it is then the object of the sacrament, however, not simply to signify in such general view, but to actuate and carry into effectual force in the very article of its own transaction. And what is thus received, we are told farther, is not the life of Christ simply as exhibited in His divine nature, but more especially His proper human life, nothing less in truth than that once crucified body in which He reigns, now risen from the dead, at God's right hand in heaven. "The Lord's Supper," it is said in plain terms, "is a visible, but in no sense a mere empty or vain sign, *wherein* all believers not only partake of all Christ's benefits, but also, since Christ thereby hath promised and therewith testifies as much, are fed and refreshed with the true, essential body and blood of Christ Himself, as really and certainly as with the visible bread and wine." Again, in terms if possible still more explicit and strong, we have the declaration: "That the body and blood of Christ are *in His Holy Supper*, and that they are therein also truly eaten and drunken, we know from God's Word, and confess as much with mouth and heart before God and all angels and men; but that He is therefore *in the bread* we find not written in God's Word." Here we have the distinction which serves to explain all. Not in the bread; but yet none the less in the transaction.[14] Not therefore in the way of any local comprehension; but yet none the less certainly, in a way transcending, for faith, all merely local relations by the power of the Holy Ghost; *actus in actu* [trans: actual actions] the working of the Spirit in His own sphere going along with the sacramental ministration in the sphere of nature, and filling out the true and proper sense of it in another order of existence altogether. In this view the fact of the Savior's glorified body being in heaven only, and not on the earth, is considered to be no bar at all to the idea of a real communion with it in the sacrament. It can seem so only to those whose minds are so preoccupied with the notion of local and physical connection, that they have no power to rise to the far higher conception of a true dynamical connection through the Spirit. Even in the sphere of nature, there are what may be called physical unions of things locally separate and distinct, which far exceed in intimacy and closeness all merely local contact or inbeing. Such is the

---

14. [Nevin was rejecting an ontological view of Christ's presence in the elements and advocating a performative view of Christ's presence in the ritual.]

union of the vine with its branches, and the union of the head with the members of the human body; which are especially employed in the New Testament to represent the very mystery of which we are now speaking, the communication of Christ's life to His people. Why then should it be thought a thing impossible for this to have place in the sacrament, so that, although "Christ is in heaven and we on the earth," we may nevertheless come into communion there with His blessed body itself, through the working of the Holy Ghost, in a way surpassing all natural understanding? "The ascension of Christ into heaven," the theologians of Heidelberg, with Ursinus at their head, here tell us,

> leaves His body indeed in the Holy Supper, but not in the bread; for the Holy Ghost, by whose power and working things far asunder as regards place are as closely bound and joined as though they were together in the same place, unites and binds us, who are on the earth, with the body of Christ which is in heaven, a thousand times more closely and firmly than the members of our body are bound together. For which reason the body of Christ is not alone in the Lord's Supper, but is also eaten therein.[15]

After all this we can feel no surprise in finding the last part of the "*Gründlicher Bericht*" devoted to the purpose of showing, that the Heidelberg doctrine of the Lord's Supper stood in no opposition whatever to the tenth article of the Augsburg Confession.

It is easy to recognize here the general sacramental system of Calvin; but we have no right to say that it was borrowed exactly from Calvin himself. It seems rather to have been reached in an independent way, as the result of what we have seen to be the Melanchthonian tendency of thought in Germany itself; though the influence of Calvin had something to do also, no doubt, with Ursinus especially, in determining the particular form of its conception and expression at certain points. With the merits of the theory we are not now concerned.[16] Let it pass for what it is worth; all we wish is to have it fairly understood that this, and no other, is the scheme of thinking, which underlies the sacramental doctrine of the Heidelberg Catechism. With all its opposition to the notion of a local presence of Christ's body in the sacrament, and the thought of everything like a corporal and carnal partaking of it in the use of the sacramental elements, the Catechism seeks just as earnestly on the other hand to save, in a different way, what may be called the proper mystery of the institution in this view, against all attempts to drag it down into the sphere of mere nature. Its view is mystical,

---

15. [Ursinus, *Gründtliche bericht vom Heilegen Abendmal*.]

16 [Nevin was aware of a debate that had arisen in Germany about the origins of the Heidelberg Catechism's doctrine of the Lord's Supper. August Ebrard described the doctrine in the Heidelberg Catechism as being "calvin-melanthonische" or "melanthonisch-calvinische." In general Ebrard interpreted the Catechism as the felicitous confluence of both Calvinist and Melanchthonian influences. In 1852 Heinrich Heppe responded by claiming that the catechism was not at all Calvinistic, but was purely Melanchthonian. See Johann Heinrich August Ebrard, *Das Dogma vom heiligen Abendmahl und seine Geschichte*, vol. 2 (Frankfurt: Heinrich Zimmer, 1846); Heinrich Heppe, *Geschichte des deutschen Protestantimus in den Jahren 1555- 1581*, vol. 2 (Marburg: Elwert, 1852).]

making heavy demands on faith; not rationalistic, requiring for its apprehension only the common reason of men.[17] So much, indeed, is evident at once from the labored effort which so strikingly characterizes the phraseology of its several questions in relation to this whole subject. The doctrine plainly struggles throughout, that in avoiding the Scylla of materialism on the one side, it may not fall over to the Charybdis of an equally false spiritualism on the other.

Reserve on the Decrees

Substantially Calvinistic as the Heidelberg Catechism is, however, in its doctrine of the sacraments, it has carefully refrained from committing itself in like manner to Calvin's doctrine of the decrees. This is the more remarkable, as both of its authors, Ursinus and Olevianus, are known to have been themselves strenuous disciples here of the great Genevan teacher; which, however, only goes again with other things to show how in this work a sort of general objective spirit, in their ecclesiastical surroundings, seems to have taken possession of them, and to have made use of them as organs for reaching its own end.[18]

There is an innate opposition here, unquestionably, between the two sides of Calvin's system, as it was taught by himself in the sixteenth century; his theory of election and reprobation can never be made to agree fully with the old church idea which he labored with so much ingenuity to conserve in his theory of the sacraments. Where an abstract unconditional decree is made to be the principle of the whole Christian salvation, in such way that this is supposed to be only for a predestinated number of the human family, and to have no real regard whatever to any who may stand from their birth outside of such election—it is not easy to see certainly, how much earnest can be made with the outward, historical, organic character of Christianity generally, or how there can be any room in particular for the conception of sacramental grace in a truly objective form.[19] And so it has been found in fact, in the history of the Reformed Church, that these two forms of thinking have not been able to exist in full force for any length of time together. Where the Calvinistic theory of the decrees has been allowed to rule the course of theology, the Calvinistic theory of the sacraments has gradually lost its meaning altogether; whereas, in proportion as the sense of the sacramental has prevailed anywhere, as in Germany especially, the doctrine of the decrees has been held only with much qualification and reserve. In any view, it must

17. [Again Nevin relies on the Romantic appeal to a faculty that is different from, and more foundational than, discursive reasoning. The continuing influence of Coleridge, Schleiermacher, and Neander is evident.]

18. [Here again the influence of Hegel is evident in Nevin's proposal that world-historical figures are exemplars of broad cultural/spiritual movements.]

19. [Nevin argues that the reception of grace through the sacraments, something which is available to everyone, is the basis of an individual's salvation, and not a person's inclusion in the restricted number of the elect.]

be considered a recommendation of the Heidelberg Catechism that it has not allowed itself to go into this labyrinth of speculation; and most of all, that it has not made a metaphysical principle, in this way, the root and regulating law of its religious teachings. For children in particular, all such constructions of Christianity are something to be deprecated and deplored. But we may go farther and say, that they are out of character in any confession or creed, designed for general church use, or proposed as the basis of common Christian communion.[20]

Universally, indeed, an extensive, complicated creed must be regarded as a great evil; and the Church is to be congratulated that can be content to measure its orthodoxy by so simple and general a formulary as the Heidelberg Catechism, to the exclusion of every less liberal standard. No platform of ecclesiastical faith should ever be less large and free; whether even this be not too circumscribed, may well be made a question.

Some have presumed to say that the Catechism carries with it an actually Arminian sense at times, in the view it takes of the plan of salvation.[21] We have seen already, that Arminius himself, and his party in Holland, affected to consider it in general harmony with their views. But we know, at the same time, that the plea was never allowed to be of any real force in their favor. The party themselves showed clearly enough that they felt the real sense of the Catechism to be strongly against them, by their persevering endeavors to destroy its authority and credit; while the Synod of Dort, speaking not simply for the Dutch Church, but for the Reformed Confession in all lands, took it fully into their confidence and trust as a true exposition of their common faith. It requires, indeed, very little examination, to perceive that the order of thinking which runs through the whole work is utterly opposed to the Pelagian scheme in every form. Nowhere do we find represented in more decided terms the helplessness of man through the fall, on the one hand, and the absolute sovereignty of God's grace in the work of his salvation, on the other.

Thus, as we know, the Catechism has its first part devoted entirely to the consideration of the misery of man in his fallen state, as something necessary to be well understood, in order that we may come to any proper knowledge of our redemption through Christ. It begins, accordingly, by asserting in the strongest manner the general depravity and corruption of our nature, brought to pass through the wholesale ruin of the fall. Not only is the fact affirmed, that all men are involved in the terrible contradiction of sin (questions 3–5); but this fact is referred also to its true ground, as holding, not just in the individual will, but in the common life of the race itself (questions 6, 7). "Our nature is become so corrupt, that we are all conceived and born

20. [See the editor's introduction to this section in this volume, 259.]

21. ["Arminianism" was a term applied to the followers of the theologian Jacob Arminius (1560–1609). Arminius had voiced concerns that the more doctrinaire Reformed leaders were interpreting God's sovereignty in ways that suggested absolute divine determinism. The Arminians typically denied the doctrines of total depravity, unconditional grace, limited atonement, irresistible grace, and the perseverance of the saints.]

in sin." The evil is as deep and broad as humanity itself, and not of a kind therefore to be ever surmounted by the individual man in himself considered. This at once strikes at the root of all Pelagianism. The ruin is organic, and as such, needs an organic redemption—a redemption of humanity in its wholeness first of all, as the only way of bringing true deliverance to any particular or single life embraced in this whole. That which is born of the flesh, the nature of man in its fallen state, is flesh, and in and of itself must ever remain such; can never leave itself behind; can never transcend really and truly its own sphere (question 8).

Our spiritual nature, in this way, is in ruins; its powers paralyzed; "wholly unapt to any good, and prone to all evil;" though still under law, and possessed of a capacity for salvation. If it be asked now, how this tremendous lapse originally took place, no attempt is made to fathom the full depth of the mystery. We are only told, in general terms, that it came not from God, but from the free will of man himself. Our first parents were holy, and had power to keep their first estate; they were under no supralapsarian necessity of falling; but by their own willful disobedience they fell in fact, and so brought sin and death upon the entire race (question 9). The origin of sin, beyond this, the Heidelberg Catechism seeks not to explain. It rejects all Manichean necessity on the one side,[22] while it rejects also all Pelagian freedom on the other; and, like the Bible itself, takes its course firmly between these two irreligious extremes, leaving the understanding to manage its own embarrassment in the case as it best can. There are truths in this way, truths too of the most important and most immediately practical sort, whose very nature it is to involve dialectic contradictions, not to be reconciled by the understanding in its common form.[23]

The mind must receive them, if they are to be received at all, through another sort of knowledge altogether. What was lost in Adam, the Catechism goes on to teach in the next place, has been recovered for us again, and more than recovered in Christ. He is the fountain of the whole Christian salvation (question 18), having in Himself all the qualifications which are needed to constitute a perfect medium of reconciliation or atonement between the human nature and the divine (questions 12–17); being in His own person in fact the fullest conjunction of both; so that "the same human nature which has sinned" is brought to make full satisfaction for sin, and to become thus the righteousness of God for the race at large, in Him and through Him as the second Adam. To the full benefit of this glorious redemption, however, only those of the race come who are united to Christ by faith; which involves the living apprehension, not simply of an abstract doctrine, but of the whole perennial fact of Christianity itself, as we have it embodied in the Apostles' Creed (questions 21–59). The great cardinal doctrine of justification by faith alone, through the imputation of Christ's "satisfaction,

---

22. [Manichean religion arose in Persia in the third century CE. It was based on a dualistic cosmology in which materiality was associated with evil.]

23. [The tension of dialectical oppositions played important roles in the philosophies of Hegel and Schelling.]

righteousness, and holiness," in opposition to the idea of any merit on the part of the believer himself, is asserted in the strongest terms (questions 60–64). But this threefold imputation is held to be of such a character, at the same time, that the grace which is thus objectively made over to us in Christ, carries along with it from the very start the principle of our personal sanctification. The apprehension and appropriation of it through faith cause it to become at once the power of a new divine life in the subject of this faith; "for it is impossible" (we are told, question 64) "that those who are implanted into Christ, by true faith, should not bring forth fruits of thankfulness." Faith itself, which thus comprehends in itself the whole force of the Christian life, is no product simply of the thinking and willing of men. The Holy Ghost "works it in our hearts by the preaching of the Holy Gospel, and confirms it by the use of the Holy Sacraments" (questions 65–85). All is of grace; and the divine sovereignty reigns supreme throughout the entire work. But now when we fall back upon the deep questions that concern the relation of this sovereignty to human freedom, the Heidelberg Catechism, as in the case of the origin of sin before, is again significantly silent. Not only does it shrink from asserting the supralapsarian theory of the decrees—the fall and ruin of the whole race ordained from all eternity, in order to open the way for the predetermined salvation of a certain limited number of the race—which is after all the only really consistent form of metaphysical Calvinism; but the whole doctrine of the decrees is left untouched; except as it may seem to be comprised in the doctrine of God's almighty and everywhere present providence. The idea of predestination to life is brought no closer than this: that of the fallen posterity of Adam those only are saved by Christ, who "by true faith are ingrafted into Him, and receive all His benefits" (question 20); or that the Son of God gathers and preserves for Himself, out of the whole human race, unto everlasting life, "a chosen communion, in the unity of the true faith" (question 54). Still less, of course, do we hear formally of anything like a decree of absolute reprobation; or of what is the necessary consequence of this, and only another manner of expressing the same thing, such a limitation of the atonement, as makes it be of no force whatever for humanity in general, but only for a fragmentary part of it, numerically settled and fixed beforehand in the Divine Mind. The Catechism knows nothing of any such particular redemption, offered to all, but intended only for some, and carrying in it for others no possibility of salvation whatever. On the contrary, regardless here of all difficulties, and true to all sound religious feeling, it plainly declares, in conformity with the unequivocal sense of the Scriptures themselves, that Christ "bore, in body and soul, the wrath of God against the sin of the whole human race" (question 37); which is of course implied also in what is asserted before of its being necessary for Him to be very man, in order that the "same human nature" which sinned in Adam might in Him again, as the new Adam, "make satisfaction for sin," and so "obtain for, and restore to us, righteousness and life" (questions 16, 17).

So also if the question be asked, whether God's grace be irresistible in the conversion of men, and incapable of being altogether lost afterward, we look in vain for any direct answer to it in the Heidelberg Catechism.[24] It holds itself here, as before, to the general, popular representations of the Bible, without pretending to solve the philosophical problems that lie behind them. As it does not teach an unconditional election, so neither does it affirm the absolute invincibleness of grace in the work of conversion; while the doctrine of what is called the necessary perseverance of the saints is left by it, in great measure at least, unmooted and unsettled.

It is a peculiarity of the Catechism, indeed, that it makes faith to include in it an assured confidence of a personal interest in the everlasting righteousness and salvation of the Gospel (question 21); on the ground of which then the believer is represented throughout as enjoying a present certainty of all that has been procured for him by Christ, on to the full blessedness of heaven itself in the end. This is brought out especially in the very first question, with great beauty and force. But in all this, regard is had not so much to the idea of a decree of election on the part of God, making salvation certain for His chosen ones in an outwardly objective view, as to the sense rather which they have in themselves of the all-sufficiency of His grace, and of their own security as being comprehended in its present power.[25]

They know themselves to have in Christ all things that pertain to godliness and salvation, not only for this world, but also for that which is to come. But no such inward persuasion, however true and clear it may be in itself, can ever authenticate the outward fact of their being predestinated, without the possibility of failure, to everlasting life; nor can it be said properly to rest at all on the knowledge of any such fact. We know, moreover, that the inward persuasion may itself fail and come to an end, at least for a time; for all admit the possibility of such temporary backslidings and defections, in the case of believers, as shall completely eclipse, while they last, any assurance they may have had before of the certainty of their own salvation. This of itself then is sufficient to show that the mere confidence of faith, however just, is not at once a conclusive argument for the continuation of its own present good estate unto the end; and so the strong language of the Catechism in regard to this confidence may agree very well, after all, with the supposition that there is such a thing as falling away hopelessly from a state of grace.

The ark may include all that is necessary to outride the flood, and land its rescued ones on Ararat in the end; and they may have, while in it, the fullest assurance of their safety in this way; but that is not just in and of itself such a foregone certainty of their final deliverance, as makes it impossible for them to forsake the ark, and so lose their

---

24. [The irresistibility of grace and the perseverance of the saints were two of the tenets affirmed by the Synod of Dort. Here Nevin was resisting the "Dutch" interpretation of the Heidelberg Catechism.]

25. [Again Nevin was treating the Catechism not as a set of objective propositions about metaphysical matters, but as an edifying text whose meaning is found in its impact on the subjectivity of its users. He then observes that the passions and experiences nurtured by the Catechism do not necessarily imply metaphysical truths, e.g., a feeling of assurance does not necessarily imply the doctrine of the perseverance of the saints.]

hold on what was real and true for them only while remaining in its bosom.[26] These two terms, as we know, the assurance of Christian hope on the one hand, and the peril of coming short of the same hope on the other, are joined together all through the New Testament, as cooperating forces or motives in the work of our salvation. We are to give diligence to "make our calling and election sure" [2 Pet 1:10]; we are to "fear lest, a promise being left us of entering into His rest, any of us should seem to come short of it" [Heb 4: 1–2]; "we are made partakers of Christ, if we hold the beginning of our confidence steadfast unto the end" [Heb 3:14].[27]

The teaching of the Catechism in regard to the perseverance of the saints goes thus far, but it cannot be said to go any farther. All back of this is a philosophical question, which it nowhere pretends to solve or settle.

Here then is a material difference between the Heidelberg Catechism and many of the larger confessions of faith which have appeared in the Reformed Church. It may be said indeed, that the Calvinistic points to which we have now referred are at least involved or implicated in its general system of doctrine. So it must have seemed, of course, to that part of the Reformed communion, for which these points had become of confessional authority; since it could not otherwise have been indorsed, as it was for instance by the Synod of Dort, as sound and orthodox. But this only shows that the Catechism leaves these points untouched; allowing room thus, as the Bible itself also does, for different methods of carrying out its general doctrine. These strong Calvinistic positions hold beyond its practical horizon.[28] The Belgic Church might consider them necessary to complete her theological system; but there has always been a part of the Reformed Church, in Germany more particularly, which has not received them, though willing enough to own the general platform of the Heidelberg Catechism. This is so constructed as to afford fair opportunity for such difference. The authors of it seem to have held their own theological convictions purposely in a certain measure of abeyance, in order that they might be true to the church life around them; which, as we know, included much that could never have been satisfied with extreme Calvinism on the subject of the decrees. Or rather perhaps, as we shall see presently, the peculiar order and method of their work, after it had been once fairly adopted, served to determine its reigning character here, with a sort of inward necessity flowing from the nature of the subject itself.

Some have gone so far as to charge the Catechism with contradicting itself, because it is thus comprehensive in its views; appearing occasionally to favor in one

---

26. [For Nevin's earlier use of the Ark as a metaphor for Christian election and assurance, see "Hodge on the Ephesians," in *One, Holy, Catholic, and Apostolic: Tome Two*, ed. Sam Hamstra Jr., The Mercersburg Theology Study Series, vol. 7 (Eugene, Or: Wipf & Stock, 2017), 98.]

27. [Nevin had argued at length against Charles Hodge that while the New Testament recognizes Christians as elected saints, it also affirms that this election can be lost: "Hodge on the Ephesians," in *One, Holy, Catholic, and Apostolic, Tome Two*, 64–72.]

28. [At times Nevin's language reflects Immanuel Kant's distinction of theoretic reason and the understanding on the one hand, and practical reason on the other.]

direction, what it may be thought to oppose again in another. But in this it only resembles the broad comprehensiveness of the Sacred Scriptures themselves; which also countenance, in some cases, what seem to be conflicting views; though it must always be assumed, of course, that they are not such in fact, but require only a deeper knowledge than we now have, to be seen in their proper concord and agreement. All great truths indeed, it has been said, are polar; carry in themselves opposing forces or powers, whose very contradiction is found to be necessary at last to the true harmony of their constitution.[29]

Conception and Plan

Much depends for the spirit of the Catechism, no doubt, on the plan of its construction. This is in a measure peculiarly its own, and differs materially from what was common in formularies of this sort before. The Ten Commandments, the Lord's Prayer, and the Creed form of course the proper basis of all right catechetical instruction, to which must be joined then some notice of the Word and Sacraments as means of grace; but it is not at once so clear in what order these general topics should be handled, and then there may be much difference of judgment also as to what exactly should be embraced under each division. The common method has been to commence with the Law, as set forth in the Decalogue, connecting with it the being of God and His general relations to the world, so as to open the way to the knowledge of sin, and the true idea of the Gospel as a system of salvation by grace. Luther's Catechism starts in this way with the Ten Commandments. So the Catechism of Zurich,[30] based on the Catechisms of Leo Juda[31] and Bullinger[32]; which, as we have said before, has much in common with the Heidelberg Catechism, but differs from it in being shorter, and also in the different arrangement of its matter.

It consists of four parts: the first treating of God, of the Scriptures, and of the Law; the second, of the articles of the Creed; the third, of thankfulness and the Lord's Prayer; and the fourth, of the Sacraments. Lasky's Catechism again has the same fourfold order, beginning with the knowledge of God and the Ten Commandments.[33] In Calvin's Catechism we have the order partially changed: first the Creed;[34] next the Decalogue; then the Lord's Prayer; and finally the Word and Sacraments;—all in answer to the general question: In what manner is God to be rightly honored? The

29. [This theme of polar tensions was typical of both Hegel and Schelling.]

30. [The original 1534 version of the Zurich Catechism was composed largely by Leo Jud (or Juda).]

31. [Leo Jud (1482–1542) was a Swiss Reformer who worked closely with Zwingli in Zurich.]

32. [See Heinrich Bullinger (1504–1575), *Catechesis pro auditioribus scripta* (Tiguri, 1559).]

33. [John à Lasco (1499–1560) was a Polish-born Reformed theologian who was active in the Netherlands, England, and Poland. His "Emden Catechism" appeared in 1551.]

34. [Nevin is alluding to the Geneva Catechism, composed by Calvin in 1542 to replace his early catechism of 1537, which was deemed to have been too complicated.]

difficulty with this whole method is that it runs almost necessarily into the form of mere didactic representation. The teaching is made to hinge too much on some speculative principle, and assumes a sort of outward character, as a scheme of knowledge simply for the understanding. Christianity comes to appear in this way a theory, rather than a living fact. It is especially worthy of note now that the preliminary, experimental Catechisms of Ursinus (larger and smaller) were themselves constructed according to this general fashion, following in particular the order of Calvin. But, strange to say, the Heidelberg Catechism came out immediately after on another plan altogether. How the authors were led to it, we are not informed. It would seem to have some connection with that idea of the Covenant of Grace which entered so largely, as we know, into the thinking of Olevianus,[35] and is foreshadowed to some extent in the spirit of his previous Catechism for children; but there is evidence enough that it belongs also to the independent judgment of Ursinus. Altogether the case is one of the singularities that so strikingly characterize the authorship of the book.

The method here followed, as it has often been remarked, is that of St. Paul in his Epistle to the Romans (with the omission of chapters 9–11); a threefold division, namely, in which we have the fact of Christianity represented in its own living, historical order, as it appears first in the fallen condition of man, then in the work of redemption, and finally in the fruits of righteousness which spring from the joyful, believing apprehension of such great mercy. The conception is easy and simple, but at the same time profound and comprehensive; and we may readily see, what a vast improvement it brings with it at once into the whole organization of catechetical instruction.

We have the old material still, the Decalogue, the Creed, the Lord's Prayer, with the Church and Sacraments; but it is no longer in the form of so many separate parts, put together in merely outward conjunction, or subordinated at best to a speculative scheme of divinity; they are worked up into the general subject to which they belong, according to what may be called the law of its own inward movement and progress. Thus, although the first part of the Catechism has to do with the knowledge of sin, which comes only through the knowledge of law, we are not referred at once for this purpose, as in Luther's Catechism, to a formal explication of the Ten Commandments. "The Decalogue," says Ursinus, "belongs to the first part so far as it is a mirror of our sin and misery, but also to the third part as being the rule of our new obedience and Christian life."[36] With good judgment, accordingly, the consideration of it in detail is reserved for this ethical sphere; while simply the sum of the law, as given by our Savior Himself, is employed to bring its scattered rays to a burning focus, in the first part, on the fact of our common human depravity, considered in its spiritual principle and root (question 4). In the second part, then, we have the Creed and the Sacraments; and along with the Ten Commandments, in the third part, also the Lord's Prayer. There is

---

35. [For Olevianus the covenant of grace was God's promise to give eternal life to all who have faith in the life, death and resurrection of Jesus Christ.]

36. [Ursinus, *The Commentary . . . on the Heidelberg Catechism*, trans. Williard, 14.]

a beautiful order in this way, from first to last, in which all these catechetical elements seem to find their appropriate place, and by means of which they enter naturally and easily into the constitution of the work as a whole. Then, as we have said, the structure of the work is not theoretical, but prevailingly practical. It is not a system of knowledge merely for the understanding, in which the truths of religion are set forth in the character of abstract thought and general theological doctrine; it is a representation rather of the great facts of religion in their own living and concrete form, so ordered as to address itself continually to the believing contemplation of the heart and soul.

The Catechism of Geneva abounds with fine devotional sentiments, which we find frequently turned to account in the Heidelberg Catechism; but somehow they seem to be farther away from us, and more a matter of cold reflection, in the first case, than they are felt to be in the second. Compare the two formularies, for example, on the topic of Divine Providence.[37] "Why dost thou call God Creator only," it is asked with Calvin, "when to maintain and preserve creatures in their condition is something; much better than to have made them at first?" Answer:

> It is not meant by this word only, that God so created His works once as to have no care of them afterward. But it must be so understood rather, that the world, as it was made by Him once, is by Him now also preserved; so that the earth, and all other things, stand not otherwise than as they are upheld through His power, and as it were by His hand. Moreover, since He has all things under His hand, it follows from thence also that He is the supreme ruler and lord of all. Therefore from His being creator of heaven and earth, it is proper to understand, that it is He alone who with wisdom, goodness, and power, governs the whole course and order of nature; who is the author both of rain and drought, of hail and other tempests, and also of fair weather; who by His benignity makes the earth fruitful, and again renders it barren by withdrawing His hand; from whom proceed both health and sickness; under whose command finally are all things and whose will they obey.

Then follow two other questions, on the subjection of bad men and devils to this universal government, and the advantage of our knowing that they are thus under God's almighty control. It is all beautiful and grand; but who can help feeling, at the same time, with how much more beauty and grandeur the same thoughts are represented to us in the inimitable, poetical simplicity and pathos of the 27th and 28th questions of the Heidelberg Catechism? We give them here in full. Question 27: "What dost thou mean by the Providence of God?" Answer: "The almighty and everywhere present power of God, whereby, as it were by His hand, He still upholds heaven and earth, with all creatures; and so governs them, that herbs and grass, rain and drought, fruitful and barren years, meat and drink, health and sickness, riches and poverty, yea all things, come not by chance, but by His fatherly hand." Question 28: "What

---

37. [See Calvin, *The Catechism of the Church of Geneva*.]

does it profit us to know, that God has created, and by His providence still upholds all things?" Answer: "That we may be patient in adversity; thankful in prosperity; and for what is future, have good confidence in our faithful God and Father that no creature shall separate us from His love; since all creatures are so in His hand, that without His will they cannot so much as move."

Calvin's Catechism is theological throughout, a theory of religion based on the doctrine of God and His relations generally to the world. So much is signified in its very first question: "What is the chief end of human life?" This is made to be such a knowledge of God as leads to His proper glorification. Then it follows: "How is He to be rightly glorified or honored?" To which we have the answer, resolving the subject theoretically and didactically into four main parts: "By our reposing in Him our whole trust; by our endeavoring to devote our whole life to Him in obeying His will; by our calling upon Him as often as we are in any need, seeking safety in Him and all desirable good; and finally, by acknowledging Him, both with heart and mouth, to be the sole author of all good things." This fourfold scheme then is made to lead and rule the entire subsequent course of instruction, imparting to it necessarily something of its own scholastic complexion. Even the Apostles' Creed, in this way, fails to exercise its proper power over the form and manner of religious thought. It determines indeed the order of the first part; but the sense of its historical significance is too much lost in its subordination to mere theological reflection.

In the Heidelberg Catechism all is different. It offers us no speculative scheme of theology, but throws itself at once into the bosom of what we may call the actual work of redemption in its historical form.

It is anthropological, beginning with the constitution of man, as it finds him in his present fallen state; and then again it is soteriological, following out the great facts of the new creation in Christ Jesus, as we have them exhibited to our contemplation in the Creed.[38] Its character in this respect is strikingly represented in its opening question, which reveals to us at once the principle and comprehensive sum of the entire work: "What is thy only comfort in life and in death?" Answer:

> That I, with body and soul, both in life and in death, am not my own, but belong to my faithful Savior Jesus Christ, who with His precious blood has fully satisfied for all my sins, and redeemed me from all the power of the Devil; and so preserves me that without the will of my Father in heaven, not a hair can fall from my head; yea, that all things must work together for my salvation. Wherefore, by His Holy Spirit He also assures me of eternal life, and makes me heartily willing and ready henceforth to live unto Him.

No question in the whole Catechism has been more admired than this, and none surely is more worthy of admiration. Where shall we find, in the same compass, a

---

38. [Nevin is proposing that the Genevan Catechism is theocentric while the Heidelberg Catechism is soteriocentric.]

more beautifully graphic, or a more impressively full and pregnant, representation of all that is comprehended for us in the grace of our Lord and Savior Jesus Christ? For thousands and tens of thousands, during the past three hundred years, it has been as a whole system of theology in the best sense of the term, their pole star over the sea of life, and the sheet anchor of their hope amid the waves of death. But what we quote it for now is simply to show the mind that actuates and rules the Catechism throughout. We have here at once its fundamental conception, and the reigning law of its construction; the key note, we may say, which governs its universal sense, and whose grandly solemn tones continue to make themselves heard through all its utterances from beginning to end.

Relation to the Apostles' Creed

It belongs to the practical, historical character of the Catechism, as now described, that it falls in readily with what may be called the natural movement of the Apostles' Creed, and allows itself to be ruled largely by its proper confessional spirit.[39]

This primitive symbol, as we know, is not a summary of doctrinal truths proposed in didactic style for the understanding, but an exhibition rather of the living process of Christianity itself for the intuitional vision of faith; a panoramic representation, we may say, of the grand facts of redemption, made to pass before the eye of the spectator, gazing upon them from within the sphere of the new creation itself to which they belong. The principle of Christianity here, that from which its whole being in the world starts and proceeds, is the revelation of God in Christ, the mystery of the Incarnation; which, where it has come to be apprehended with true faith, in the spirit of St. Peter's memorable confession, "Thou art the Christ, the Son of the Living God" [Matt 16:16] is found to involve, with inward, necessary, historical consequence, all the other articles of the symbol, out to the resurrection of the body and the life everlasting. Where the Creed is allowed to exert its natural and proper influence as the original norm of all right Christian thinking, we shall have always a theology and a church life materially different from what will be found to prevail where this is not the case. By holding the mind to the true Christological and historical point of observation, it serves to keep it from the tether of a merely speculative or metaphysical construction of Christian doctrine. A theology which flows in the order of the Creed, and breathes the spirit of the Creed, becomes in this way concrete, and not simply abstract; organic, and not simply logical and systematic; historical, and not simply dogmatic; and with all this churchly also and sacramental, and not simply didactic and preceptive.

---

39. [Nevin wrote a series of articles in 1849 on the importance of the Apostles' Creed for *The Mercersburg Review* and then rewrote and published them as *The Apostles' Creed: Its Origin, Constitution, and Plan*. See *The Early Creeds*, ed. Charles Yrigoyen. In those writings he repeatedly identified Peter's confession in Matthew as the seed of all subsequent genuine confessions of faith.]

It follows then, that where the system of religious thought has already fallen away seriously from this order, there will be no proper sense for the symbolical authority of the Creed, and no power to use it in a free and natural way. It could not be incorporated at all, for example, into the Westminster Catechism, which, with all its merits, moves from first to last in a wholly different order of thought. It suffers also a certain measure of constraint, as we have seen, in the admirable Catechism of Geneva. But with the Heidelberg Catechism the case is altogether different. We will not say, that even this is fully answerable in all respects to the genius of the Creed, or that the Creed finds in it everywhere its natural sense and right exposition. We can easily enough see that a theological interest is allowed at times to bend the symbol from its true course; as in the arbitrary gloss, for example, on the descent to hades, adopted in the 44th question from Calvin.[40] But with all this, there is a real inward correspondence between the Catechism and the Creed, which in the circumstances is truly remarkable. The Creed is here not simply as an outward text made to accommodate itself to the purposes of religious instruction in one part of the Catechism; but as the central basis rather of the whole work, in which all its parts come together and find their true construction and sense. However it may have come to pass, the fundamental idea of the Catechism, the scheme on which it is projected, leads over of itself to the "articles of our catholic, undoubted Christian faith," as they are presented to us in the Creed; the exposition of which then follows, in the second part, as a simple history of the great work of redemption, carrying forward with natural ease the general theme proposed in the first question. The spirit of the Creed, in this way, seems to enter into the whole constitution of the work, influencing its course of thought, and giving form and complexion to its conceptions, even beyond what was designed always or distinctly premeditated in the mind of its authors. For it is not too much to say, that in the composition of the Catechism we have something more than mere outward thought and reflection. It carries in it, unquestionably, to some extent, the genial inspiration of a true work of art; in which the mind of the artist is seized and borne away by what we may call the mind of his subject, so as to become for it the more or less passive organ simply of its own self-production.[41] Only in such view can we account for much that must otherwise ever appear strange and perplexing in the authorship of the book.

40. [The meaning of Christ's "descent into Hell" had been hotly debated in the Reformation era. Lutheran and Reformed theologians were divided among themselves on this issue. Calvin had rejected the belief that Christ had liberated the deceased faithful who had lived before Christ and were imprisoned in Hell, and regarded the phrase as pointing to the completion and severity of Christ's earthly sufferings (*Institutes of the Christian Religion*, Book 2, chapter 16). Many subsequent Reformed theologians proposed that the phrase pointed to Christ's spiritual anguish before his death as an aspect of his bearing of the terror of God's judgement upon the sin. Nevin sought to recover the older patristic sense of the doctrine, suggesting that the concept indicated Christ's victory over death and separation from God and his pledge to the deceased that they would be raised from their "intermediate state." See Erb, *Nevin's Theology*, 336.]

41. [The theme that a beautiful work of art is generated when a subject matter expresses itself through the spirit of an artist was a commonplace of many varieties of Romantic and Idealist aesthetic

Only for the Sphere of Grace

It is a distinguishing feature of the Heidelberg Catechism, showing its general affinity with the spirit of the Creed, that its teachings throughout are more confessional than didactic, uttered everywhere from the stand-point of faith and personal experience, rather than from that of mere knowledge and outward consideration. How different in this respect is the style of instruction that meets us in the Catechism of Geneva. "What is the chief end of life?" Answer: "That men may know God, by whom they have been created." "What reason have you for saying this?" Answer: "Because He has created us, and placed us in this world, that He might be glorified in us; and it is just certainly, that our life, which has its beginning from Him, should be referred to His glory." "But what is the highest good of man?" Answer: "This same thing." "Why do you hold this to be the highest good?" Answer: "Because without it our condition is more unhappy than that of any sort of brutes." And so on to the end of the chapter. All is general and theoretic; question and answer are alike external to their object, stand as it were on the outside of it altogether, and look toward it only through the medium of dry, frigid reflection. So [it is] with the more modern Westminster Catechism. "What is the chief end of man?"—general again, and philosophically theological, as before. Answer: "Man's chief end is to glorify God, and to enjoy Him forever." "What rule hath God given, to direct us how we may glorify and enjoy Him?" Answer: "The word of God, which is contained in the Scriptures of the Old and New Testaments, is the only rule to direct us how we may glorify and enjoy Him." "What do the Scriptures principally teach?" Answer: "The Scriptures principally teach what man is to believe concerning God, and what duty God requires of man." [This is] doctrine for the understanding simply, matter of theoretic contemplation at best, from first to last. [It is] an admirable compend of metaphysical divinity, after its own order and in its own kind; but all impersonal and ideal, a description of Christianity in the abstract, more than the felt appropriation of it in any way as a living and present fact.

Contrast with this now, the tone and manner, in which the voice of religion is made to address us from the Heidelberg Catechism; and who can help feeling that we are introduced by it into another spiritual element altogether. Question and answer move here from the very start, in the actual bosom of the new life of grace itself, and involve all along the practical acknowledgment of the great facts of the Christian salvation in the form of experimental, personal faith.

The standpoint of the whole Catechism, in this respect, is significantly proclaimed in its first question, the echo of whose silvery music we seem to hear in all that follows. "What is thy only comfort in life and in death?" Not: What is God? Nor yet: What is the chief end of man? Nor even: What is the comfort of a true Christian in this world? But with an application brought home at once to the learner's own case: What is Christianity in thee and for thee, O child of Adam, planted in Christ? In full keeping

---

theory, which Nevin sometimes taught to students at Franklin and Marshall College.]

with which then we have the magnificent answer before quoted, all couched in the same intensely personal terms, and breathing the same spirit of faith.[42] It is nothing less than a full appropriation of the grace of the Gospel, answerable for example to the import of those great words of St. Paul: "Who hath delivered us from the power of darkness, and hath translated us into the kingdom of His dear Son; in whom we have redemption through His blood, even the forgiveness of sins" [Col 1:13]. I am not my own, the catechumen is made to say, I belong to my faithful Savior Jesus Christ; He has died for me; has fully satisfied for all my sins, and delivered me from all the power of the Devil; He preserves me with His almighty power, and by His Holy Spirit assures me of eternal life. So [it goes] throughout the Catechism. All is so constructed as to hold continually, not only in the element of personal experience, but in the element of such experience advanced to the consciousness and sense of a true personal interest in the salvation of Jesus Christ.

Thus true faith is described to be (question 21) "not only a certain knowledge whereby I hold for truth all that God has revealed to us in His word; but also a hearty trust, which the Holy Ghost works in me by the Gospel, that not only to others, but to me also, forgiveness of sins, everlasting righteousness, and salvation are freely given by God, merely of grace, only for the sake of Christ's merits." So on the topic of God's work of creation under the first article of the Creed (question 26), the question is not just what we are to understand by it; to which the answer might be: "His making all things of nothing, by the word of His power, in the space of six days, and all very good." It looks rather to what is involved in the apprehension of the fact as an exercise of faith—that faith by which "we *understand* (Heb. 11: 3) that the worlds were framed by the word of God." It is an inquiry into the relation of a believing Christian to this foundation truth of religion. "What dost thou believe when thou sayest, I believe in God the Father, Almighty, Maker of heaven and earth?" Answer:

> That the eternal Father of our Lord Jesus Christ, who of nothing made heaven and earth, with all that in them is, who likewise upholds and governs the same by His eternal counsel and providence, is for the sake of Christ His Son, my God and my Father; in whom I so trust, as to have no doubt that He will provide me with all things necessary for body and soul; and further, that whatever evils He sends upon me in this vale of tears, He will turn to my good; for He is able to do it, being Almighty God, and willing also, being a faithful Father.

Another classical example truly of the reigning mind, as well as of the peculiar force and beauty, of the Catechism.

Take again the 32nd question, where, after the explanation of the name Christ, or Anointed, in its reference to our Savior's threefold office of Prophet, Priest, and King, it is suggestively asked: "But why art *thou* called a Christian?" No merely general and impersonal view of the case will suffice; the interrogation goes at once to the interior

42. [Nevin emphasizes the self-involving force of the Catechism's rhetorical style.]

life of the subject, and the answer must come again from the respondent's own soul: "Because by faith I am a member of Christ, and thus a partaker of His anointing; in order that I also may confess His name; may present myself a living sacrifice of thankfulness to Him; and may with free conscience fight against sin and the Devil in this life, and hereafter, in eternity, reign with Him over all creatures."

The prophetical, priestly, and kingly functions are all in this way not simply copied but, as it were, actually transfused into the believer, through his living union as a Christian with the living Christ.[43] The 52nd question, on the second coming of our Lord Jesus Christ, the 56th, on the "forgiveness of sins," the 57th, on the "resurrection of the body," the 58th, on the "life everlasting," the 60th, on justification, might all be quoted here, as so many rich examples, in the same inimitable strain, of the peculiarity now under consideration—the way, namely, in which the Catechism refers all Christian truths to the standpoint of actual personal faith and experience; and there is a strong temptation to quote them, certainly, in the intrinsic beauty of the questions themselves. But we find it necessary to forbear, and content ourselves at present with simply making mention of them in this general way.

This very peculiarity of the Catechism, however, on which the beauty and power of it so largely depend, has been made at times a matter of objection to it; as being supposed to encourage in all who use it the thought that they are true Christians, when many of them may not be so in fact. It is not safe, especially, we are told, to put the language of personal piety, in such strong terms, into the mouths of children and young people generally; they are in danger of being deluded by it into the notion, that they have in their mere outward connection with the Church all that is required for their salvation, so as to take no interest in the subject of religion under any more inward view.[44]

The Catechism, in other words, is so constructed, it has been imagined, as to foster spiritual ignorance, presumption, and carnal security, in the minds of those for whom it should be a discipline rather of conviction and conversion; a purpose which it might serve much more effectually, according to this view, if it were so framed as to represent the idea of religion in a general theoretic way, holding the mind of the catechumen steadily on the outside of it, and leaving the question of his personal relations to it open always for separate adjudication at the bar of his own conscience.

The objection is plausible, and falls in well especially with what may be considered perhaps the reigning tone of religious thought at the present time; but it becomes of no force, as soon as we reflect that it holds against the general faith and practice of

---

43. [Here Nevin is making a strong case that the individual's sharing in the benefits of the work of Christ is based on impartation through the communication of Christ's life to the believer rather than on imputation alone. See Evans, *Imputation and Impartation*.]

44. [Samuel Hopkins (1721–1803) advanced the controversial claim that unconverted individuals may actually grow worse by partaking of the means of grace offered by the church, including prayer and catechesis. Hopkins was a student of Jonathan Edwards who served pastorates in Connecticut and Newport, Rhode Island.]

the Church in past ages, and against the whole teaching of the New Testament, just as strongly as it holds against the Heidelberg Catechism. The Church, from the beginning, has always considered her children sacred to God, and in covenant with Him, by Holy Baptism; and on the ground of this relation has sought to instill into them, from the first, the consciousness and sense of their being Christians, as the necessary condition of their growing up in the nurture and admonition of the Lord.[45]

In this way also Christianity is made to be a matter of personal appropriation throughout in all the early Creeds; they move in the orbit of the Christian life itself, and not on the outside of it; they are the language of faith for the faithful only. The spirit of the Catechism in this respect, then, is in full harmony with the spirit of the Apostles' Creed, from which indeed it seems to be in large measure derived.[46]

What is of still more account, however, it is in full harmony also with all Apostolic teaching, as we have it especially in the New Testament Epistles. This too proceeds everywhere on the assumption that those to whom it is addressed belong already to Christ and not to the world. It is Christian instruction for such as are considered to be within the bosom of Christianity; not a scheme of doctrines and duties offered for the consideration of those who are still on the outside of it, and personally strangers to its grace. This is so palpable, that it is only wonderful how it should be so frequently forgotten or overlooked.

These Epistles, as we all know, address themselves to the "elect," to those who were "called to be saints," to the "faithful in Christ Jesus," and go on the hypothesis throughout that these titles were not idle, nominal distinctions only, but designations rather of a real state of grace, which laid the foundation for all that they were expected to be or to do as followers of Christ. No fear was felt, it seems, that the acknowledgment of such a general state of grace, in the case of those who belonged to the Church, might lead to indifference or presumption; on the contrary, it is made the main argument and motive always for a holy life. "Ye are bought with a price" (1 Cor. 6: 20, in the very spirit of the 1st question of the Catechism), "therefore glorify God in your body and in your spirit, which are God's." Let the fact of your election, with its glorious opportunities, privileges, and powers, engage you to all diligence (2 Pet. 1: 10) in making "your calling and election sure." Having such promises (2 Cor. 7: 1), "let us cleanse ourselves from all filthiness of the flesh and spirit, perfecting holiness in the fear of God." Such is the tenor everywhere of these New Testament instructions and exhortations. All relations, for those addressed, are held to be Christian relations; all duties, growing out of them, find their ultimate sense and force only in Christ. He is the principle of the new ethical creation into which husbands and wives, parents and

---

45. [Nevin objected to the notion that baptism was a testimony to a grace that was experienced in the general subjective religious life of an individual, quite independently of the ecclesial context of the ritual. Rather, the sacramental rituals, situated in the ongoing life of the church, have the power to accomplish what they promise. For Nevin's writings on baptism, see *Born of Water and the Spirit*, ed. David W. Layman. See especially Layman's introduction to "Noel on Baptism," 80–81 in that volume.]

46 [See Nevin, "The Apostles' Creed," in *The Early Creeds*, ed. by Charles Yrigoyen, 87.]

children, masters and servants, have here come by their common Christian character and profession. All depends on their having power to know and honor the fact of their own heavenly distinction in this view, so as to "walk worthy of the vocation where with they are called" [Eph 4:1]. Children, we see, as well as others, have place in this glorious citizenship of the saints, however we may suppose them to have come into it; and being there, they are to be known, and also to know themselves, as being "in Christ " no less than their believing parents, and not simply as being candidates for the Christian profession at some future time. They come in, with other classes, for their full proportion of Apostolic counsel and care, subject to no dismal exclusion whatever from the membership of Christ's Church. They are exhorted to obey their parents "in the Lord" (Eph. 6:1; Col. 3: 20); which implies, of course, that they are "not strangers and foreigners, but fellow citizens with the saints, and of the household of faith;" and it is charged upon fathers (Eph. 6:4; Col. 3 : 21) to treat them—not as children of the Devil—but as children of God, by reverencing their tender personality, and bringing them up "in the nurture and admonition of the Lord."

What we mean now by all this, is simply to show that the New Testament Epistles have the same religious bearing toward those whom they address, which we have seen to be held by the Heidelberg Catechism toward its probationers and pupils. In both cases alike, the teaching is "from faith to faith," the utterance of Christianity for the use of such as are supposed to stand within its own sphere. This would seem to be a sufficient vindication, then, of the peculiar construction of the Catechism in this respect. It is not a system of instruction for unbelievers, and such as are outside of God's covenant.

Like the Lord's Prayer and the Creed, it is for those only who have been initiated into the life of the Church; and in putting the full confession of Christianity into their lips, it cannot be said certainly to venture more than St. Paul does, when he says (1 Cor. 6: 11) to the Corinthian Christians collectively: "Ye are washed, ye are sanctified, ye are justified, in the name of the Lord Jesus, and by the Spirit of our God;" or to go beyond his strong language to the sorely erring Galatians (Gal. 3: 26, 21): "Ye are all the children of God, by faith in Christ Jesus; for as many of you as have been baptized into Christ, have put on Christ."

It will not do to say, of course, that St. Paul's assumption in this whole case was both for his own mind, and in actual fact, a mere complimentary or benevolent fiction—as when a physician, for example, tries to inspire his patient with the confidence of returning health, though knowing him to be under the power of a deadly disease. No one knew better than the Apostle himself that many of those whom he addressed as Christians were in a condition of great spiritual unsoundness and defect; and no one could be more ready to charge home upon them this mournful fact, in the most sweeping and unreserved terms. But with all this, he never allows himself to question for a moment the value of their Christian estate in itself considered; and what seems strange, he is never willing to have it questioned either, or doubted, in their own minds. Where the tact of a modern revivalist would be ready at once to discourage every such ulterior ground of trust as a refuge of lies, the different wisdom of St. Paul forces it into view, and lays all stress upon it, for the highest purposes of religion itself. It is with him, we repeat, no fiction, but a glorious reality, lying at the foundation of the whole grace of the Gospel. It is nothing less in truth than that doctrine of the Church, that great idea of organic, sacramental Christianity, which runs through his universal teaching, and forms with him the basis of all faith and piety in every less general view.

In making its catechumens to be Christians, the Heidelberg Catechism proceeds undoubtedly on the same general theory of religion; it is not an ecclesiastical fiction merely that is put forward in the case; they are taken to be, not hypothetically only, but really and truly, in the state of grace and salvation which they are instructed to lay claim to as their own. This does not mean, of course, that they are held to have come in all cases to such a clear, firm sense and assurance of their good estate as the Catechism puts into their lips; but it does mean that this good estate is theirs by heavenly right, and that it is their privilege and duty to be assured of it, and to lay claim to it, in this way. The theory is, that they are Christians by being in the Church, and thus in actual covenant with God through His Son Jesus Christ; and that all they need to make them personally righteous and holy is that they should believe this great fact, and accord to it its proper influence over their hearts and lives. Substantially the same view, indeed, was held by the entire Protestant Church in the beginning; as it had been held by the Catholic Church also, through all previous ages; and it was considered one of the monstrous innovations of the fanatical Anabaptists (as well as of the rationalistic Socinians)[47] that they would hear of no such objective sanctification and grace. Both the Lutheran and the Reformed communions, it deserves to be well considered, stood here on the same ground.

So far as the matter of covenant relation to God through union with the Church is concerned, the Heidelberg Catechism at least goes quite as far as the Catechism of Luther. They differ, it is true, in the force they assign to Baptism, the sacrament of introduction into this state of grace. With Luther, it is itself the thing it represents, God's act of mercy, setting the subject over at the time from the power of darkness into the kingdom of His dear Son. To the question, "What doth Baptism profit?" he answers without any sort of hesitation: "It works remission of sins, delivers from death and the Devil, and gives eternal salvation to all who believe in it, according to the word and promise of God."[48] In the Heidelberg Catechism, the sign and the thing signified are held as it were more apart; but still the sacrament is taken to be a seal and certification of the grace it represents, an authenticating act on the part of God, which makes

---

47. [Socinianism was a cluster of nontrinitarian movements that arose in the sixteen and seventeenth centuries, often associated with the work of Faustus Socinus (1539–1604). Strong in Poland and Transylvania, Socinians were identified with the denial of the pre-existence of Christ, original sin, and Christ's substitutionary atonement. As a term of abuse, eventually "Socinian" was used almost interchangeably with "Unitarian."]

48. [See Martin Luther, *Luther's Small Catechism*, 18.]

it to be objectively present and sure for the baptized person, as much as if it were in the outward sign itself, requiring only faith on his part to give it full efficacy for the purposes of his salvation. The force of it in this view is strikingly represented in what is said of Infant Baptism in the 74th question; where it is asked: "Are infants also to be baptized?" To which the answer follows:

> Yes; for since they as well as their parents belong to the covenant and people of God, and both redemption from sin and the Holy Ghost, who works faith, are through the blood of Christ promised to them no less than to their parents; they are also by Baptism, as a sign of the covenant, to be ingrafted into the Christian Church, and distinguished from the children of unbelievers, as was done in the Old Testament by Circumcision, in place of which in the New Testament Baptism is appointed.

The amount of all plainly is that Baptism, if it be not itself the origin and ground of that gracious relation to God which is denominated the covenant, is nevertheless such a ratification of it under the immediate hand of God Himself, that all who are baptized must be held to be within the range of the covenant, and to have its benefits assured to them, if only they can be brought to believe and improve the fact in the most actual and real way. But this is at once nothing less than that idea of baptismal grace, potential Christianity, sanctification to the service of God by being in the Church, of which we are now speaking; and which, as we say, underlies and conditions the teaching of the Heidelberg Catechism from beginning to end. It addresses itself everywhere to those who are considered to be really within the covenant of grace; and it addresses them therefore as Christians, whose duty as well as right it is to respond to the claims of this gracious condition, and to make its benefits their own through the joyful appropriation of faith.

Educational Religion

In all this we have the proper conception of educational religion, which entered so largely into the whole catechetical system of the sixteenth century, but for which, unfortunately, with much of our modern Christianity, the power of appreciation seems to have passed away altogether. Education, of course, supposes always the existence and presence potentially of that which it is expected to bring out in the way of actual development and growth. As a stone cannot be cultivated into a plant; and as no training again can cause a plant to become an animal; so in the spiritual world also it is not possible, by mere nurture of any sort, to carry the evolution of life beyond the principles and germs which are already imbedded in its own constitution. This applies emphatically to the new creation in Christ. It can never be brought to pass, in the way of simple derivation from the powers and possibilities of our common human nature, in its fallen Adamic state. That which is born of the flesh—we are solemnly assured—is flesh; it remains as such hopelessly bound to its own sphere, and can in no way be brought to transcend it.[49] If it were pretended then to take such as by their natural birth are in this state only, and to train them into Christianity by mere teaching and discipline, as they might be trained for example into the knowledge of some worldly art or science, the pretension would well deserve to be rejected as both false and vain. The idea of educational religion in such form would be neither more nor less than Pelagianism without disguise; and if there were no room to conceive of any other foundation on which to build, in the case of children, than such as is exhibited to us in their original condition, we can easily enough see that it must involve a contradiction to think or to speak of building them up as Christians in any such way. Then the modern Puritanic or Baptistic sentiment after all would be right, and the old Catholic sentiment wrong; we must look upon our children, and teach them to look upon themselves, as without lot or portion in God's family—"the children of wrath even as others" [Eph 2:3]—until such time as they might come, in their isolated, separate capacity, to a true awakening and conversion by the Spirit of God, on the outside of the Church altogether. For such thinking, as a matter of course, the old catechetical system, the old sacramental system, the old church system in general, can never appear reliable and satisfactory; for the simple reason that it has no faith whatever in that which lay at the foundation of all this old Christianity, a gracious condition, namely, supposed to be already at hand in the case of all who belonged rightfully to the Church, in virtue of which they were considered to be no longer nature or flesh only, but to have part also in the supernatural economy of the Spirit. The capacity for Christianity which Pelagius heretically pretended to find in the birth of nature, St, Augustine referred to a higher birth of grace, which was effected, as he believed, by the sacrament of Baptism; and in one form or another, the same view substantially has always been held, wherever the idea of educational religion has been found to carry with it any sort of practical force.

Only in such view, indeed, can we understand what educational religion means, or have any right sense of what it is to bring up our children in the nurture and admonition of the Lord. In some way we must be assured that they belong to Christ, and not to Satan, if we are to encourage in them at all the Christian consciousness, which the conception of such culture implies from the very start. There must be a basis here on which to build—not in nature merely, or our own willful imagination, but in grace; of whose presence, then, we need to have some outwardly objective evidence and pledge. In that

---

49. [Nevin argues that the Christian education of human beings in their fallen state requires the presence of a new capacity supplied by grace; reliance upon natural endowments alone would make Christian pedagogy impossible. That essential supernatural capacity is acquired through the individual's inclusion in the covenantal life of the church, as assured by baptism. Nevin does not claim that the ritual of baptism is the cause of this grace, but it is the objective certification of the bestowal of this grace. Consequently, it can legitimately be called "baptismal grace." Nevin's earlier thinking on "baptismal grace" and "educational religion" can be found in *Born of Water and the Spirit*, ed. David W. Layman, The Mercersburg Theology Study Series 6, 34–115.]

case, it will be possible for us to look upon our children as Christians from the beginning, and so to make them the subjects of a positively Christian culture throughout, according to the injunction of St. Paul, for which otherwise there would be no room whatever. Then religious education for the young will not be negative merely, an outward discipline intended to prepare the way for Christ at some future time, or a moral training for the purposes only of the present life; nor will it stand simply in lessons and rules presented to the understanding; but it will aim rather, as all true education does, to reach its subjects through the power of the life which is supposed to belong to them in common with their teachers. In other words, it will be organic, reproductive, the continuous ongoing, we may say, of the "law of the spirit of life in Christ Jesus." [Rom 8:2.] For any such process the idea of the Church is indispensable; for with this only can we have the supernatural element—in distinction from the element of mere nature—in which it may be felt possible at all for the work of the Spirit to proceed in such manner. To be brought up and educated in the Lord is to be first planted in the life of the Church; and then to be so comprehended in this, and so nurtured by it from the beginning, in the trustful use of all its means of grace and salvation, that the soul shall have the sense of it formed into itself as part of its own consciousness, and grow up in it always as the natural home and habit of its thoughts; just as in the order of nature, the life of a family, or the constitutional spirit of a whole people, is found to pass onward from one generation to another in the same organic way.[50]

This does not imply, by any means, that such covenant relationship to God involves of itself a natural, spontaneous growing up into the maturity of the Christian life, without obstacle or let, and with no farther care, from the beginning. There must be, of course, the proper conditions of outward Christian training—the vivifying action of spiritual light, and air, and heat, in the family and in the Church—and the proper inward disposition of obedience and faith also on the part of the subject, (come whence or how it may), to secure any such result as that; and as these terms of success are in general only most imperfectly at hand in the actual state and character of the Christian world, it need be no matter of surprise that the grace of God, in the form of which we are now speaking, should seem to be bestowed upon very many altogether in vain; or that where this may not be the case, it should be found reaching its object at last only in the way of more or less violent reaction and conversion from a life of sin. But with all this, the reality of the grace itself, in its own positive, objective character, must not be questioned or undervalued. "For what if some did not believe?" St. Paul exclaims (Rom. 3: 3, 4), referring to this very subject in its relation to the Jews; "shall their unbelief make the faith (or fidelity) of God without effect? God forbid: yea, let God be true, and every man a liar." That is, in the Christian economy: If ten thousand baptized members of the Church despise their birthright in God's family,

---

50. [Nevin proposes that there are necessary connections among the themes of God's objective covenantal grace promised to the church, the certification of that grace through baptism, and receptivity to catechetical instruction.]

like Esau, shall their unbelief nullify the reality of God's grace made sure to them in the holy sacrament of Baptism? Nay rather; though all prove false to the covenant of salvation thus signed and sealed in their favor by the hand of the Almighty, let us not dare to turn into fiction the sign manual of the Almighty Himself. Baptismal grace is no fiction; it is the real possibility of salvation, conferred, by divine gift, upon all whom Christ thus blesses and brings into full union with His Church; and for all the purposes of educational religion, nothing is more necessary than that both Christian parents themselves, and their baptized children, should be thoroughly imbued with the believing sense of this truth.

The Heidelberg Catechism now, we say, is constructed on this theory or scheme of Christianity altogether. It assumes that the baptized children of the Church are sealed and set over to the service of God by the sanctifying or separating act of their Baptism itself, that they belong to the congregation and people of Christ, that they have part in the covenant of grace, that they are of the household of faith; and it aims accordingly everywhere to stir up their minds to a knowing and believing apprehension of this great grace, that they may be engaged by it to die unto sin and live unto holiness. In this respect, however, it was only in keeping, as we have already said, with the general thinking and practice of the Church in the age of the Reformation; and it is not difficult to see that the entire catechetical system, in particular of the sixteenth century, owed its whole interest, and vigor, and success, to the same theory of Christianity and no other. It is not intelligible on any other ground; and with the giving way, accordingly, of the old belief in baptismal grace, and educational religion, we find that it has in fact lost its hold upon the practice of our modern Churches in large measure altogether,

Modern Baptistic Theory and Practice

For that such a general falling away from the old church belief on this subject has actually taken place with a large part of our modern Protestant Christianity is a fact too plain, we think, to be disputed by any intelligent student of history. In this country especially, we meet with the painful evidences of it in every direction. We have whole denominations among us, large and powerful, which may be said to have started into existence on the very principle of undervaluing all organic and educational piety, and which glory in being a sort of practical protest, in this way, against the sacramental and churchly views of other times. A sacramental religion is for them a religion of forms only and nothing more; and educational piety they take to be a mere soporific delusion for the most part that rather hinders than helps the great work of coming to Christ. As for themselves, they have found out what they conceive to be a far more excellent way. For what have been supposed to be the objective factors of the new creation in Christ Jesus, they throw themselves upon the purely subjective side of the process; making the work of Christianity to be an inward transaction wholly between each individual singly considered and his Maker, on the outside of the Church altogether; in which, by dint of certain spiritual experiences, he is held to pass from death unto life, and so to be qualified for the communion of the Church below, as having his citizenship already with the true Israel of God on high. We are all familiar with the way in which this theory tends to discourage and bring into discredit everything that is not found to agree with its own chosen machinery for the accomplishment of religious ends. For all especially that carries with it here the character of the gentle and the continuous God's "still, small voice," as it causes itself to be felt in the daily light, and air, and dew of heaven—it has no sympathy or understanding. It must have the Holy Ghost—or what it takes to be the Holy Ghost—in the form of whirlwind, tempest, and fire, or it will not believe in His presence at all. The common beauty of the sanctuary, thus, is without comeliness in its eyes. Baptism is of less solemn significance for it than the anxious bench. It owns no household religion, in any full and proper sense of the term. Catechisms, and the entire apparatus of catechetical instruction as it once prevailed, have come to seem to it no more than the useless lumber simply of the long-buried past. We have whole sects, we say, a church membership amounting altogether to millions in our American Christendom, whose ecclesiastical life is openly based on this unchurchly foundation alone. But the change of which we are speaking goes far beyond these bounds, and is but too apparent everywhere in those denominations also which still profess to make account of their historical descent from the age of the Reformation. Neither the Lutheran Church, nor any part of the Reformed Church in this country, Dutch, Scotch, or German (to say nothing now of the Episcopal Church, or of the Congregationalism of New England), can be said to stand here firmly on the ground which was occupied by their religious ancestry in the beginning. There is not the same faith among them which there was of old in sacramental grace, in the church membership of children, and in the possibility of bringing them up as Christians in the nurture of the Lord, from their earliest years. The Baptistic principle, as it may be called, has entered widely into their theology and church life, bringing them to make large concessions practically to the unchurchly spirit around them; so that they find it hard to bear up against its assumptions and pretensions, and are more and more in danger always of being swept away by it from their ancient moorings altogether, and driven forth into the open sea of spiritualistic fanaticism and unbelief. This unquestionably is the great reason, why in certain quarters, within these communions, such small stress has come to be laid on Infant Baptism; why so little account is made of church schools; and why the systematic catechization of the young, as a door of introduction to the Lord's table, has fallen into such general neglect. The faith which once lay at the foundation of these things has been secretly undermined, till there is no power at last of dealing with them in any truly earnest way.

Let it be well understood and considered, then, that there is a necessary connection between the catechetical practice of former times, and the general theory of Christianity in the bosom of which it flourished and had power; and that it is vain to dream of restoring it to honor or force in any other connection. Where the old idea of educational religion, based on the sense of covenant relation to God and baptismal grace, has come to be regarded with distrust; where the use of confirmation, or some equivalent mode of bringing the young into full communion with the Church, has fallen into neglect or disesteem, and the only safe way of making Christians is supposed to be that of experimental, subjective excitement and stimulation, on the outside of these church appliances altogether; there, most assuredly, the old idea of catechetical instruction also will be found to have lost its meaning, and there will be no longer any power to use a church catechism at all in the manner of the sixteenth century. If there be any semblance left at all of such teaching, it will be only in the milk-and-water style of such Bible lessons as are made to serve their ephemeral purpose in Sunday schools, following no fixed rule, and leaving behind them no solid indoctrination whatever. It is not possible for an altogether unchurchly Christianity to be a truly catechetical Christianity, whether this unchurchliness show itself in the pietistic or in the openly rationalistic form. Socinianism and Anabaptism had indeed their catechisms; but they never entered into the religious life of the bodies to which they belonged. Arminianism in Holland could never stomach the church use of the Heidelberg Catechism; it was all for the Bible, unbound by any formulary of this sort. So in modern times, we cannot conceive of any vigorous system of catechetical instruction—in the fashion, for example, which we find reported to have been common throughout the whole Reformed Church at the Synod of Dort—as being upheld and prosecuted now among Unitarians, Quakers, Baptists, Methodists, or any of the openly unchurchly sects that go to make up the mass of our American Christianity.

They move, and have their being, in a wholly different order of religion. They are, we may say, constitutionally uncatechetical as well as unchurchly; and must belie their own existence, should they think of asserting or perpetuating their life now in any such churchly way.

Present Alternative

It is thus a very great and solemn question, which is brought home to the German Reformed Church in America at this time, in connection with the Tercentenary Jubilee of the Heidelberg Catechism. It is not simply whether we shall continue, or not, to honor the Catechism, as it has been honored by the Church before us in other lands; but this rather, whether we are prepared, or not, to abide by the theory and scheme of Christianity to which it belonged in the beginning, and without which all honor shown toward it can deserve to be considered no better than an empty farce. We have seen for what purpose it was originally framed, in what way it was used of old, and of what ecclesiastical system it formed all along an integral part. It stands before us as a witness for what was the church faith and church practice of the whole Evangelical Protestant world in the beginning, both Lutheran and Reformed. The faith and the practice went hand in hand together; so that neither can be rightly understood now, or earnestly honored, in separation from the other. In this age of catechisms, it was part of the general Christian creed to believe in the Church, as being in an important sense the Mother of all Christians—without whose continual intervention, according to Calvin (Inst, iv, ch. 1, § 4) there can be no true regeneration or growth unto everlasting life, as "beyond her bosom also neither remission of sins is to be hoped for, nor any salvation." Along with this went the idea of ministerial powers and forces in the Church, which were held to be superior to the order of mere natural gifts and workings of the Spirit there, as they were to be found nowhere else; sacramental mysteries, which were not only signs of the heavenly and invisible, but certifying seals also of its objective presence; outward covenant rights and privileges; baptismal grace, and the sanctification of children to the service of God in this way, as truly as if Christ had laid His hands upon them, and blessed them for such purpose. This, we say, was the reigning belief; and because it was so, the age addressed itself vigorously everywhere, as we have seen, to the work of educational religion, aiming to build in such style on the foundation which was supposed to be at hand in the established order of the Church. Hence the full and universal subordination of the school to the sanctuary. Hence the significance of the Catechism, as an organ of Christian instruction. Hence the catechetical system, in all its ramifications of discipline, whether private or public, kept up continually, as the grand support of both altar and pulpit, from one end of the year to the other. We are surrounded now, as we have just seen, with a wholly different practice which is the fruit and evidence also of a wholly different faith. What that faith is, or rather what it is not, has been mentioned already in general terms. It is the absence of all belief in that side of Christianity, which is represented to us in the idea of the Church, as being in any way the organ and medium of grace for the children of men. In this respect, our modern sects generally are of one mind. Calling themselves evangelical, and professing to be wholly governed by the Bible, they yet shut their eyes systematically to the plain sense of half the New Testament, and turn into a nullity every part of it that owns the fact of sacramental grace, or makes account of outward covenant interest in Christ. They will have it that there is no such covenant, other than that into which the world at large is brought, by the death of Christ, and by the free offer of salvation now in His name. They are all of them thus constitutionally Baptistic; having no power to see in the church membership of infants and young children anything more than an empty form, and never daring to make any practical earnest with the thought of their sanctification to God. Such has come to be the reigning habit of thought, it is but too plain, with our American Christianity in general at the present time; leading everywhere, with inward logical necessity, to what we have just seen to be its proper counterpart in ecclesiastical life and practice.

Between these two different systems, then, the German Reformed Church is required now deliberately and intelligently to make her choice. The Heidelberg Catechism belongs to one of them, and it does not belong at all to the other. If it is to be maintained still in true honor, as a symbolical book, it must be with the free acknowledgment of the old church views and ways with which it was joined in the beginning. It cannot be dissociated from these, without being shorn at the same time of its proper spirit and life. No attempt to ingraft it into a constitutionally different church system can ever be successful.

Taken out of its own original surroundings, like an exotic plant in strange soil, it can only languish and die. It cannot be made to flourish, with any true confessional force, where there has come to be a want of faith in the old idea of Christian nurture, founded on covenant sanctification and baptismal grace. It can never be incorporated effectually with any scheme of religious thinking which has lost the power of understanding what is meant by Confirmation, and along with this all sense of the true motherhood of the Church in relation to her baptized children. There may be, indeed, in such circumstances, an affectation of zeal for the venerable symbol, ostentatiously assumed for effect. There may be a readiness, at such a time as this especially, to join in glorifying its merits, and in garnishing the sepulchers of the righteous men to whom it owes its birth. But all such honor will prove to be in the end hypocritical and vain. In the midst of it, the Catechism itself will be quickened into no real life. It will be honored only as a dead monument of the past, without the possibility of its being restored to any enduring practical use.

General Merits of the Catechism

In every view, we may say, the Catechism of the Palatinate, now three hundred years old, is a book entitled, in no common degree, to admiration and praise. It comes before us as the ripe product of the proper confessional life of the Reformed Church, in the full bloom of its historical development, as this was reached at the time when the work made its appearance. Its wide-spread and long-continued popularity proclaims its universal significance and worth. It must have been admirably adapted to the wants of the Church at large, as well as admirably true to the inmost sense of its general life, to come in this way into such vast credit. Among all Protestant symbols, whether of earlier or later date, there is no other in which we find the like union of excellent qualities combined and wrought together in the same happy manner. It is at once a Creed, a Catechism, and a Confession; and all this in such a manner, at the same time, as to be often a very Liturgy also, instinct with the full spirit of worship and devotion. It is both simple and profound; a fit manual of instruction for the young, and yet a whole system of divinity for the old; a textbook, suited alike for the use of the pulpit and the family, the theological seminary and the common school. It is pervaded by a scientific spirit, beyond what is common in formularies of this sort; but its science is always earnestly and solemnly practical.[51] In its whole constitution, as we have seen, it is more a great deal than doctrine merely, or a form of sound words for the understanding. It

---

51. ["Science" here suggests the logical arrangement of topics so that their interconnections and mutual implications can be discerned.]

is doctrine apprehended and represented continually in the form of life. It is for the heart everywhere full as much as for the head.

Among its characteristic perfections deserve to be noted always, with particular praise, its catholic spirit, and the rich mystical element that pervades so largely its whole composition.

Its catholicity appears in its sympathy with the religious life of the ancient Church, in its care to avoid the thorny dialectics of Calvinism, in the preference it shows for the positive in religion as opposed to the merely negative and controversial, and in the broad and free character generally which distinguishes the tone of its instructions.

Considering the temper of the times, and the stormy relations in the midst of which it had its birth, it is remarkably free from polemical passion and zeal. We have seen how largely it is imbued with the historical spirit of the Creed. It not only makes use of it as an outward text, but enters with hearty interest and affection also into its general spirit; with the sound and most certainly correct feeling that no Protestant doctrine can ever be held in right form, which is not so held as to be in truth a living outgrowth from this primitive Christian symbol in the consciousness of faith.

The mystical element of the Catechism is closely connected with its catholic, historical spirit. This is that quality in religion by which it goes beyond all simply intellectual apprehension, and addresses itself directly to the soul, as something to be felt and believed even where it is too deep to be expressed. The Bible abounds in such mysticism. It prevails especially in every page of the Apostle John. We find it largely in Luther. It has been often said, that the Reformed faith, as distinguished from the Catholic and the Lutheran, is unfriendly to religion in this form; that it moves supremely in the sphere of the understanding, and so is ever prone to run into rationalism; and it must he confessed that there is some show of reason for the charge, so far at least as regards what may be considered the constitutional tendency here of the Reformed Confession.[52] Zwingli's great fault, as well as his chief strength, lay in the clear intellectuality of his nature.

Calvin had a deeper sense of the mystical, but along with this a still vaster power of logic also, which made it difficult for the sentiment to come with him to its proper rights. His theory of the decrees, for example, does violence continually to his theory of the sacraments.

As we have it in the Heidelberg Catechism, however, the Reformed system rises happily superior to all objection of this sort. Free regard is had in it throughout, indeed, to the lawful claims of the understanding; one of its authors at least was thoroughly versed in all the dialectic subtleties of his age, and an uncommonly fine logic in truth distinguishes its composition in every part. But along with this runs, at the same time, a continual appeal to the interior sense of the soul, a sort of solemn undertone sounding from the depths of the invisible world, which it needs an unction from the

---

52. ["Reformed Confession" in this context indicates the Reformed tradition as a whole, not any particular confessional document.]

Document 5: "Historical Introduction"

Holy One fully to hear and understand. The words are often felt to mean, in this way, more than they literally express. Simple, beautiful, and clear, in its logical construction, the symbol moves throughout also in the element of fresh religious feeling. It is full of sensibility, and faith, and joyous childlike trust. Its utterances rise at times to a sort of heavenly pathos, and breathe forth almost lyrical strains of devotion.

In this way, the inward spirit of the formulary communicates itself with powerful effect even to its outward form; so that its very language and style are found to be in large measure, as a late German writer expresses it, "unübertrefflich schön "—beautiful in the highest degree.[53] This is to be understood, of course, as holding good especially of the German original; where thought and language are more immediately of one birth, and the first shines through the last as the direct genial utterance of its own life. But the eloquence of thought becomes necessarily eloquence of speech also, into whatever tongue it may be translated, in proportion precisely to the fidelity with which the translation is made. Thus it is that the Bible has a character of simplicity, beauty, and grandeur in its style, which it is not in the power even of a bad version wholly to destroy. Its thoughts clothe themselves with a sort of necessary eloquence, in all languages. And in the same way it is easy to perceive and feel the peculiar force of the Catechism also, in almost every form of translation or version; while, however, the nearer any version may come to the exact sense of the original, the more in the nature of the case may it be expected to come near to it also in such outward grace of expression. The English language in particular, by reason of its native affinity with the German, admits this kind of translation in the case to the fullest extent; so that nothing more is needed here than a version, following as closely as possible, in the use of old Saxon words, the very letter of the original, to represent the quality of which we are now speaking with full effect. The Catechism speaks the language of faith and deep personal conviction; its words come from the heart, and take hold upon the heart. It speaks the language of life; its words are pictorial, concrete, of universal meaning and sense, significant for all classes and conditions alike. It speaks the language of devotion in words that breathe communion with the Spirit of God. It speaks everywhere the language of authority and power in words that carry with them no uncertain sound, but go always directly and precisely to their own point. A certain priestly solemnity and unction are felt, in this way, to run through all its teachings; so that, in listening to them, we seem indeed to hear the voice of the Church itself, and not the words simply of any single teacher speaking in its name. It was the sense of this in part, no doubt, which led some formerly to challenge for the composition of the Catechism a sort of supernatural character; something of inspiration in fact, or at least an extraordinary baptism of the Spirit, embracing both matter and form, which might be said to approach toward inspiration. Always simple, often beautiful, it becomes at times even grand and sublime. Portions of it, at least, are like "a

---

53. [See Jakob Theodor Plitt, *Theologische Studien und Kritiken*, vol. 36 (1863). Plitt (1815–1886) was a pastor and professor in Heidelberg and one of the founders of the German Evangelical Alliance, as well as the catalyst of many home mission initiatives.]

very lovely song of one that hath a pleasant voice, and can play well on an instrument" [Ezek 33:32]. There is music in its tones, and not unfrequently the very rhythm and cadence of unconscious poetry in its whole movement. Quite a number of questions, rivalling or approaching more or less the magnificent beauty of the first, might easily be quoted as examples of such rhetorical felicity; but it is enough to refer to them now in this general way. One of the most striking peculiarities of this grand old Catechism, unquestionably, is its religious eloquence.

Representing, as we have seen it do, the general confessional life of the Reformed Church in the age of the Reformation, the Heidelberg Catechism carries with it a special historical force for all times. We may say indeed, that its existence is interwoven with the very being of Protestantism itself; inasmuch as we have in it the genial, living expression of what was a necessary constituent of this vast religious movement in the beginning. It belongs to the creative period of the two great Protestant Confessions; and comes before us here as the spontaneous utterance of the Reformed type of faith, in its difference from the Lutheran, as well as in their common opposition to that which prevailed in the Church of Rome. Its polemical relations in this way, more generally silent than expressed, are at the same time plastic forces, which go everywhere to determine its positive constitution and character[54]; making it to be for the integral idea of Protestantism what no catechism or confession could ever possibly have become under other circumstances. It is a mirror of the mind and spirit of the Reformed Confession, as this was comprehended organically in the entire movement of Christianity and the Church, when the distinction first arose; a particular symbol, reflecting throughout the lights and shadows of what may be denominated the comparative symbolism of the age. [55] In this view, history shows it to be of vital account for the whole course of the Reformation. In the original antithesis of the Confessions, it was recognized on all sides as the representative banner of the entire Reformed Church. With the triumph of Rationalism in later times, it became more and more an empty name, till we find it sunk at last into almost universal neglect. Indifference to all positive religion, and contempt for the Catechism, went hand in hand together. And now that this period of spiritual dissolution, in the old world, has come to be followed again with a wholesome reaction, which is bent on building up in new form what it was the fashion before to pull down and destroy, one of the most striking facts connected with it is the resurrection of the Heidelberg Catechism once more to life and honor. Even the Confessional Union, which has for its object the consolidation of the Reformed and Lutheran Communions into a single Evangelical Protestant Church, is felt to require this; since there can be no positive taking up of the full, whole sense

---

54. [Nevin learned the language of "plastic forces" from Frederick Rauch, who defined "plastic power" as "the principle of individual life and its preservation, which . . . will confine the form of each individual to its species" (*Psychology*, 28–29). To once again translate this into Aristotelian terms: "polemical relations" (over against both Rome and Lutheranism) manifest or embody the "essence" of "the Reformed type of faith," which then operates or manifests itself throughout its "positive constitution".]

55. [Nevin is referring to the distinction of the Reformed and Lutheran traditions.]

of the Reformation in any such way that shall not be found to involve in the end a real synthesis, or true inward reconciliation, of its old opposing forms of faith. All attempts to provide for such confessional amalgamation by wholly new formularies have signally failed; and it has come to be generally understood now, that if the union is ever to be anything more than a lifeless relation between dead Churches, it must embrace in it the substantial spirit of the self-same symbols, in which is enshrined still the power of their original life. Thus we have what has been called a resuscitation of the Heidelberg Catechism in the new Catechism of Baden,[56] as well as in other catechisms lately produced for the use of the Evangelical Union in Germany; and along with this a general reawakening of interest in the formulary, which has made the Tercentenary of its formation on the other side of the Atlantic only less memorable than the observance of the same jubilee, during this year of secular terrors and sorrows in the United States.

It is hardly necessary to say that the zeal which has been thus renewed for the old classical symbol of the Reformed Church is no blind devotion to it as a mere outward tradition, and has no tendency whatever to promote an exclusive, sectarian spirit. It is wide-hearted and free, moving throughout in the hallowed interest of Christian love, and studying the things that make for unity and peace. It is zeal, not for the letter that enslaves and kills, but for the spirit which works always toward freedom and life. It does not hold the Catechism to be the end of all wisdom, absolutely faultless and in every respect complete; and it involves no disposition to make it a stiff, unyielding sarcophagus for the thinking of the Reformed Church at all points, to the end of time. It is honored simply for what is felt to be in it the positive substance of a once gloriously spoken martyr faith, which can never pass away; and occasion is now taken, by means of it, to emphasize and intone the rights of this faith, as St. Paul magnified his special office of Apostle to the Gentiles, not for the purpose of division, but to make room rather for the end of all strife, through the full integration of the doctrine of Christ, on a higher plane, under a new, more broadly catholic and perfect form.

Altogether, the German and Dutch Reformed Churches in this country have good reason to glory in their common symbol, and to cling to it with abiding affection as the most precious heirloom of their denominational existence. Though not for them here the palladium of civil and political rights, as it has been in times past for Churches in other lands, it is still the charter and warrant of their proper ecclesiastical constitution, without which they can have no right to continue their existence as particular Churches at all. They owe it to the world, as well as to themselves, to remain confessionally and ecclesiastically true to their own historical life; and they can claim for themselves no more honorable distinction, in the Christian Commonwealth, than to be known and spoken of as the CHURCHES OF THE HEIDELBERG CATECHISM.

---

56. [In 1821 the Lutheran and Reformed communions in the Grand Duchy of Baden (in which Heidelberg was located) were united. The new catechism for the union church was an amalgam of Luther's Catechism and the Heidelberg Catechism.]

Bibliography

Adam, Melchior. *Dignorum Laude Virorum*. Frankfurt: Johann à Sande, 1705.

Alpen, Heinrich Simon van. *Geschichte und Litteratur des Heidelbergischen Katechismus*. Frankfurt am Main: Hermannischen Buchhandlung, 1800. Translated by Joseph Berg as *The History and Literature of the Heidelberg Catechism*. Philadelphia: William S. and Alfred Martien, 1863.

Alting, Heinrich. *Historia Ecclesiæ Palatinæ*. Groningen, 1728 (originally published 1644).

Ames, William. *Christianae catecheseos sciagraphia*. Franekeræ: Berentsma, 1635.

Appel, Theodore. *The Life and Work of John Williamson Nevin*. Philadelphia: Reformed Church Publication House, 1889.

Aubert, Annette. *The German Roots of Nineteenth-Century American Theology*. Oxford: Oxford University Press, 2013.

Baars, Arie. "'The Simple Heidelberg Catechism . . . ' A Brief History of the Catechetical Sermon in the Netherlands." In *Power of Faith: 400 Years of the Heidelberg Catechism*, 159–67. Edited by Karla Apperloo-Boersma and Herman J. Selderhuis. Göttingen: Vandenhoeck & Ruprecht, 2013.

Baronius. *Institutes of Ecclesiastical History*. New York, 1839.

Barrett, Lee. "The Distinctive World of Mercersburg Theology: Yearning for God or Relief from Sin?" *Theology Today* 71, no. 4 (2015) 381–92.

Bayle, Pierre. *Dictionaire Historique et Critique*. Vol. 4, third edition. Rotterdam: Michel Bohm, 1720.

———. *Historische and Critische Wörterbuch*. Leipzig: Breitkopf, 1740–44.

Berg, Joseph, translator. *The History and Literature of the Heidelberg Catechism*, by Heinrich Simon van Alpen. Philadelphia: William S. and Alfred Martien, 1863.

Beza, Theodor. *Kreophagia sive Cyclops*. Conradus Badius, 1561.

Bierma, Lyle D. "The Sources and Theological Orientation of the Heidelberg Catechism," in *An Introduction to the Heidelberg Catechsim*, 81–86. Edited by Lyle Bierma. Grand Rapids, MI: Baker, 2005.

Böckel, E. G. Adolf. *Die Bekenntniss-Schriften der Evangelisch-Reformirten Kirche*. Leipzig, 1847.

Buddeus, Johann Franz. *Isagoge Historico-Theologica*. Leipzig: Thomas Fritch, 1727—30.

Bunyan, John. *The Holy War Made by King Shaddai upon Diabolus, to Regain the Metropolis of the World*. London: Dorman Newman, 1684.

Calvin, John. *The Catechism of the Church of Geneva*. Translated by Elijah Waterman. Hartford: Sheldon and Goodwin, 1815.

———. *Institutes of the Christian Religion*. Edited by John T. McNeill. Translated by Ford Lewis Battles. 2 volumes. Philadelphia: Westminster, 1960.

Cave, William. *Scriptorum Ecclesiasticorum Historia Literaria*. London, 1688.

Clark, R. Scott. *Caspar Olevianus and the Substance of the Covenant*. Grand Rapids: Reformation Heritage Books, 2008.

Coleridge, Samuel Taylor. *Aids to Reflection in the Formation of a Manly Character*. London: Taylor and Hessey, 1825.

Coomhert, Dirck. *Proeve van de Heydelbergische Catechismus*. Gouda: Jasper Tourny, 1583.

Conser, Walter H. *Church and Confession: Conservative Theologians in Germany, England, and America, 1815–1866*. Macon, GA: Mercer University Press, 1984.

Coppenstein, Johann Andreas. *Uncalvinisch Heydelbergische Catechismus, Veruncalvinisiert*. Heidelberg: Leonhart Neander, 1624.

Davenant, John. *An Exposition of the Epistle of St. Paul to the Colossians*. Translated by Josiah Allport. London: Adams, Hamilton, and Co, 1832.

DeBie, Linden J., ed. *Coena Mystica: Debating Reformed Eucharistic Theology*. By John Williamson Nevin and Charles Hodge. Edited by Linden J. DeBie. Mercersburg Theology Study Series, vol. 2. Eugene, OR: Wipf & Stock, 2013.

———. *Speculative Theology and Common-Sense Religion: Mercersburg and the Conservative Roots of American Religion*. Eugene, OR: Pickwick, 2008.

Dennison, James T., ed. "The Confession of Frederick III (1577)." In *Reformed Confessions of the 16th and 17th Centuries*. Vol. 3. Grand Rapids: Reformation Heritage Books, 2012. 439–57.

Dingel, Irene. "The Heidelberg Catechism in Sixteenth-Century Confessional Debates." In *Power of Faith: 400 Years of the Heidelberg Catechism*, 41–49. Edited by Karla Apperloo-Boersma and Herman J. Selderhuis. Göttingen: Vandenhoeck & Ruprecht, 2013.

DiPuccio, William. *The Interior Sense of Scripture: The Sacred Hermeneutics of John W. Nevin*. Macon, GA: Mercer University Press, 1998.

———. "Nevin and Coleridge." *New Mercersburg Review*, no. 17 (1995) 59–63.

Dubbs, Joseph Henry. *History of Franklin and Marshall College*, Lancaster, Franklin and Marshall Alumni Association, 1903.

Eames, Wilberforce. *Early New England Catechisms*. Charles Hamilton: Worcester, Mass, 1898.

Ebrard, Johannes Heinrich August. *Christliche Dogmatik*. Königsberg: August Wilhelm Unzer, 1851.

———. *Das Dogma vom heiligen Abendmahl und seine Geschichte*. Frankfurt: Heinrich Zimmer, 1845.

Erb, William H. *Dr. Nevin's Theology, Based on Manuscript Class-Room Lectures*. Reading, PA: I. M. Beaver, 1913.

Ersch, Johann Samuel, and Johann Gottfried Gruber. *Encyclopädie der Wissenschaften und Künste*. Leipzig, 1818–42.

Evans, William B. *A Companion to the Mercersburg Theology*. Eugene, OR: Cascade Books, 2019.

———. "General Introduction." In *The Incarnate Word: Selected Writings on Christology*. By John Williamson Nevin, Philip Schaff, and Daniel Gans. Edited by William B. Evans. Mercersburg Theology Study Series, vol. 4. Eugene, OR: Wipf & Stock, 2014.

———. *Imputation and Impartation: Union with Christ in American Reformed Theology*. Eugene: OR: Wipf & Stock, 2008.

BIBLIOGRAPHY

Feldberg, Michael. *The Philadelphia Riots of 1844: A Study of Ethnic Conflict.* Westport, Conn: Greenwood Press, 1975.

J. V. Fesko. *The Theology of the Westminster Standards.* Crossway: Wheaton, Illinois, 2014.

Gieseler, Johann Karl Ludwig. *Lehrbuch der Kirchengeschichte.* 6 volumes. Bonn: Adolph Marcus, 1824–57. English translation by Samuel Davidson as *A Compendium of Ecclesiastical History.* 2 volumes. New York: Harper & Brothers, 1849.

Goebel, Max. *Geschichte des christlichen Lebens in der rheinisch-westphälischen evangelischen Kirche.* Coblenz: Baedeker, 1849.

Good, James. *History of the Reformed Church in the US in the Nineteenth Century.* New York: Board of Publication of the Reformed Church in America, 1911.

Griffioen, Arie J., "Nevin on the Lord's Supper." In *Reformed Confessionalism in Nineteenth Century America*, 113–24. Edited by Sam Hamstra, Jr., and Arie Griffioen. Lanham, MD: Scarecrow Press, 1995.

Guerike, Heinrich Ernst Ferdinand. *Handbuch der Allgemeinen Kirchengeschichte.* 4th edition. Halle, 1840.

Gunnoe, Charles D. "The Reformation of the Palatinate and the Origins of the Heidelberg Catechism," 15–47. In *An Introduction to the Heidelberg Catechsim.* Edited by Lyle Bierma. Grand Rapids, MI: Baker, 2005.

Hambrick-Stowe, Charles, ed. "North Carolina Classis, Minutes." In *Living Theological Heritage.* Volume 3. Cleveland: Pilgrim Press, 1998.

Harbaugh, Henry. *The Life of Rev. Michael Schlatter.* Philadelphia: Lindsay and Blakiston, 1857.

Hart, D. G. *John Williamson Nevin: High Church Calvinist.* Phillipsburg, NJ: P&R, 2005.

Hase, Karl August (von). *Evangelische Protestantische Dogmatik.* 4th ed. Leipzig: Breitkopf and Härtel, 1850.

———. *Hutterus Redivivus, oder Dogmatik der Evangelisch Lutherischen Kirche.* Leipzig: Johann Friedrich Leich, 1833.

Hase, Karl August (von), ed. *Libri symbolici Ecclesiae evangelicae, sive, Concordia.* 2nd ed. Leipzig. 1837.

Hatch, Nathan O. *The Democratization of American Christianity.* New Haven, CT: Yale University Press, 1989.

Heppe, Heinrich. "Der charakter der deutsch-reformiten kirche," *Studien and Kirtiken.* Edited by Carl Ullmann, July, 1850, vol. I.

———. *Die Einführung der Verbesserungspunkte in Hessen von 1601–1610.* Kassel: J. C. Kruger, 1849.

———. *Geschichte des deutschen Protestantimus in den Jahren 1555– 1581.* Volume 2. Marburg: Elwert, 1852.

Herder, Johann Gottfried (von). *Ideen zur Philosophie der Geschichte der Menschheit.* 3rd ed. Leipzig: Johann Friedrich Hartknoch, 1828.

———. *The Spirit of Hebrew Poetry.* Translated by James Marsh. 2 vols. Burlington: Edward Smith, 1833.

———. *Treatise on the Origin of Language (1772).* Translated by Michael N. Forster. Cambridge: Cambridge University Press, 2002.

Heshusius, Tilemann. *Verae et Sanae confessionis de praesentia corpus Christiin Coena Domini.* Kirchener, 1562.

Hommius, Festus. *Schat-boeck der verclaringhen over de Catechismus der christelicke religie.* Leiden: Andries Clouck, 1617.]

Hodge, Archibald Alexander. *The Life of Charles Hodge.* New York: Scribner's Sons, 1880.

Hodge, Charles. "The Idea of the Church." *Biblical Repertory and Princeton Review*, vol. 25, no. 2 (1853) 249–90.

———. Review of *The Inspiration of Holy Scripture, Its Nature and Proof*," by Henry Lee. In *The Biblical Repertory and Princeton Review*, vol. 29, no. 4, (Oct., 1857) 660–698.

———. *Systematic Theology.* 3 vols. New York: Scribner, Armstrong, 1873.

Holifield, E. Brooks. *Theology in America: Thought from the Age of the Puritans to the Civil War.* New Haven, CT: Yale University Press, 2003.

Hopkins, Samuel. *Enquiry Concerning the Promises of the Gospel.* Boston: McAlpin and Fleming, 1765.

———. *The System of Doctrines.* 2 volumes. Boston: I. Thomas and E. Andrews, 1793.

———. *Two Discourses.* Bennington, VT: Anthony Haswell, 1793.

Klaasens, Harry. "The Reformed Tradition in the Netherlands." In *The Oxford History of Christian Worship*, 463–68.. Edited by Geoffrey Wainwright and Karen Westerfield Tucker, Oxford: Oxford University Press, 2006.

Kœcher, Johann Christoph. *Katechetishe Geschichte der Reformirtne Kirche.* Jena: Cröker, 1756.

Köllner, Heinrich Dorotheus Eduard. *Symbolik aller christlichen Confessionen.* Hamburg: Friedrich Perthes, 1844.

Layman, David W. "Was Nevin Influenced by S. T. Coleridge?" *New Mercersburg Review*, no. 17 (1995) 54–58.

Lenfant, Jacques. *L'innocence du Catechisme de Heidelberg.* Amsterdam: Pierre Humbert, 1723 (originally published 1688).

Littlejohn, W. Bradford. *The Mercersburg Theology and the Quest for Reformed Catholicity.* Eugene, OR: Wipf & Stock, 2009.

Locke, John. *The Reasonableness of Christianity, as Delivered in the Scriptures.* Edited by John C. Higgins-Biddle. Oxford: Clarendon Press, 1999.

Luther, Martin. *Luther's Small Catechism.* Philadelphia: Lindsay and Blakiston, 1855.

———. *The Small Catechism.* Edited by Timothy Wengert and Mary Jane Haemig. Minneapolis: Fortress, 2017.

The Lutheran Observer. 17, no. 38 (September 21, 1849).

Maxwell, Jack Martin. *Worship and Reformed Theology: The Liturgical Lessons of Mercersburg.* Pittsburgh: Pickwick, 1976.

Melanchthon, Philip. *Apologia pro Luthero, adv. furoisum Parisiensium Theologastrorum Decretum.* Wittenberg: Melchior Lotter, 1531.

———. *Iudicium de controversis Coena Domini, Responsio.* Geissler, 1560.

Michelet, Jules. *Mémoires de Luther.* Paris: L. Hachette, 1835.

Mieg, Ludwig Christian. *Monumenta Pietatis & Literaria.* Franfurt am Main: Johann Maximilian, 1701.

Morrell. John Daniel. *The Philosophy of Religion.* London: Longmans, 1849.

Mosheim, Johann Lorenz. *Institutionum historiae ecclesiastica antiquae at recentiors libri quator ex ipsis fontibua insigniter emendati.* Helmstedt: Christian Frederick Weygand, 1755. English translation by Archibald MacLaine as *An Ecclesiastical History: Ancient and Modern, from the Birth of Christ to the Beginnings of the Present Century.* 4 volumes. New York: Collins, 1821.

Neander, August. *Allgemeine Geschichte der christlichen Religion und Kirche.* 6 volumes. Hamburg, 1825–52. Translated by Joseph Torrey as *General History of the Christian Religion and Church.* 9 volumes. Edinburgh: T & T Clark, 1847–55.

———. *Lectures on the History of Christian Dogmas*. Translated by Jonathan Edwards Ryland. London: Henry G. Bohn, 1858.

Nevin, John. "Antichrist; or the Spirit of Sect and Schism." in *One, Holy, Catholic, and Apostolic: John Nevin's Writings on Ecclesiology (1844-1849)*, Tome One, 163-232. By John Williamson Nevin. Edited by Sam Hamstra Jr. Mercersburg Theology Study Series, vol. 5. Eugene, OR: Wipf & Stock, 2017.

———. *The Anxious Bench*. In *One, Holy, Catholic, and Apostolic, John Nevin's Writings on Ecclesiology (1844-1849)*, Tome One, 26-103. By John Williamson Nevin. Edited by Sam Hamstra Jr. Mercersburg Theology Study Series, vol. 5. Eugene, OR: Wipf & Stock, 2017.

———. "The Apostles' Creed." *The Mercersburg Review* vol. 1, number 2 (1849). The three parts of the series were: I. "Outward History of the Creed," (March 1849) 105-27; II. "Its Inward Constitution and Form," (May 1849) 201-21; III. "Its Material Structure or Organization," (July,1849) 314-47.

———. *The Apostles' Creed: Its Origin, Constitution, and Plan*. Mercersburg, PA: H. A. Mish, 1849. Also contained in *The Early Creeds*. By John Williamson Nevin, Philip Schaff, and John Williams Proudfit. Edited by Charles Yrigoyen and Lee Barrett. Eugene, OR: Wipf & Stock, Mercersburg Theology Study Series, vol. 8, 2020.

———. "Athanasian Creed." *Mercersburg Review* (Oct., 1867) 624-27.

———. "Athanasius." *Mercersburg Review* (July, 1867) 445-57.

———. "Brownson's Quarterly Review." *Mercersburg Review* 2 (1850) 33-80.

———. "Catholic Unity." In *One, Holy, Catholic, and Apostolic, John Nevin's Writings on Ecclesiology (1844-1849)*, Tome One, 118-19. By John Williamson Nevin. Edited by Sam Hamstra Jr. Mercersburg Theology Study Series, vol. 5. Eugene, OR: Wipf & Stock, 2017.

———. "Christianity and Humanity," *The Mercersburg Review* 20 (1873) 469-86.

———. *College Chapel Sermons*. Philadelphia: Reformed Church Publishing House, 1891.

———. "The Dutch Crusade." *Mercersburg Review* 6 (1854) 67-117.

———. "Evangelical Radicalism." *Mercersburg Review* 4 (1852) 508-12.

———. "Faith." *The Weekly Messenger* (February 12, 19, 23; March 4, 11, 18; 1840).

———. "The Heidelberg Catechism," *The Weekly Messenger* (December, 1840-August, 1842).

———. "The Heidelberg Catechism." *Mercersburg Review*, III, Number 2 (March 1852) 172.

———. *History and Genius of the Heidelberg Catechism*. Chambersburg, PA: Publication Office of the German Reformed Church, 1847.

———. *My Own Life: The Early Years*. Lancaster, PA: Historical Society of the Evangelical and Reformed Church, 1964.

———. *The Mystical Presence*. In *The Mystical Presence and the Doctrine of the Reformed Church on the Lord's Supper*. By John Williamson Nevin. Edited by Linden J. DeBie. Mercersburg Theology Study Series, vol. 1. Eugene, OR: Wipf & Stock, 2012.

———. "Religion a Life." *Pittsburgh Friend* 2, no 25 (December 25, 1834) 198; no. 28 (January 15, 1835) 222-23; no. 29 (January 22, 1835) 230; no. 30 (January 29, 1835) 238-39. Reprinted in *New Mercersburg Review*, no. 17 (1995) 37-45.

———. "The Sect System. In *One, Holy, Catholic, and Apostolic, Tome 1*, 233-71. By John Williamson Nevin. Edited by Sam Hamstra Jr. Mercersburg Theology Study Series, vol. 5. Eugene, OR: Wipf & Stock, 2017.

———. "Unity of the Apostles' Creed." *Mercersburg Review* 16 (April 1869) 313-17.

———. "Zacharias Ursinus." *The Mercersburg Review*, vol. III (1851) 490-512.

Newman, John Henry "The Episcopal Church Apostolical, Tract 7." *Tracts for the Times*. London: Rivington, 1840 (original 1833-34).

Nichols, James Hastings. *Romanticism in American Theology: Nevin and Schaff at Mercersburg.* Chicago: University of Chicago Press, 1961.

Niemeyer, H. A., ed. *Collectio Confessionum in Ecclesiis Reformatis publicatarum.* Leipzig: Klinkhardt, 1840.

Nolt, Steven. "Liberty, Tyranny, and Ethnicity: The German Reformed 'Free Synod' Schism," *The Pennsylvania Magazine of History and Biography*, vol. XXV, nos. 1–2 (Jan/April, 2001) 35–60.

Nowell, Alexander. *A Catechisme.* London: John Daye, 1573.

Olshausen, Hermann. *Biblical Commentray on the Gospels.* Translated by Thomas Brown. Edinburgh: T & T Clark, 1848.

Pareus, David. *In Divinam ad Romanos S. Pauli Apostoli Epistolam Commentarius.* Franfurt: Johannes Lancelloti, 1608.

Payne, John. "John Williamson Nevin: The Early Years." *The New Mercersburg Review* 36 (Spring 2005) 4–35.

Penzel, Klaus. *The German Education of Christian Scholar Philip Schaff: The Formative Years, 1819–1844.* Lewiston, NY: Edwin Mellon, 2004.

Penzel, Klaus, ed. *Philip Schaff: Historian and Ambassador of the Universal Church: Selected Writings.* Macon, GA: Mercer University Press, 1991.

Plank, G. J. *Geschichte der protestantischen Theologie von Luthers Tode bis zu der Einführung der Konkordienformel.* Leipzig: Siegfried Crussius, 1799.

Plitt, Jakob Theodor. *Theologische Studien und Kritiken.* Volume 36, 1863.

Porter, T. C. "Review of *Private Judgment—Address to the Suffolk North Association of Congregational Ministers, with Sermons on the Rule of Faith, the Inspiration of the Scriptures, and the Church*, by J. P. Lesley." *Mercersburg Review*, vol. 1 (September 1849) 515–19.

Proudfit, John Williams. "The Apostles' Creed." *The Biblical Repertory and Princeton Review* vol. 24, no. 4 (October 1852) 602–77.

Proudfit, John Williams, "The Mercersburg Theology." *The Puritan Recorder.* July, 1849.

Proudfit, John Williams, and John Forsyth. *Memoire of the Late Rev. Alexander Proudfit, DD.* New York: Harper and Brothers, 1846.

Purvis, Zachary. *Theology and the University in Nineteenth-Century Germany.* Oxford: Oxford University Press, 2016.

Rauch, Frederick. "Faith and Reason." *Mercersburg Review* 8 (1856) 80–94.

———. *Psychology; or, A View of the Human Soul.* Fourth Edition. New York: M. W. Dodd, 1846.

Richards, George Warren. *History of the Theological Seminary of the Reformed Church in the United States, 1825–1934.* Lancaster, PA: Rudisell, 1952.

Rittmeyer, Christian. *Catholische Anmerkungen uber den Heydelbergischen Catechismus.* Heidelberg: J. Mayer, 1707.

Rothe, Richard. *Die Anfänge der christlichen Kirche und ihrer Verfassung.* Wittemberg: Zimmermann, 1837.

Salig, Christian August. *Vollständige Historie der Augsburgischen Confession.* 3 volumes. Halle, 1730.

Schaff, Philip. *Christ and Christianity.* New York: Charles Scribners' Sons, 1885.

———. *The Creeds of Christendom.* 3 volumes. 4th ed. New York: Harper Brothers, 1919.

———. *Geschichte der Christlichen Kirche.* New York: Rudolph Garrigue, 1851.

———. *The Principle of Protestantism*. In *The Development of the Church: "The Principle of Protestantism" and Other Historical Writings of Philip Schaff*, 25–205. By John Williamson Nevin. Edited by David R. Bains and Theodore Louis Trost. Mercersburg Theology Study Series, vol. 3. Eugene, OR: Wipf & Stock, 2017.

Schlatter, Michael. *The Case for the German Protestant Churches Settled in the Province of Pennsylvania in North America*. London, 1753.

Schlegel, Friedrich. *Philosophische Vorlesungen*. Vienna: Carl Schaumburg and Co., 1830.

Schleiermacher, Friedrich Ernst Daniel. *Der christlich Glaube nach den Grundsätzen der evangelischen Kirche im Zusammenhang dargestellt*. 2nd ed. Berlin: Reimer, 1830. Translated and edited by H. R. Mackintosh and J. S. Stewart as *The Christian Faith*. London: T & T Clark, 1999.

———. Über *die Religion: Reden an die Gebildeten unter ihren Verächtern*. Hamburg: F. Meiner, 1958. English translation by John Oman as *On Religion: Speeches to its Cultured Despisers*. New York: Harper, 1958.

Schmucker, Samuel. *The American Lutheran Church*. Springfield, Ohio: Harbaugh, 1851.

———. *Elements of Popular Theology*. 2nd edition. New York: Leavitt, Lord, and Co., 1834.

Scultetus, Abraham. *Medulla theologiae Patrum, Pars Secunda*. Neapoli Nemetum: Nicolaus Schrammins, 1605.

Seisen, D. *Geschichte der Reformation zu Heidelberg*. Heidelberg: J. C. B. Mohr, 1846.

Spruner, K. L. "Covenant Theology." In *Dictionary of Christianity in America*. Edited by Daniel G. Reid, Robert Linder, Bruce Shelly, and Harry Stout. Downers Grove, IN: InterVarsity, 1990.

Strauss, David Friedrich. *Leben Jesu kritische bearbeitet*. Tübingen: C. F. Osiander, 1835–36. Trans. by George Eliot as *The Life of Jesus, Critically Examined*. Philadelphia: Fortress, 1973.

Synesius, *Opera*. Edited by D. Petavius. Paris, 1612.

Taylor, Nathaniel. *Lectures on the Moral Government of God*. 2 volumes. New York: Clark, Austin, Smith, 1859.

Tillemont, Louis S. *Memoirs pour servir à l'histoire eccles*. Brussels, 1693–1712.

Thornwell, James. "Lectures on Theology." In *The Collected Writings of James Henley Thornwell*. Edited by John B. Adger. 3 volumes. Richmond: Presbyterian Committee of Publication, 1871, I, 462.

Ullmann, Carl. "Sketches from the History of the Heidelberg Catechism in the Land of Its Birth." In *Tercentenary Monument in Commemoration of the Three Hundredth Anniversary of the Heidelberg Catechism*, 125. Edited by Henry Harbaugh. Philadelphia and New York: Kieffer & Co, 1863.

Über die Sündlosigkeit Jesu. Hamburg: Friedrich Perthes, 1833.

———. Über den unterscheiden *charakter oder das Wesen Christenthum*. Hamburg: Friedrich Perthes, 1845.

Ursinus, Zacharias. *Admonitio Christiana De Libri Concordiae*. Neustadt, 1581.

———. *Admonitio Neostadiensium*. Neustadt: Harnish, 1581.

———. *Catechismus, oder kurtzer underricht christlicher lehre*. Neustadt: Herborn, 1595.

———. *The Commentary by Dr. Zacharias Ursinus on the Heidleberg Catechism*. 2nd edition. Translated by George Washington Williard. Columbus, OH, 1852.

———. *Corpus doctrinae Christianae Ecclesiarum*. Geneva: Tornaesium, 1622.

———. *Corpus doctrinae Christianae Ecclesiarum*. Hanover, 1634.

———. *Corpus doctrinae Orthodoxae Sive Catecheticarum Explicationum D. Zachariae Ursini Opus absolutum.* Edited by David Pareus. Rhodin, 1612.

———. *Corpus doctrinae Orthodoxae sive Catechetarium Explicationum D. Zachariae Ursini.* Heidelberg: Johannis Lancelloti, 1612.

———. *D. Zacheriae Ursini theology celeberrimi, Opera theological.* Edited by David Pareus and Quirinius Reuter. Three volumes. Heidelberg: Johannis Lancelotti, 1612.

———. *Explicationum catecheticarum D. Zachariae Ursini Silesii.* Heidelberg: Harnish, 1591.

———. *Explicationum catecheticarum D. Zachariae Ursini Silesii.* Neustadt, 1593.]

———. *Gründtliche bericht vom Heilegen Abendmal.* Heidelberg: Mayer, 1564.]

———. *De Libro Concordiae quem vocant.* Neustadt: Harisch, 1581.

———. *The Summe of Christian Religion.* Translated by Henry Parry. Oxford, 1587.

Ussher, James, Archbishop of Armagh. *The Summe and Substance of Christian Religion.* London: Ranew and Robinson, 1670.

Van den Honert, Johannes, ed. *Schat-Boek der Verklasingen over den Nederlandschen Catechismus.* Gortinchen: Nicolas Goetzee, 1763.

Vierordt, Karl F. *Geschichte der Reformation im Grossherzogthum Baden.* Karlsruhe: G. Braun, 1847.

Walch, Johann Georg. *Historische und theologische Einleitung in die Religionsstreitigkeiten der evangelishe-lutherischen Kirche.* 5 volumes. Jena: Johann Meyers Wittwe, 1733–39.

———. *Introductio in libros Symbolicos ecclesiae Lutheranae.* Jena: Meyer, 1732.

Weber, Georg Gottlieb. *Kritische Geschichte der Augspurgischen Confession.* Frankurt, 1782.

Westphal, Joachim. *Farrago et Confusanaerum et inter se Dissentium Opinionum de Coena Domini.* Hamburg, 1552.

Wette, Wilhelm Martin Leberecht de. *Commentar über die Psalmen.* 3rd edition. Heidelberg: J.C.B. Mohr, 1829.

Widder, J. *Erbauliche Betrachtungen uber die in dem Heidelbergischen Catechismo.* Frankfurt, 1753.

Winebrenner, John. "Letter 4," *Gospel Publisher* (Nov. 1, 1843).

Index

Absolute Reprobation, 135, 278
Absolution, 148
Adam, Melchior, 193
Adolphus, Gustavus, 101
Agricola, Rudolph, 65
Ailing, Henry, 194
Albigenses, 236
Alexander, Archibald, 3, 37, 308
Alting, Heinrich, 52, 82, 83, 92, 94, 130, 157, 168, 186, 195, 196, 232, 268, 305
Ames, William, 113, 305
Anabaptists, 8, 94, 149, 191, 292
Andreæ, James, 90, 91, 140, 170, 270
Andrews, Jedidiah, 119
Anti-pedobaptists, 241
Anti-Trinitarianism, 94
Apollos, 185
Apostles' Creed, 5, 56, 139, 144, 145, 164, 167, 182, 188, 190, 235, 236, 239, 241, 258, 269, 277, 284, 285, 290, 309, 310
Appel, Theodore, 1, 2, 3, 37, 38, 45, 164, 257, 305
Aristotelianism, 65, 235, 303
Arianism, 44
Arminianism, 17, 29 53, 56, 98, 106, 112, 113, 133, 174, 185, 195, 242–49, 259, 260, 268, 269, 276, 298
Aubert, Annette, 20, 305
Augsburg Confession, 7–12, 21, 22, 27, 48, 55, 56, 67–79, 81–93, 96, 111, 139–43, 161, 162, 173, 193, 243–49, 261–64, 272
Augustine, 187, 294
Augustus of Saxony, 93

Baptism, 16, 29, 40, 56, 119, 126, 139, 146–59, 170, 191, 239, 241, 258, 290–302
Barrett, Lee C., vii, x, 1, 24, 40, 167, 305, 309
Bayle, Pierre, 157, 159, 176, 192, 305
Belgic Confession, 13, 16, 61, 62, 86, 110, 127, 137, 148, 249, 253
Belgic Catechism, 111

Bellarmine (Bellarmini), Robert, 207, 215
Benthem, Heinrich Ludolph, 88
Berg, Joseph, 3, 64, 84, 103, 305
Beza, Theodore, 11, 17, 61, 79, 82, 97, 98, 135, 174, 175, 215, 247, 305
Bierma, Lyle D., 7, 14, 15, 305
Billican, Theobald, 66
Böckel, Adolf, 232, 305
Bocquin, Peter, 75, 76, 79, 90, 170, 191
Bœhm, John Philip, 28, 119, 121
Bogardus, Everardus, 116
Bomberger, J. H. A., 147
Brentius, Johann, 170
Brenz, Johannes, 7, 170, 270, 271
Bres, Guido de, 17
Bucer, Martin, 11, 61, 66, 68
Buddæus, 190
Bullinger, Henry, 61, 79, 90, 106, 107, 131, 159, 191, 202, 206, 281
Bunyan, John, 184, 305

Calvin, John; Calvinism, 11–17, 25, 26, 32, 37, 40, 45–61, 67–98, 107–13, 118, 127, 129, 132–37, 140–46, 159–75, 190–93, 203–24, 232, 238, 241–52, 275–86, 299, 301, 305
Campbell, Thomas, 22
Canisius, Peter, 15
Casimir, John, 56, 92, 93, 96–99, 147, 173, 174, 193, 194
Catabaptists, 191
Catechism of Emden, 111, 281
Catechism of Geneva, 62, 111, 191, 283, 286, 287
Catechism of Luther, 62, 106, 132, 292
Catechism of St. Gall, 107
Catechism of Zurich, 107, 281
Catholic Church, Roman Catholicism, 7, 8, 16, 17, 20, 21, 28, 34, 47, 182, 234, 235, 266
Charles V, 6, 7, 66, 91, 142
Charles of Baden, 89
Christopher of Wirtemberg, 76

313

INDEX

Church of England, 29, 61, 116, 125, 140, 185, 195, 219
Church of Holland, 60, 121, 122
Claudius, Matthias, 237
Clement of Alexandria, 187, 237
Cocceius, 109, 114, 130, 164, 269
Colloquy of Maulbronn, 170
Common Sense Scottish Philosophy, 1, 32, 38
"communicatio idiomatum," 78, 140, 263, 271
Confession of Sigismund, 142, 243
Confirmation, x, 45, 56, 126, 139, 150, 183, 298, 300
Consensus of Zurich, 78
Conser, William, 20, 306
Coornhart, Dirck Volkartz, 111
Coppenstein, Johann Andreas, 110, 204, 306
Cotton, John, 19
Council of Braques, 188
Council of Mentz, 188, 189
Council of Trent, 9, 85, 103, 167, 183, 190, 208, 209, 216, 225, 226, 229, 236
Council of Tourain, 188, 189
Covenant of Grace, 77, 163, 164, 269, 282, 293, 296
Covenant Theology, 17, 77, 109, 164
Cranmer, Thomas, 61
Cromwell, Oliver, 18, 139
Cyril of Jerusalem, 186

Daub, Karl, 3
Davenant, John, 195, 216, 306
Davies, Samuel, 25
DeBie, Linden, 35, 130, 134, 264, 265, 306
Declaration of Thorn, 142
Deistism, 39
Demetrius, Bishop of Alexandria, 188
Depravity, 10, 13, 36, 134, 242, 245, 276, 282
Diet of Augsburg, 7, 55, 81, 87
D'Outrein, John, 109, 186
Dubbs, Joseph Henry, 3, 306
Duncan, Martin, 111
Dunkers, 119

Ebrard, Johannes H. A., 157, 231, 245, 274, 306
Edward VI, 61
Edwards, Jonathan, 25, 26, 27, 30, 37, 289
Erastianism, 230
Erb, William, 36, 38, 39, 145, 286, 306
Ersch, Johann Samuel, 52, 232, 306
Eucharist (Lord's Supper), 8-16, 21, 58, 61, 68-71, 76, 81, 94, 140, 160, 161, 168, 170, 183, 189, 193, 215, 219, 223, 224, 239-45, 249, 261-66, 271
Eusebius, 187

Evans, William, 38, 39, 40, 135, 281, 306

Farel, William, 82, 141
Fatalism, 134
Faukelius, Herman, 17
Ferlinghuysen, Theodor, 25
Fesko, J.V., 18, 307
Finney, Charles, 26, 29, 30, 33, 41, 46
First Confession of Basel, 61
First Helvetic Confession, 61
Flatt, Friedrich, 32
Fleury, Andre-Hercule de, 190
Formula of Concord, 14, 21, 22, 70, 78, 90, 97, 98, 108, 132, 138-42, 161, 170, 174, 249, 261, 263, 270, 271
Francis I, 189
Frederick I, 65
Frederick IV, 99, 100
Frederick V, 100, 101, 195
Frederick, John (of Gotha), 76
Frederick, John (of Saxony), 75, 91
Frederick III, the Pious, 8, 67, 72, 74, 82, 91-98, 147, 162, 173, 174, 183, 193
Frederick II, the Wise, 7, 66
Free Synod, 124, 125
French Catechism, 107

Gabriel, Peter, 111
Gallaher, James, 26
Gallic Confession, 61
Gerlach, Ernst Lugwig von, 21
German Reformed Church, 1-11, 22-31, 38, 45-48, 51-55, 68, 77, 84, 88, 96, 98, 109, 115-27, 140-50, 170, 177
Gerson, Jean, 189
Gnesio-Lutherans, 9, 10, 11, 15, 40, 48, 61, 76, 82, 89, 90, 169, 262, 270
Goebel, Max, 167, 231, 307
Gomarus (Gomer), Franciscus, 249
Goodwin, Thomas, 18
Goudse Catechism, 17
Gruber, Johann Gottfried, 52, 232, 306
Guerike, Heinrich Ernst Ferdinand, 88, 307
Gunnoe, Charles D., 307

Hall, Joseph, 195
Hardenberg, Albert, 71, 83, 160
Hatch, Nathan, 23, 307
Helvetic Formula, 249
Hengstenberg, Ernst Wilhelm, 145
Henry, Otto (or Otho) the Magnanimous, 7, 8, 67
Heppe, Heinrich, 243, 244, 249, 250, 274, 307
Heshusius (or Hesshuss), Tilemann, 55, 73-79, 89, 140, 160, 162, 169

314

INDEX

Hodge, Charles, ix, 13, 32, 35, 37, 38, 168, 207, 280
Holifield, Brooks, 26, 308
Holy Spirit, 39, 73, 136, 162, 201, 284, 288
Hommius, Festus, 113, 196, 307
Hopkins, Samuel, 26, 149, 289, 308
Huss, John, 189

Iconoclasm, 8, 146
Idolatry, 8, 85, 103, 104, 167, 183, 188, 208–23, 231
Illyricus, Matthias Flacius, 10, 15, 89, 91, 169, 245
Imputation, 35–39, 134, 135, 277, 178, 289
Incarnation, ix, x, 33–39, 164, 239, 258, 262, 263, 285
Infralapsarianism, 249

Jerome, 187
Jesuits, 53, 103, 190, 212, 218
Jesus Christ, 14, 30, 38, 39, 60, 78, 81, 92, 99, 136, 142, 167, 176, 206–12, 217, 231, 237, 263, 264, 272, 282–96
Johnson, Samuel, 210, 230
John the Baptist, 184
Juda, Leo, 107, 281
Junius, Francis, 98, 174, 175, 177, 215
Justification, 36, 39, 83, 93, 119, 126, 133, 134, 160, 164, 166, 208
Justin Martyr, 186

Keckermann, Bartholomew, 197, 198
Klebiz, William, 73, 74, 162
Knox, John, 60, 107
Koecher, Johann Christoph, 53, 210, 308
Krauth, Charles Porterfield, 22, 27

Lampe, Frederick Adolphus, 109, 164
Lasco, John à, 111, 281
Latitudinarianism, 21, 109, 110, 204, 244, 248
Law, third use, 14, 138
Leipsic Conference, 142
Lenfant, James, 52, 53, 103, 212, 308
Livingston, John H., 117–18
Louis the Pacific, 65, 66
Loyola, Ignatius, 190
Ludwig V, 7
Lubbert, Sibrand, 196, 198
Luther, Martin; Lutheranism, 15, 20–29, 46–48, 55–71, 73–99, 108–10, 124–32, 137–45, 159–74, 189–95, 203, 205, 211–18, 224, 231–34, 238–50, 253, 259, 261–65, 268–72, 281, 282, 286, 292, 297, 298, 301–4

Maclaine, Archibald, 243, 308

Mann, Julius, 27
Marburg Colloquy, 8, 14, 261
Marshall College, 3, 84, 124, 147, 155, 164, 287, 306
Maulbron Conference, 271
Maurice of Saxony, 66
Maximilian II, Holy Roman Emperor, 9, 75, 83, 93–94, 168, 308
Mayer, Lewis, 85, 103, 124, 155, 160, 261, 272, 310, 312
Melanchthon, Philip, 7–12, 14–15, 40, 48, 55, 67, 69, 71, 73, 75, 78–79, 81, 83–84, 138, 140–41, 143, 158–62, 167, 176, 186, 192, 208, 213, 215, 229, 232, 242–43, 248, 250, 261–62, 272, 308
Mennonites, 25, 29, 88
Methodism, 125, 151
Michelet, Jules, 215, 308
Miller, John Peter, 119
Moreri, Louis, 190, 192, 196
Morlin (or Mörlin), Maximilian, 75
Morlins of Lower Saxony, 77
Mosheim, Johann Lorenz, 242–43, 248, 308
Mystical Presence, 35–36, 39–40, 70, 130, 134, 137, 161, 219, 257, 264–65, 309
Mysticism, 168–69, 205–7, 233, 236–38, 301

Naumburg Convention, 8, 68
Neander, Johann August, 110, 130, 132, 204, 236–37, 275, 306, 308
"Neology," 31
Neuser, Adam, 94, 168
Nevin, John Williamson, ix–x, xii, 1–4, 6, 8, 10, 12–19, 22–24, 26–28, 30–40, 43, 45–48, 52, 57–59, 61, 67, 73, 80, 82–84, 88, 94, 98, 103, 108–10, 115, 119, 123, 125–27, 130–34, 136–40, 142, 144–46, 153, 155–56, 159, 161, 164–68, 174, 179, 181–84, 198–99, 202–16, 218–21, 223–26, 229–36, 239, 242, 255, 257–68, 273–75, 279–81, 284–90, 294–95, 303, 305–11
life, 1–19
and Mercersburg, ix, 33–41
theology, 33–41, 45–50, 155–56, 181–82, 223–24, 257–66
"New England Theology," 26
New Church Order of 1816, 18
New Covenant, 148
"New Side" Presbyterianism, 3, 29
Nichols, James Hastings, 21, 24, 310
Niemeyer, Hermann Agathon, 142, 192, 194, 210, 226, 228, 232, 243, 310

Œcolampadius, John, 7, 61, 65–66, 107

INDEX

Old Palatinate Liturgy, 56, 139
Old Scotic Confession, 61
Olevianus, Frederick Caspar, 11, 55–56, 77, 80–84, 89–90, 93–94, 96–97, 163–64, 168, 170, 173, 183, 191, 229, 231, 257, 275, 282, 306
Olshausen, Hermann, 237, 310
Origen, 187
Otterbein, Philip William, 29

Pacification of Passau, 67
Paganism, 188
Pantænus, 187
Pareus, David, 56, 96, 99–100, 113, 155, 172, 175, 177, 192, 194, 196, 200, 220, 310, 312
Pareus, Philip, 197–98
Parry, Henry, 155, 177, 199–200, 250, 312
Pascal, Blaise, 218
Paul (the Apostle), 107, 131, 185–87, 190, 197, 237, 238, 282, 288, 291–92, 295, 304, 306, 310
Paulicians, 236
Peace of Augsburg, 7, 9
Peace of Westphalia, 101
Pedobaptists, 241
Pelagianism, 56, 112, 129, 133–34, 244, 252, 277, 294
Perkins, William, 19
Peter the Hermit, 184
Philip II, 196
Philip the Upright, 65
Philippists, 10, 90, 170, 262, 270
Philosophes, 30
Piscator, John, 98, 130, 174, 269
Pithopceus, 194
Planck, G. J., 52, 91–92, 141, 157
Pomp, Nicholas, 147
Pomp, Thomas, 3
Pope Urban VI, 65
Possevin, 190
Prasmovius, Andrew, 108
Predestination, 12, 14, 18, 69, 112, 135, 160, 164, 193, 203–4, 224, 242–50, 260, 278
Presbyterian Church, 26, 107, 181, 200
Prince Louis, 98, 174
Protestantism, 3–7, 15, 21, 34, 36, 47–48, 57–60, 67, 77, 101–2, 131, 143–46, 162, 164, 189, 219, 235–41, 261, 303, 311
Proudfit, John Williams, xii, 127, 156, 166, 181–84, 188, 191, 198, 201, 204, 206, 162, 164, 189, 219, 235–36, 240–41, 261, 303, 311 07, 215, 219, 224–27, 230, 232–33, 235–36, 238–42, 244, 246–48, 250–53, 259, 270, 309–10
Providence, 82, 135, 161, 278, 283–84, 288

Prussian Church, 56, 139
Puritanism, 18–19, 24, 34, 125, 127, 139, 144, 146, 150–51, 234–35, 239–40, 253

Quakers, 191, 298
Queen Elizabeth, 60, 107
Quirinus, 194, 197–98

Ramsay, William, 30
Rationalism, 15, 27, 30–32, 40, 124, 144–45, 168, 205, 224, 234–35, 238, 253, 301, 303
"Rationalistic Supernaturalism," 32
Rauch, Frederick Augustus, 3, 31, 52, 56, 58, 124, 126, 131, 139, 155, 165–66, 235, 303, 310
Redemption, 35–38, 56, 129, 131, 134, 147, 164, 184, 243, 245, 247, 259, 261, 276–78, 282, 284–86, 288, 293
Reformed Church, ix, x, 1–2, 4, 13, 17–18, 28–32, 46, 51, 55–63, 267–70, 275, 280 297–310
Reformed Dutch Church, 56, 115, 118, 148, 195, 229, 233, 240, 249, 252–53, 267
Regeneration, 146, 186, 299
Reiley, James, 29
Religious Toleration, 67, 112, 192
Remonstrants, 13, 17, 86, 112–13, 191, 203
Reuterus, Quirinus, 197
Revelation, 23, 31–32, 57, 206, 285
Richard of Simmeren, 91
Richards, George, 28, 30–31, 119, 310,
Ridley, Nicholas, 61
Righteousness, 29, 35–39, 131, 134–35, 185, 194, 264, 277–79, 282, 288
Rittmeyer, Christian, 103, 310
Rollock, Robert, 19
Roman Catholic Church, 7, 102, 140, 187–89, 207, 214, 236, 270
Rupert, Elector, 64–65

Sacramentarianism, 58, 70, 83, 160–61
Sacraments, vii, ix, 5, 27–28, 33–34, 40, 56, 78, 127, 129, 135, 137, 140, 146–47, 159, 168, 189, 201, 205, 235, 239–40, 242, 244, 249, 253, 261–62, 269, 275, 278, 281–82, 301
Salig, Christian August, 141, 310
Salvation, ix, x, 5, 10, 13, 15, 25, 35, 38, 92, 97, 112, 131–36, 146, 164, 191, 194, 203, 208, 239, 243, 245, 252, 259–63, 275–81, 284, 287–89, 292–96, 299
Sanctification, 5, 29, 35, 39, 134–35, 185, 204, 246, 258, 278, 292–93, 299–300
Saravia, Adrian, 110
Scaliger, Joseph, 101
Schaff, Philip, ix, 21–22, 27, 33–34, 37, 57, 147, 182, 257, 306, 309–11

INDEX

Schlatter, Michael, 120–22, 307, 311
Schmalkaldic League, 7, 47, 66–67
Schmucker, Samuel, 27, 241, 311
Schnepf, Ehrhard, 66
Schultens, A., 130, 269
Scottish Presbyterianism, 18
Second Helvetic Confession 16, 61
Sectarianism 30–31
Seisen, D., 157, 231, 246, 311
Senfftel, Johann Jakob, 101
Sieben-Tœger (Dunkers), 119
Sigismund, John, 108–9, 142, 243
Sin, 5, 8, 13–14, 31, 35–40, 56, 97, 129, 133–36, 138, 142, 145, 148–49, 187, 190–91, 199, 213, 217, 233, 247, 252, 259–61, 276–82, 284, 286, 288–89, 292–93, 295–96, 299, 305
Smaller Catechism, 107, 164
Socinianiam, 31, 191, 203, 292
Stephens, Robert, 62
Storr, Gottlob Christian, 32
Stossel (or Stössel), John, 75
Stuttgart Confession, 140
Stuttgart Synod, 140, 270
Supralapsarianism, 135, 249, 278
Sylburg, Frederick, 107
Sylvan (or Sylvanus), John, 94, 168
Synod of Dort, 13, 16–18, 29, 56, 62, 86, 106, 110, 112, 118, 127, 133, 135–36 139, 195, 204, 215–16, 224, 242, 244, 247–50, 253, 259, 276, 279–80, 298
Synod of Emden, 17, 71, 111, 281
Synod of Gravenhagen, 195
Synod of Middleburg, 195
Synod of the French Protestant Church, 60
Synod of Wesel, 195

Ten Commandments, 5, 14, 137, 189, 258, 281–82
The 80th Question, 85, 87, 93, 103–4, 110, 167, 208–12, 214, 220, 225–32, 270
Theophilus, 185
Thirty-Nine Articles, 219
Thirty Years' War, 56, 96, 100–101, 104, 195
Thornwell, James, 37, 311
Tilly (Bavarian general), 100, 195
Timann, John, 71
Tossanus, Daniel, 94, 98, 174
Total Depravity, 10, 13, 242, 245, 276
Trautwein, Margaret, 173, 193
Tremellius, Immanuel, 62, 191, 193
Trent, Council of, 9, 85, 103, 167, 183, 190, 208–9, 216–17, 225–26, 229, 236
Triennial Convention, 127–28
Turretine, John, 13, 215–16

Ubiquity of Christ, 78, 140, 171, 262–63, 265
Ullmann, Karl, 16, 130, 236, 249, 307, 311
Unconditional Election, 136, 142, 279
Unitarianism, 234
United Evangelical Church, 143, 145
Universal Atonement, 164
Ursinus, Zacharias, 11–12, 14, 55–56, 76–77, 79–85, 88, 90–91, 96–100, 113, 130–31, 141, 143, 147, 155–64, 166–67, 169–70, 172–77, 181–84, 191–94, 196–203, 205–11, 213–15, 223, 225–33, 242, 246–48, 251–52, 257, 261, 268, 271–72, 274–75, 282, 309, 311
Usher, Bishop, 215
Utenhoven, John, 111

Van Alpen, Heinrich Simon, 3, 52, 64, 83–84, 88, 103–4, 106, 113, 157, 195, 227–28, 305
Van den Honert, Johan, 192, 195, 312
Vanderkemp, 195
Vermigli, Peter Martyr, 12, 69, 160, 193
Vierordt, Karl Friedrich, 157, 231, 246, 312
Viret, Pierre, 141

Waldensians, 34, 57, 189, 236
Weis (or Weiss), George Michael, 119, 121
Wesley, John, 29, 185
Wessel, John, 65
Westminster Assembly, 18, 107, 202, 204, 244
Westminster Confession, 3, 16, 18, 61, 134, 182, 249, 261
Westphal, Joachim, 69–71, 75, 77, 90, 140, 160, 170, 270, 312
Whitefield, George, 25, 185
Wickliffe (or Wycliffe), John 189
Wigands of Lower Saxony, 77
Wilhelm, Frederick III of Prussia, 8, 20, 67, 74, 76, 82, 91, 95–96, 142, 147, 162, 173, 193, 306
William, Philip, 29, 56, 96, 102
Williard, George W., 155–56, 177, 181–84, 198–202, 211, 213, 220, 225, 228, 250–52, 282, 311
Wimpheling, Jacob, 65
Winebrenner, John, 22, 23, 29, 45–46, 312
Wittenberg Concord, 11, 68
Wolfgang of Neuburg, 89

Yrigoyen, Charles, 24, 144, 167, 204, 207, 214, 216, 219, 225, 285, 290, 309

Zanchius, Jerome, 98, 135, 174, 247
Zinzendorf, Nikolaus, 29
Zwinglianism, 81, 137, 140, 245

www.ingramcontent.com/pod-product-compliance
Lightning Source LLC
Chambersburg PA
CBHW082003150426
42814CB00005BA/206